W9-CYY-241

WITHDRAWN

WITHDRAWN

WITHDRAWN

Elizabethan Players

IN SWEDEN 1591-92

&c.

ERIK WIKLAND

Elizabethan Players

IN SWEDEN 1591–92

&c.

Second edition
Revised, enlarged and in great part rewritten

> First soldier: What say you to his expertness in war?
> Parolles: Faith, sir, has led the drum before the English
> tragedians.
> (Wm. Sh.sp., *All's Well*, 4.3.295 ff.)

ALMQVIST & WIKSELL

STOCKHOLM

257838

First published May 1962
Second edition September 1971

© ERIK WIKLAND 1971

Translated by

PATRICK HORT, M.A.

Translations from the Latin by

CARL ERIK HOLM

Design by

JERK-OLOF WERKMÄSTER

Set in Monotype Modern Extended,
Series 7, 10/12, 9/10 & 8/10

by

EVA SUNDGREN, *monotyper,*

LARS ROOS, *hand compositor*

and

JAN PÅLSHEDEN, *make-up man*

PN
2590
E5
W513
1971

Library of Congress Catalog Card Number: 68-11434

Standard Book Number: 0 85132 009 0

PRINTED AND BOUND IN SWEDEN BY

Almqvist & Wiksells

BOKTRYCKERI AKTIEBOLAG

UPPSALA 1971

CONTENTS

TABLE OF ABBREVIATIONS AND SHORT TITLES

Add. Mss — Additional Manuscripts. British Museum.

App. — Appendix.

BM — British Museum, London, W.C.1.

Cal. Car. IX — Calendaria Caroli IX.

Cotton Mss — Cotton Manuscripts, British Museum.

Danish RA — Rigsarkivet (Danish National Archives), Copenhagen.

DBL — Dansk Biografisk Lexikon (*Dictionary of Danish National Biography.*)

DNA — Algemeen Rijksarchief (Dutch National Archives), The Hague.

DNB — Dictionary of National Biography.

H — Calendar, 1883–1940, of the Manuscripts of the Most Hon, the Marquis of Salisbury preserved at Hatfield House, 1–18 (The Cecil Papers).

Harl. Mss — Harleian Manuscripts, British Museum.

Hamlet, F 1 — Hamlet in William Shakespeare's First Folio 1623.

Hamlet, Q 1 — Hamlet, First Quarto Edition 1603.

Hamlet, Q 2 — Hamlet, Second Quarto Edition 1604/05.

KA — Kammararkivet (a department of the Swedish National Archives), Stockholm.

KB — Kungl. biblioteket (Royal Library), Stockholm.

Krigsarkivet — Swedish Military Record Office, Stockholm.

L.C. — Lord Chamberlain's records, PRO.

Lansdowne MSS — Lansdowne Manuscripts, British Museum.

n. — footnote.

Ms, Mss — Manuscript, manuscripts.

PHT — Personhistorisk tidskrift (Periodical of the Swedish Genealogical Society), Stockholm.

PRO — Public Record Office, London, W.C.2.

RA — Riksarkivet (Swedish National Archives), Stockholm.

SA — Slottsarkivet (The Archives of the Royal Palace), Stockholm.

SAOB — Svenska Akademiens Ordbok (dictionary), Lund.

SBL — Svenskt Biografiskt Lexikon (Swedish Dictionary of National Biography), Stockholm 2.

Sh.Jahr. — Jahrbuch der Deutschen Shakespeare-Gesellschaft.

SP — State Papers, Public Record Office, London, W.C.2.

SUB — Svensk Uppslagsbok, 2 edition (32 vols.), 1947–55. (Encyclopædia.)

UUB — Uppsala universitetsbibliotek (University Library), Uppsala.

'Research has revealed that the appearance of the Elizabethan players at the Nyköping court of Duke Charles between 1591–92 was not an isolated occurrence, since there is also evidence of English theatrical activities in Sweden and Finland around 1598–1600. The details of this latter activity have only been treated briefly and in conclusion, but I hope that it may be possible in due course to continue with investigations in this period.'

So I wrote nine years ago in the preface to the first edition. In bringing out a new issue of this work, I have sacrificed some of the comeliness of that edition in order to render it accessible to a larger number of students of 'Shakespeare on the Continent'. The book has been thoroughly revised and brought up to date: redundant and peripheral material has been discarded, new results of researches in archives and libraries have been added and parts of the book completely rewritten. At least its enlargement, a graver labour than I anticipated, has served as a refresher course, and I can only hope that the book in its new form will help others to a fuller understanding, perhaps even to a fuller appreciation of 'Shakespeare overseas'.

My researches did not follow the line originally envisaged. Extensive investigation in Sweden and Finland failed to disclose any additional information about the theatrical activities in 1598–1600 and instead I had to pursue other approaches. To gain further insight into the theatrical significance of the events in Nyköping in the early 1590's I have been obliged to search the records extant from other theatrical activities in Sweden during this period up to the coronation of Gustavus II Adolphus at Uppsala in October 1617. Danish declared accounts from embassies to England (particularly with respect to the London of Shakespeare's day) have also been consulted. There is also a comparison with the activities of a company of Italian players on the occasion of Sigismund's coronation in February 1594. Most of these events in the history of the theatre have not been considered before. I am also gratified that the contacts established between James Hill, Tobias Hume and the sign of the Boare's Head have made it possible to link up Duke Charles's Nyköping with Shakespeare's London. Research at the Vatican yielded particularly interesting results in that the Fondo Borghese documents in Archivio Segreto della Santa Sede were found to contain a papal licence issued on 13 January 1607 for John Messenius Sr. after the completion in 1603 of theological studies at the Seminary in Braunsberg, permitting his ordination notwithstanding certain formal objections arising from canon law.

My book is not confined to the history of Swedish theatre—it aims at the wider purpose of throwing more light on the 'overseas' activities of the English travelling companies. Details of Swedish history have had to be considered in certain contexts to explain the setting for theatrical events.

Among the new sources that have been consulted for this second edition, particular mention should be made of 'Baron von Moersperg's journal of 1592' from journeys in Denmark, Norway, Sweden (Lapland) and the Baltic states. This manuscript has been known at secondhand from printed sources and during my researches it was located at the library in Sondershausen, East Germany. I am much indebted to the Vice-President of the German Shakespeare Association, Weimar, Professor Otto Lang, for his valuable help in sending microfilm of the manuscript to Sweden. This manuscript is chiefly of topographical interest and I have used it mainly for some of its illustrations, but I hope that it may be possible in due course to publish an edition of this German, for the most part Low German, manuscript translated and compiled with footnotes and an index.

Only one of the illustrations in the first edition has been reproduced here and most of the new illustrations for this second edition are unique in their way.

There remains the pleasant duty of acknowledging the numerous forms of assistance which it has been my good fortune to receive over the many years of interrupted work on this edition. Special mention must be made of the archivist, Vello Helk, D. Phil., Danish National Archives of Copenhagen, who has helped me so much in my reasearch ever since the publication of the first edition and provided valuable guidance and contributions. The former Keeper of the Swedish National Archives, Dr. Ingvar Andersson, and the former head of the Drottningholm Theatre Museum, Professor Agne Beijer, have continued to follow my work and advise me in my research procedure. Professor Beijer had led me to understand, before the first edition appeared, that historians of the theatre wished to locate 'Baron von Moersperg's journal of 1592' and to establish the identity of Salvator Fabris, the Italian playwright, player and fencing-master who was involved in the plot to murder Duke Charles during the celebration of Sigismund's coronation in Uppsala in 1594. I am happy to say that both these tasks have now been undertaken. I should also like to thank the Keeper, Dr. Åke Kromnow, and the other officers of the Swedish National Archives; Dr Bertil Broomé, head of the Swedish Military Record Office; and the chief librarian, Dr Uno Willers, and all the librarians of the Royal Library, Stockholm, for their unstinted efforts in helping me to locate facts about the Elizabethan Players in Sweden. The character of the work has necessitated research in numerous foreign archives in Denmark, England, Finland, France, Germany, Holland, Italy, Poland, Russia and the USA. The heart-warming and generous helpfulness of scores of scholars and institutions 'overseas' has been such that I do not know how to acknowledge it adequately or even how to cite all my benefactors by name. In England I am particularly indebted to the officers of the Public Record Office and the librarians of the Department of Manuscripts of the British Museum; furthermore to the College of Arms, where the Garter Principal King of Arms, Sir Anthony Wagner, has followed my work with interest and given me valuable assistance concerning English heraldry and genealogy; and to the Director of Research, Anthony J. Camp, Society of Genealogists, London. My sincere thanks also go to Dr. James Mc Manaway, formerly at the Folger Shakespeare Library, Washington, and to the chief librarians of the Huntington Library, San Marino, Cal., and of the Library of Harvard University, Cambridge, Mass., USA, for their valuable assistance in letting me have microfilms of their rare 'Album Amicorum' of the period. Finally I should like to thank the head of the Department of Manuscripts at the Saltykov-Shchedrin Library in Leningrad, Madame Bernadskaja, for the valuable help I received during visits to Leningrad in 1967 and 1968.

The completion of certain parts of the research has been made possible through grants from the King's Fund (Konung Gustaf VI Adolfs 80-årsfond för svensk kultur) in 1963 and the Längman Cultural Foundation (Längmanska kulturfonden) in Sweden in 1964.

Kivik, Sweden, September 1971   *Erik Wikland*

The object of this work has been to examine the activities of the English players who were at Nyköping in Sweden between 1591–92. A secondary problem has been to investigate the remarkable parallelism of details which prevails between the Baltic background of William Shakespeare's Hamlet and the Swedish plays by Johannes Messenius the Elder and Magnus Olai Asteropherus about the turn of the century (1599–1600). Certain aspects of the work, therefore, have had to be treated in considerable detail; for example, the appendix on Johannes Messenius's brother-in-law, Duke Charles's physician-in-ordinary, Dr. Teofilus Homodei, is much more extensive than it would have needed to be for a purely theatrical historical study.

Research has revealed that the appearance of the Elizabethan players at the Nyköping court of Duke Charles between 1591–92 was not an isolated occurrence, since there is also evidence of English theatrical activities in Sweden and Finland around 1598–1600. The details of this latter activity have only been treated briefly and in conclusion, but I hope that it may be possible in due course to continue with investigations in this period.

Now that this work, which was begun in 1956, is being published, I should like to extend my sincere thanks to all those who have helped me in Sweden. The Keeper of the Swedish National Archives, Dr. Ingvar Andersson, and the head of the Drottningholm Theatre Museum, Professor Agne Beijer, have followed my work, at one time or another read parts or all of the manuscript and advised me in my research procedure. I should also like to thank the officers of the Swedish National Archives, the late Baron Gustaf Rudbeck, formerly the King's archivist, the late Mr. Arvid Berghman, formerly Comptroller of accounts and the King's armorist, Dr. Birger Steckzén, formerly head of the Swedish Military Record Office, and the chief librarian, Dr. Uno Willers, and the staff of the Royal Library, Stockholm, for their unstinted efforts in helping me to obtain rare volumes from abroad. I am indebted to Dr. Arthur Bygdén for a number of different pieces of research, particularly concerning Henry Francklin's album, to Docent Bror Danielsson, who offered me the benefit of his wide experience in research among English archives and libraries, and to Docent Emil Schieche, who during the

10

course of several years has helped me with the transcription of documents of the period.

The character of the work has necessitated research in numerous foreign archives in Denmark, England, France, Germany, Holland, Italy, and Poland. The heart-warming and generous helpfulness of scores of scholars and institutions overseas has been such that I do not know how to acknowledge it adequately or even how to cite all my benefactors by name. In England I am particularly indebted to the staff of the Public Record Office and the Department of Manuscripts of the British Museum; to the College of Arms, where the Garter Principal King of Arms, Sir Anthony Wagner, has followed my work with interest since the beginning of 1957 and given me valuable assistance concerning English heraldry and genealogy; to the late Sir Walter Greg, formerly President of the Malone Society, who until shortly before his death March 4, 1959, helped me and read parts of the manuscript; to his successor, Professor F. P. Wilson and the Hon. Secretary of the Society, Miss Kathleen M. Lea; and to Professor Allardyce Nicoll and the staff of the Shakespeare Institute, Stratford-on-Avon. Several German archivists, principally Dr. Papritz and Dr. Franz, both from Marburg, have supplied me with valuable material concerning the activities of English players in Hesse-Cassel during the 1590's. Valuable discoveries in Dutch archives were made possible through the help of various officials at the Dutch National Archives in the Hague, and the Municipal Archives of Amsterdam and Leyden. The contribution to my researches represented by transcriptions of collections of early Dutch letters (1593–94) by Dr. Annie Versprille at the Municipal Record Office in Leyden, was invaluable. An extensive correspondence with, and a couple of visits to, the Danish National Archives in Copenhagen brought new facts to light concerning the activities of the Elizabethan players in Denmark. In this respect I should like to express my thanks in particular to the Keeper, Dr. Svend Aakjær, and also to Professor Astrid Friis of the University of Copenhagen.

The completion of the research and the publication of this book has been made possible through various scholarships and grants from the King's Fund (Konung Gustaf VI Adolfs 70-årsfond för svensk kultur), the Längman Cultural Foundation (Längmanska kulturfonden), and the Swedish Humanistic Research Council (Statens humanistiska forskningsråd) in Sweden.

Stockholm, May 1962   *Erik Wikland*

CHAPTER 1

Henry Francklin goes to England in 1591. A company of English players is engaged to perform at Nyköping

Towards the end of the sixteenth century, when England was facing the threat of war with Spain and Queen Elizabeth was championing the Protestant cause, Sweden was ruled by John III.

Gustavus Vasa had died in 1560, leaving the throne to his son Eric XIV and various territories to Eric's three half-brothers; John received Finland, Magnus Ostrogothia and Charles Sudermania, Neriche and Vermelandt. Eric XIV, whose suspicious nature gradually degenerated to the point of insanity, was deposed and imprisoned in 1568 and John became king. Duke Magnus and Duke Charles retained their inheritance, which they ruled very much after the manner of the minor German princes of the period. While foreign policy was in fact the king's business, Duke Charles in particular interested himself in this sphere. As John III grew older and more and more infirm, Duke Charles managed an increasing amount of the business of government for him and supervised a number of foreign negotiations.

During the 1580's Duke Charles's policy on behalf of Sweden was directed towards furthering an alliance with England. News of the impending clash between England and Spain was brought to Nyköping, where the Duke resided, and in a letter of October 31, 1587, he informed Queen Elizabeth that he had sold a man-of-war to her navy through his English agent, Thomas Fisk, and that he wished to present a second warship, fully equipped, to the Queen, to whom he refers as the Defensor of the Faith. This was only nine months before the Armada sailed in the summer of 1588, so it is not surprising that Duke Charles was regarded with favour in England. He used the occasion to ask permission to buy some horses and several hundred bales of cloth[1] and at the

---

[1] SP 95/1, fol. 20 and 25, PRO.

same time he himself allowed English merchants to trade in Sweden. By now there were several countries in Europe which either sympathized with or else already supported Calvinism; they included England and Scotland, the Netherlands, the Palatinate and Hesse, as well as Duke Charles's domains in Sweden. It is true that The Established Church of England was Henry VIII's Anglican foundation, but during the 1590's the number of Puritans increased considerably in spite of Archbishop Whitgift's efforts to suppress them. In Sweden, John III had Catholic leanings, influenced as he was by his Queen, the Polish-born Catherine Jagiello, and her sister and brother-in-law, Anne and Stephen Báthory, the King of Poland. There was also his mother-in-law, the Italian-born Queen of Poland, Bona Sforza. On the other hand, Duke Charles, whose first wife had been Mary of the Palatinate and who had also been influenced by the Reformist spirit of Heidelberg, was privately an ardent Calvinist.

Duke Charles's first wife, Mary of the Palatinate, died in the summer of 1589, leaving her husband with their five-year-old daughter, Catherine Vasa, the maternal ancestor of the Swedish Royal House of the Palatinate. In the same year Sweden and Russia started a war that was to last for six years. In July John III had journeyed to Tallinn for a meeting with Sigismund of Poland, his son. He waited three weeks for Sigismund, who, when he finally arrived, was unable to guarantee an alliance with Sweden against the Russians. John had hoped that Sigismund would return to Sweden with him after their meeting, though in this he was opposed by the majority of the representatives of the Swedish nobility.[1]

In the autumn of 1587 Princess Anne Vasa had accompanied her brother Sigismund to the Royal Election at Cracow; she stayed in Poland until August 1589, when she went with Sigismund to Tallinn. From there John III took her back to Sweden with him. It was not only her father who wanted her to return home. Anne was a Protestant and while she had been at the Polish court Lutheran services had been held in private for her and her Swedish ladies-in-waiting, much to the annoyance of the Catholic Poles. Moreover, she had considerable influence with her brother and was suspected of furthering her father's plans for marrying Sigismund to Princess Christine of Holstein-Gottorp, who was later to become Duke Charles's second wife. There were powerful forces at work

[1] Letter from Thomas Fisk to Sir Francis Walsingham, Dec. 8, 1589; SP 95/1, fol. 36 r, PRO.

in the Polish court to separate Anne from Sigismund by having her return to Sweden.[1]

The war against Russia came to a head in 1590. On Christmas Eve, 1589, a Swedish–Finnish force had burned the monastery of Petsamo on the Arctic coast and after the New Year the Russians ravaged East Bothnia in Finland, advancing as far as the coast on the Gulf of Bothnia.[2] A truce signed on February 23 to last until January 6, 1591, laid down that Iwangorod and Koporie on the Baltic front were to be handed over to the Russians. Since it was clear that Sweden would have to increase her war effort, Duke Charles was unable to travel abroad that summer, as he had planned the previous autumn.[3]

John III's court was at Uppsala from the beginning of September until the end of December 1590[4] and with the King were his Queen, Gunilla, and his daughter, Anne Vasa. John, who was ill part of the time, summoned Duke Charles to his bedside to confer with him about the war against Russia. While Duke Charles was at Uppsala from October 24 to December 17,[5] it is probable that the subject of his remarriage was discussed. On December 17, the last day of his stay, Anne Vasa wrote a letter of introduction to Queen Elizabeth on behalf of Henry Francklin, a court chamberlain born in England who, having served King Sigismund, was now also Duke Charles's man:

... M. Vestrae significantes latorem harum Hendricum Francklein Anglum

iam aliquot annos Sereniss^{mo} Poloniae Regi Magno Duci Lithuaniae Russiae Prussiae Marsoviae &c. nec non Regnorum

Sueciae Gothiae et Vandaliae proxime haeredi et futuro Regi Fratri Nostro carissimo fideliter inservisse quam-

obrem ipsius M^{ti} summopere erat acceptus ut ipsum libenter in servitio Suo aulico. Ser^{us} Rex frater Noster carissimus

et honorandissimus diutius detiunisset nisi ipsi in Patriam ob privata sua negocia redeundum esset prout hac de re testi-

monium scriptum nactus est. Quod cum ita sit et dictus Henricus Franklein nunc profectionem suscipere statuerit petiit a

Nobis obnixe ut Nostris quoque literis ipsum causamque ipsius quam in patria expeditam libenter cupit M. Vestrae com-

---

[1] *SBL* II, 22 ff.   [2] Cf. pp. 210 ff.

[3] Johan IIIs registratur (riksregistraturen) 1590, I–II, and 1591, Hertig Karls registratur 1592, RA, and SP 95/1, fol. 36 r, PRO.

[4] Johan IIIs registratur (riksregistraturen) 1590, I–II, RA.

[5] Hertig Karls diarium 1566–92, RA.

mendaremus, quod quidem et hisce quam diligentisseme facimus M. Vestram
obnixe vocantes ut praefatum Henricum

Franklein sibi commendatissimum esse ipsique gratia et favore Suo Reginali
complecti dignetur Etenim non dubitamus

quin ipse sese facile vel quovis beneficio dignum reddat ...[1]

During Francklin's stay in Poland, King Sigismund had written a
letter of introduction—dated Warsaw, August 12, 1590—to Queen
Elizabeth concerning a journey to England, containing the following
passage:

... Serenissima Princeps; domina consanguinea charissima, quandoquidem
praesentium exhibitor, nobilis Henricus Franchelinus subditus Ser:[tis] V[rae],
Nobis aliquot annos non minus diligenter quam bene inservierit, et iam
rebus eius ita postulantibus, in patriam remeare statuit, eum absque singulari
Nostra commendatione dimittere noluimus. Quare eum nimium Ser[ti] V[rae]
maiorem in modum hijsce comendatum cupimus. Quia vero Ser[tem] V[ram]
aut Nobis servitij quaerendi gratia vel alicuius negotii causa forte adibit,
pergratum Nobis fuerit, si eum huius commendationis aliquem fructum
apud Ser:[tem] V[ram] cepisse intellegimus. Id quod vicissim pari vel maiori
vice erga Ser:[tem] V[ram], singulari Nostra benevolentia recompensaturi sumus
...[2]

[1] 'We hereby inform Your Majesty that the bearer of this letter, Henry Francklin, an Englishman, has for several years now served the Most Gracious King of
Poland, Grand Duke of Lithuania, Russia, Prussia, Marsovia &c. as well as immediate heir to and future King of the realm of the Swedes, the Goths & the Vandals,
Our Most Beloved Brother. For which reason he was very dear to His Majesty, so
that His Most Gracious Majesty, Our dear and highly esteemed Brother would have
been happy to have kept him in service at court had not private business obliged
him (Franklin) to return to his native country, as certified in a document given to
him. As this is the case and the said Henry Francklin has decided to make his
journey, he has earnestly requested Us that We too with Our letter might commend
him and the business that he wishes to do in his native country. This We do with
this letter as diligently as possible, in that we earnestly entreat Your Majesty to
condescend to allow the aforementioned Henry Francklin to be well commended to
You and extend to him Your royal grace and favour. For We have no doubt that
he will readily prove himself worth every occasion for benevolence ...'; Mss Cottonian, Vespasian F III, 137, BM.

[2] 'Beloved Cousin, since the bearer of this document, Henry Francklin, nobleman
and a subject of Your Majesty's, has served Us both diligently and well for several
years and has now, thereto obliged by his affairs, decided to return to his native
country, We have been unwilling to let him go without Our special recommendation.
Therefore with this letter We clearly wish to commend him most strongly to Your
Grace. And since he may wait upon Your Majesty, either with the intention of
rendering Us a service or on some other account, it would give Us great pleasure if

In this letter from King Sigismund there is no suggestion that Francklin will approach the Queen concerning Poland's need of English cloth. Two months later, on October 13, 1590, Sigismund issued credentials for John Haas, a cloth merchant, to buy up some twelve hundred bales of cloth in England and if possible to ship them out of the country duty free:

..., amice rogantes, ut huic servitori Nostro Johanni Haas vel plenipotenti illius ad mille ducentos pecios ex dicto panno, Nostro nomine coemere liceat, simul etiam potestatem illi concedat, eumdemque pannum absque telonio et vectigali ad nos asportari ...[1]

Poland's need of English cloth was also pointed out to Sir Christopher Parkins, who was in Warsaw and other parts of the country at the turn of the year. Sir Christopher's 'A diurnall of the affaires in Poland' includes the following passage for February 25, 1590–91:

... The XXIst of the said month (21 December 1590) two of the king's (Sigismund III) secretaries came to me to dinner, declaring unto me, in the king's name that his Maiestie had written unto England to requir free passe for one thousand CC clothes, and that his Majestie required of me to write also in the same behalf. I understanding that one of their two called Johannes Bulsious[2] was very neare the king thought good to take occasion of some further talk with him ...[3]

Queen Elizabeth replied to Sigismund's requests in May and June 1591. Concerning Henry Francklin, she wrote in June 1591:

... Valde nobis iucundum fuit intelligere Henricum Franklineum, fidelem et dilectum subditum Nostrum cum e Regno Poloniae discederet tam gratam servitij sui memoriam apud Serenitatem Vestram reliquisse. Ac fuit quidem ille Nobis antea suo nomine peracceptus quem in omni officio virum industrium fidumque cognovimus nunc vero ad superiorem eius gratiam cumulum non levem adiecerunt. Literae Ser[tis] V[trae] quae grato admodum sermone ostenderunt subditum Nostrum praenominatum apud eos principes quos scivit a Nobis sijncere diligi officia sua prudenter collocasse.

We sensed that he had received some benefit from this recommendation to Your Majesty. For this We in turn would display Our gratitude to Your Majesty through Our great good will in some similar or more important matter. ...'; Mss Cottonian, Nero, B II, fol. 181 v ff., BM.

[1] '... We therefore wish to enquire whether it may be granted to Our emissary, John Haas, or his accredited representative, to buy up in Our name some twelve hundred bales of this cloth and at the same time grant him a licence to ship out the some quantity of cloth to Us without customs dues and fees ...'; Mss Cottonian, Nero, B ii, fol. 214 v, BM.

[2] John Tidiksson Bultius. Cf. Index.

[3] SP 88/1 (Poland); fol. 159 r; PRO. Cf. Pollard, 'Sir Edward Kelley', pp. 49 f.

Quare cum favorem in Franclinium contulimus quem eius rationes haec in Anglia postularunt ea etiam benignitate hominem cum usus fuerit complectemur ut subditi Nobis perdilecti et a Serenitate Vestra commendatissimi rationem debitam habuisse videamur. Interea Serenitatem Vestram valde oramus ut solitum in eum favorem augere et quibus rebus oportunum videbitur Nostra causa ornare velit ...[1]

Earlier, in May 1591, the Queen had dealt with Sigismund's request that John Haas be permitted to buy up cloth and ship it to Poland duty free:

... Scribit ad Nos, Ser^{tas} V^{tra}, de mille ducentis pannis in Anglia ad usus suos coemendis et absque telonio aut vectigali e Regno Nostro transportandis idque negotium Joanni Haas illiusve procuratori datum esse ut eum numerum mercetur et in Poloniae Regnum quam fieri potest citissime invehat. Cui petitioni libere sine ulla exceptione satisfacere voluimus si id recte facere potuissemus resque in integro esset et in manu nostra posita. Verum ita res est ut pannorum Anglicorum exportandorum vectigal conductoribus quibusdam subditis Nostris ante annos aliquot locaverimus quibus locationis fructum omnem adimere non potuimus nisi magno cum eorum detrimento pactionum Nostrarum fidem infringere velimus. Eas tamen mille ac ducentas pannas coemere Ser^{tis} V^{trae} ministro potestatem dedimus eique praerogativam plane eandem portoriis solvendis quam subditis Nostris libentissime detulimus.

Qua in re ita Ser^{ti} V^{trae} commodare studuimus ut eum plane sibi persuadere velimus ad vestras regnique vestrae rationes promovendas nullum nobis unquam egregiae voluntatis propensionem esse defuturum ...[2]

---

[1] 'It has given Us great pleasure to learn that Henry Francklin, Our trusty and beloved subject, on departing from Poland left such a favourable impression of his service with Your Majesty. He was already in great favour with Us, as We have found him in every respect to be an energetic and faithful man. His earlier esteem with Us has been not inconsiderably enhanced by Your Majesty's letter, which eloquently intimates that this Our subject has shown wisdom in the performance of his duties on behalf of the princes whom he knows We truly love. Having given Francklin the mark of favour required by his position here in England, We shall also, when the occasion arises, cherish him with such goodwill that it can be considered that We have duly looked after Our most beloved and by Your Majesty warmly recommended subject. We earnestly entreat your Majesty to increase Your favours towards him and for Our sake honour him in the most appropriate manner. ...'; Mss Additional no. 36774, fol. 16 v, BM.

[2] 'Your Majesty writes to Us concerning the purchase of twelve hundred bales of cloth in England for Your use and the shipping of these bales from Our realm without customs duty or fees and further that this matter has been entrusted to John Haas or his accredited representative, to buy this number and import them to Poland as soon as possible. We would have wished to grant this request freely

Both John III and Anne Vasa clearly hoped that Christine of Holstein-Gottorp would marry Sigismund. It was therefore desirable that Duke Charles, who had also considered marrying Christine, should have his attention drawn elsewhere; however, since Sigismund had in fact already begun negotiating with Christine, it would seem that Duke Charles had withdrawn already and was looking for a bride elsewhere. Thomas Fisk, the Duke's agent in London and a draper, had visited Sweden in 1589. In November, before returning home, he had been informed by the Duke that the latter intended visiting England during the course of his travels the following summer. Fisk drew Walsingham's attention to this[1] but added that the Duke's journey abroad probably would be undertaken primarily for the purpose of visiting John Casimir of the Palatinate, an uncle of Duke Charles's late wife.

Thomas Fisk, besides acting as a cloth merchant, had involved himself in diplomacy with the aim of improving Anglo–Swedish relationships, pursuing this task from the time of Helena Northampton's visit to Sweden in 1581–82 until the end of Queen Elizabeth's reign in the early seventeenth century. Two questions were particularly sensitive at this time. One concerned Sweden's trade in war materials and supplies with Spain in the years before and after the defeat of the Spanish Armada in 1588, the other the shipment of arms from England to Archangel during the war of 1589–95 between Russia and Sweden.

A draft dated March 1591 from Elizabeth to Duke Charles—replying to a letter from the Duke and Thomas Fisk's personal communication when he delivered this letter—contains the following passages:

... Praecipue vero quam sollicite elaboraverit ut pro Litterarum Nostrarum tenore arma instrumenta bellica frumentum navesque et armamenta navalia ex illo regno in Hispaniam quamdiu rex ille nobis hostis erit transportari

and without restriction had We been able and if We had a free hand in this matter. As it is, however, the customs revenue from the export of English cloth has for many years been farmed out to certain contractors who are Our subjects and whom We cannot deprive of all their earnings by a breach of contract to their great disadvantage. We have nevertheless granted Your Majesty's emissary permission to buy these twelve hundred bales of cloth and with the greatest pleasure granted him the same privileges concerning the payment of harbour dues as apply to Our own subjects. In this matter We have striven to show Your Majesty such consideration that Your Majesty may be fully convinced that We are by no means lacking in goodwill and a desire to promote Your own and Your realm's interests ...'; Mss Additional no. 36774, fol. 15 r, BM.

[1] SP 95/1, fol. 36 r, PRO.

edicto regio prohiberentur ... Quod igitur vice versa Ex:ᵃ Vᵗʳᵃ a Nobis postu-
lat ne mercatores Nostri in Russiam navigantes pulverem tormentorium aut
instrumenta bellica quibus Muscus hostis Vester armetur in Muscoviam im-
portent id nos aequissimum esse censemus: ideoque Nos illis regio Nostro
mandato quod nullatenus violari volumus severe interdiximus ne deinceps
eas muntiones aut tormenta bellica quovis colore in Russiam advehere
audeant, uti magis particulatim Fiscus iste referre poterit. Cuius etiam fidei
commisimus ut Ex:ᵃᵉ Vᵗʳᵃᵉ significet quam grato animo accepimus amicis-
simum illud officium in particulari negotio ostensum quod ille Nobis fuse
explicavit ...¹

The order preventing English merchants from trading war materials
with Russia was officially confirmed in a letter dated June 1591 from
Elizabeth to John III:

... Per subditum Nostrum fidelem Henricum Franklinium Serenitas Vʳᵃ
ad Nos scribit varia tormentorum genera aliamque instrumenti bellici ma-
teriam per mercatores Nostras in Russiam navigantes Mosco hosti Vestro
subministrari et velut fomitem alendo bello adhiberi ideoque petit ut talium
rerum importationem in Moscoviam prohibeamus. Nos certe pro veteri
Nostra amicitia ac necessitudine Serᵗⁱˢ Vʳᵃᵉ desiderio in singulis satisfacere
cupientes et pacem inter principes Christianos praecertim fieri optantes
postulato Vestro amice ac libenter accquievimus.²

¹ '... but in particular with what diligence he brought about, in accordance with
Our letter, that a royal decree should prohibit the export from Sweden to Spain
of arms, war materials, grain, ships and naval equipment for as long as the Spanish
king remains Our enemy ... Concerning that which Your Highness thus requires
of Us in return, namely that Our merchants, when they sail to Russia, shall not
carry thence 'guns, powder and lead' with which Your Highness' Russian enemy
can arm himself. We consider this entirely proper and have accordingly by Our
Royal Decree, which We do not wish to be violated, strictly forbidden Our merchants hereafter to carry any war materials to Russia, as the above-mentioned
Thomas Fisk can report in more detail. We have also instructed him to explain to
Your Highness that We have most gratefully received the above-mentioned service
shown to Us and recounted in detail by Thomas Fisk. Thomas Fisk will also in
turn relate Our opinion in this matter to Your Highness. We also hope that Your
Highness will grant him Your confidence'; Mss Additional No. 36774, fol. 29 r.

² '... Through Our trusty subject Henry Francklin, Your Majesty has written
to Us that by Our merchants sailing to Russia with various kinds of cannon and
other war materials We have supported Your Majesty's Muscovite enemy. It is
therefore requested that timber exports for an extension of the Spanish war be
forbidden at the same time as similar war materials be prevented from entering
Russia. Without hesitation, for the sake of Our long friendship and the need to
satisfy Your Majesty's wish to maintain peace between the Christian princes, We
acquiesce amicably to Your request'; Mss Additional No. 36774, fol. 16 r.

Henry Francklin[1] accompanied Duke Charles when he left Uppsala in the late autumn of 1590; he was with the Duke at Gripsholm Castle over Christmas and at Nyköping Castle in January 1591.[2] In addition to the letter of introduction from Anne Vasa he received, on January 23, 1591, a passport to England from Duke Charles for the purpose of purchasing cloth.[3] Since Francklin remained at Nyköping until January 24, it would seem that he received this document direct from the Duke before leaving the next day for Stockholm to arrange the details of his journey. On the same day as he received this first passport to England, Francklin was also given 121 daler by the Duke's treasurer for a journey he had made to Poland the previous year.[4]

It is not improbable that the Polish purchase of cloth was mentioned in this context. Duke Charles considered similar purchases necessary for the pursuance of the Swedish–Russian war of 1589–95 and consequently Francklin was commissioned personally to buy cloth during his stay in England. The Polish and Swedish purchases in England were arranged somewhat differently. Sigismund III issued credentials on August 12, 1590, for Henry Francklin to Queen Elizabeth and then waited two months, until October 13, before instructing his commissioner, John Haas, to buy twelve hundred bales of cloth in England. In Sweden, on the other hand, Francklin himself was commissioned on January 23, 1591, to buy cloth in England and only nine days later, on February 1, he received credentials to Elizabeth for the journey to England. In the case of the Polish commission, both documents are still extant at the Public Record Office, whereas of the Swedish there is only the letter to Elizabeth on Francklin's behalf dated Nyköping, February 1, 1591. Drafts of two recredentials from the Queen to King Sigismund, dated May and June 1591, are now in the British Museum, as are drafts of correspondence with John III and Duke Charles of Sweden in the years

---

[1] According to his own album, fol. 74 r, Henry Francklin was in Warsaw on August 27, 1590. After this there are no further entries until the beginning of June 1591, when he was in England. (These albums—Latin *album amicorum*, German *Stammbuch*, Swedish *stambok*—were a kind of diary common from the middle of the 16th century until the 19th. In them the friends and acquaintances of the owner signed their names, often adding a motto, their coat of arms or something of the kind. *SUB* 27, 193.)

[2] Kungl. Hofförtärningen 1591–92, SA.

[3] Riksregistraturen (Johan III) 1591, and Hertig Karls diarium 1566–92, RA.

[4] Hertig Karls räntekammare 1590–97, fasc. 5, Håkan Larsson 1591, fol. 43 v, KA.

1590 and 1591—but no reply to the Swedish request to purchase cloth, though there is a recredential for Francklin's return journey to Sweden. Duke Charles's order for Francklin to buy cloth in England was either not presented or else it went straight to Thomas Fisk and to the leaseholder for cloth exports who is mentioned in connection with the Polish purchase. It is highly probable that this leaseholder was Sir Walter Raleigh. He had received the patent for similar export dues from Queen Elizabeth in 1576.[1] According to Thomas Fisk's accounts, large quantities of cloth were imported to Sweden from England in 1591 and 1592, while somewhat smaller amounts were obtained in 1593 and 1594.[2]

Duke Charles issued a second passport for Francklin's voyage to England, dated at Nyköping on February 1, 1591, though there is nothing about the purpose of this in the entry in the Duke's accounts.[3] It was presumably handed to Francklin's servant at Svartsjö, where both the Duke and King John III were staying at the time. Francklin's servant left Duke Charles's court shortly afterwards, to return on April 8, 1591.[4] This would suggest that Francklin left for England about April 1. The entries in his album show that he was certainly in England by June 2 and he probably arrived somewhat earlier.[5] The draft of Queen Elizabeth's reply to Francklin's passport of February 1 is dated June 1591; May has been written and crossed out.[6]

While it has not been possible to find the passport dated January 23, the one dated February 1 is in the Public Record Office. The Duke made no mention in it about the engagement of a company of players at his expense, but then he was primarily concerned to inform the Queen that Francklin intended to marry 'a maiden[7] now living in Our daughter's gynaeceum'. He wrote:

..., M^{ti} V^{ae} felix novi anni auspicium, Sui Regni continuum incrementum, contraque inimicos et adversarios victoriam a Deo precamur Vosque pro-

[1] SP 12/239, No. 101, Gorhambury 29.7.18. Eliz. (1576); PRO. Cf. *DNB*, 47, 189, col. A. (Walter Raleigh).
[2] Op. cit., fol. 15 r–28 r; Hertig Karls räntekammarböcker. Räkningar med diverse personer; KA.
[3] Riksregistraturen (Johan III) 1591, and Hertig Karls diarium 1566–92, RA.
[4] Kungl. Hofförtärningen 1591–92, SA.
[5] Henric Francklyns stambok, fol. 74 r.
[6] Mss Additional 36774, fol. 17 r, BM.
[7] Constantia Eriksdotter, the illegitimate daughter of Eric XIV of Sweden and Agda Persdotter.

spera adhuc uti valitudine constare volumus. Cum enim Nobis occasio daretur ad M^{tem} V^{am} per praesentem eius subditum Hinricum Frenclinum nostras literas mittendi, eam occasionem praetermittere noluimus. Idem enim Frenclinus Nobis aliquot annis in Nostra aula ministravit, Nobisque industriam et fidelem operam sedulo navavit et honeste modesteque se gessit, in animum denique induxit ad coniugium aspirare, atque cum virgine in filiae nostrae Gynaeceo degente matrimonium contrahere, prius vero quam nuptia celebrentur, res suas in patria expedire constituit, quibus in rebus M^{tis} V^{ae} auxilio indigere se nobis humiliter significavit, utque se intercessione nostra juvaremus demisse rogavit. Cum igitur is vita se gesserit, ut supra commemoravimus. commendamus eum M^{ti} V^{ae} majorem in modum amice rogantes, ut M^{tas} V^{a} eum clementer juvare dignatur, ut sua negocia in Anglia quamprimum expedire possit, quod facturam M^{tem} V^{am} non dubitamus, eumque ita promoturam, ut is intelligat, hanc Nostram commendationem sibi plurimum profuisse. Mandavimus eidem Henrico Frenclino ministro Nostro, ut M^{ti} V^{ae} quaedam, Nostro nomine, coram et oretenus commemoraret et referret, quae M^{tis} V^{ae} Regno utilia et in rem esse poterunt, et ad utriusque Regni nempe Anglici et Suetici mutuam benevolentiam non solum alendam sed etiam augendam spectant, quapropter rogamus M^{tem} V^{am} ut ex eo talia cognosci curet ...[1]

---

[1] '... We pray God for a happy start to the New Year for Your Majesty, for a continuous expansion of Your realm and for victory over enemies and opponents, and wish that Your Majesty may continue to enjoy good health and prosperity. For We would not wish to lose this opportunity of sending a letter from Us to Your Majesty through Your subject Henry Francklin, who is staying at present in Our country. The same Francklin has in fact served Us for several years at Our court, giving Us faithful service with diligence and willingness, conducting himself honourably and nobly. He has now finally decided to conclude a marriage with a maiden dwelling in Our daughter's gynaeceum. But before celebrating the wedding, he has determined to settle his affairs in his native country. He has humbly let it be understood that in these affairs he requires assistance from Your Majesty and has asked Us in all modesty to help him with Our recommendation. Since he has thus displayed such honourable conduct as We have mentioned above, it is all the more warmly that We recommend him to Your Majesty and kindly request that Your Majesty be graciously pleased to assist him, so that he may soon settle his affairs in England. We do not doubt that Your Majesty will acquiesce and promote his business in such a way that he may understand that this Our recommendation has been to his great benefit. We have moreover commanded the same Henry Francklin, emissary in Our service, that he should on Our behalf personally and confidentially to Your Majesty recount and relate certain matters as may be to the gain and advantage of Your Majesty's realm and such as are intended not only to maintain but even to strengthen the mutual bonds of friendship between the two kingdoms of England and Sweden, for which reason We pray that it may please Your Majesty to receive these communications from him'; SP 95/1, fol. 54 r ff., PRO.

The Queen's reply, June 1591, to this is an acknowledgement 'in amplissima forma' of Francklin's competence:

...Commendavit Nobis Cel:° V^a Literis ex arce Nicopiana, mense Februario datis fidelem subditum Nostrum qui has refert Henricum Franklinium ut eum in negotiis quibusdam hic in Anglia expediendis iuvaremus et favore nostro prosequi dignaremur. Quod nos et libenter fecimus et deinceps continuo facturae sumus, si qua in re illius commodis ac utilitatij prospicere poterimus maxime cum V^{tram} Cel^m multos iam annos ita inservierit ut obsequij et servitij sui tam illustre testimonium videatur meruisse. Eum itaque iam in Sueciam revertentem quam sibi pro patria matrimonij futuri iure destinasse videtur hijs literis commitari voluimus a Cel:^{ne} V^{tra} vicissim efflagitantes ut solitum vestrum favorem in eum Nostra causa ita augere dignetur ut nostra commendatione novus gratiae—quasi cumulus adjiciatur. Eius etiam fidei quaedam Cel:^{nl} V^{trae} exponenda comisimus quae mandatis ijs quae Vestro nomine ore tenus significavit, responsionem desiderio Vestro conformem continent ...[1]

It is probable that the questions which Duke Charles entrusted his emissary to put in person concerned the possibility of an English partner for the Duke's second marriage, though it has not been possible to discover who the lady or ladies in question may have been. A tangible result of these negotiations was the engagement of the company of English players which arrived in Nyköping with Francklin on the latter's return.

A certain parallel to these marriage negotiations is to be found in the activities of Ivan the Terrible in 1583 when he sought the hand of Lady Mary Hastings, daughter of Henry, Earl of Huntingdon.[2] Lady Mary

---

[1] 'In a letter from Nyköping Castle, dated February, Your Highness has recommended Our faithful subject Henry Francklin, who carries this letter in reply, so that We should assist him in the conduct of certain business here in England and be pleased to show him Our favour. This We have been pleased to do and should do again in the future, were We in some respect able to be to his advantage and benefit, the more so since for many years he has served Your Highness in such a manner as to deserve such an excellent testimony of his affection and diligence. Since he (Francklin) is now to return to Sweden, which country he by virtue of his coming marriage would seem to have chosen for his future home, We have seen fit to honour him with this letter in which We in return beseech Your Royal Highness so to increase Your favours to him (Francklin) on Our behalf that through Our recommendation further honour may be added to his name. We have also entrusted him with certain information to be imparted to Your Highness, the purport of which is a fervent agreement to those questions which he (Francklin) has put to Us by word of mouth alone ...'; Mss Additional 36774, fol. 17 r, BM.

[2] Chambers, *Sir Henry Lee*, 204 f.

24

was not attracted by the Czar's offer, however, and his death the following year put an end to this episode. At the turn of the century the question arose again. This time it was Boris Godunov who accepted Queen Elizabeth's offer to negotiate a marriage for his son, for whom the Queen had in mind an eighteen-year-old daughter of the late Ferdinando, Earl of Derby. When, in 1601, it became known that Boris Godunov's son was only thirteen, however, negotiations were broken off. A year later the Queen wrote again to the Czar, though without mentioning anyone by name, to inform him that she had now found 'a pure maiden, nobly descended by father and mother, adorned with graces and extraordinary gifts of nature ... at the Emperor's service'. With the Queen's death in 1603 this too came to nothing.[1]

In Duke Charles's household accounts for 1590–92 there appears the following entry:

Hendrich Francklyn begärer:
1. haffuer han utlagdt på Engelske ressen aff sitt egit till at ahntage Engelske spelemen — 79 Engelotter och bekommit icke mere för stycket igen än — 10 marker klippingz mijnt, säger at honom är skedt förkort och stiller thet uthi h.f.n:s behagh, huadh h.f.n^e wele betenkie honom för sin skadhe.
2. Item haff^r han vthlagt på ressen till leapolis när han köpte then vngerske hesten aff sitt egitt 148 slagne dal(er) och bekom igen 4½ mark^r klippingz mijnt för huar daler, begärer och therföre något för sin skadhe.
3. Säger han att min n: förste haffuer skenckt honom till norrbottens ressen — 12 alnar samet och 8 alnar Engelsk hvilket honom i hans besoldningh är affrechnat löper i penningar 64 daler.
4. Säger han at min n: förste haffuer tilsagdt honom på tredie höst sedhen om kijrcketiendhe huadh h:f:n:^e täckes unna honom therför.[2]

[1] Chambers, *Sir Henry Lee*, 204 f.
[2] 'Henry Francklin charges: (1) Paid on the journey to England of his own money to engage English players—79 Engelots (*Eng. gold coin also used in Sweden, 5.184 grammes, stable currency*) for which he has received no more than 10 Klippingz coin for every Engelot (*Klippingz, an unstable currency, were issued when coinage had to be minted in a hurry as during John III's reign*). This he claims is not enough and trusts that it will please His Royal Highness to make good his losses. (2) The same occurred on his journey to Lemberg where he bought the Hungarian horse with his own money, 148 minted daler for which he received only 4½ mark in Klippingz coin for each daler; he therefore requests something towards his losses. (3) That the Duke for the North Bothnia journey (July–October 1592; cf. App. VI) has given him 12 yards of velvet and 8 yards of English cloth, for which 64 daler have been deducted from his pay. (4) That the Duke had granted him church tithes two years

In the margin is written:

än haffuer min n: förste skenckt honom på norbotenz ressen som til-
förendhe är affrechnet:

64 daler 5 öre 8 penningar samet .... 12 alnar ⎫
30 daler 10 öre 16 penningar Engelst .... 8 alnar ⎭ 64 daler
94½ daler

Restadhe honom på hans före rechningh
i penningar 18 daler 6 öre
176 daler 22 öre[1]

According to Duke Charles's accounts[2] Francklin received 20 daler
for his personal outlay on his journey to England. This he received on
September 8, 1591, or only about a week after his return to Nyköping.
The more detailed bill quoted above concerned various expenses that
Francklin had had in the course of three journeys in 1590, 1591 and 1592
respectively. It was probably submitted after November 7, 1592, when
he returned to Nyköping from the journey to North Bothnia.[3]

When he left for England, Francklin had no funds advanced to him
for the engagement of the company of players with whom he returned
and he was obliged to draw on his own money. This suggests that the
decision to engage these players was taken while he was in London,
probably in July 1591, not long before his return.

As has already been mentioned, Duke Charles's agent in London at
this time was Thomas Fisk. The accounts for the years 1586–94[4] show
that the Duke purchased great quantities of cloth from Fisk, whose
colleagues were the Englishmen John Coote[5] and Rubrich Allem[6]

ago (1590) and hopes that His Royal Highness will be graciously pleased to give
him the money'; Hertig Karls räntekammare 1589–92, fasc. 4. fol. 17 v—21 v, KA.
(During 1590–92 Sweden suffered from severe inflation and the rate of exchange probably rose all the time.)

[1] 'Furthermore the Duke has given him, for the North Bothnia journey, total
94½ daler. The Duke's debt on the bill previousley submitted by Francklin is 18
daler 6 öre. Total 176 daler 22 öre'; Hertig Karls räntekammare 1589–92, fasc. 4,
fol. 17 v—21 v, KA.

[2] Handling^n och Betalning^n anno &c. 91, Hertig Karls räntekammare 1590–95,
fasc. 5, Håkan Larsson 1591, fol. 43 v, KA.

[3] Cal. Car. IX, 7.11.1592, p. 82.

[4] Hertig Karls räntekammarböcker. Räkningar med diverse personer 1586–95,
fol. 15 r—32 r, KA.

[5] Ibid., and Henric Francklins stambok, fol. 143 r.

[6] Hertig Karls räntekammarböcker. Räkningar med diverse personer 1586–95,
fol. 15 r—32 r, KA.

(Robert Allen?). To judge from the contents of Henry Francklin's first passport for his journey to England in 1591, it would seem that one of his most important missions on the Duke's behalf was to come to an agreement with Thomas Fisk as to the price and other details concerning the different cloths that were to be delivered to Nyköping.

As we have seen, Francklin was in England from the end of May until the end of July 1591. His album contains the following entries from this time:

Thomas Petevine[1]	London	2/6
Teofilo Homodei D.M.[2]	London	8/6
Petrus van Heile, Belga[3]	London	13/6
Severine John[4]	Greenwich	23/6
Thomas Burgh[5]		4/7
J. Wolley[6]		5/7
Ham. Charleton[7]		5/7
Camillo Cardoini[8]	London	9/7
John Cowell, Dr.[9]	Cambridge	19/7
William Dethick[10]	London	21/7

Francklin's album also contains an anonymous coat of arms[11] in the British style with the motto 'Virtutis amore'; this too may have derived from his embassy to England. The origin of this remarkable coat of arms and crest incorporating a figure of the World has been located at the College of Arms in a manuscript of uncertain origin entitled:

A Noate of some few coates and creasts lately come to my hands geven by William Dethick when he was York Herald and sithence he hath executed the Office of Garter King of Armes.

The entry of the anonymous coat in Francklin's album occurs on fol. 19 (20) of the manuscript together with the following ironical remarks by William Dethick:

Thes Armes and Crest is given to William
Saunderson of London, Fishmonger, by
Garter which William is the first that ever
bear or quartered any of the fower Coates.
The Crest is not fitt for soe mean a person

---

[1] Henric Francklyns stambok, fol. 22 r.   [2] *Ibid.*, fol. 30 v.   [3] *Ibid.*, fol. 141 v.   [4] *Ibid.*, fol. 160 r.   [5] *Ibid.*, fol. 53 r.   [6] *Ibid.*, fol. 52 r.   [7] *Ibid.*, fol. 54 r.   [8] *Ibid.*, fol. 76 r.   [9] *Ibid.*, fol. 44 v.   [10] *Ibid.*, fol. 52 v.   [11] *Ibid.*, fol. 72 r. For the motto, 'Virtutis amore', cf. Chassant–Tausin, II, 743 and Dielitz, 367.

but rather for one that pocesseth the whole wourlde.'[1]

William Saunderson, a wealthy merchant and fishmonger, advanced money to Swedish merchants in London.[2]

The three most prominent men in the above list were J. Wolley, William Dethick and Lord Thomas Burgh.

Mr. John Wolley, Esquire, had been Chancellor of the Order of the Garter since 1589 and was also Secretary for the Latin Tongue to the Queen's Most Honourable Privy Council.

William Dethick had been Garter King of Arms since 1586. The last and one of the most important private matters which Francklin settled during this embassy to England was clearly the renovation of his patent of nobility, which was Dethick's responsibility. Dr. Cowell's entry in Francklin's album is dated from Cambridge, July 19, 1591, and Dethick's is from London two days later, on July 21. Concerning Henry Francklin's coat of arms, it can be mentioned that his simple shield with a 'lion rampant', representing his paternal lineage, was renovated (final approval dated May 20, 1592) to give a division with the lion in the lower half and, in the upper, a spread eagle flanked by royal crowns, representing his maternal line. The eagle is described in the renovation certificate as follows:

... In superiore autem ceruleo Aquilam aliis utrinque distentis inter duas regum coronas auro gemmisque micantes ...[3]

---

[1] Dethick's grants X; College of Arms. London, E.C.4.

[2] Cf. Söffring Jönsson's accounts from a journey to England 1590–91, fol. 3 r, according to which William Sanderson advanced a total of £54 to Jönsson; Diplomaträkenskaper 1570–93, Vol 5. Furthermore, the Caesar papers include a document entitled 'A treatice of Exchange and of the King's Majestie's Royal Exchangers office in his emenent place of dignity. ...' The author, whose name was William Sanderson, Gent., a schemer and projector in the reign of James I, may be identical with William Saunderson. He calls his work 'A present for the King's most sacred Majestie and the Prince His Highnes' and maintains that he shall enable His Majesty to gain £400,000 and the Prince half that sum. And afterwards 'a yeerely rent of fortie Thousand Pounds ...'; Mss Lansdowne 768, BM. William Sanderson is also one of the merchants in England who are reported as having claims on Sweden after the death of Charles IX; The Britaniskes Rechningh 1612, 1613 och 1614; Likvidationer Ser. 91:18; KA.

[3] 'In the upper half the field is charged with the spread eagle flanked on either side by a royal crown or, studded with precious stones'; op. cit.

Francklin belonged to an ancient noble family, as witness the record drawn up on June 2, 1592, at the College of Arms in conjunction with the renovation of his patent:

... Henricus Francklyn Anglus filius Rowlandi Francklyn generosi ...[1]

One interesting fact to emerge from the heraldic search is that the arms of Henry Francklin are quite unlike the arms granted to various members of the Franklin or Frankland family originating at Skipton-in-Craven in Yorkshire and represented in one line by Sir James Assheton Frankland of Thirkelby, twelfth Baronet. While this is no indication that Henry Francklin was not of Yorkshire origins, it does suggest that he came from a family unconnected with that anciently settled at Skipton-on-Craven.

It is interesting to speculate over the inclusion of the spread eagle[2] (Casa dell'Impero) and the royal crowns in Francklin's renovated arms. Some guidance can be found in the genealogies of the Swedish nobility and from Thomas, Lord Burgh, the third of the prominent men listed above. Henry Francklin was probably born about 1550. According to the pedigrees[3] of the Swedish House of Nobility, 'his father was an Englishman Roland Francklijn and his mother Dorotea Patavin, otherwise called Dorotea Ellmont (Ellmout) and by von Schantz[4] entitled Princess'. Dorotea Patavin (Ellmont, Ellmout) cannot be located—the names Patavin and Ellmont (Ellmout) in the pedigrees are apparently corruptions. von Schantz's claim that Dorotea Patavin was of princely origin probably came from Palmskiöld (1719). In the Palmskiöld collection at Uppsala, under Koskull,[5] we find: Dorotea Patavin, en furstes dotter uti Engeland.[6]

The man who was perhaps most interested in the theatre was Thomas Burgh, Lord Burgh de Gaynesboro from 1567 to 1597. He was the son of William, Lord Burgh, who was born about 1521, died on September 10, 1584, at Lambeth and was buried on October 2, 1584, at Lingfield in Surrey. William Burgh was one of the peers involved in the great lawsuit

---

[1] 'Henry Francklin Englishman, son of Roland Francklin, gentleman'; Vinc. Old. Gr., fol. 518, 530 and 537; College of Arms, E.C. 4.

[2] The heraldic emblem of royalty.

[3] *Elg.*, II, 817.

[4] C. L. von Schantz, 'Adliga släkten Frankelin, no. 48'.

[5] Henry Francklin's daughter, Mary Catherine, married Baron Andrew Koskull.

[6] 'Dorotea Patavin, daughter of an English royal person.'

against the Duke of Norfolk in 1572. He married Catherine, the daughter of Edward Clinton, Earl of Lincoln, and Elizabeth Blount, Dowager Baroness Tailboys.

Elizabeth, daughter of Sir John Blount, of Kinlet, Shropshire, was a maid of honour to Queen Catherine between 1512 and 1514. Henry Fitzroy, her illegitimate son by King Henry VIII, is said to have been born at Blackmore, Essex, in 1519. He was created Duke of Richmond in 1525. His mother married about 1519 Gilbert Tailboys of Kyme, Lincolnshire, who was created Lord Tailboys in 1529 and died in 1530. They had two sons and a daughter: George, Lord Tailboys, who died without issue in 1540; Robert, Lord Tailboys, who died unmarried in 1541 and Elizabeth, Lady Tailboys, who was born about 1520, married first Thomas Wymbish, secondly Lord Ambrose Dudley, who was created Earl of Warwick and died without issue in 1563. Her mother, Elizabeth, Lady Tailboys, married secondly about 1531 Edward, Lord Clinton, who was later created Earl of Lincoln. They had three daughters: Bridget, who married Robert Dymoke of Scrivelsby, Lincolnshire, Catherine, who married William, Lord Burgh, and Margaret, who married Charles, Lord Willoughby of Parham.[1]

William Francklyn, Archdeacon of Durham and subsequently Dean of Windsor and Court Chaplain to Henry VIII, may have been closely connected with Henry Francklin's grandfather Hugh Francklyn. William's arms as Archdeacon of Durham admittedly include a lion but differ greatly in other respects from those of Henry Francklin described above:

Argent on a pale between 2 Saltires couped and engrailed gules a Dolphin haurient argent on a chief azure a lion between 2 Dove's or cillared azure.[2]

William and Hugh Francklyn probably belonged to the same generation but their relationship cannot be established. William Francklyn was closely associated with Henry VIII, particularly as a mediator with the clergy, and played an active part in arranging the royal divorces in the manner desired by the King. He also received a salaried appointment as chancellor resident with Henry Fitzroy, Duke of Richmond, the natural son of Henry VIII alluded to above.[3] It is worth noting further that Hugh Francklyn was granted Longworth in Berkshire (not far from Windsor and Reading) by Henry VIII in 1538.[4]

[1] College of Arms, London, E.C. 4; various sources.
[2] Muniment Room, Box 15, Roll 25, No. 477; College of Arms, London, E.C. 4.
[3] *DNB* 19, 204 f. and the sources listed there.
[4] Lists and Indexes No. 13. The Star Chamber; and Cal. State Papers Henry VIII.

Lord Burgh's seat was Starburgh Castle in Surrey. Thomas, Lord Burgh, was the English governor at Briel in Holland from 1589 to 1597. From there he was posted to Ireland but died soon after his arrival in October 1597.[1] His post as Lord Deputy of Ireland was later conferred upon Essex.[2] His wife was Frances Vaughan, only daughter of John Vaughan of Sutton-on-Derwent in Yorkshire and his wife Anne, who in her turn was the daughter and heiress of Sir Christopher Pickering. Anne's second husband was Sir Henry Knyvet, so that Lady Burgh was step-sister to Thomas Knyvet, Lord Knyvet of Escrick, known as the man in Parliament who disclosed the Gunpowder Plot of 1605. Frances Vaughan's paternal grandfather was Thomas Vaughan of Porthamal in the county of Brecknock. The Vaughan family was very well known at that time and the majority of its branches lived along the Welsh border.[3]

Lord Burgh was patron of 'Lord Burgh's Company', that acted in the provinces and appeared at Ipswich, Norwich and York in 1590–91, 1594 and 1596–97.[4] With these dates in mind, and the fact that, as his album shows, Henry Francklin had been in touch with Lord Burgh, one is tempted to assume that it was this company that was engaged to perform at Nyköping during 1591–92. The records at Ipswich and Norwich, however, clearly show that 'Lord Burgh's Company' performed in these two towns on July 18 and August 25, 1591, respectively, i.e. after the 'Nyköping' company had left for Sweden.

Apart from his patronage of a dramatic company, Lord Burgh's literary interests declared themselves in other ways. One of the rare editions in the British Museum is Thomas Bradshaw's *The Shepherd's Starre*, with the subtitle 'being a paraphrase upon the third of the Canticles of Theocritos in prose, part with songs interspersed'.[5] Thomas Bradshaw is described as a 'Gentleman late of the Right Worthie and honorable the Lord Burgh his Companie & retinue in the Briell in North-Holland', and the volume is dedicated to the Earl of Essex and Lord Burgh. Alexander Bradshaw, Thomas Bradshaw's brother, prefixes a letter to the author dated 'from the court of Greenewich upon Saint George's day, 1591, April 23', in which he explains that he has taken the liberty of publishing the book while the author is abroad. The preliminary

---

[1] *Complete Peerage*, 2, 424.
[2] *Ibid.*, 5, 142.
[3] College of Arms.
[4] John T. Murray, *English Dramatic Companies*, 2, 78.
[5] Stationers' Register, 2, 579.

poems, by I. M. and Thomas Groos, deal with Thomas Bradshaw's departure from England. The author's own style in the preface is highly affected and probably influenced by John Lyly's *Euphues* from 1580. The Theocritean Canticle reads all the more pleasantly.

The three most important literary and theatrical events at Court during Francklin's stay in 1591 were Edmund Spenser's *The Tears of the Muses*, dedicated to Alice Spencer, Lady Strange, entered in the Stationers' Register on December 29, 1590,[1] and published in 1591 ('Imprinted for William Ponsonbie, dwelling in Paule's Churchyard at the signe of the Bishop's head'), Thomas Bradshaw's above mentioned play *The Shepherd's Starre*, and the publication of three plays by John Lyly, namely *Endimion*, *Galathea* and *Midas*, which were entered in the Stationers' Register on October 4, 1591.[2] Although Henry Francklin had left England before these three plays were published, he may nonetheless have been there when they were performed at court.[3] The title page of the quarto edition of *Endimion*, printed in 1591, runs 'Playd before the Queenes Maiestie at Greenwich on Candlemas day at night, by the Chyldren of Paules'. It is thus not unlikely that during his stay in England Francklin saw a performance of one or several of Lyly's plays at the Court at Greenwich. On January 1, 1592,[4] Edmund Spenser dedicated his *Daphnaida—an Elegy upon the death of the noble and virtuous Douglas Howard, daughter and heir of Henry Howard, Viscount Bindon, and wife of Arthur Gorges, Esquire* to Helena Northampton;[5] in the form of a pastoral, Spenser has Alcyone complain of the death of his Daphne.

During 1591 and 1592 Duke Charles had a considerable correspondence with Helena Northampton[6] in England. Born in Sweden in 1549, she was a member of the ancient family of Bååt (Snakenborg). She accompanied Cecily Vasa to England in 1565. Queen Elizabeth soon became very attached to her and gave her a post at court. She advanced quickly to become First Lady of the Privy Chamber. In 1571 she married William Parr, the brother of Catherine Parr. Six months after their

[1] Stationers' Register, 2, 570.
[2] *Ibid.*, 2, 596.
[3] Cf. Bond, *John Lyly*, 2, 417 ff. and 3, 5 ff. and 106 ff.
[4] Presumably January 1, 1591. Cf. Edmund Spenser, *Variorum Edition*, 7, 435 ff.
[5] Cf. pp. 167–9 and Edmund Spenser, *Variorum Edition*, 7, 435 ff.
[6] Cf. p. 172.

marriage William Parr died, and about 1578 Helena Northampton married again, this time Sir Thomas Gorges of Longford. She died in 1635. Unfortunately, most of her correspondence with Duke Charles has been lost. Helena Northampton's secretaries, Laurentius Bilefelt and Otte Lodskin, were in Sweden in the summer of 1591; Duke Charles was one of those who assisted them in transferring to England their mistress's inheritance from her mother. Thus 800 dalers' worth of grain was placed at Laurentius Bilefelt's disposal for export to England, as follows:

Dalehamn 12.7.1591. Till Palne Erichsson för fru Eliens till Nortens tienare Lars Billefeldt be^{dh}, att upkiöpa spannmål i Östergötland för 800 D^r.[1]

Stockholm 18.5.1592. Till Palne Erichsson för fru Helenes Margrevinnen till Nordhemtons tienare Lorens Bilefeldt den Spannemåhl i Söderkiöpingh Uthan Taxering Uthskepa låtha.[2]

Bilefelt was again in Sweden in 1592.[3]

Another factor of importance was the close relationship as well as the friendship between Sir Walter Raleigh and Sir Arthur Gorges. They were first cousins once removed[4] who had known each other since childhood and had studied together in Devon and at Oxford. Sir Arthur Gorges was the nephew of Sir Thomas Gorges of Longford, Helena Northampton's second husband. Sir Walter Raleigh was well acquainted with Duke Charles and kept in touch with him for some time.[5]

While on an embassy to England in 1589–90, Count Eric Brahe[6] and Andrew Keith[7] had borrowed money from Helena Northampton. When the loan was not repaid, she requested that the yield from the estates of these two noblemen should be distrained until such time as full payment was made.[8] Duke Charles, in his reply of August 10, 1591,[9] requested that Helena Northampton should see to it that Queen Elizabeth put a

[1] 'Dalehamn, July 12, 1591. To Palne Erichsson for Helena Northampton's secretary Lars Bilefeldt, permission to buy grain in Östergötland for 800 dalers'; Hertig Karls diarium 1566–92, 12.7.1591, RA.

[2] 'Stockholm, May 18, 1592. To Palne Erichsson for Helena, Margravine of Northampton's secretary Lorens Billefeldt, permission to export the grain in Söderköping free of duty'; Hertig Karls diarium 1566–92, 18.7.1592, RA.

[3] *Ibid.* and Henric Francklyns stambok, fol. 160 v.

[4] Cf. pp. 166 ff. and Index.

[5] Edmund Spenser, *Variorum Edition*, 7, 433 ff. Cf. pp. 97, 99, 108, 169–172.

[6] Cf. Index.

[7] *Ibid.*

[8] Hertig Karls registratur, 10.8.1591, fol. 132 v f.

[9] *Ibid.*

stop to the export to Russia via Archangel of 'muskets, powder and shot' so long as Sweden and Russia were at war. This was certainly by no means an easy task, since the Muscovy Company in London counted many ministers and courtiers among its members, including Cecil, Walsingham and Leicester.[1] Nevertheless, in her reply Queen Elizabeth agreed that the trade in arms should be forbidden.[2]

Dr. Teofilus Homodei was Duke Charles's physician-in-ordinary. His name is one of the first to appear among the entries in Henry Francklin's album from the latter's stay in England in 1591.[3] Dr. Homodei writes:

> Per amicitia et fraternita perpetua scrisse
> in Londra. L'anno 1591 a di 8 Giugnio
> Teofilo Homodei D.M.

He had been sent to England to study the extent of this export of arms to Russia and to further certain commercial and political matters. It is not unlikely that he also assisted Francklin to engage a company of players.[4]

Severine John (Severinus Joannis Suecus, Söffring Jönsson) was dockmaster at Duke Charles's naval yard outside Nyköping; it was he who commanded the Spanish venture. He too was in England at this time helping Dr. Teofilus to clear up the problems connected with the loss at sea of the Duke's ship *Elephanten*. While he was there he lent Henry Francklin a sum of money.[5]

It would seem that it was Helena Northampton, assisted by Sir Walter Raleigh and William Dethick,[6] who managed to obtain permission for an English company of players to be engaged at Duke Charles's court at Nyköping from 1591 to 1592. Dethick was also a staunch supporter of the theatre. On a later occasion—September 1603—when the insignia of the Garter were to be bestowed upon Duke Frederick of Württemberg, the English ambassadors, Lord Spencer and Sir William Dethick, took with them a company of players. While we do not know who the members of this company were, we do know that they performed a play en-

---

[1] M. S. Andersson, *Britain's Discovery of Russia 1553–1815*, 32.

[2] Mss Additional 36774, fol. 16 r, BM.

[3] Cf. p. 27 and Henric Francklyns stambok, fol. 30 v.

[4] Cf. pp. 185 ff.

[5] Cf. Diplomaträkenskaper 1570–1593, fasc., Söffring Jönssons räkning från en resa i England 1590–91, KA.

[6] Cf. pp. 27 and 33.

titled *Suzanna* in Württemberg and that in 1604 in Nordlingen they performed *Romeo and Juliet* and *Pyramus and Thisbe*.[1] William Dethick is perhaps best known to students of Shakespeare's life as the man who signed the first draft of the grant of arms for John Shakespeare in 1596, with a final document in the assignment of 1599.[2]

Shortly after Francklin left for England, Duke Charles sent a personal letter to his sister, Princess Elizabeth of Mecklenburg, dated April 14, 1591. This is the first indication we have of the Duke's negotiations for a German marriage, and as yet he was making extremely tentative enquiries. He asks his sister to

beflite sig åm te try Conterfei: Hålsten Brandeburg och Anhaltt.[3]

His hopes rest on Christine of Holstein, but if this cannot be arranged then he asks his sister

att bevise ett wenstycke, och försöke på ett anett sett ... til ewentyrs, medh ten yngste kåme till godh ende tett såm medh ten elste först war begynt.[4]

Duke Charles was thus prepared to consider no less than four alternatives, one princess from the house of Brandenburg, one from the house of Anhalt and two from the house of Holstein.

The correspondence between Duke Charles and Princess Christine together with other documents connected with the arrangements for their wedding have been preserved in the *Landesarchiv Schleswig-Holstein*. The first letter from Duke Charles, dated June 20, 1591, was a letter of introduction to the Dowager Duchess of Holstein on behalf of the Duke's good friend, Ludbert Kaver, one of the gentlemen of his bedchamber. Thus it would seem that Charles was already concentrating on the house of Holstein, though his letter took two months to arrive. Ludbert Kaver was still in Stockholm on July 13 and it was not until August 21 that his credentials were handed over to the Dowager Duchess. He had arrived at Travemünde on August 4 and was at Schöneberg in

---

[1] Chambers, *The Elizabethan Stage*, 2, 283.

[2] C. W. Scott-Giles, *Shakespeare's Heraldry*, 36 ff.

[3] '... be active and hand over his three portraits to the Princesses of Holstein, Brandenburg and Anhalt'; Staatliches Archivlager, Göttingen (Paket 348 der Auswärtigen Akten des Staatsarchivs Schwerin).

[4] '... to be his friend and try some other means ... perhaps with the youngest Princess, whereby a happy ending might be reached in that affair that was begun with her eldest sister'; *ibid*.

Mecklenburg on the 11th.[1] He spent the whole autumn travelling apparently aimlessly between Lübeck, Rostock, Hamburg and Schöneberg waiting to learn how the negotiations were proceeding. In the beginning of November he received his instructions from Nyköping, dated October 19, 1591. He was ordered to proceed at once to Elizabeth of Mecklenburg and ask her to put Duke Charles's proposal of marriage in person to Princess Christine; if he was successful in this, he was to go to the mother of the Duke's bride-to-be and enquire which wedding gift the two Princesses would prefer, Gripsholm Castle or Eskilstuna City; he was to make it known that it was the Duke's personal wish that mother and daughter should, if possible, leave for Sweden before the frosts came and celebrate the wedding at Nyköping the same autumn; he was to buy an ornament of rubies and diamonds for 1500 to 2000 daler from the Duke's agent, Marc Meus of Lübeck, and this gift he was to hand over to Princess Christine on the occasion of the proposal of marriage; finally, he was to remain on the Continent so as to keep Duke Charles informed of developments and was to wait for further instructions at the Duke's inn at Rostock. He was to accompany the Princesses when they left for Nyköping.[2]

Around December 1, 1591, Kaver received a letter from Elizabeth of Mecklenburg inviting him to come to Schöneberg after she had returned from a short journey. The negotiations seemed to be bearing fruit, and Kaver arrived at Schöneberg in the middle of December. He did not leave until some time in the middle of January 1592.[3]

Charles's negotiations with the house of Holstein were complicated by the fact that his nephew, Sigismund Vasa, King of Poland and heir to the Swedish throne, was also seeking Princess Christine's hand at this time. He too had sent her his portrait and expensive gifts[4] through the same Princess Elizabeth of Mecklenburg who was involved in Duke Charles's affairs.[5] However, negotiations begun in May were finally

---

[1] Diplomaträkenskaper 1570–93, fasc. 'Ludbert Kavers räkning från en resa i Tyskland 1591–92', KA.

[2] Hertig Karl av Södermanland m. fl. Handlingar rörande politiska och personliga förhållanden, K 348, RA.

[3] Enskilda arkiv. Arkivfragment (Fasc. 'Brev till Ludbert Kaver'), RA.

[4] Werwing, 1, 104.

[5] Nachrichten von der Vermählung ..., fol. 6 r and v, Landesarchiv Schleswig-Holstein.

concluded towards the end of 1591 for a marriage between Sigismund and Anne of Hapsburg, and this took place in May 1592.

Thus Sigismund entered into negotiations with the house of Hapsburg at the same time as Duke Charles was negotiating with the house of Holstein. In March 1591 Cardinal Radziwill and Sigismund's chamberlain, Gustavus Brahe, arrived at the Dowager Princess Mary's seat at Graz to obtain permission to approach the Emperor Rudolph II in Prague officially on Sigismund's behalf for the hand of one of her daughters.[1] The court at Graz was in deep mourning at this time, but Gustavus Brahe's task of selecting a wife for Sigismund was made easier by his being allowed to look through the arras at the two Princesses, Anne and Catherine, without their veils. Gustavus Brahe's proposal of marriage on Sigismund's behalf was accepted both by Princess Mary as the mother, by the Emperor Rudolph II as the chief guardian and by the Princes Ernest and Matthew as the guardians of the fatherless Princesses.[2]

It was soon clear, however, that the Poles, who at this time were about as enthusiastically Protestant as the north Germans, were strongly opposed to their king marrying an archduchess.[3] Some time later, Sigismund informed the Emperor of the arrival in Prague of his mediators, Hieronimus Rozdroz, Bishop of Wladislaw, and Albert Radziwill, Duke of Olyka. Sigismund wished the wedding to take place *per procuram* in Prague on November 10, 1591, but this proved impossible to arrange[4] and the ceremony was postponed until Easter 1592. After Sigismund had written to the Archduchess Mary in December 1591 about this delay, the date was finally fixed for May 1592.[5] News of this arrangement was sent to Philip II's Spanish court in December 1591.[6]

The letter from Elizabeth of Mecklenburg that put Duke Charles's marriage negotiations on a firmer footing is dated from Schöneberg on

[1] Familienakten Kart. 24, Bericht Westermachers an Erzh. Mathias, 19. März, 1591. Österr. Staatsarch., Vienna.

[2] *Ibid.*

[3] Archduke Ernest in a letter to the Archduchess Mary, June 30, 1591, Österr. Staatsarch., Vienna.

[4] Letters to the Emperor Rudolph II from the Archduchess Mary and the Archduke Ernest, dated 27.9.1591 and 28.9.1591 respectively, Österr. Staatsarch., Vienna.

[5] Letter to the Archduchess Mary from the Emperor Rudolph II, dated 14.12. 1591, Österr. Staatsarch., Vienna.

[6] Arch. Gen. de Simancas Secret. de Est. Cap. con la casa de Austria, 1493–1796, fol. 698.

January 16, 1592 to the Dowager Duchess Christine; in it she requests an answer to her previous enquiries on Duke Charles's behalf:

... Demnegst machen wir unss keinen zweiffel, E.L. sich guter maßen werden zu entsinnen wissen, wass wir an dieselbte unlangst schrifftlich haben gelangen lassen, darauff unnss zwar noch zur zeitt keine andwordt wiederumb zukommen. ...[1]

Ludbert Kaver was at Gottorf Castle at the beginning of February; the preliminary marriage contract was drawn up there and it was arranged that the wedding should take place the following midsummer. On his way back to Sweden Kaver received a letter from Berndt Stedingk, the legate of the house of Holstein, dated from Kiel on February 16, 1592. This letter expressly states

... unnd ist deß Frewleins guetter wille.[2]

The Dowager Duchess Christine had originally intended the wedding to be held in Holstein. John III, however, was definitely opposed to this and wrote to the court at Holstein on March 24, 1592:

Nachdeme uns auch mehrhochgedachter unser bruder bericht, da E.L. an S.L. freundtliche begehret, da S.L. zu volnziehung gemelts christlichen heiraths sich in das furstenthumle Holstein verfuegen wolte, so mugen wir E.L. darauf freundtlich nicht volhalten, da es itziger zeit dieses reichs zustandt und gelegenheit nicht geben will, da sich S.L. ausserhalb landes begeben solte, dan wir S.L. gegenwart nicht entrathen khonnen; ...[3]

At the same time John extended a welcome to Princess Christine as the future wife of Duke Charles and promised her the same rights and privileges as Princess Mary, Duke Charles's first wife, had had:

[1] 'Soon We shall not be able to doubt that Your Highness has had sufficient time to consider the matter about which We quite recently wrote to the person concerned, to which question We at present have yet to receive an answer'; Nachrichten von der Vermählung ..., fol. 6 r f., Landesarchiv Schleswig-Holstein.

[2] '... and the young lady has agreed'; Enskilda arkiv. Arkivfragment (Fasc. 'Brev till Ludbert Kaver'), RA.

[3] 'According to what Our Gracious Brother also relates, Your Highness requests that His Royal Highness shall travel to Holstein for the completion of the aforementioned Christian marriage. To this We must amiably object that Sweden's present state and circumstances are such that His Royal Highness cannot leave the country since We are unable to spare him'; Nachrichten von der Vermählung ..., fol. 11 r, Landesarchiv Schleswig-Holstein.

... nemblichen das schloß Gripsholm, die Stadt Strengnes, auch das haus Lundelsöö und Refsnass ...[1]

It had thus taken Charles longer than he had expected to arrange his second marriage. Circumstances had changed in the interval between the engagement of the company of players in England in June–July 1591 and this company's arrival at Nyköping towards the end of August the same year. The Duke was obliged to retain the company in his service for no less than thirteen months, a far longer period than was usual for the English companies that travelled abroad at that time. It is probable that special permission was required from Queen Elizabeth.

Since, according to the entries in Duke Charles's diary, the marriage was not definitely agreed upon until March 1592, by which time the English company had been in Nyköping for over half a year, this company can hardly have been engaged specifically for the Duke's wedding with Princess Christine. On March 5, 1592, Charles wrote in his almanac:

5. fick iagh uette, att gudh alzmechtigh haffuer tett så behagett, att fröken Kirstin är migh medh wenners rådh och samtycke tilsaghd, är tett gudh behageligett och migh nyttight så werdiges gudh videre hielpe i saken till en lycksaligh begynnelse och saligh endelychtt, amen.[2]

In the entry for May 1, 1592, he again mentioned the plans for his marriage:

1. fick iagh tett förste breff i frå fröken Chirstin, gudh late ware skett i en lycksaligh stund, Hans v. Rostock förde breffuett.[3]

The negotiations for an English marriage, initiated during Francklin's mission to Queen Elizabeth, were suspended while Charles was investigating his chances on the Continent; it is clear that Christine of Holstein was his first choice. After his return from England in August 1591, Francklin stayed at Nyköping until the middle of July 1592, when Duke Charles dispatched him on a mission to North Bothnia. He was thus not present at the wedding, which finally took place at the end of August 1592.

[1] '... namely Gripsholm Castle, Strängnäs Town and the Manors of Lundelsöö [Tynnelsö?] and Räfsnäs'; Drottning Kristinas d.ä. Morgongåvebrev, RA.

[2] '5. Learned this day that it has pleased the Almighty God that Princess Christine on the advice and approval of many friends is to be my wife. May it further please the Almighty to help the matter to a prosperous beginning and a blessed conclusion'; Cal. Car. IX, 74.

[3] '1. Received today the first letter from Princess Christine. May the Almighty God have done it in a happy hour. Hans von Rostock carried the dispatch'; ibid.

CHAPTER 2

The Elizabethan players cross to Sweden and are engaged at Duke Charles's court at Nyköping

The last entry in Henry Francklin's album from his mission to England is dated July 21, 1591. The company he engaged probably left England late in July. Though we do not know for certain, it seems likely that they crossed to Elsinore in Denmark and then proceeded to Nyköping. It is possible that they were on board the vessel that carried the assortment of cloth purchased by Francklin in England for Duke Charles. According to the Sound Toll Registers of the Danish king, seven vessels loaded with cloth from England sailed eastwards about this time, most of them registered in London, and the names of their captains were Petter Witt, Jann Stoffuadt, Thomis Smitt, Michel Merell, Vibrand Jacobßen, Herman Cornelißen and Willum Sather. The ship destined for Nyköping waited at Elsinore a while for a Swedish pilot before proceeding round the coast of southern Sweden with its cargo of cloth, probably also the English players and Henry Francklin. A letter from Duke Charles to Laße Weßgiöthe, dated August 24, 1591, runs as follows:

> Karl med Guds nåde, Sueriges Rijkis
> Arffurste, Hertig till Sudermanne-
> land, Neriche och Wermeland &c.

Wår gunst och nåde tilförende &c. Efther Wij förnimme, Laße Weßgiöthe, att ett Engels skep med allehande slagz Engelz kläde som Wij ther gennom Henrich Engilsman hafue beställe lathit skall med thz förste warde förwentendes in i Orsund och the ödmiukeligⁿ ähr begärendes en Wiß Styreman som han beledsagedt der ifrå och in åth Nijköping Derföre ähr Wår willie och befalning, att thu betinger en god Stijreman der i staden anthen Anders Bertilßon eller någen annen som wiß ähr eller och ther wår eigin tienere Finnen wore tilstädes och hwilkenter thu bekommer då wele Wij att thu strax skijnder, hijt, så wele Wij med en egen Enspennere lathe fölgie in till Sundet.* Dett bestellendes. Af Gripzholm then 24 Augusti Åhr.[1]

* såsom och nu strax hijt sende Olof Jönßon om han ther wid Nyköping stadde ähr.

---

[1] 'Charles by the Grace of God Hereditary Prince of the Kingdom of Sweden, Duke of Södermanland, Nerike and Värmland &c. With Our grace and favour &c. Since, Laße Weßgiöthe, We have learnt that an English ship with all manner of

Severine John and the gunfounders engaged by him were on board as far as to Elsinore, but it would seem that they proceeded overland from there to Gripsholm, where they arrived at the latest on August 15, 1591.[1] The first mention of the players at Nyköping is in the kitchen accounts for 1591:

för 12 Engliske spelemän som dhe förtärtt haffue i Grijpen ifrå 27 Aug^{tl} intil 8de 7^{bris} th är i 12 dagar efter werdens Hans Krög^s rechningh. Pening^r .... 37 dal^r 13 öre[2]

From September 8 the players were lodged at Duke Charles's Nyköpingshus (Nyköping Castle).

Among the gifts listed in the Duke's accounts for 1591 there appears the following:

skänchte H.F.N. 5 engilsche trommetter som ankomen
31 Aug^{ti} $\overline{91}$ til at presentere H.F.N. sin tiänst
Ung^{sch} gyllen .... 10 sty^r
Udi lijke motte och same dagh 6 engilsche instrumentist^r
Ung^{sch} gyllen .... 12 sty^{r3}

Duke Charles had been staying at Gripsholm Castle during August and returned to Nyköping on the 30th. The English company was presented to him on the following day. Francklin's name, which last appeared in

English cloth ordered by Us through Henry (Francklin) Englishman is waiting in The Sound and respectfully requests an experienced pilot to take them from there into Nyköping, it is accordingly Our wish and command that you engage a good pilot from the town, either Anders Bertilßon some other skilled person, possibly Our own servant the Finn, if he is there, whichever of these you can engage as pilot, We wish that the pilot and you as soon as possible make haste to Us here at Gripsholm. According to Our wishes one of Our one-horse vehicles shall drive the pilot down to the Sound. We wish also that you immediately send Us Olof Jönsson to Gripsholm if you can get hold of him in Nyköping. This is ordered. At Gripsholm 24 August 1591'; Kungl. arkiv. Brev till ståthållare m. fl. Fasc.: 'Brev till Laße Weßgiöthe', K 353, RA.

[1] Cf. Söffring Jönssons räkning 1590–91, fol. 16 r, KA. Hertig Karls diarium 1566–92 den 15 augusti 1591, and Hertig Karls brev till Laße Weßgiöthe, 24 augusti 1591, K 353, both RA.

[2] '... to 12 English players their board at Grijpen's Inn from August 27 to September 8, 1591, i.e. for 12 days according to Hans Kröger, the innkeeper's bill'; Hertig Karls räntekammare 1590–97, fasc. 5, Håkan Larsson 1591, fol. 52 v, KA.

[3] 'Given by His Royal Highness to 5 English trumpeters who arrived August 31, 1591, to present their services to him ... (Hungarian) ducats 10. The same the same day to 6 English *Instrumentister* ... ducats 12'; Skänchningar 1591, Hertig Karls räntekammare 1590–97, fasc. 5, Håkan Larsson 1591, fol. 62 r, KA.

the Nyköping kitchen accounts of January 1591, is mentioned again from August 30 onwards.[1]

On their engagement at court various sums[2] were paid to the members of the company[3] as follows:

Engilske Instrumentister

Edwardus Stackman	13 daler 3½ marker
Willam Kupertt	4 daler 1 öre
Edwardus Tamset	14 daler 1 öre
Ricard Havel	41 daler
Ricard Bluett	13 daler 3½ marker
Matteus Bruck	13 daler

Engilske Trommetter

Johannes Huss	8 daler 3 marker
Ricard Raaff	3 daler 10 öre
Philip Bruggiss	20 daler
Johan Wahan	35 daler
Rubertt Wahan	43 daler
Niclas König dr^eg	11 daler 1 öre på sin kleder

Only five trumpeters are mentioned in the list of gifts presented to members of the company on their arrival. The sixth, Nicholas King, was only an apprentice and as such received no more than money for his apparel.

Shortly after the arrival of the Englishmen the Duke also engaged six, probably Swedish players:

> Nykiöping 7 september 1591
> Bestälning för Sex stycken Spelmän
> H:F:N: antagit hafver.[4]

Although in fact nothing is mentioned here about the nationality of these players, it is highly probably that they were the same six trumpeters whose names are listed elsewhere in the accounts for this period:

Trommetter

Matz Hindersson pukslagare[5]	30 daler
Casper Rebock	7 daler

[1] Kungl. Hofförtärningen 1591–92, SA.

[2] Bestälningar Anno 1591, Hertig Karls räntekammare 1590–97, fasc. 5, Håkan Larsson 1591, fol. 24 v–25 r, KA.

[3] Cf. App. I (Wikland, *Eliz. Pl.*, 1. ed., 1962.)

[4] 'Nyköping September 7, 1591. Warrant for 6 Players engaged by the Duke'; Hertig Karls diarium 1566–92, RA.

[5] *Pukslagare* = drummer. Hertig Karls räntekammare 1590–97, fasc. 5, Håkan Larsson 1591, fol. 21 v, KA.

Jöns Nilssonn	24 daler
Hans Pålach	16 daler
Jörgin Reboch	16 daler
David Festhe	16 daler

There were thus eighteen players, musicians and trumpeters at Nyköping during the latter part of 1591, twelve of them English and six
Swedish. Others were engaged during the spring of 1592, so that the company numbered about thirty all told[1] at the time of the Duke's wedding
celebrations on August 27–28, 1592.

The warrant containing the names of the Elizabethan players quoted
above also included the English specialists engaged by Severine John for
the Duke's shipyard at Nyköping:[2]

Skipbygger[2]	Tomos Walter engilßman	118 daler
Engilske	Johan Forne	55 daler
bössegiutere[4]	Edemont pinsebech	43 daler
	Hindrich v. Meklnb. tolch[5]	17 daler

The English gunfounders who accompanied Severine John from England presumably went with him to Gripsholm.[6] Duke Charles's letter
from Gripsholm dated August 24, 1591,[7] to Simon Erichsson

om några engeländer som äre antagne och skole bewijsa sine mesterstycken[8]

most probably refers to these.

The name of Hindrich v. Meklnb., interpreter, in the above list is immediately followed by the names of the twelve players. His name suggests that he was a German-speaking interpreter employed for the same
reason as the man who followed the English company that in September
1586 left Denmark for Saxony.[9] Although the English gunfounders with
whom Hindrich v. Meklnb. is bracketed in the accounts probably required the services of an interpreter, the English players must have

[1] K. klädkammaren 1592, vol. 48, 2, fol. 64 r ff., SA. Cf. pp. 53–54 and App. II
(Wikland, *Eliz. Pl.*, 1. ed., 1962)

[2] Cf. pp. 34 and 184–185.

[3] Shipbuilder.

[4] English gunfounders.

[5] Interpreter.

[6] Hertig Karls diarium 1566–92, 24.8.1591, RA.   [7] *Ibid.*

[8] '... concerning certain Englishmen who have been engaged and are to demon-
strate their masterpieces (English guns)'; cf. *SAOB*, 17, M 2040.

[9] Cf. Chapter 9.

needed him much more. On August 10, 1592, less than three weeks before the wedding, Hindrich v. Meklnb. was issued with expensive apparel and other items;[1] this would hardly have occurred had he not been assisting the players. Moreover, the bracket uniting his name with those of the 'English gun-foundrymen' has been emended in a different ink at a later date; the initial *R* has been written next to the bracket opposite Edemont pinsebech's name and a tick entered on the line between this and the sum paid, 43 daler. What probably happened was that the bracket was simply drawn too far down in the first place.[2]

The people of Nyköping can hardly have known enough English for the players to be able to manage without an interpreter. This is not to say that the English plays had to be translated word for word; the interpreter would have been used during, for instance, the prologue and the epilogue and, off the stage, for negotiations between the players and the Duke's officials.

One would naturally like to know whether this company was known in England and from what circles its members were drawn. Two of the players, Richard Bluett and William Cooper, are mentioned in Joseph Foster's *Alumni Oxonienses*. From this list of students at Oxford,[3] the Heralds' Visitations books and the pedigree of the Bluett family[4] it has been possible to compile the following:

Bluett, Richard (Blewet), of Somerset, arm. Father: John Bluett, of Greenham, Somerset, esq., died 1587. Grandfather: Sir Roger Bluett, of Holcombe Rogus, Devon. Mother: Dorothy Bluett, daughter of William Blount, Lord Mountjoy. Hart Hall, matriculation entry under date 1568, aged 19; buried at Holcombe Rogus, Devon, March 18, 1614/15. He m. Mary Chichester, and had a son, Arthur, b. 1591.

What is of particular interest here is Richard Bluett's relationship, via the Blounts, to Lord Thomas Burgh.[5]

Alumni Oxonienses[6] tells us the following about William Cooper:

Cooper, William, of Salop, pleb. Brasenose Coll., matriculation entry under date July 4, 1579, aged 20; B.A. Feb. 22, 1581 [–2], M.A. July 8, 1584.

[1] K. klädkammaren 1592, vol. 48, 2, fol. 71 v, SA.
[2] According to Swedish usage a tick indicates that something is inaccurate or erroneous.
[3] Op. cit., 1, 142.
[4] College of Arms.
[5] Cf. pp. 29, last §, f. and App. 7 (Wikland, *Eliz. Pl.*, 1. ed., 1962).
[6] Op. cit., 1, 325.

Thus at the time when the company arrived at Nyköping, Bluett would have been 41 and Cooper 31 years old and it is not improbable that it was in fact they who were two of the players. Richard Bluett, it is true, belonged to the English gentry and it was unusual for such a man to become a player. Nevertheless, in this particular case, involved as it was with the plans for Duke Charles's second marriage, Bluett's birth need not be regarded as evidence against this identification.

According to the Lord Chamberlain's records[1] a certain Thomas King[2] was engaged in 1582 as 'the Queen's Drum player'. The young trumpeter whose name appears last on the list quoted above may well have been Thomas King's son or near relation; not only had they the same profession but also the same surname [Sw. *Konig* (*König*) = King].

In James Hill's dispatches[3] from the Nyköping of Duke Charles's day mention is made of Johannes Huss (John Howse), Philip Bruggis (Briggis) and Richard Havel (Havill). Otherwise the members of the company are unknown to us.

---

[1] Cf. pp. 129–132.
[2] *Ibid.*
[3] SP 95/1, fol. 70 ff., and Dom SP 12/274, PRO. Cf. also p. 94.

CHAPTER 3

The English company at Nyköping 1591–92

The records tell us little about the activities of the English company during their thirteen months' stay at Duke Charles's court at Nyköping. However, one of the entries relating to Richard Bluett runs:

> hafver h.f.n^d honom skienckt till
> H. Karl Stures bröllop .... Kledhning ....
> 1 mz all tillbehör.[1]

Thus Bluett and probably all the Englishmen performed on October 17, 1591, at the wedding between Charles Sture and Catherine Joensdotter, daughter of Joen Carlsson of Mem and Sjösa. Sture, who was born in 1555, inherited Tullgarn Castle from his father and was a chamberlain at the court of John III in 1571. He joined Duke Charles's party, however, and became one of the Duke's most trusted advisers.

Catherine Joensdotter received Tullgarn Castle as her morning-gift when she married Charles Sture; the document confirming this, dated October 18, 1591,[2] is sealed both by its originator, Charles Sture, and also by his sisters and brothers-in-law.[3] From this it would seem that these relatives were present at Charles Sture's wedding and at the celebrations in connection with this on October 17 and 18. Though it has not been possible to find any record of the guests of the bride at this wedding, it is very likely that many of Joen Carlsson's relatives were also present. Thus the occasion would have assembled many members of the Swedish nobility. A number of the signatories to the document mentioned above

[1] 'His Royal Highness has granted him for Charles Sture's marriage ... apparel ... 1 complete set'; Hertig Karls räntekammare 1589–92, fasc. 4, fol. 76 r, KA.

[2] According to a letter *Giffwith Nyköping aderthende octobri Åhr efter Christi byrdh 1591*, Catherine of Sjösa received Tullgarn as a morning gift. Pergamentsamlingen 18.10.1591, RA.

[3] Sigrid Sture of Geddeholm, Eric Gustafsson (Stenbock), Baron of Öresten, &c. (married to Magdalene Sture), Hogenskild Bielke, Baron of Läckö (married to Anne Sture), Gustavus Axelson Banér of Djursholm (married to Christine Sture) and Ture Bielke (married to Margaret Sture).

later supported Sigismund when he attempted to retain the Swedish crown after his coronation as King of Sweden in 1594, and they were subsequently beheaded at Linköping in 1600 after Charles had successfully evicted his nephew.

At the time of Charles Sture's wedding the following names are included in the record of those who received board at Nyköping Castle on October 15 and during the week of the 17th to the 24th:

Duke Gustaf of Saxony,	Axel Ryning,
Mauritz Stensson Lewenhaupt,	Jost Kurtzel,
Doctor Zacharias Vheling,	Karl Karlsson Gyllenhielm,
Doctor Teofilus Homodei,	Jakob Koskul,
Count Geronimus Strozzi,	Hindrich Kumhusen,
	Bo Ribbing &c.[1]

Among the guests from abroad, the presence of the Italian Count Geronimo Strozzi is of particular interest. The following entry is to be found in Duke Charles's household accounts:

> Schenchte H.F.N. en Italiener b[d] Jeronimus
> Stratzzij sendebudh frå(n) her lasky i Påland
>   dat. Nycöping: 19 8[b] 91
> En guld kiädh wogh . . . .   77 cronr
>   ther udi hengiende
> Ett M.N.H. conterfeij wogh . . . . 15½ crone.[2]

This gift to Geronimo Strozzi must have been a token of the Duke's sympathies with the Calvinist reformation in Poland, later to be crushed by the Catholic counter-reformation.

For October 15 the list mentioned above includes six English trumpeters. Although they do not appear again the following week, when the wedding was held, this does not mean that they were not present but only that they did not eat in the Duke's dining hall.

The Duke's kitchen accounts contain the following entries for board for '6 Foreign English Players':[3]

[1] Förtäringsräkenskap 1591–92 (October 1591–January 1592). Kungl. Hofförtärningen 1591, SA.

[2] 'Gift from His Royal Highness to an Italian Geronimo Strozzi, envoy from Herr Lasky in Poland, dated Nyköping October 19, 1591, A gold chain weighing— 77 cronor (*1 crona = ca. 3.3 gm*) from which there hung A Portrait of His Royal Highness, weight 15½ crona'; Hertig Karls räntekammare. Håkan Larssons m. fl. räkenskaper 1590–97, fasc. 5, 1591, Skänckningar a° 91, fol. 62 r, KA. (*Such a gift was common in princely circles from about 1550–1650.*)

[3] Kungl. Hofförtärningen 1591, SA.

Den 28/11– 4/12 1591	1 dag
den 5/12–11/12 1591	7 dagar
den 12/12–18/12 1591	1 dag[1]
den 19/12–25/12 1591	1 dag
den 26/12 1591–1/1 1592	5 dagar
den 2/1– 8/1 1592	2 dagar
den 9/1–15/1 1592	1 dag
den 16/1–22/1 1592	1 dag
den 19/3–25/3 1592	1 dag
den 27/3–2/4 1592	5 dagar
den 3/4–9/4 1592	1 dag

From these entries it would appear that the Englishmen sat at the Duke's table for a longer or shorter period each time they performed. According to an entry in the wardrobe accounts for 1592 Richard Raph married while he was at Nyköping:

Thend 20 Martii $\overline{92}$ skenckte W.N.
Herre en Engels Spelemant Trumetter
benemdt Rickertt Raff till sitt
Bröllop
Trijp .... ½ st Blomerdt.[2]

This marriage was probably one of eight that were celebrated on March 27, 1592:

Bröllop för
Brudgummer 8
Bruder 8
med följe 63

Summa 79 personer

Avrest Bröllopsfolk
den 29/3 .... 79 personer.[3]

While no mention of it is made in Duke Charles's almanac for 1592,[4] it is clear from the register of persons at the Duke's table that the English company contributed to the celebrations on this occasion.

[1] On this occasion the register refers to 6 English trumpeters.

[2] 'March 20, 1592, His Royal Highness presented an English Player Trumpeter named Richard Raaff for his wedding, Trijp (type of woollen cloth) ½ piece with flower pattern'; op. cit., vol. 47, fol. 95 r, SA.

[3] 'Marriage for Bridegrooms—8, Brides—8, with train—63, Total 79 persons. Marriage guests departed, March 29—79 persons'; Hovförtäringsräkenskap 1591–92, SA. Cf. p. 76, 6th §.

[4] *Cal. Car. IX*, 75.

A Swedish trumpeter, David Festhe, and three unnamed English trumpeters accompanied Duke Charles when he went to Södertälje on May 8, 1592, and presumably went with him to Stockholm next day. Two other members of the English company appear in the accounts after this:

Lengden opå hoffsens förtärningh pro anno etc $\overline{92}$

....

	Willam Kuper haffver bekomit effter hans gådes sedel iffrå 22 maij til 19 julii	
	runde M(ark)st.	12 daler
engilske	Philpuss trumetere iffrå then 9 maij	
spelmen	in thil then 19 julij	
	runde M(ark)st.	16 daler[1]

Thus a player and a trumpeter received their board away from Nyköping Castle during the summer months. In both cases the account was closed on July 19, five weeks before the Duke's own wedding, so that presumably Cooper and Briggis took their meals at the castle from then on.

From July 21 until August 5, 1592, six English players and as many English trumpeters appear regularly in the kitchen accounts.

During the winter months the players naturally gave their various performances indoors, probably in much the same manner as another company[2] had entertained the court of Saxony five years earlier with theatricals, music and tumbling. According to an inventory drawn up in 1649 there was at Nyköping Castle

Huite Salen med ett rum derinnenföre ...[3]

with no less than 53 windows; it was probably here that the entertainments were held. As soon as the weather permitted, performances were given in the open air. According to Indebetou's book, the *Lillträdgården* (the Small Garden) lay directly in front of the castle with the *Bollhuset* (the Ball-house) close by.[4] This Ball-house was where the cour-

---

[1] 'The payroll of the court kitchen accounts for 1592—William Cooper has received according to Hans Gåde's bill from May 22 to July 19 in round Mark pieces 12 daler. Philip Briggis the same from May 9 until July 19 in round Mark pieces 16 daler'; Hertig Karls räntekammare 1590–97, fasc. 7, Hindrich Hinderssons räkenskaper 1592, fol. 34 r, KA.

[2] Cf. pp. 130 f.

[3] 'White Hall with a room within.' This inventory was made in 1649, i.e. before the Great Fire at Nyköping Castle in 1665. Södermanlands landskapsbok för år 1649, Södermanlands landskapshandlingar, KA.

[4] See the map, Plate 6 (Wikland, *Eliz. Pl.*, 1. ed., 1962).

tiers and the young men of Nyköping took exercise; it could well have been converted for use as a stage—this was in fact done with a similar building at Stockholm about forty years later.

West of the river but east of the castle and directly opposite the royal gardens lay the *Spelegårdsholmen* (Play-yard Island), a piece of land with a canal between it and the castle. At the end of the 16th century this island, besides being surrounded by water, was covered with trees. The inventory mentioned above describes the *Spelegården* as an enclosed space with portals and means by which it could be shut and locked. It is known today as *Spelhagen*. Thus when the weather was fine performances could be given in the open air in the *Spelegården* and when it was wet there was the *Bollhuset*.

While the English company was at Duke Charles's court, a carpenter was employed at the castle to work on the *spelebanen*,[1] which Henrik Schück considers was probably some sort of stage. The bill for this work runs as follows:

Oloff Snickare Haff[r]
arbetat widh Nyköpings Slotth
uthi Spelebannen på sin egenn kost
uthi — 3 wikŭr. Ther på Jöns
mortenßons bewijs $\overline{92}$.

Affrecknad thn 12 $\Big\{$ Löp[r] uthi
Octob. $\overline{93}$.[2] $\big\lfloor$pnr ... 6 Dal[r] 24 öre

The performances given by the English company at Duke Charles's wedding clearly took place on an open-air stage. An eye-witness, Michael Heberer von Bretten, described the occasion thus:

... / und haben sich auch dabey Engelländische Comoedianten und Springer finden lassen / die ihrem Gebrauch nach zimliche Kurtzweil geübet und gemacht / ...[3]

[1] Playyard or stage. Cf. Henrik Schück, 'Englische Comoedianten in Skandinavien', *Skandinavisches Archiv 1892*, I, 371. At this time the Swedish word *spelebannen* was used in two senses: 'players' yard' and 'stage'. Cf. Jacob Schroderus, Regium donom eller konungzlig förähring, Företal 1, 1606, *SAOB* arkiv.

[2] 'Olaf the carpenter has worked at Nyköping Castle on the 'spelebannen' without board for 3 weeks. Thereto Jöns Mortensson's account $\overline{92}$. Paid October 12, 1593, 6 daler 24 öre'; Hertig Karls räntekammare, Likvidationer 1592–93, vol. 91, 12, KA. Jönß Mortenßon was *c.* 1592(–93) bailiff of Nyköping Castle. Cf. the bill of Mester Petter Dionysii Bygmestere (Master-builder) *ibid.*

[3] '... /and were on this occasion English strolling players and tumblers present (in Nyköping), who according to their manners and customs performed a great deal of rather good entertainments/ ...'; *Aegyp. Serv.*, 626.

Von Bretten had been in Cracow a few months earlier for the wedding between Sigismund and Anne of Hapsburg and there he had seen an entertainment performed on May 25, 1592. He has left us the following description:

Das Achte Capitel

. . . .

Uff der ein seiten des Saals / war ein Teatrum auffgericht / mit Rohtem Tuch überzogen / darauff uff die 1.000 Personen stunden und saßen / so dem Spectacul zusahen.

Das Neundte Capitel

. . . .

Baldt öffnet sich die Pforten des Thurns / und gieng erstlich herausser ein Sanno, in Mascaladen vermummet und gekleidet / so Italienisch redete / zu welchem sich nochmals zween andere verfügten / und machten groß Gelächter / mit kurzweiligen Italienischen reden.[1]

This entertainment was thus given indoors. A comparison of the author's two descriptions from Cracow and Nyköping suggests that the latter performance was given outdoors and without any elaborate settings.[2] In writing about the wedding celebrations in Poland, von Bretten mentions that after the masque both Queen Anne of Poland and Princess Anne Vasa of Sweden were invited to the dance by the three zannies of the comedy. Clearly these[3] cannot have been professional actors but must have been important noblemen who, as wedding guests, gave an amateur performance. Arrangements had, however, been made for an entertainment. Westermacher, the Austrian secretary, gives the following account, dated June 6, 1592, in a description of the wedding celebrations at Cracow:

Sonst ist auf diesen tag ferner nichts fürgenommen worden, dann daß man nach der mahlzeit ein tantz gehalten, und auf den abent ist angestelt gewesen, daß man auf dem neugepauten und zuegerichten tantzsal ein mascarada und etliche andere spectacl hette ediern sollon. Weyl aber ein solcher großer platzregen kurtz vor abents gefallen, welcher das theatrum

---

[1] '*Chapter 8.* ... On one side of the hall a theatre was built with a red carpet unfolded on which more than 1000 spectators of the play stood and sat. *Chapter 9.* ... The doors of the tower were soon opened. First a masked Italian-speaking sanno (player) came out. Furthermore two other sannos, all Italian-speaking, making comical jests, resulting in bursts of laughter from the spectators'; *Aegyp. Serv.*, 555. Cf. Beijer, *Fossard*, 5 ff.

[2] Cf. Hodges, *The Globe Restored*, 15 ff.

[3] *Aegyp. Serv.*, 556.

etlichermassen verderbet, ist das spectacl und mascarada disen abendt auch noch gepliben.'[1]

It will be remembered that Anne Vasa, Sigismund's sister, wrote a letter of introduction for Henry Francklin before he went to England and engaged the Elizabethan players for Duke Charles. As it turned out, she remained in Poland[2] after her brother's wedding and missed the Duke's marriage in August; she may therefore never have seen the players whom she indirectly helped to engage.

[1] 'Otherwise no events this day except some dancing after dinner. In the evening at the new dancing-pavilion a masquerade and some other entertainments were to have been performed. Because it was raining shortly before evening, and the downpour to a degree damaged the stage, the performance and the masquerade were called off again this evening'; Familienakten Kart. 24, 25 und die Handschrift Böhm—Supplement 8, Österreichisches Staatsarchiv, Vienna.

[2] *SBL* 2, 22 ff. and *PHT 1938* (S. U. Palme, 'En politisk giftermålshandel').

CHAPTER 4

The English company at Nyköping
reinforced, Spring 1592

Two more Englishmen joined the company at Nyköping in the spring of 1592. From the wardrobe accounts[1] it is clear that Philip Kingman, 'Timlare',[2] and Philip Gibson served with the company at Nyköping at the latest from May 1, 1592, onwards. These two most probably accompanied the English and Dutch mercenaries engaged by Duke Charles for the Swedish–Russian war,[3] in which case they would have travelled from Emden via Lübeck to Nyköping. That their names do not appear on the Lord Admiral's passport dated February 10, 1592, for Robert Browne and his companions[4] may mean that they had already accepted another engagement and that Henry Francklin, during his mission to England when the rest of the Nyköping company was engaged, came to an agreement with these two that they should join the other players in Nyköping at a later date.

A directive concerning Kingman's and Gibson's pay appears to have been embodied in the following:

Stockholm 17 Maius 1592

Swar opå Håkan Larßons Schriffwelse om godzet i Norkiöping, dee Engilske Spelemäns och Arbetzfolkets Penningar.[5]

The pay for the members of the company who had been at Nyköping since the summer of 1591 had already been adjusted in another warrant;[6]

---

[1] Kungl. klädkammaren 1592, vol. 48, 2, fol. 65 v, SA. Cf. App. 2 (Wikland, *Eliz. Pl.*, 1. ed., 1962).

[2] *Timlare*, an old Swedish word also used of a player, *SAOB* arkiv.

[3] Cf. pp. 187 ff.

[4] Cf. pp. 135 ff.

[5] 'Stockholm, May 17th, 1592. Reply to Håkan Larsson concerning the cargoes at Norrköping, and the pay for the English players and the workmen'; Hertig Karls diarium 1566–92, RA.

[6] Cf. pp. 41 ff.

it is therefore reasonable to assume that it was Kingman and Gibson who had their conditions of service determined on May 17.

Among those listed as being quartered at Nyköping Castle at the time of Duke Charles's wedding there is a section headed 'Players' which includes the following:[1]

Spelemän

M. Zion 3	L. Philip ⎫		
Matz Stender 1	Måns ⎬ drenger (*apprentices*)		3
Peter 2	Hans ⎭		
Torpanŭs ⎫	Matz Pukslager (*kettle-drummer*)...	2	
Gabriell ⎪	Trummeter (*trumpeters*)	13	
Niclaŭs ⎪ 6	Drenger (*apprentices*)	4	
Willam ⎬	Wulf Cantor	18	
Richardt ⎪	Lacheijer (*lackeys*)	6	
S. Philip ⎭			

Most probably, S. (*Store* = Big) Philip and L. (*Lille* = Little) Philip were Philip Kingman and Philip Gibson respectively; at all events, there were no other players, Swedish or English, who would fit the occasion better. Willam and Richardt would have been William Cooper and Richard Havill. The other members of the English company were lodged elsewhere and thus do not appear in this list.

On an earlier page in these records the French-born Willem Cratell,[2] who was responsible for the fireworks at the wedding celebrations,[3] is listed between two interpreters and four painters. It would thus seem that only those whose presence was vital to the success of the celebrations were lodged at the castle itself. If this was so, one would be justified in according William Cooper, Richard Havill, Philip Kingman and Philip Gibson a special position among the members of the English company.

Philip Kingman was a well-known figure in Shakespeare's London, and it seems that he came from Herefordshire.[4] He may have been in Cassel in 1594–95 with Robert Browne, i.e. not long after the present company had departed from Nyköping. According to two undated warrants[5] both Browne and Kingman entered the service of Maurice the

---

[1] Kungl. Hofförtärningen $\overline{93}$, SA.

[2] Cf. p. 189.

[3] Cf. *Aegyp. Serv.*, 626.

[4] Cf. *Coryat's Crudities*, 2, 183.

[5] Urkundenbestand. Best/Comoedianten, Staatsarchiv Marburg, Marburg/Lahn. Cf. Gustaf Könnecke, *Neue Beiträge zur Gesch. der Engl. Komödianten*, and Chambers, *Eliz. Stage*, 2, 277.

Learned, Landgrave of Hesse-Cassel. A bill,[1] dated December 1594 from Ludwig Brockman, a German shoemaker in Cassel, to the Landgrave, contains a demand for the expense of providing lodging for two English lutenists for fifteen weeks; from this it would seem that a sizeable English company had arrived at Cassel sometime around the beginning of August and that some of its members had had to be lodged out in the town. At all events Robert Browne was the Landgrave's man by April 16, 1595, when an order was issued permitting the export of a consignment of bows and arrows from England to Cassel and Browne was in England to collect them.[2] This entry in the Hatfield MSS is confirmed by the settlement between John Wroth, a London banker, and Landgrave Maurice according to which Wroth, among other items, paid 20 pounds to one Roberto Braun in London in 1595.[3]

Browne's and Kingman's above-mentioned warrants are not alike. Kingman's has the following paragraph:

Neben dißen soll er jeder Zeitt, wan wir ihme ein Argument oder Inhalt einer neuen Comoedien oder Historien sagen werden schuldig sein, dieselbig in seine Sprach zu transponieren und zu einer comoedien oder Spill zu zurichten.[4]

This clause does not appear on Robert Browne's warrant. Instead, he is engaged specifically as a

... Comoediant und Musicus ...[5]

whose duty it was to entertain the Landgrave not only with comedies and tragedies but

... sowohl in Musica Vocali als Instrumentali ...[6]

to train a boys' choir made up of Hessian or foreign pupils and to remain in Cassel unless he had permission to leave. No mention of either music or a choir is made in Philip Kingman's warrant.

[1] Best. 4b, 46a, Nr 1, Blatt 2, 1594 Dezember, Staatsarchiv Marburg, Marburg/Lahn. Cf. Richard P. Wülcker, *Engl. Schausp. in Kaßel*, and Chambers, *Eliz. Stage*, 2, 277.

[2] H. 5.174. Cf. Chambers, *Eliz. Stage*, 2, 277.

[3] Best. 4f England, Nr 33, 1595, Dezember 18, Staatsarchiv Marburg, Marburg/Lahn.

[4] 'Moreover, he shall every time, when We give him the plot of a new comedy or history, be obliged to translate this into his own tongue and arrange it as a comedy or play'; op. cit.

[5] '... player and musician ...'

[6] '... both in the Vocal and the Instrumental Music ...'

From these discrepancies it would seem that Kingman's most important task was to be the Landgrave's playwright, while Robert Browne was to be responsible for the music and singing. A parallel to this arrangement is to be found in connection with the permit to build the Porter's Hall in 1615. Here Philip Kingman, in order to erect a new theatre, went into partnership with Philip Rosseter, who was perhaps the foremost lutenist of his day.[1]

Nearly four years after the Nyköping venture, Philip Kingman became the leader of an English company of strolling players in August 1596; in the same month he obtained permission to give performances in Strasburg. The following entry from the *Straßburger Rathsprotokolle* is of interest in this connection:

Samstag, den 7. August 1596.

Philipp Konigsman (Kingman) sambt noch eilff personen aus Engellandt Comoedispieler obergeben per Bittelb(ron) ein supplication; darin sie bitten, m(eine) H(erren)[2] wollen Ihnen zulassen, dz sie hie auch gleich in andern Stätten wie auch bei Fürsten vnnd H(erre)n Ire Comoedias Tragoedias spielen mögen vnnd von den zusehern 1 batzen oder 4 dolchen nehmen mögen. Den sie wegen der zehrung irer selbs vnnd Roß vnd Fuhrman vil uncosten anwenden müssen.

Erkannt: Sollen Ihnen die 14 tag hie zu spielen erlaubt sein, doch dz sie nuhr 3 dolchen von der person nehmen sollen.[3]

Thus Kingman and his men performed both comedies and tragedies in Strasburg.

We also know that Philip Henslowe, the well-known London theatre manager, used 'Mr Kyngman the elder' to witness a bond on April 16, 1599[4] and thus we can be certain that there were two actors named

---

[1] Cf. below and p. 57, 2nd to 4th §§.

[2] This refers to the Council of the city of Strasburg, which at this time consisted of a mayor and 30 councillors—10 noblemen and 20 citizens.

[3] 'Sunday, August 7th, 1596. Philip Kingman and a further eleven persons from England, Comedians, have sent a petition from the City of Bittelbron, in which they apply to Your Lordships for permission to perform their Comedies and Tragedies here in Strasburg as in other Cities and also for Princes and Lords, and tentatively to take from the spectators 1 batzen or 4 dolchen per head, which money they must dispose for food for themselves, horses and drivers and sundry other expenses. Granted: Permission to play a fortnight; as entrance fee, however, only 3 dolchen per head'; *Straßburger Rathsprotokolle*, 21, 238 r. Cf. Crueger, 113 f.

[4] *Henslowe's Diary*, 1, 205.

Kingman at this time, Philip and Robert, probably brothers to judge from a similar case.[1]

Philipp Rosseter, Philipp Kingman, Robert Iones and Raphe Reeve are mentioned by name in a building permit dated June 3, 1615, for a theatre at Blackfriars—the Porter's Hall previously referred to. Authority was given on the following conditions:[2]

> ... scituate and being within the Precinct of the Blackeffryers neere Puddlewharfe in the Suburbs of London, called by the name of the lady Saunders house, or otherwise Porters hall, and now in the occupation of the said Robert Iones ... one convenient Playhouse for the said children of the Revelles, the same Playhouse to be vsed by the Children of the Revelles for the tyme being of the Queenes Maiestie, and for the Princes Players, and for the ladie Elizabeths Players ...

The exact position of the theatre is not clear, but there must have been a porter's lodge[3] not far from the King's Men's Blackfriars theatre and Shakespeare's Gatehouse.[4]

Robert Kingman,[5] probably Philip Kingman's younger brother, was a member of Robert Browne's company when it performed at Heidelberg, Frankfort on the Main and Strasburg in 1599 and at Frankfort on the Main during Easter 1601. Shortly afterwards he left the stage and his career as a strolling player to become a merchant and citizen of Strasburg, where Coryat[6] met him in 1603. Later he assisted Robert Browne

---

[1] Arber, 2, 726, 'Master John harrison the Yo(u)nger, brother of master John harrison th(e) elder.' *Ibid.*, 2, 251. This freeman is called 'John Harrison the yo(u)ngest' on January 19, 1601.

[2] Chambers, *Eliz. Stage*, 2, 472.

[3] *Ibid.*, 2, 55, 472 and 516–17. *Collections*, 1, 1, 43–100. *Ibid.*, 1, 3, 277–79. *Ibid.*, 1, 4 and 5, 374. *Ibid.*, 2, 3, 320 (The Malone Society 1907, 1909, 1911 and 1931, respectively). William Shakespeare, *Third Variorum*, 1821, 3, 52. Additional facts concerning the struggle between the London authorities and Rosseter, Kingman and their associates have been published by F. P. Wilson in 'More Records from the Remembrancia of the City of London, *Collections*, 4, 55–65 (The Malone Society, 1956).

[4] This was acquired by William Shakespeare on March 10, 1613, from Henry Walker, 'Citizen and Minstrel of London' for £140. Cf. Chambers, *William Shakespeare*, 2, 154 ff.

[5] Nung., *Dict. of Act.*, 226.

[6] *Coryat*, 2, 183.

and other English actors, when, for instance in 1618, they again visited Strasburg.[1]

Less is known about Philip Gibson. There are a number of notes which include the name Gibson in the margins of prompter's copies preserved in the British Museum (Egerton MS 1994). In most cases, however, only the surname has been written, e.g. 'Enter: Gibs', and even in the three cases where an initial appears, this has been written so indistinctly that it cannot be interpreted with certainty. In fact, it looks like an 'H' at first sight, but it may well be some other letter.

In *The Captives* Gibson appears as a merchant, in *The Two Noble Ladies* as a soldier and in *Edmund Ironside* as a messenger. All these plays are in the Egerton MS 1994. Their style has led to their being dated 1590–95 but as they were performed during the 1620's and 1630's it is not possible to say with certainty whether the notes in the margin were made at the time they were written or later, when they were performed. It is thus impossible to tell if the Philip Gibson of the Nyköping company was the same person as the Gibson of the Egerton manuscripts.[2]

[1] Herz, 15, 22, 31 and 37.
[2] Nung., *Dict. of Act.*, 152.

CHAPTER 5

The celebrations at Nyköping on the occasion of Duke Charles's wedding with Princess Christine of Holstein, August 25 to September 3, 1592

Once the marriage between Duke Charles and Princess Christine of Holstein had been agreed upon and the Duke had received the first letter from his wife-to-be,[1] Axel Ryning and George Blancke[2] were dispatched on May 3, 1592, to certain German states to make the formal arrangements for the wedding. Axel Ryning returned to Nyköping July 16[3] and George Blancke, who had been to Hesse and elsewhere, probably later. Ludbert Kaver had returned to Sweden from his lengthy mission in Germany in the beginning of June and he remained at Nyköpingshus from June 28 until after the wedding celebrations.[4]

Moreover, two letters[5] were issued on May 3, one to Olaf Hård and the other to Boo Ribbingh, instructing each of them to investigate a separate route by which the wedding party might approach Nyköping. Boo Ribbingh's alternative, which ran from Varberg through Marck 'härad' direct to Hegnetorp, was rejected because there was a lack of suitable lodging places along the route. The road from Halmstad to Jönköping, which Olaf Hård had investigated, was therefore chosen and Hård received 200 daler[6] with which to purchase wine and German beer in Halmstad to meet the needs of the party from Holstein and to provision the places between Halmstad and Jönköping where the party would be staying overnight.

---

[1] Cf. p. 39.

[2] Cf. *Cal. Car. IX*, 76 and 78 *f.*

[3] Cf. *ibid.*, 79.

[4] Cf. *Cal. Car. IX*, 78 and 79 and Diplomaträkenskaper 1570–93, vol. 5, fasc. 9.

[5] Hertig Karls registratur 1592, fol. 122 v, RA.

[6] Quitentzier och Szedler Anno etc. 92, fasc. 7, 'Hindrich Hinderssons räkenskaper 1592', fol. 71 r, Hertig Karls räntekammare 1590–97, KA.

On August 6, 1592, Duke Charles left Nyköping for Westrogothia.[1] He was bound for the Manor of Hegnetorp (now Höjentorp in the parish of Eggby, about eight miles as the crow flies east-north-east of Skara), the southernmost limit of his Duchy. Here he was to meet Princess Christine. The route he took was as follows:[2]

Nyköping	6/8	—
Julita gård	7/8	(1 måltid) (1 *meal*)
Segersjö gård	7/8	(1 måltid)
Örebro slott	8/8	—
Kumla prästgård	8/8	(1 måltid)
Bodarne	9/8	(1 måltid)
Hova prästgård	9/8	(1 måltid)
Marieholms gård	10/8	—
Hegnetorp	11/8	—

The Duke was accompanied by most of his closest advisers and officials, with an escort of halberdiers and knights. The Holstein account of the journey[3] makes special mention of six pages, twelve trumpeters, a kettle-drummer, six footmen in red satin liveries and thirty halberdiers dressed in red with black velvet trimmings. One of the trumpeters, Philip Briggis, was the only member of the English company in the Duke's retinue.[4] Three other Englishmen, John Howse, John Vaughan and Robert Vaughan,[5] had arrived at Hegnetorp a few days earlier as members of a party of ten trumpeters, three servants and Matz, the kettle-drummer. Thus altogether four English trumpeters left Nyköping on this occasion. Presumably the two trumpeters Richard Raph and Nicholas King, the apprentice, and the English players stayed behind to arrange the performances to be given during the wedding celebrations.

Princess Christine, her elderly mother, the Holstein and the Hessian wedding parties began their long journey from Kiel on July 15, 1592. They travelled by the following route:[6]

[1] Cf. *Cal. Car. IX*, 80.

[2] *Ibid.* and Kungl. Hofförtärningen 1592–93, SA.

[3] Nachrichten von der Vermählung ... fol. 46 r, Landesarchiv Schleswig-Holstein.

[4] Kungl. Hofförtärningen 93.

[5] *Ibid.*

[6] Nachrichten von der Vermählung ... fol. 37 r ff., Landesarchiv Schleswig-Holstein. The dates and distances given here are taken from this document. 1 mil = 10 kilometers = ca. 6 ¼ miles. Cf. Bring No 21; Ord och Bild, 26, 177–188; Ahnlund *Storhetstidens Gryning*, 1–37, and Ilsøe No 19.

Kiel–Schloß Gottorf	15/7	6 mil (60 km)
Rested	16/7–17/7	—
Schloß Gottorf–Flensburg	18/7	4 mil
Flensburg–Aabenraa	19/7	4 mil
Aabenraa–Haderslev	20/7	3 mil
Haderslev–Kolding	21/7	4 mil
Rested	22/7	—
Kolding–Middelfart	23/7	2 mil
Crossed the Little Belt		
Middelfart–Odense	24/7	6 mil
Odense–Nyborg	25/7	4 mil
Rested	26/7	—
Nyborg–Korsör–Slagelse	27/7	2 mil
Crossed the Great Belt		
Rested	28/7	—
Slagelse–Ringsted	29/7	4 mil
Ringsted–Roskilde	30/7	4 mil
Roskilde–Slangerup	31/7	4 mil
Slangerup–Kronborg	1/8	4 mil
Rested	2/8	—
Kronborg–Ängelholm	3/8	3 mil
Crossed the Sound		
Ängelholm–Laholm	4/8	4 mil
Laholm–Halmstad	5/8	3 mil
Rested	6/8	—
Halmstad–Nissaryd	7/8	8 mil
Nissaryd–Villstad	8/8	5 mil
Villstad–Öreryd	9/8	5 mil
Öreryd–Jönköping	10/8	8 mil
Rested	11/8–12/8	—
Jönköping–Sandhem	13/8	5 mil
Sandhem–Karleby	14/8	4 mil
Karleby–Hegnetorp	15/8	4 mil

On August 1 an estafette, Daniel von Boventer,[1] was dispatched from Elsinore to Nyköping and met the Duke's party at Segersjö on the 7th. Duke Charles's entry in his almanac that day runs:

7. kåm Daniell v. Båuenter från H(ertighinnen) aff Holsten och skildes från henne i Helsinggeör gudh werdigges widere beuare tett hele föllie medh sine helige englerer, amen.[2]

[1] A court chamberlain in the service of Duke Charles at Nyköping Castle. Cf. Håfflöningⁿ för håffiunckare Anno 1591. Hertig Karls räntekammare 1590–97, fasc. 5, Håkan Larsson 1591, fol. 19 v, KA.

[2] '17th. Daniell von Båuenter arrived from the Princess of Holstein, having left her at Elsinore. May it please God to continue to follow her with his holy angels, amen'; Cal. Car. IX, 80.

The arrangements for the royal party's stay at Kolding in Denmark on July 21–23 were dictated by the Danish regency council as follows:

... 18. Om Verelserne paa Koldinghuus at lade tilflye of Forraad at skaffe till Hertugindens at Holsten Ankomst &c. 1592. 7. Julii.

Christian thend Fierde &c. Wiid, eptersom thend Hogborne Forstinde Frw Christina Hertuginde til Sleßwig, Holsten &c. er nu til sindz att tage Hindis Kierlighetz Reigse her igiennom Riigit, med Hindis Kierlighetz Hogborne Datter Froicken Christina och medhaffŭendis Folck ind ŭdi Swerige. Och epter begge theris Kierlighetter ere formodendis diid thil Slottit til den 21. Julii förstkommendis, och ther paa tho Natters Thiid att fortsffŭe, Tha bede Wii dig och wille, attŭ lader bestille beqŭeme Losementer ther paa Slottit for theris Kierlighetter sielff, och lader dennom drage och tilflie, paa the beste Maade, och epter thend Leilighed skee kand. Och attŭ vdi Forraad lader bestille med Wiin och anden fremmede Drik, och hŭis andet som til en Forstelige Underholding och Tractering hörer och wil formoden gioris. Sammeledis attŭ ŭdi Byen lader forordne guode Losementer til theris Kierligheters medhaffŭendis Folck, och Stallerom til deris Heste, og siden bestiller, att theris Kierlighetter med ald deris medhaffuendis Gesinde och Heste bliffŭer frii udqŭiterit. Disligeste attŭ bestiller nottorftige Wogne ther till, Saa the fremmede, saa wel som wore egne Undersotter aff Adelen, thennom paa wore wegne geleide schŭlle, kŭnde med deris Folck och Guodtz bliffue tilborligen befordrit. Wii schicke Dig herhoß en Foreer Zeddel, hŭor epter Dŭ kand haffŭe Dig att rette, och altingist vdi Forraad att lade bestille och forordne. Ther med skeer Wor Wilge, Befalendis dig Gud. Skreffŭit paa Wort Slott Kiøpnehauffn thend 7. Julii Anno 1592. Under Wort Signet,

Hogbemelte Wor allernaadigste
udŭolde Herre Printz och Konnings
tilforordnede Regierings Raad

| Nils Kaas | Jørgen Rosenkrantz | Hack Ulfstand |
| egen handt | egen handt | egen handt[1] |

---

[1] '18. Concerning the arrangement of accommodation at Koldinghus Castle and the procurement of supplies for the arrival of the Princess of Holstein, &c. Anno 1592. *July 7*. Christian the Fourth &c. We, ..., whereas Her Grace, Lady Christine, Princess of Schleswig, Holstein &c is now to make her royal progress through this realm, with Her Grace's daughter, the Lady Christine and entourage on their way to Sweden. And whereas both Their Graces are expected at the Castle on July 21 next, continuing therefrom after two nights, therefore is it Our wish and desire that you shall arrange comfortable lodgings at the castle for Their Graces themselves and have everything made ready, in the best manner, and as circumstances permit. And from the stores order up wine and other foreign drink and do whatever else besides is fitting for a princely entertainment and upkeep. Furthermore that in

Attached to these instructions is an account which contains the most complete list of the Holstein members of the bridal party:

Furier und Futter Zettel unser gnedigen Furstin und Frauwen, der Furst-lichen Holsteinischen Witwen, auf der Reyse nach dem Reiche Schweden (Victuals and forage for Her Ladyship and Princess, the Dowager Duchess of Holstein during Her Highness's journey to Sweden)

Vor Furstl. Gn. Wagen (Before Her Ladyship's coach)	6 Pferde (horses)
Vor Freuwlin Christinen Wagen (Before Lady Christine's coach)	8 Pferde
Vor das Frauenzimmer Wagen (Before the Gynaeceum coach)	4 Pferde
Vor 2 Megde Wagen (Before Maids' coach)	8 Pferde
Vor den Silber Wagen (Before the table silver coach)	4 Pferde
Vor Furstl. Gn. Rustwagen (Before Her Ladyship's baggage cart)	4 Pferde
Vor Freuwlin Christinen Rustwagen (Before Lady Christine's cart)	4 Pferde
Vor des Frauwenzimmers Rustwagen (Before the Gynaeceum cart)	4 Pferde
Vor des Befredigers und Medici Wagen (Before the Chaplain's & Doctor's coach)	4 Pferde
Vor dem Cantzley Wagen (Before Chancellery coach)	4 Pferde
Vor noch einen Rustwagen (Before yet another baggage cart)	6 Pferde

Der Herrn Räthe und Junckern Wagen und Wagen-Pferde

(Coaches and coach-horses of the Councillors and Gentlemen)

Henrich von Ahlefelt	4 Pferde
Otto von Qualen	4 Pferde
Gerhart Steding	4 Pferde
Otto von Bestenböstel, Hofmeister (Keeper)	3 Pferde

the town you arrange good lodgings for Their Graces' company, stabling for their horses, and order so that Their Graces with all their retinue of men and horses incur no expense themselves. Finally that you order sufficient carriages so that the guests, as well as Our own noble subjects who are to accompany them along Our highways, can be properly conveyed with their retinues and baggage. We send you herewith instructions to follow and use when ordering and arranging everything from the stores. This to be done according to Our will, as the Almighty commands. Written at Our Castle of Copenhagen, July 7, 1592. Under Our Signet, &c'; Danske Magazin, 5, 52, 123–126, 1751.

Hof-Junckern (Chamberlains)
Volradt von der Decken,
  Hofmarschalk (Master
  ot the Household)
Luder von der Lithe   fünf
Herman von der Decken   Gutzschen   20 Pferde
Johan Rodenhausen   (five
Gotsche Ratlenow   drivers)
Matthias Rantzouw
Ciriacks Kluver
Johan Bremer

Edle Knaben ⎱ Arndt Søhe
(Boys of old families) ⎰ Detleff Brocktorff
Benedictus Hundersmarck   3 Pferde

Gereysige (Outriders)

Unser gnedigen Furstinne und Frauw (For Her Ladyship
  and Princess)   3 Pferde
Der Räthe (The Councillors)   6 Pferde

Einspenninger (One-horse vehicles)

Hans Wulff	1 Pferd
Claus von Lübeck	1 Pferd
Hans Buntmacker	1 Pferd
Lorentz Bolte	1 Pferd
Johan Keding	1 Pferd
Dirich Hoyer	1 Pferd

Trompter (Trumpeters)

Jacob	1 Pferd
Marcus	1 Pferd
Peter	1 Pferd
Clammers Junge (Clammer's Boy)	1 Pferd
Christoffer	1 Pferd

Trabanten (Yeomen) = 12
Hufschmit (Blacksmith)
Rademacher (Wheelwright)[1]

While in Denmark, the Holstein and Hessian wedding guests had been
accompanied by a Danish escort. At the Danish–Swedish border, which
at that time ran between Villstad and Öreryd, they were met by a Swedish escort sent by John III and led by Baron Schenck of Lautenburg,
Baron Horn of Åminne and Jörgen Eriksson, governor of the fortress of
Elfsborg.

[1] Danske Magazin, 5, 52, 123–126, 1751.

On several occasions accommodation for the travellers was extremely limited. There is a note of resentment in the Holstein account of conditions at the border:

In diesen beiden Dorffen haben wir unser Tag- und Nachtlager unter den wilden Thieren gehabt.[1]

It was about three o'clock in the afternoon of August 15, 1592, when the Holstein and Swedish parties met at Hegnetorp. Duke Charles delivered an address of welcome, and this was replied to on behalf of the two Princesses by Henry von Ahlefelt.[2] In addition to her mother, the Dowager Princess Christine, Princess of Hesse by birth, Princess Christine of Holstein was accompanied by her two sisters Anne and Agnes. Her brother John, Archbishop of Bremen and reigning Duke of Holstein, was unable to be present in person and was represented by Henry von Ahlefelt, Otto von Qualen and the chancellor, Gerhard Stedingk. The royal ladies were waited on by the bride's lady of the bedchamber, Veronica von Mandelslo, two noble ladies, one of them the wife of Henry von Ahlefelt, and five noble maidens.[3] In addition, Princess Christine had with her no less than five Holstein trumpeters, namely Jacob, Marcus, Peter, Clammer's Boy and Christopher[4] and five servants for these.

The combined Swedish and Holstein parties totalled about 635 persons during the journey from Hegnetorp to Nyköping,[5] the route for which was as follows:[6]

Rested	16/8	—
Hegnetorp–Marieholm	17/8	6 mil (60 km)
Rested	18/8	—
Marieholm–Hova	19/8	5 mil
Hova–Bodarne	20/8	—
Bodarne–Kumla	21/8	5 mil
Kumla–Örebro	22/8	4 mil
Örebro–Julita	23/8	8 mil
Julita–Floda	24/8	4 mil
Floda–Nyköping	25/8	9 mil

---

[1] 'In both these hamlets we have had our abode by day and by night amongst the wild animals'; Nachrichten von der Vermählung ... fol. 44 v, Landesarchiv Schleswig-Holstein.

[2] *Ibid.*, fol. 46 r.

[3] Ahnlund, *Storhetstidens gryning*, 18.

[4] Kungl. Hofförtärningen 93, SA, and *Danske Magazin*, 5, 52, 125, 1751.

[5] *Ibid.*

[6] Nachrichten von der Vermählung ... fol. 46 r ff., Landesarchiv Schleswig-Holstein. Cf. *Cal. Car. IX*, 80.

Naturally enough, the accommodation was sometimes minimal. At Bodarne (now Ramundaboda at Tiveden), for example, there was only a small parsonage for the women in the party, and the Duke and the others had to camp out under canvas.

From what we know of Duke Charles's first wedding, at Heidelberg in 1579, it would seem that his second followed very much the same programme.[1] For the latter there are two contemporary accounts extant, namely Michael Heberer von Bretten's eye-witness description printed in *Aegyptiaca Servitus* (Heidelberg 1610) and the anonymous, unpublished diary from the journey from Gottorf Castle in Schleswig to Nyköping and back. This diary, which is now in the *Landesarchiv Schleswig-Holstein*, is unfortunately lacking in details of the stay at Nyköping, there being only the laconic statement that the bridal party was there for four weeks and two days.

Nyköping was reached on August 25, 1592. Other guests had already arrived, namely Counts John and Christopher of East Friesland, nephews to Duke Charles, and the Palatine embassy under Henry von Schwerin and Michael von Bretten.[2] Duke Charles entered his capital on a white roan to the accompaniment of trumpets and kettledrums and a salute fired from the castle tower; the citizens of Nyköping were there to express their joy over the coming wedding. After the bride had left her wedding carriage, she was conducted by the Danish[3] and the Holstein[4] envoys to Nyköping Castle.

Among the guests of honour the chief ladies were Duke Charles's stepmother Catherine Stenbock—widow of Gustavus Vasa—and his sister Sophia, wife of Duke Magnus of Saxony-Lauenburg. King John of Sweden had lain ill for some time and Queen Gunilla could not leave him. The King was represented by Eric and Arvid Stenbock and his Queen by a sister of Charles Sture.

On the following day, August 26, the Palatine and Hessian envoys had

---

[1] Hertig Karls reseräkning 1577–78, Nr D*583, KB. Cf. Block, *Karl IX som teolog*, Lund 1918.

[2] *Aegyp. Serv.*, 616.

[3] According to a dispatch of July 27, 1592, the Danish envoys to Duke Charles's wedding were to be Councillor Sten Brahe of Knudstrup and Judge Nicolaus Theophilus. Udenrigske akter vedrørende forholdet mellem Sverige og Danmark. Danish RA. Cf. *DBL*, 3, 580 ff. and 23, 480 f.

[4] The envoys from Holstein were Henry von Ahlefelt and Otto von Qualen. Mantalsregistret 25/8–3/9, 1592, Kungl. Hofförtärningen 93, SA.

an audience of Duke Charles.[1] The Palatine embassy, which had travelled overland from Germany, was headed by Henry von Schwerin, councillor of the Elector Palatine and a native of Pomerania, with Michael Heberer von Bretten as secretary. The legation from Hesse, which accompanied the Holstein bridal train from Lubeck–Kiel,[2] consisted of two representatives, John Louis von Harstall for William, Landgrave of Hesse-Cassel, and Christopher von Berlepsch for Louis and George, Landgraves of Hesse-Marburg and Hesse-Darmstadt respectively. It was a long journey for these embassies to make, but Duke Charles's two wives were closely related to these princely houses. Mary was a member of the house of Palatinate, Christine was Princess of Holstein, and the Hessian landgraves William and Louis were uncles on the mother's side of each. The audience over, the wedding celebrations commenced with a gala banquet, music and dancing.[3]

The following day, the 27th, saw the performance of the actual wedding ceremony. A magnificent bed with a canopy embroidered in gold and silver stood in a great chamber of the castle; the walls were hung with tapestries. The wedding procession entered, led by Henry von Schwerin of the Palatinate, Christopher von Berlepsch of Hesse and Duke Charles's nephew, Count Christopher of East Friesland. They were followed by Duke Charles with his brother Duke Magnus on his right and his nephew Count John of East Friesland on his left. Duke Magnus, who was subject to fits of madness, was clearly having one of his normal periods. Von Bretten describes him as 'an old man from Sweden, of royal birth'.[4]

Next came the wedding guests and after them Princess Christine of Holstein with her sisters and Duke Charles's daughter Catherine Vasa. Bringing up the rear were the dowager queen, the dowager princess and the ladies-in-waiting. The ceremony began with a sermon in German by Master Petrus Jonae, the Superintendent[5] of Strängnäs, after which the Holstein chancellor Gerhard Stedingk made a speech and placed the

---

[1] *Aegyp. Serv.*, 623.

[2] Nachrichten von der Vermählung ..., fol. 37 v, Landesarchiv Schleswig-Holstein. *Aegyp. Serv.*, 623, states that the Hessian legation travelled from Lubeck by sea direct to Nyköping, but this is probably a misunderstanding on Michael Heberer von Bretten's part.

[3] *Aegyp. Serv.*, 623.

[4] *Ibid.*, 622.

[5] The title 'Superintendent' was used controversially instead of 'Bishop' by extreme Protestant reformers of the 16th century. *New Eng. Dict.*, 9, 2, p. 183.

young princess in the Duke's care and safe-keeping. Stedingk made a point of expressing the wish that the Duke would allow his wife to pursue in freedom the religion in which she had been brought up. Charles Sture replied for the Duke, also in German, and said that Princess Christine would be permitted to practice the Lutheran faith as it had been established by the Confession of Augsburg. Von Bretten, who described this scene, adds by way of explanation that the house of Holstein was not alone in suspecting the Duke of Calvinist sympathies. Von Bretten, who was himself a Calvinist, goes on to describe how Duke Charles unhesitatingly put forward his theological position, making a point of explaining his view on the doctrine of the Holy Communion and attempting to refute the Lutheran doctrine 'Ubique' with quotations from the scriptures.[1] The ceremony was concluded with music.

On the 28th the ceremony of handing over the bride's morning gift was performed and valuable presents were bestowed by the noble guests. According to a list,[2] wedding presents were also sent by the following:

> Duke John of Holstein
> Christian IV and the Dowager Queen of Denmark
> The young Elector Palatine of Heidelberg[3]
> A princess of the Palatinate[4]
> The landgraves William, Louis and George of Hesse
> Duke Ernest Louis of Pomerania's widow
> John III of Sweden
> The Dowager Queen Catherine Stenbock, Duke Charles's stepmother

Neither King Sigismund of Poland nor Queen Elizabeth of England sent representatives to the wedding, nor did either of them send any wedding gifts. According to a letter of July 2, 1592,[5] King Sigismund was invited, but it has not been possible to discover any record of an invitation having been sent to Queen Elizabeth.

The Duke thanked his guests through his friend Ludbert Kaver and the Elizabethan players then performed for their entertainment. These

---

[1] *Aegyp. Serv.*, 625.

[2] Nachrichten von der Vermählung ..., fol. 24 r ff., Landesarchiv Schleswig-Holstein.

[3] Frederick IV, Electoral Prince of the Palatinate.

[4] Anne Mary of the Palatinate, who had been invited, together with her children, by Duke Charles.

[5] Hertig Karls registratur 1592, fol. 148 r, RA.

wedding festivities were undoubtedly the climax of the English company's engagement at Duke Charles's court.

Jousting and tilting at the ring had been arranged too, probably along the lines of the entertainment at Woodstock[1] on the afternoon of September 11, 1575, performed by Sir Henry Lee for Queen Elizabeth, Leicester's feast of St. George at Utrecht on April 23, 1586[2] or the celebrations in honour of the newly-wed King and Queen of Scotland arranged on January 21, 1590, at Kronborg Castle in Denmark.[3] Duke Charles was particularly fond of this type of entertainment. We still have a collection of 'Rules and Regulations' for jousting dating from the Nyköping of the Duke's day.[4] Due attention was paid to both chivalry and burlesque. On one occasion a prize of a velvet costume was offered to the one who could make the most graceful entry into the lists. On another, the prize was a costume of silk taffeta for the one who could make himself most ridiculous doing the same thing. Other items were the entries of 'Hector defensor', 'Ajax inquietus' and 'Achilles conquestor', who issued challenges to each and every one of the contestants. These, then, were probably some of the ingredients that made up the tournament at the Duke's wedding. A stately display of fireworks was held as darkness fell over the scene.

The Duke was liberal in his hospitality. In the kitchen accounts there is a list for the issuing of provisions showing how this was arranged at Nyköping Castle.[5] There was beer and wine in abundance, perhaps even to excess. The Holstein trumpeters, at least, drank so much of the sweet Spanish wine that they preferred the Rhenish thereafter.

The celebrations were an unqualified success, though for von Bretten the sight of the pitiful Muscovite prisoners carrying out menial tasks proved an unhappy reminder both of the fact that Sweden was still at war and also of the time when he himself had been taken prisoner-of-war. Nor was this the end of the festivities. Maurice Leijonhufvud was to marry Amelia von Hatzfeld at Nyköping on September 3 and all the guests

[1] *The Queenes Maiesties entertainment at Woodstock*, 1575, printed for Thomas Cadman, 1585, BM.

[2] Cf. pp. 111 f.

[3] Slange, *Christian IV*, 1, 33. Cf. pp. 132 f.

[4] K 349, fasc. 'Torneringar i Nyköping 1584–1602', RA. Ahnlund, *Storhetstidens gryning*, 32 ff. Meyerson, *Adligt nöje*, 142 f.

[5] The value of this as a social document would seem to justify its being reproduced in full. Cf. App. 3 (Wikland, *Eliz. Pl.*, 1. ed., 1962).

were invited to be present. The same ceremony was probably used, albeit in a somewhat simplified form. It is also very likely that the English company performed at this wedding too.

Summer was drawing to a close. The wedding had been celebrated from the 26th to the 28th of August, which by the modern calendar would be the 4th to the 6th of September. The first of the foreign guests to leave Nyköping were the members of the Hessian delegation, who sailed direct to Lubeck.[1] Duke Charles's letter of thanks[2] to William of Hesse-Cassel is dated August 31, so the party can scarcely have been able to stay for Maurice Leijonhufvud's wedding. They were doubtless anxious to return to Landgrave William, whose health had been bad when they left him.

Henry von Schwerin and Michael Heberer von Bretten had received commissions in Denmark, so they decided to return as they had come, by land. They left Nyköping on September 5[3] with two riders in their train and entered Denmark at the old border station of Ulvsbäck near Markaryd, heading for Helsingborg.

The relatives from Holstein stayed longest at Nyköping. They originally intended to leave on September 18 but it was not until the 24th that they finally got away. With autumn in the air it was natural that they chose the old continental road: Nyköping–Norrköping–Linköping–Jönköping–Markaryd–Helsingborg. The Duke and his bride accompanied them for part of the way, as the following extract from his almanac for September bears witness:

24. drog min frumoder H(ertiginnen) aff Holsten till Lunde prestegård.
25. till Kuillinge.
26. till Nårköping.
27. låge wi der stille.
28. skildes wi ått, gudh förlene henne en lycksaligh rese, ...[4]

Among those who accompanied the Duke to Lunde parsonage were 11 trumpeters and 4 trumpeter apprentices.[5] The former included four

[1] *Aegyp. Serv.*, 631.
[2] Aktenbestand 4 für Schweden, Staatsarchiv Marburg, Marburg/Lahn.
[3] *Aegyp. Serv.*, 631.
[4] '24th. Brought my mother-in-law to Lunde parsonage. 25th. To Kvillinge. 26th. To Norrköping. 27th. Rested there. 28th. We parted. May God grant her a safe journey ...'; *Cal. Car. IX*, 81.
[5] Kungl. Hofförtärningen 93, SA.

Englishmen, namely John Howse, Robert Vaughan, John Vaughan and Philip Briggis. In addition there was Richard Havill, one of the English players. In other words, more or less the same Englishmen who had gone to Hegnetorp to meet the party from Holstein on August 15 now accompanied the Dowager Princess Christine on the first leg of her long journey home.

The travellers, including the six Holstein trumpeters, were escorted by five Swedish noblemen. Their journey was not without difficulties. They were forced by bad weather to wait two weeks at Korsør before they could cross the Great Belt, and it was not until November 25 that they reached Kiel, which they had left more than four months previously.[1]

The papers concerning John Louis von Harstall's embassy to Nyköping as the representative of Landgrave William IV of Hesse are to be found in *Staatsarchiv Marburg*.[2] Von Harstall's presence at the Duke's wedding is of particular interest in the light of subsequent activities by English companies on the Continent.

Duke Charles had sent the Landgrave an invitation to the wedding through the Duke's envoy, George Blancke, in June 1592. Landgrave William replied that, while he could not attend in person, he was sending John Louis von Harstall to Nyköping as his accredited representative. Von Harstall had been appointed governor of Werra Castle in Eschwege in 1591. However, his arrival at Nyköping coincided with the death of the Landgrave on August 25, 1592. From the entry in Duke Charles's almanac (October 6, 1592) it would appear that there had been more than a purely formal relationship between himself and the Landgrave:

6. fick iagh tiende, att gudh hade kallett aff tenne iemmerdall landtgreff Willam, huars siell gudh euinnerlige hugsuale och förlene en saligh stund, ner wi skulle föllie efter, amen.[3]

Landgrave William IV was succeeded by his son Maurice 'the Learned', who from 1586 to 1588 had had von Harstall as one of his chamberlains. Maurice now took von Harstall into his service once more and, as of

<hr>

[1] Nachrichten von der Vermählung ... fol. 37 r ff., Landesarchiv Schleswig-Holstein.

[2] Aktenbestand 4 für Schweden (No. 34) and other references compiled by Dr. Papritz and Dr. Franz, Staatsarchiv Marburg, Marburg/Lahn.

[3] '6th. Learned today that God has called from this vale of sorrows the Landgrave William, whose soul may God eternally bless and grant a blessed while when we shall follow after him, amen'; op. cit., 81.

January 1, 1593, confirmed his appointment as governor of Werra Castle, a post which he still held in December 1616.

Mention has already been made[1] of the circumstance that Philip Kingman was engaged by Landgrave Maurice in Hesse-Cassel in 1594–95, not long after the Duke's marriage in 1592. There is thus a certain historical connection between Philip Kingman's performances at Nyköping and in Hesse-Cassel.

[1] Cf. pp. 54 ff.

CHAPTER 6

The English players return to England, October 1592

At the end of their term of service with the Duke, the English trumpeters and players received each a sum of money as shown in the following list reproduced from the bills in the Duke's household accounts.[1]

	Trummethere	
Jahannes Huss	7/9 1591–4/10 1592	75 daler 1 mark
Philip Bryggis	7/9 1591–30/4 1593	110 daler 3 mark 2½ öre
Jahan Wahn	7/9 1591–4/10 1592	75 daler 1 mark
Robert Wahnn	7/9 1591–4/10 1592	75¼ daler
Ricardus Raff	7/9 1591–8/6 1595	215 daler 1 mark
	Spelemän	
William Coper	7/9 1591–5/10 1592	110 daler 29 öre 16 pr
Edhwardus Tamsetth	7/9 1591–5/10 1592	110 daler 29 öre 16 pr
Ricardus Blueth	7/9 1591–5/10 1592	110 daler 29 öre 16 pr
Ricardh Haffuell	7/9 1591–5/10 1592	110 daler 29 öre 16 pr
Matthias Bruck	7/9 1591–5/10 1592	110 daler 29 öre 16 pr

According to these accounts, one of the trumpeters, Nicholas King, the apprentice, only received payment in kind. Nor is there a record of any payment to Edward Stackman, one of the players for whom a warrant was issued at the time of their engagement in 1591. It seems that Stackman left his fellow-players after January 27, 1592. At all events, the last payment recorded in the kitchen accounts for 1591 was as follows:

> Til 12 Engilske Spelemän i 28 dagʳ, nemb:
> ifrå 30 10ᵇ til 27 Janu: 92
> Penninger .... 73 1/2 dalʳ²

Unfortunately, although we have the household accounts for 1591 and 1593, as kept by the treasurer Haakon Larsson, those for 1592 are

---

[1] Hertig Karls räntekammare 1589–92, fasc. 4, fol. 69 r–78 r, KA. *Trummethere* = trumpeters, *spelemän* = players.

[2] 'To 12 English players for 28 days, namely from 30 December to 27 January 1592, coin ... 73½ daler'; *ibid.*

missing. Moreover, the kitchen accounts, which contain information about who sat at the Duke's table, are also lacking in detail here. It is thus not possible to tell exactly when Edward Stackman left Nyköping. The players received about 100 daler per annum in addition to certain payments in kind. The account drawn up for the five English players at the end of their period of service includes the following entries:

For Richard Bluett:

> Anno, etc. 92
> Hafver H.F.N.^{d} honnom skienckt:
> till H. Karl Stures bröllop
> Kledhningh .... 1 mz all tilbehör
> till H.F.N.^{ds} eg:^{t} bröllop
> Kledhningh .... 1 mz all tilbehör[1]

For William Cooper, Edward Tamset and Matthew Bruck individually:

> Hafver h.f.n.^{e} honnom skienckt till ährecledningh:
> Kledning .... 1 mz all tillbehör.[2]

For Richard Havill:

> Hafver h.f.n.^{d} honnom skienckt till ährecledning på h.f.n.^{ds} bröllopshöghtid
> $\overline{92}$
> Kledning .... 1 mz all tillbehör.[3]

It would thus appear that Richard Bluett, who received two suits of apparel in all, was the chief member of the company engaged in August 1591.[4]

The six trumpeters were paid at a lower rate. They received about 70 daler per annum in cash as well as payment in kind in the form of clothing for different occasions. The entries in the accounts are differently worded for some of the trumpeters.

Thus the account for Robert Vaughan is worded the same as those for William Cooper, Edward Tamset and Matthew Bruck:

---

[1] 'His Royal Highness has granted him: for Charles Sture's wedding—Apparel 1 complete; for His Royal Highness's own wedding—Apparel 1 complete.'

[2] 'Anno &c. 1592. His Royal Highness has presented him with a suit of clothing: Apparel 1 complete.'

[3] 'Anno &c. 1592. His Royal Highness has presented him with a suit of clothing on His Highness's marriage 1592: Apparel 1 complete.'

[4] Cf. pp. 44 f. and Appendices 1 and 2 (Wikland, *Eliz. Pl.*, 1. ed., 1962).

Hafver h,f,n^d honnom skiencht till ähreklädhning.[1]

while John Howse's runs:

Hafver h,f,n^d honnom skiencht till h,f,n^d bröllop.[2]

Richard Raph's:

Hafver h,f,n^d honnom skiencht till sin bröllopshögtidh.[3]

and those for Philip Briggis and John Vaughan:

Hafver h,f,n^d honnom skiencht och giff^t.[4]

Philip Briggis also paid for a musket which he bought from the Duke's armourer:

Af Petter Krig^{er} Rust: $\overline{91}$
K: Bössa .... 1 för .... 4 dall^{r}[5]

Two of the players, Richard Bluett and Edward Tamset, had some of their pay issued in England in English currency, presumably for the benefit of their families:

Szå hafver han fåt öfwerskrifningh till Johan Kuth i Engelandh på — 28 st^n Richsdall^r — 5 skilling^r huilcka her icke äre för afdraghne thz hans rechningh vthuiser som mz honnom giordh är then 11 aprilis åhr $\overline{92}$ löper i S: Penning^r: — 31 dall^r 21 öre 8 pr.[6]

This transaction also appears in Thomas Fisk's accounts:

Item haffuer Jahan Kwt öfferschriffuit
2 Engilske Spelemen på Min n: förstes
   wegne till theres Besoldningh på
   stycket — 4½ marker — Slagne Daler — 56 stycken för — 63 Dal^r S:[7]

[1] 'His Royal Highness has presented him with a suit of clothing.'

[2] 'His Royal Highness has presented him to His Highness's marriage.'

[3] 'His Royal Highness has presented him to His Highness's wedding celebrations.'

[4] 'His Royal Highness has presented and given him.' The word *honnom* does not appear in Bruggis's account.

[5] 'Received by Petter Krig^{er}, Armourer: 91, Short musket — 1 for ... 4 daler.'

[6] 'Remittance for him to John Coote in England—28 Richsdaler—5 shillings. This sum has not been deducted from his bill drawn up on 11 April 1592 amounting in Swedish money to cash—31 daler 21 öre 8 pr.'

[7] 'Item John Coote has remitted to 2 English Players on His Royal Highness's order their pay thus: 4½ marks every Daler, 56 for 63 Daler specie'; Hertig Karls räntekammarböcker. Räkningar med diverse personer 1586–95, fol. 26 r, KA.

John Coote was a companion of Thomas Fisk, Duke Charles's agent in England.[1] While he was in Sweden in 1590–91, Coote delivered large quantities of clothing and materials on Thomas Fisk's behalf. These were probably intended for the furnishings at Nyköping Castle, for the Duke's servants, the mercenaries, the players, stage-properties and the wardrobe.[2] Henry Francklin's album also contains an undated entry in 1590 by John Coote.[3]

On January 18, 1591, a letter of introduction was issued for John Coote:

Öpet brev för Johan Kuth till att handla med uppstädes borgare om thet goda som honom i hans handel kan tienligt wara, för den summa penninger som han bekommit hafver.[4]

A similar letter[5] was issued for Jacobo Homodei, brother of Dr. Teofilus Homodei; Jacobo was a silk cloth merchant.

John Coote[6] returned to England for a short period in the first half of 1592. He probably returned to Sweden at the same time as Philip Kingman and Philip Gibson arrived at Nyköping to reinforce the English company.

Richard Raph married a Swedish girl—probably a member of the Duke's household at Nyköping Castle—on March 27, 1592, and the nuptials in Nyköping Cathedral were attended by the Duke himself, the court chamberlains and ladies-in-waiting.[7]

On September 2, 1592, von Bretten visited on board the Duke's warships. From his account it is clear that there were several vessels ready to sail at this time:

Fuhren also in einem kleinen Pott oder Schifflein von Newcöpping uff zwo Meil wegs zu den gemeldten Schiffen / deren Sechs nach einander / allerdings

---

[1] SP 95/1, fol. 70 ff., PRO.

[2] Hertig Karls räntekammarböcker. Räkningar med diverse personer 1586–95, KA.

[3] Op. cit. fol. 143 r.

[4] 'To whom it may concern. John Coote is licensed to trade with the citizens of the inland towns in such goods as may be suitable for his commerce for the money at his disposal'; Hertig Karls registratur 1591, fol. 13, RA.

[5] *Ibid.*

[6] Hertig Karls räntekammare begynnelseåren 1590–92, fol. 75 r and 76 r, KA.

[7] Kungl. Hofförtärningen 27.3.1592. Cf. p. 48.

mit munition und Geschütz stattlich versehen / und sonsten nach notturft außgerüstet / zu Ancker lagen.[1]

Duke Charles's almanac contains the following entry for October 5, 1592:

war iagh medh min gemall och besågh tett nye skeppett.[2]

Since this was the date of the final account for the players, it is reasonable to assume that the vessel in which they sailed from Nyköping weighed anchor on about October 9.

Shortly after the majority of the players and trumpeters had left Nyköping, the following warrant was drawn up:

Wij Karl &c. Göre witterligt att wij hafwe tagit och annammat thenne brefwijsere Reckert Hawin (Richard Havill) uthi wår tiänst för en Spelleman och honom till åhrligh löhn och vnderhåld nådigst tilsagdt och efterlatit, som wij och nu med thette wårt öpne bref honom nådigst tilsigie och efterlåthe penningar 20 daler, kledning Ehn om 20 daler, Rogh 6 tynner, malt 6 tynner, humbla ½ (pund), oxe ehn, fåår 2, Swin itt, strömming ½ t:na, smör 4 (pund), salt ½ t:na och ther till frij disk och förtäring wid hofwet, der wår Cammerer Fougde och andre måge wette sigh efter rette, låtandes honom för:te Parzeller och annen deel som för:t är åhrligen och i retten tid vt bekomma, enär han them opå fordrer.

Gifwit Nyköpingh 25 Octobris åhr 92.[3]

Certain other records have been found concerning those Englishmen who had their period of service as trumpeters to the Duke extended. After the wedding the following players received new warrants for 1593 and remained in the Duke's service until various dates the same year.

---

[1] 'Thus we were conveyed in a small sailing craft or schooner from Nyköping about two nautical miles to the aforementioned ships, which lay at anchor six in a line. These ships were well fitted with cannon and plentifully equipped with ammunition while they also had the bare necessities in other respects'; *Aegyp. Serv.*, 627.

[2] '... was with my wife and saw the new ship'; op. cit., 81.

[3] 'We Charles &c., hereby do make known that we have engaged the holder of this letter Richard Havill in our service as a Player and to him as annual pay in money and in kind have graciously decided and acknowledged as we now with this our open letter do decide and acknowledge cash 20 daler, apparel one for 20 daler, rye 6 barrels, malt 6 barrels, hops ½ (pound), oxen one, sheep 2, pigs one, Baltic herring ½ barrel, butter 4 (pounds), salt ½ barrel and thereto free board at the court, where our treasurer and other persons shall deal accordingly and shall allow him the said provisions and such else as may be due to him yearly when he so requires'; Hertig Karls registratur 1592, fol. 232, RA.

Ricard Hauell
Pnr .... 20 dal:r
Johan Wahan
Pnr .... 11 dal:r
Philip Bruggis för clede och pnr
Pnr .... 19 dal:r 22 öre afbtalt (sic)
Niclaß König på sin cledning bland 3 dal:r af cledcam:en
Pnr .... 7 dal:r
Ricard Raaff trommetter
Slagne dal:r .... 2 st:r
Pnr .... 3 dal:r[1]

Judging from the list drawn up at their engagement in 1591, there were one player and four trumpeters who stayed behind in October 1592. The other four players, namely William Cooper, Edward Tamset, Richard Bluett and Matthew Bruck, together with one of the trumpeters, John Howse, would appear to have returned to England by sea in one of the warships that sailed to Dr. Teofilus in the Netherlands.[2] John Howse, however, left Nyköping at the turn of the year when he carried a letter from James Hill to Lord Burghley.[3] Although apparently no warrant was issued for 1593 for Robert Vaughan, he is mentioned in the wardrobe accounts for that year, so one may assume that he too had his engagement extended. The names of Philip Kingman and Philip Gibson only appear in the wardrobe accounts for 1592,[4] though the reference to 'Big Philip' and 'Little Philip' as players in the kitchen accounts for 1593[5] must surely refer to them. Nevertheless, it would appear that they left Sweden either before or else in company with the four players for whom no warrants for 1593 were issued.

During 1593 Richard Raph served as a trumpeter on board the Duke's ship *Suanen*, as is clear from his final account:

Ricardus Raff
af Johannes Derfelt när han var på Suanen

---

[1] 'English Players. Richard Havill, cash 20 daler. John Vaughan, cash 11 daler. Philip Briggis for cloth and cash 19 daler, 22 öre deducted. Niclas König for his apparel 3 daler from the wardrobe, cash 7 daler. Richard Raph Trumpeter, minted daler 2 pieces, cash 3 daler'; Hertig Karls räntekammare 1590–95, Fasc. 8, Håkan Larsson 1593, fol. 16 r and v, KA.

[2] Hertig Karls diarium 1566–92, August 6, 1592, RA.

[3] Cf. p. 94.

[4] K. klädkammaren 1592, Vol. 48, 2, fol. 65 v, SA.

[5] Mantalsregistren 25/8–24/9, 1592, Kungl. Hofförtärningen 93, SA.

til Franckerijket $\overline{93}$
Peningar . . . . 1½ daler[1]

According to the kitchen accounts Nicholas King also received a sum of money when he left Nyköping on May 11, 1593:

2 dal Niclaß König trommetter d(reng) mz
greffverne aff Ostfrisland åth
Elfzborgh 11 maj $\overline{93}$,[2]

This is the last time that the young trumpeter's name appears in Duke Charles's accounts. According to the kitchen accounts[3] Philip Briggis also left Nyköping the same day and his name does not appear again either. Prior to this, however, he had accompanied the Duke to Uppsala, where they stayed from March 11 to March 20, 1593,[4] in connection with the Synod there.

The names of three English trumpeters occur again in the accounts for 1594:

Engilshe Trommetter
Johan Wahan
Pngr . . . . 8 dal:r 4 öre
Ricard Raaff
Pngr . . . . 4 dal:r 30 öre
Ricard Hauel
Pngr . . . . 4½ dal:r[5]

Thus if the absence of the names of Philip Briggis and Nicholas King from the accounts for 1594 means that these two had left Nyköping, the number of players there was reduced from five in 1593 to three in 1594. It is interesting to note that all five are referred to as *Spelemän* (players) in the warrant for 1593, whereas in the warrant for 1594 Richard Havill, who was originally engaged as an instrumentalist and later described as a player, is now grouped with the English trumpeters.

[1] 'Richard Raph from Johannes Derfelt when he was on the *Swan* bound for France $\overline{93}$, Cash ... 1½ daler'; Hertig Karls räntekammare 1593–97, fasc. 2, fol. 40, KA.

[2] '2 daler Nicholas King, trumpeter (pupil) when with the Counts of East Friesland (John and Christopher) to Elfsborg (now Gothenburg) May 11, 1593'; *ibid.*, Fasc. 8, Håkan Larsson 1593, fol. 26 r, KA.

[3] Kungl. Hofförtärningen 1592–93, vol. 4, SA.

[4] *Ibid.*

[5] 'English Trumpeters. John Vaughan, cash 8 daler, 4 öre. Richard Raph, cash 4 daler, 30 öre. Richard Havill, cash 4½ daler'; Hertig Karls räntekammare 1593–97, Fasc. 9, Håkan Larsson 1594, fol. 16 v, KA.

According to the Duke's registry for 1595, the following letter was written to the King of Denmark on September 9:

> Förschrifft för Richartt Raf trummetere
> til Konu. W:de i Danmark. Af Nyköping
> den 9 septemb. åhr &c. 1595.

Wår naboelige wenlige helsenn &c. &c.

Stormechtige högborne Konungh, besynnerlige gode wen och nabor. Wi kunne E:rs Konu. W:de naboerligen och wenligen icke forholle, att effter brefwisere Richartt Raaf Engelschman hafwer sigh på någre åhr her uthi Wår tienesth för een trummetere bruke lathie och Wi hans tienesth i så måthe nu icke lenger behöfwe, såsom han och dessföruthan hafwer lust sigh widere att försökie, hafwe Wi fördenskuld honom uthaf förbe:te Wår tienesth gunsteligen förlowedt. Och medan han helst begärer til at lathe sigh bruke uthi E:rs Konu. W:ds hoff, hafwer han af Oss uthi underdånigheet ödmiukeligen bedit om thenne Wår förschrifft til E:rs Konu. We:de, hwilcken Wi icke hafve kunnedt honom förneke, uthan nådeligen meddeele lathitt serdeeles effter han icke annorlunde uthi Wår tienesth sigh hafwer förhollit än som Oss hafwer behagedt och honom borth hafwer. Ähre fördenskuld uthi then naboerlige och wenlige tilförsicht, att hwar E:rs Konu. We:de hans tienest kan behage, att E:rs Konu. W:de will då honom uthi E:rs Konu. W:ds tiänesth antage och annamme eller och elliesth till någen annen godh befordringh förhielpe och i så måthe lathe honom thenne Wår förschrifft till godhe niuthe. Wi göre och altidt gärne thet E.K.M. till naboerligit och wenligit wälbehag ware kan och befale E:rs Konu. We:de &c. &c. Datum ut supra.[1]

---

[1] 'Reference for Richard Raph, trumpeter, to the King of Denmark. At Nyköping, September 9, Anno &c 1595. With Our neighbourly, amicable greetings &c., &c. Most sovereign and illustrious King, particularly good neighbour and friend. We could not desist out of neighbourliness and friendship from informing Your Majesty that the bearer of this letter, Richard Raph, Englishman, has served Us as a trumpeter for some years and We now no longer require his services, besides which he is desirous to try his fortune further, wherefor We have graciously released him from Our service. And being chiefly desirous of an engagement at Your Majesty's court, he has humbly and respectfully requested this Our recommendation to Your Majesty, the which We could not deny him, but graciously convey, particularly as he has never in Our service conducted himself otherwise than has pleased Us and befitted him. For which reason be neighbourly and amicably assured that if Your Majesty can find pleasure in his service, then engage him thereto or else assist him to some other good appointment and thereby benefit from this Our reference. We always willingly do whatever may be to Your Majesty's neighbourly and amicable well-being and command &c., &c. Dated as above'; op. cit., Pars 1, 9/9 1595, fol. 256 r f, RA.

There is no record, however, of this letter having been received by the Danish regency council, nor any evidence to show that employment was found for Richard Raph in Denmark. Raph appears in Hinrick Hindersson's accounts for 1595–97 as follows:

Ricart Trumeter

Rickert Trummetare i sin siukdom
som Johan Kuuth anammade
then 20 Decembris anno etc 96
Penningar . . . . 4 dal:r 1½m[1]

which may mean that illness prevented him from travelling to take up an appointment in Denmark. At all events, he did not enter Danish service before 1597 while, as the following document shows, he re-entered Duke Charles's service on August 17, 1599:

Bestälningz bref för Rickardt trummetare.
Af Stockholm den 17 augusti åhr &c. 99 &c.

Wij Carl giöre witterligitt att efther Wij hafwe ahntagitt thenne bref-wijsere Reckardt Raff uthi Wår tienisth för een trummetare, szå på thett han thess troligere och fliteligere uthi samme tienisth må och skall bruke och befinne lathe, desföre hafwe Wij nådigest undt och effterlatitt honom till åhrligh löhnn päninger fämtio daler, klädningh een om tiugu daler, deslikest och frij disk och förtärningh, hvilkett kläde och päninger han åhrligen af Wår ränthe och kläde cammar bekomme skall. Der Wåre cammererere, renthemästere och klädeskrifware måge wette sigh effter rette. Datum ut supra.[2]

Moreover, on July 16, 1600, Raph was called by John Coote as a witness in his lawsuit against James Hill in the courts in Stockholm.[3] Later, on August 30, 1602, Richard Raph was given 'Mester Didriks hus'

[1] 'Paid Richard Trumpeter during his illness, which money John Coote received December 20, 1596, Cash ... 4 daler 1½ marks'; Hertig Karls räntekammare 1593–97, fasc. 11, fol. 15 v, KA.

[2] 'Letter of Appointment for Richard Trumpeter. At Stockholm, August 7, Anno &c. 99 &c. We Charles make it known that as We have engaged the bearer of this letter Richard Raph in Our service as a trumpeter, in order that he shall the better be able to perform and maintain the same dutifully and diligently, We have graciously granted unto him an annual wage in money fifty daler, clothing one suit for twenty daler, in addition to free board and food, which clothing and money he shall receive annually from Our treasury and wardrobe. Our chamberlain, treasurer and wardrobe master to act accordingly. Dated as above'; Riksregistraturen (Duke Charle's) 17.8.1599, fol. 71 v, RA.

[3] *Stockholms stads tänkeböcker från år 1592*, 3, 1600, p. 93. Cf. pp. 102 ff.

in the street known as Österlånggatan near Stockholm Castle in fief, a decision that was confirmed by King Gustavus II Adolphus on January 21, 1620.[1] Raph appears in the accounts as a member of the royal orchestra in the years 1602–21[2] and he probably died in Sweden shortly after 1621. It is interesting that he appears to have acted as a music teacher while in Sweden, as witness the following royal letter, October 12, 1613:

Trompetaren Richard att lära två poikar som sändes till honom.[3]

The Duke's papers for 1605 also include the following title deed:

Förläningz Bref för H.F.N.[s] Spelman, Rijckert Hawill benempt, på een behållenn Kyrkie tiendtt vdi Tingsta Sockn i Bierkindz heredhtt i Östergötlandh. Datum Stockholm denn 17 Januarij, Åhr 1605.[4]

Richard Havill, too, was confirmed in his right to a church tithe by King Gustavus Adolphus on December 19, 1614,[5] and he probably died early in 1616 since a letter was issued on June 18 that year to

Richert spelemans enka at njuta frihet på des heman samt 12 tunner årligen til underhåld.[6]

---

[1] Riksregistraturen 30.8.1602 and 21.1.1620, fol. 162 r and 24 r, respectively, RA.

[2] Norlind–Trobäck, *Kungl. Hofkapellet 1526–1926* p. 272.

[3] 'Richard, Trumpeter, to teach two boys who where sent to him'; Riksregistraturen 12.10.1613, fol. 639 r /2, RA.

[4] 'Writ of enfeoffment on behalf of His Highness's Player Richard Havill with church tithes in the Parish of Tingsta in the county of Bjärkind in Ostrogothia. Stockholm, 17.1.1605'; Riksregistraturen, fol. 2 v, RA.

[5] Riksregistraturen 19.12.1614, fol. 1303 r f, RA.

[6] 'Richard the Player's widow to enjoy the freedom of their homestead together with 12 barrels annually in maintenance'; *ibid.*, 18.6.1616, fol. 233 r, RA.

CHAPTER 7

Erich Lassota's diary

Apart from the sources already mentioned, it has unfortunately not been possible to discover any contemporary letters with eye-witness accounts of the wedding celebrations at Nyköping in 1592. The present chapter is based upon a diary of, *inter alia*, a visit to various places in Sweden during the years 1590–93. Though the activities of the English players are not directly mentioned, the diary is of interest not least for the glimpses it gives us of Duke Charles, Nils Gyllenstierna and the Nyköping of those days. It also provides some interesting sidelights on the difficulties Sigismund of Poland must have had in the early years of his reign before he married Anne of Hapsburg.

In the Gersdorff-Weicha library at Bautzen near Dresden there is a sixteenth-century manuscript entitled 'Diarium des Erich Lassota von Stebelow'. It was published in Germany by Dr. Reinhold Schottin in 1866, and it is to this edition that reference is made in *Ord och Bild* from 1908. In his preface, Schottin writes:

Um den Freunden deutscher Vorzeit im allgemeinen und den Historikern von Fach insbesondere einen Dienst zu erweisen, lasse ich das Tagebuch des Erich Lassota in einem diplomatisch-getreuen Abdruck erscheinen,[1]

which would seem to justify the assumption that Schottin's is a reliable edition.

The Lassota von Stebelows (also spelled Lesota, Lesata) were one of Silesia's most ancient noble families. During the sixteenth century many of its members held high office both in Silesia and in Poland.[2] Erich Lassota probably grew up on the Blaschewitz[3] estate. At all events, ac-

---

[1] 'As a service to the friends of German history and, in particular, professional historians, I hereby publish Erich Lassota's diary in a documentary edition that is as close to the original as possible'; op. cit., v. Cf. Cordt No. 95, Bring No. 19 and Ilsøe No. 22.

[2] Schottin, 4.

[3] Also Bläschwitz.

83

cording to his diary he always returned there after his long journeys and used it for his preparations for new ones. He makes no mention of his parents in his diary, and a brother who died at an early age is only referred to in passing. Erich Lassota went to school in Görlitz and from there he entered the University of Leipzig. About December 1573 he travelled to Italy with his brother Friedrich and his maternal uncle Georg Stofel. He writes that he studied at the University of Padua until 1576 and that it was here that he met a number of highly-placed Swedes such as Axel Leijonhufvud, Ture Bielke and Eric and John Sparre; these friendships were later to stand him in good stead.[1]

Together with another maternal uncle, Hans Sitsch von Stiebendorff, Lassota left Padua in June 1576 and arrived home at Blaschewitz on July 16 the same year. He was at Prague when the news came that Philip II of Spain had obtained the Emperor's permission to raise a regiment of German mercenaries for his war against Portugal. Without more ado, Lassota decided to place his services at the disposal of the Spanish monarch. He returned to Blaschewitz to collect the necessary equipment and, with his young cousin, Ludwig Lassota, as his servant, crossed the Brenner Pass into Lombardy, where the regiment was to assemble. His commanding officer was Count Hieronymus von Lodron, and Lassota enlisted at Cremona on August 24, 1579. He was posted to Captain Kripp von Freydeneck's company as a private; he was probably what was known as a *Doppelsoldner*, as were several other noblemen whom he mentions by name.[2]

After a long sea voyage the regiment reached Cadiz. It took part in the conquest of Portugal, as well as in a series of expeditions to the Azores, and, its numbers decimated, returned home on July 6, 1584, after five years' service. Lassota's diary contains a detailed account of all these adventures.

Lassota stayed at Blaschewitz for a while after his return[3] but on March 13, 1585, he was appointed a groom of the bedchamber to the Emperor Rudolph II. It is not clear what his duties were, though his frequent journeys to Silesia and Poland, together with the fact that he had an audience of the Archduke Maximilian in 1586 immediately after the death of Stephen Báthory, king of Poland, suggest that he was some

---

[1] Cf. Schottin, 149. Concerning Lassota's biography cf. *Allgemeine Deutsche Biographie*, 17, 193–94.

[2] Cf. Schottin, 4.

[3] *Ibid.*

sort of political agent, especially as Maximilian questioned him about conditions in Poland.[1]

After Henry of Valois had declined the throne of Poland in 1574, Báthory, as the candidate of the gentry, was elected king in the face of the Emperor Maximilian, who was the choice of the magnates. Báthory married Anne, the sister of Sigismund Augustus II and Catherine Jagiello, who was Queen of Sweden, and secured his brother-in-law, John III of Sweden, as his ally in a war against Russia, which was successfully concluded in 1582 after the Russians had been driven out of Lithuania. However, he died in 1586 and his queen put forward Sigismund Vasa, her sister's son, as candidate for the throne of Poland. The other candidates were Czar Fyodor of Russia and the Archduke Maximilian of Austria. Supported by the chancellor, Zamoyski, Sigismund was elected in August 1587 upon his promise to transfer Esthonia from Sweden to Poland. As a result of Sigismund's success in this election, relations were severely strained for a while between him and the two unsuccessful candidates, whereupon John III of Sweden took his son's side.[2]

Lassota had accompanied Maximilian to Poland for the election in 1587, and in 1590 he was dispatched to Boris Godunov, regent for Czar Fyodor, with dispatches that can hardly have boded good for either Sweden or Poland.[3] He left Prague on September 5[4] in the company of Ernst Lindeinern of Schleywitz, Salomon Pühlern of Pühlberg and Hans Förstern of St Annaberg, equipped with letters and orders from the Archduke and letters of introduction from the Emperor Rudolph. They had been directed to reach Moscow as best they could and, on arrival, to go to Boris Godunov. Lassota travelled to Lubeck, where he took ship on October 6. He should have landed at the Russian port of Iwangorod but was misled by the captain into disembarking on October 15 at Narva, which was under Swedish rule. Lassota and his entire party were stopped and imprisoned by the Swedes outside Narva. Cross-examined, Lassota's servant-boy disclosed the whereabouts of the party's baggage and documents. Lassota had tried to extricate himself and his companions by spinning some fictitious tale but he was now

---

[1] *Ibid.*, 5.
[2] *SUB* 25, 1074.
[3] Schottin, 5.
[4] New style.

forced to contradict himself. The Swedes, growing suspicious, decided to refer the entire matter to their king, John III.[1]

A long time passed before Lassota and his company reached Sweden. They arrived at Helsinki on November 22 and were joined by Johan Sterneman, Lassota's German interpreter, who had been captured and had disclosed everything he knew about the mission to Russia. On December 19, 1590,[2] they came to Waxholm. From there they were taken via Djursholm to Uppsala, arriving by sleigh on the morning of December 22. Lassota was examined by Duke Charles the same day, the former describing their meeting as

'ein selzam gespräch'[3]

Lassota refused to tell the Duke everything the latter wished to know and so he was given two days to think things over. On the 24th[4] the Duke tried using threats and when Lassota reminded him of the *jus gentium* he replied, threateningly,

Was Jura? Wir verstehen uns alhier in Schweden auf keine Jura.[5]

At this point the Duke was interrupted by the old chancellor, Nils Gyllenstierna, and Lassota notes:

Nach diesem fragt Mich der Herr Obrist Canzler der Cron Schweden Herr Niels Guldenstern ein feiner alter Man, etwan bey siebenzig Jahren, Wie Ich heiße, Ich antwortet, Mein Nahm wer Erich Lassota von Steblaw, da fehrt Er fort und sagt, Mein lieber Lassota, Wie Ich in meiner Jugend zu Wittemberg[6] studirt, hab Ich einen Ewers Nahmens und Stammes gahr wohl gekant, und ist mein Vertrautter freund und gesell gewesen, Wer also Mir von Herzen leid, wen es etwa mitt Euch böse Wege gewinnen solt, ...[7]

Gyllenstierna and the Duke now had a heated debate which the latter ended by saying:

[1] Schottin, 123 ff.
[2] New style.
[3] 'a curious conversation, to say the least.' Schottin, 143, last §.
[4] New style.
[5] 'What Law? We know nothing here in Sweden of any Law.' Schottin, 148, 1 st §.
[6] *Alb. Ac. Viteberg*, 196 b, 29. 'Nicolaus Guldenstern, Suecus, entered June 1542.'
[7] 'After this the Chancellor of the Realm, Herr Nils Guldenstern, a fine old man of about seventy, turned to me and asked my name. I replied: "Erich Lassota von Stebelow." Guldenstern continued: "My dear Lassota. When studying at Wittenberg in my youth I was closely acquainted with a person of your name and family. He was my close friend and comrade. I am deeply unhappy and troubled lest you should come into some misfortune, ..."; Schottin, 148, last §, f.

Was, meint Ihr, wen ich gleich den Kerll hencken lies, der Kayser würde wegen seiner einen Krieg anfangen?[1]

after which Lassota was led out of the room. At the door he turned and burst out:

Der Teufl möcht forthin Fürsten und Herrn dienen, Wen einer mit des andern Diener also umbgehen wolt.[2]

After several days at the guard-house of Uppsala Castle Lassota was sent[3] to Vesterås on January 2, 1592,[4] and was kept there until March 4. He notes that the castle there is not particularly large but that it is well and gracefully built.[5] From Vesterås he travelled to Stockholm, arriving in the afternoon of March 6. He was imprisoned in the pavilion on Helgeandsholm; his room, which had formerly been occupied by clerks, was fitted with iron bars across the windows to prevent him from escaping. On March 9 he was examined again but this time by a commission made up of two of the king's secretaries, namely Olof Sverkersson and Ambrosius Palm, the governor Jakob Bagge and others. The questions were put by the two secretaries in turn. The hearing was as brutal as those in Uppsala, for the King had ordered that torture was to be resorted to immediately if Lassota refused to talk. The commission told him that they would certainly forward his plea for mercy to the King, but both the secretaries and others assured him that their efforts would be of no avail. Once again he was given two days to think things over. After two troubled and sleepless nights, however, the storm died down once more.[6]

According to his diary, Lassota ran into Duke Charles on March 27, 1591, while he was still in Stockholm. They passed each other while crossing the bridge which at that time joined Helgeandsholm to Gamla Stan just by Storkyrkan. They exchanged a few words, from which it was clear that the Duke was astonished to find Lassota still in Stockholm and at large.

On April 3, 1591, presumably on the Duke's initiative, Lassota was removed from Stockholm to Svartsjö, where he stayed until the beginning

[1] 'Do you mean to say that the Emperor would start a war for his sake if I had the man hung immediately?'; *ibid.*, 149.

[2] 'It's the very devil to serve princes and nobelmen when one prince behaves like this towards the other's servant'; *ibid.*, 149 f.

[3] *Ibid.*, 151.

[4] New style.

[5] Schottin, 152.

[6] *Ibid.*, 152 ff.

of August. He notes that Svartsjö had once been a monastery but that this had been destroyed by Gustavus Vasa. The castle had been begun by Eric XIV and completed by John III, who named it Svartsjöborg. It stood on the shore of a beautiful lake and had gardens and a park. A stately church had recently been erected and behind this there was a tall runestone that particularly fired his imagination. Nevertheless, his stay at Svartsjöborg was not a pleasant memory. On April 13 he complained that all his clothes and in particular his shoes were worn out. In this respect at least he found some comfort. During the course of the summer Christian and Gustavus Oxenstierna took pity on him and sent him both clothing and a sum of money.

Finally, John III ordered that Lassota be brought to Uppsala once more and on August 3 he arrived at Sigtuna on his way there. On his arrival at Uppsala he found to his relief that one of the master builders there was a countryman of his, Antonius Watz, from Breslau. Watz had come to Sweden with several other German craftsmen to take part in the works designed by the Pahr family, which were to have such an influence on Swedish renaissance architecture. Their common origins led to Watz treating Lassota with 'much respect and great friendship', as a result of which the latter's treatment by his gaolers also improved.

On September 28, 1591, Hans Bischoff von Han, a draper from Silesia, left Uppsala and took with him in secret three letters from Lassota to Wolff Rumpfen, Jacob Kurzen and Carl von Seretein respectively. On April 28, 1592, Lassota gave another letter to one Georg Goßman, a barber-surgeon from Bâle; this one was addressed to the Imperial court at Prague and Lassota gave Goßman 50 daler for his trouble.

Duke Charles was in Stockholm between February 23 and March 12, 1592; shortly after his arrival he must have come to some agreement with Nils Gyllenstierna. The entry in the Duke's almanac runs as follows:

26. tog her Nils Gyllenstierne sin affsked ifrån migh, finnes wi icke mer i tette liuett, så gudh geffue tett sker i tett eugie liuett.[1]

Clearly Gyllenstierna had done everything in his power to help Lassota, for it had been decided around the end of February that the latter was to be moved to Nyköping where he would come under Duke Charles's

---

[1] '26th. Lord Nils Gyllenstierna took his farewell of me, if death should come may God grant that we meet again in the life eternal'; *Cal. Car. IX*, 74.

jurisdiction.[1] Gyllenstierna was seemingly very much afraid, certainly not without reason, that something would happen to Lassota while he was at Nyköping.

It would seem that, when, on his return to Silesia, Lassota compiled his diary, he had at his side several of the letters which he had sent from Sweden while he was in prison. After April 28, 1592, when he dispatched the letter with Goßman, his dates become uncertain and one can only suppose that he was writing from memory several years later. A number of the entries are not in chronological order and do not agree with the entries in Duke Charles's almanac. Thus the entries for August 19 to August 23, 1592, probably refer to events which in fact took place about two months earlier.[2]

Lassota probably arrived at Nyköping in the middle of June 1592 and remained there until a day or two before the Duke's wedding on August 27.[3] In spite of his fears, his stay was relatively uneventful and his dealings with the Duke's closest men were more or less pleasant. Lassota found himself on particularly good terms with Laße Weßgiöthe, Duke Charles's governor at Nyköpingshus. He took charge of Lassota on his arrival, supplying his needs and treating him as a distinguished prisoner. To start with, Lassota was quartered in the guardhouse of the castle. He summed up his impressions of Nyköping as follows:

New Köpingen ist ein lustiges offenes Stedlein, darbey ein schön, und doch nicht groß gemauertes Schloß, auff welchem Herzog Carl Hoff helt, ligt 12 Meiln von Stockholm, an einem schönen Strom, daruber eine lange hölzerne Brucken gehet.[4]

In the last week of July, while Lassota was still at Nyköping, Baron Augustin von Moersperg und Beffort arrived on a visit to Duke Charles.[5]

---

[1] Schottin, 168.

[2] *Cal. Car. IX*, 78 f.

[3] Cf. *ibid.*, 78. Schottin, 169.

[4] 'Nyköping is a pleasant little open town with a very attractive but not large walled castle where Duke Charles has his court. This town is 120 kilometres from Stockholm, on a beautiful river crossed by a long wooden bridge'; Schottin, 169.

[5] *Ibid.*, 168. Cf. *Cal. Car. IX*, 79. According to E. H. Kneschke, *Neues allgemeines Adels-Lexikon*, VI, 1865, Baron Augustin was known for his lengthy journeys, which he described himself, through Sweden, Denmark, Norway and other countries. His unpublished account was available to Martin Zeiller when the latter was working on his topographical description of Denmark–Norway, published as *Neue Beschreibung der Königreiche Dennemarck vnnd Norwegen, auch derselben einverleibten Landschafften, furnembsten Stätten und Plätzen sambt einer Vorrede von den*

On one occasion while the Duke was entertaining this man, who was a knight of the Order of Malta, Lassota sat at table with him together with Laße Weßgiöthe, a number of the Duke's councillors and others. On or around August 24,[1] Lassota and his companions were moved from Nyköping to Gripsholm, where their movements were severely restricted. He complains that they were not even allowed to leave the attic where they had their quarters. After a couple of months, on November 19[2] orders came to move them out to Tynnelsö but, as the ice was not yet thick enough, they stayed at Räfsnäs instead and were allowed a certain amount of freedom.

John III died on November 17, 1592.[3] At the Emperor Rudolph II's request, King Sigismund released Lassota, despite Duke Charles's strenuous protests. This was on February 28, 1593,[4] and it was not until April 29 that Lassota was able to sail from Stockholm, bound for Lubeck and home.

In this connection there are two matters that are of particular interest. The first is the fact that Nils Gyllenstierna (Niels Guldenstern) studied at Wittenberg, and the second that Lassota and his companions were at Nyköping from June 14 until August 24, 1592,[5] at the same time as the English players with Philip Kingman among them.

The theory that Nils Gyllenstierna was Shakespeare's model for Guldenstern has already been put forward by August Strindberg.[6] Gyllenstierna in fact spelt his name Guldenstern, which is not far removed from the spellings in the early editions of *Hamlet*.[7] Moreover, Shakespeare includes several references to Wittenberg. In one part of *Hamlet* there is every

---

in den Historien so hoch berumbten Normännern ..., Vlm 1648. Zeiller's book contains excerpts from Baron Augustin's descriptions (Elsinore on pp. 164–5, Kronborg Castle on pp. 169–70, Copenhagen on p. 179, Uraniborg on pp. 252–5) but he does not deal with the Swedish part of the Baron's travels. However, Kneschke seems to have known where to find the Baron's manuscript while he was engaged in publishing his *Adels-Lexikon* in 1865, although he does not explicitly state its location. During the course of my research I have found that the document is still extant at the library in Sondershausen (Die Moersperger Handschrift; Sondershausen—Wissenschaftliche Bibliothek der Stadt Erfurt, Michaelisstraße 39, 50 Erfurt, East Germany).

[1] Old style.   [2] New style.
[3] Old style.   [4] New style.
[5] New style.
[6] August Strindberg, *Hamlet* 22.
[7] F 1, Guildensterne; Q 1, Gilderstone; Q 2, Guyldensterne.

indication that Hamlet, Horatio, Guildenstern and Rosencrantz had all been there.[1] Nils Gyllenstierna was in London on Eric XIV's behalf in 1561 to 1562 and it has previously been held that this was too early for him to have had any certain connection with Shakespeare's England.[2] However, the fact that there was an English company at Nyköping from 1591 to 1592 would seem to put the matter in a different light, for the players must surely have got to know about the old chancellor.

[1] *Hamlet*, I. ii. 113, 119, 164 and 168.
[2] Ingvar Andersson, *Hamletdramats nordiska miljö*, 138, note 2.

CHAPTER 8

James Hill

The Public Record Office, the British Museum, Hatfield House and other sources in England contain several dispatches from James Hill to Lord Burghley, Sir Thomas Heneage, Lord Buckhurst and others, written in Nyköping or Stockholm and containing reports on Duke Charles's court at Nyköping during the early nineties and at the turn of the sixteenth century. Hill in his turn first appears in the Duke's kitchen accounts[1] in the middle of October 1592 about two months after the wedding.

James Hill's second letter to Mr. Vice-Chamberlain (Sir Thomas Heneage at that time) is dated January 12, 1593, from Stockholm. A note about Hill has been written on the back in another hand and runs as follows:

This Hill was a student at the law in Lincoln's Inn[2] who procured a licence to travel and at his departure was with Mr. Vice-Chamberlain to know if he would command him in any service for her Majesty. A very proper man, and of a good behaviour, otherwise Mr. Vice-Chamberlain knows him not. This is the first letters of his have been received, and by Mr. Alderman Salternstall's[3] means.[4]

If his own version in the above letter is to be believed, Hill was favourably received at Nyköping on his arrival in Sweden. His acquaintanceship with the Duke in particular flourished; he was invited to sit at the same table, he hunted with the Duke and conversed with him the while.[5] One of Hill's earlier letters, to his step-father, Mr. Rudolph

---

[1] Mantalsregistret, Kungl. Hofförtärningen 93, SA.

[2] No record of a James Hill is to be found in the list of students at Lincoln's Inn. On the other hand, a person of that name was admitted as a student of Gray's Inn in 1571. Joseph Foster, *Reg. Adm. Gray's Inn*, 42.

[3] Mr. Alderman Salternstall = Sir Richard Saltonstall. Cf. Index.

[4] SP 95/1, fol. 68 v, PRO.

[5] SP 95/1, fol. 64 r, PRO.

Scryvener in Ipswich,[1] mentions that he was not content unless the Duke had drunk his health at least once a day. Hill's comment on Sweden was concise,

I think it to be the coldest country in the world.

For the Duke, however, he was full of admiration and he wrote towards the end of 1592,

He is a courteous Prince, and wise, and hath the hearts of all the whole land.

Quite soon after his arrival in Sweden James Hill's loyalty to Queen Elizabeth and her ministers was put to the test. Another Englishman, who went under the name of Thomas Cornwallis at Nyköping but whose real name was Christopher Graye, had fled from England via Scotland to Duke Charles's court, where he was engaged 'for entertainment' in August 1592. Graye took Hill into his confidence, much against the latter's will, and disclosed to him that while in England he had been mixed up in treason, murder and other foul deeds, all of which Hill faithfully reported back to Burghley and Heneage. Unfortunately it has been impossible to discover much about Graye's real past in England, though his account seems somewhat improbable.

Hill, anxious to learn more about Graye's affairs, became his close friend and confidant, and was thus able to send copies of letters in Graye's possession to Heneage. Duke Charles also came to hear of Graye's doings and had him thrown into prison in Nyköping. While waiting for a reply from England as to how Graye's case was to be dealt with, it was considered necessary to arrest Hill as well.[2]

The Englishmen at Nyköping took Graye's side in the question and were much incensed by his imprisonment. Graye, moreover, answered the charges against him ably, and Hill comments 'for his naye is better than my yea'. In particular, 'one of the baser sort — this Briggis that playeth the Jester to the Duke', informed the Duke and his councillors that Hill had dealt as he had out of spite and that in fact Hill was himself a much more dubious character than Graye. Philip Bruggis (Briggis)[3] declared

---

[1] Cf. the letter dated 4.10.1596 from Princess Elizabeth of Mecklenburg to Mr. Rudolph Scryvener, Ipswich. Staatl. Archivlager, Göttingen.

[2] SP 95/1, fol. 64 v, 68 and 70–71, PRO.

[3] Cf. p. 45, last §, and App. I A (Wikland, *Eliz. Pl.*, 1. ed., 1962).

that Hill was 'but a player in England' and that he had been obliged to flee the country.

Nor was Bruggis entirely wrong. The earliest letter by James Hill is dated August 1584 from one of the London prisons. Presumably Hill was suspect by reason of his fanatical Puritanism. So as to be set free, he offered his services to Sir Francis Walsingham and to prove his sincerity added a list of persons known to him to have Catholic leanings and to have hidden Jesuits and Catholic fugitives in their homes; he also attached a list of these people's addresses.[1]

The letter dated January 12, 1593, from Hill to Mr. Vice-Chamberlain has a postscript that runs:

> The first letter[2] I directed to your honour was by one John Howse Anglius that served the Duke as a Trumpeter, and willed him to deliver it to one John Coote, Tho. Fishes man, the Duke's Inglische merchant, which I hope is safely delivered ...

According to the warrant from 1591, both Howse and Bruggis were trumpeters. It is interesting to note that Hill writes of the first as 'the Duke's Trumpeter' and of the second as 'the Duke's Jester'.

James Hill left Sweden some time in 1593 and returned to England.[3] In a dispatch[4] to Duke Charles 'Datae in Curia ad Hamtoncourt V Martij 1593'[5] and signed by the Privy Council[6] on behalf of the Queen, James Hill is cleared of all suspicion. The passage runs as follows:

[1] Harl. Mss 286, fol. 52 r ff., BM.

[2] James Hill's letter to Sir Thomas Heneage, January 5, 1593. Landsdowne Ms 73, fol. 72 f., BM.

[3] Anglica. Förhandlingar 1559–1632, No. 531. Letter 5.3.1593 conc. James Hill, RA.

[4] *Ibid.*

[5] 5 March 1594 by the modern calendar.

[6] The dispatch was signed by Dr. John Whitgift, Lord Archbishop of Canterbury; Sir John Puckering, Lord Keeper of the Great Seal of England; Robert Devereux, Earl of Essex, Master of the Horse; Charles Howard, Baron of Effingham, Lord Admiral of England, Knight of the Garter; Henry Carey, Lord of Hunsdon, Lord Chamberlain, Knight of the Garter; Thomas, Lord Buckhurst, Lord High Butler of England, Knight of the Garter; Sir Thomas Heneage, Vice-Chamberlain of the Queen, Chancellor of the Duchy of Lancaster; Sir Robert Cecil; Mr. John Wolley, Esq., Secretary for the Latin Tongue, Chancellor of the most Honourable Order of the Garter; Mr. John Fortescue, Esq., Master of the Great Wardrobe, and Under-Treasurer of the Exchequer. Since there is a gap in the records between 26.8.1592 and 1.10.1595, it has not been possible to find a copy in the Acts of the Privy Council of England, Vol. XXV.

...; ita non postremum testimonium in causa dilecti nobis, ac fidelis suae M:^tis subditi Jacobi Hill Generosi, apparuit, quam pro debito suo in Sacram R. M:^tem obsequio, contra malevolum et temporum M^tis suae obtrectatorem, pudorisque nescium, Thomam Cornewallis, in Regno Vestro instituit, et ob quam commodius hic coram nobis legitime Magistratu suo persequendam, Angliam natale suum solum repetiit ...[1]

Hill returned to Sweden in 1594 as Duke Charles's English agent[2] and in 1595 he made the following entry in Henry Francklin's album:[3]

expecta et spera
Audi vide tace: si vis vivere in pace.
Jacobus Hyll
Anglius A° 95

Early in 1595 James Hill was a member of Duke Charles's court at Stockholm Castle on the occasion of Prince Gustavus Adolphus's christening.[4]

During 1596 marriage negotiations were conducted between James Hill and Elizabeth von Zeulen, a lady-in-waiting to Princess Elizabeth of Mecklenburg. In this connection the Princess wrote two letters from Stockholm, dated October 4, 1596, to Hill's step-father Mr. Rudolph Scryvener of Ipswich and to Helena Northampton, asking in each for details of James Hill's ancestry, &c.

The letter to Mr Scryvener contains the following passage:

... Quod si e re tui privigni (ut certum erit) futurum putabis, clementer a te exigimus ut consensum tuum litteris testeris et matrimonij feliciter suscipiendi ergo mille Joachimicos, quos vocant unciales vulgo thaleros, privigni tuo in subsidium huc ad nos transmittere quam primum velis ...[5]

---

[1] '...; here now a witness—not the last—has been found in the case of our good friend and Her Majesty's faithful servant, James Hill, Gentleman, which he in accordance with his bounden duty to Her Most Blessed Majesty forwarded in Your realm against the scoundrillous upsetter of Her Majesty's rule, the shameless Thomas Cornwallis. It was in order the better to be able to pursue this action before us, his lawful rulers, that he again visited England, the land of his birth ...'; Förhandlingar 1559–1632 (Fasc. 1583–1611). Letter 5/3 1593 conc. James Hill; RA.

[2] Likvidationer 91/13. Köpmäns Rechninger pro Anno 94 och 95, fol. 83 r–84 r, KA.

[3] 'Wait and hope. Hear, look about you, be silent: if you prefer to live in peace. James Hill, Englishman. 1595'; op. cit., fol. 19 r.

[4] Kungl. Hofförtärningen 95. Cf. Ch. 9, pp. 154 f.

[5] '... If you consider that it would benefit your stepson (as it certainly would), we kindly ask that you certify your approval in a letter and that, for a happy

And that to Helena Northampton the following:

... Quae res si eum, quem speramus, sortiri debet exitum, in primis
necessarium esse videtur, ut mos in hisce regionibus solemnis observetur,
quo ij qui se nobili stirpe editos profitentur, suae geniturae praesertim hoc
in casu perspicua et evidentia adferre iubentur documenta ...[1]

Replies to these letters could not be found in the German archives or
elsewhere, but it seems that James Hill concluded his negotiations in
Mecklenburg, though hardly before the turn of the century.
The following entry for August 2, 1602, appears in 'Riksregistraturen':

Öppet bref för Ingeborg, Jacob Hilles efterlefverska, på 12 tunnor spannmål årligen at bekomma i Västerås län i sin lifstid af oförlänt kyrkotionde.[2]

This entry possibly serves as an indication of the time when James Hill
married Elizabeth von Zeulen. Hill's Ingeborg seems to have been a
contentious woman, as witness the irritation expressed in a further entry
on the same matter by Charles IX in 1608:

Till Nils Bengtsson, att han skall låta Ingeborg, Jacob Hilles, bekomma
så mycken bespisning, som hon kan sig med behjälpa, så att Wi därom måge
blifwe obesvärade.[3]

Later Hill was commissioned by Duke Charles as a captain in the
Swedish forces,[4] took part in the expedition of 1598–99 to Finland and

commencement of the marriage, you will send over one thousand Joachim daler
as soon as possible for the upkeep of your son ...'; No. 375. Staatliches Archivlager,
Göttingen.

    [1] '... If these marriage negotiations are to have the outcome for which We hope,
it would seem chiefly necessary that the traditional custom of this country is
followed, according to which a person claiming to be of noble birth is charged with
presenting clear and irrefutable evidence of his descent and that particularly so in
a case such as this ...'; No. 376. Staatliches Archivlager, Göttingen.

    [2] 'Official letter for Ingeborg, James Hill's Swedish mistress, to receive 12 barrels
of corn annually in Västerås County during her lifetime out of unappropriated church
tithes'; Riksregistraturen 2.8.1602, fol. 92 r; RA.

    [3] 'To Nils Bengtsson, who is to allow Ingeborg, James Hill's, to receive as much
food as she may be in need of, in order that We be not troubled by the matter';
Riksregistraturen 9.8.1608, fol. 355 r; RA.

    [4] James Hill, letter to Lord Buckhurst 25.9.1598. MS. Additional, fol. 87, BM.

was promoted to colonel on December 12, 1600.[1] During the aftermath of this campaign Hill was entrusted by the Duke with the task of informing those sentenced to death that they would be executed shortly.[2] A letter to Lord Buckhurst[3] 'from my tent at Sand Haven[4] in ffyndland' dated September 25, 1598, contains the following note in a postscript:

To Sir Walter Raulegh great thankes from the Duck[5] for our interteynment and that the Duke will send 12 shippes from Guiana and joyne with him in any good order yf Sir Walter will send his meaning unto me I will informe His Exclencye and wright him His Graces answer, for vittall mene and shipps will the Duck provide at Newlyes[6] in the west seas, the Imperor of Rusland lyes with a great army of men ready to serve the Duck apon the borders if need so require, which indeed I wish we had fewer, for we poverish the Countreye when we come and the very name of D. Charles takes the stomackes of our Enymyes, the Governor of Obowe[7] sent the D. word this day when he can see his person here then will he yeld upp the Castill, who is the the chiefe of ffyndland.[8]

The opening sentence confirms that an English company of players appeared in some guise in Sweden between 1598 and 1600.

Hill's opinion of the Duke underwent a change during these years, as witness his comment in this letter:

... I know no stranger better, none hyer prefeored in the Courts or ffield, & yett none more hated ...

Hill returned from Finland to Sweden in the autumn of 1598 and was present at the Diet of Jönköping, which lasted from January 26 to February 13, 1599, and considered the question of Sigismund's continued right to the crown and Duke Charles's actual position in the country. The assembled estates wrote to Sigismund, presenting specific demands and complaints. The King of Denmark, Christian IV, was represented at the

[1] Riksregistraturen 1600, Pars II, fol. 363 r; RA.
[2] Anthoni I, 177.
[3] James Hill, letter to Lord Buckhurst 25.9.1598; MS. Additional 6177, fol. 87; BM.
[4] Sandhamn, an island near Sveaborg outside present-day Helsinki.
[5] Duke Charles.
[6] Nylödöse, now Gothenburg.
[7] Turku (Swedish Åbo).
[8] Cf. E. Edwards, *Sir Walter Ralegh*, I, 199; *SBL* 7, 199 ff.; *Engl. Hist. Rev.* 1899, 84; V. T. Harlow, *Guiana*, ci; *Hist. Tidskr.* 1899, 72; and Abraham Cabeljau's report from his voyage to Guiana 1598, 'Archief Staten-Generaal, Loketkas V.O.C., No. 2, *DNA*.

diet by Sten Brahe and Henry Ramelius, who negotiated with Duke Charles.[1] James Hill was sent as Swedish ambassador to Queen Elizabeth of England, extensive instructions being issued for him at Jönköping on February 13, which was the last day of the diet.[2] Hill's embassy elicited the following comment in William Camden's *Annales:*

1599

... Eodem fere tempore Carolus, Regnorum Sueciae, Gothiae & Vandaliae Princeps Dei gratia haereditarius (hoc enim titulo usus est) ad Reginam misit Hillum Anglum, qui calumnias, quasi novis rebus Sueciae regnum contra nepotem Sigismundum Poloniae Regem affectando studeret, apud Reginam dilueret; rogavitque ut fidem calumniantibus derogaret & ipsi *ad conservandam & propugnandam synceram & verbo Dei fundatam Religionem concilio & auxilio adesset.* Illa publice audivit, extemplo respondit, & optavit, ut fidem Nepoti datam syncere servaret, ne in iustitiam, naturam propinquitatis iura peccaret, & officium magis comiter quam fideliter colere videretur.[3]

The embassy also warranted the attention of Fugger's agent in Amsterdam in a brief note as follows:

660. Amsterdam, May 4th, 1599 ...
The Swedish ambassador has had an audience with Her Majesty in the name of Duke Charles. ...[4]

On May 14, 1600, shortly after the estates had met in Linköping, Duke Charles again issued credentials for James Hill to Queen Elizabeth.

---

[1] T.K.U.A.; Speciel Del. Sverige; A II: Akter og Dokumenter vedr. det politiske Forhold till Sverige: Nr 33. Akter vedr. Sten Brahes og Henrik Ramels Hverv (1599). Danish RA.

[2] Riksregistraturen 1599/I, fol. 118 r–121 r; RA.

[3] '... At about the same time, the Englishman Hill was sent by Duke Charles, Hereditary Prince of Sweden, the Goths and the Vandals (which is the title used by him), to the Queen to wipe out the slander to the effect that Duke Charles was scheming to take the Swedish throne by a coup d'état from his nephew Sigismund, King of Poland; and Duke Charles asked that the Queen refuse to believe those who slandered him and instead support by word and deed his efforts to maintain and defend the true religion founded on the Word of God. The Queen received the message standing, replied at once without a draft and expressed her wish that Duke Charles honestly keep the oath of alleigance he had given to his nephew as otherwise he would go against justice, nature and the laws of kinship. The Duke should perform his duty, moreover, not as a courtesy but faithfully and from the heart ...'; William Camden, *Annales*, I–II, 1615 and 1625; *Annales sub anno 1599*, II, pp. 188 f.

[4] Fugger[2], No. 660.

Prior to this, Hill had written in person to the Queen concerning his dispute with Lennard Tucker and the English comedians in Nyköping. Elizabeth did not grant an audience similar to that of the year before and Hill's official commission for Duke Charles in 1600 was confined to the purchase of horses and cloth &c. in England.[1]

Later Hill again fell foul of the English players, in particular of Lennard Tucker(tz), a Gentleman. I quote James Hill's letter to Queen Elizabeth I from the 'Court of Swethen', last of April, 1600, about his dispute with Tucker(tz) et consertes:

Vouchsafe to understand of an intolerable injury here lately offered me by one Lennard Tucker, by myself preferred to His Grace's service upon the recommend of Sir Walter Raulegh, who unjustly procured here the death of a brother of mine, who had been late my lieutenant—general in the field, whose corpse the Duke's Grace and Duchess', with the young Princes, and Holsten Ambassadors graciously vouchsafed to accompany to the grave; and has so falsely slandered me that in regard of the speech of the court and common people, I can no way by law be thereof here disburdened until Your Highness Council vouchsafe to certify to His Excellency of his lewd and inordinate life in England, which is too notorious.[2]

The record in English of the preliminary hearing, drawn up at Nyköping on May 4, 1600, concerning various costumes that Hill was accused of having stolen, runs as follows:

Att Nicopen in Swethen this iiii[th] of may in the yeare of our lord God (1600).

We whose names be heare under written remaininge in Swethen doe certifye unto those to whom theis presents shall come
That Leonard Tucker one countriman hath heare in open courte approached the worshipfull Mr. James Hill for a Shellom which is in theis partes the greatist name of infamy, that can be spoken to the meanest or vilest person.
And that Mr. Hill hath also buggered a boy of his owne wherewith it appeared he charged him but in a wag of requitall for that Mr. Hill in the late Finland voyage havinge him a shippbourde with him, & seeinge him to use more then ordinary familiarity towards his boy, did in friendly manner after give him warninge thereof.

[1] Credentials for James Hill by Duke Charles 14.5.1600 to Elizabeth I; Duke Charles to Elizabeth I 15.5.1600, RA. SP 95/1, fol. 136 f, PRO. Recredentials for James Hill by Elizabeth I 7.6.1600 to Duke Charles, Diplomatica, Anglica 7, Strödda handlingar, No. 531, RA.
[2] James Hill to Elizabeth I 30.4.1600. H.X. 130 f.

And that further Mr. Hill had bene hearebefore a player, & having stolen away
their apparell, came into this countrey of Swethen, where he nowe
remaineth in service by his excellencie
And that also Mr. Hill had bene a Taylor, & that he had heareby bene an
apprentice unto a Taylor in Ipswich, Which is in Suffolk.

All which he againe denied when he was driven to his proufes therefore att a
new courte day commanded by his excellencie to be held for that
purpose, which if he had not then denied, beinge notable to make due prouf
thereof himself had by the Lawes of this lande bene made unto a Shellom
with many other fauls informacons & malicious speches, tending greatly
to Mr. Hills whereof it appeareth his excellency is well satisfied
& had notwithstandinge stopped Mr. Hills determinacon for his jorney unto
England touchinge these matters, but in regarde of the censure of the com-
mone
sorte of people whose mouthes may not well in such cases be stopped without
due & publick clearinge of himself, which for that he is a strauger may
not well be donno without some certificat from the Queenes majestie or her
majesties honorable privy counsaile obteyned to that purpose.

All which matter is of discorde grewe only upon this, that he shoulde lay to his
chardge that he was a principall cause of the death of a brother of his in
bringinge a quarrell betwene him & a Scottish man, which upon the whell
proceedinge
of the matter & upon his owne open confessinge to have reported the wordes
which bread the quarrell, wee have lykewise cause to thincke which wordes
Mr. Hills brother did in his liest tyme in the hearinge of some of us utterlye
deny to have spoken unto the same Leo. Tucker.

For the better triall of which matters Mr. Hill not desiringe to followe the lawe
upon him in a straunge countrey, hath obteyned of his Excellency, that
he shoulde heare make othe to appeare shortly in person before her majesties
saide counsell the Lord chief justice of England, to answere him as well to
those as to suche other matters, as he shall there obiecte against him
myself hearde not of the words, stolen away but of takknge away their
apparrell & get stolen away & stood upon the record of the cort which
myself hearde read openly.

per me Joannem Caunton
Johannes Nicolai

That the sayd Tucker did call him shellam player Roge & taylor
I de testifie the same

per me William Greene

I Thomas Fisk concerninge the players apparrell heard according to Mr.
Cantons testymony and was present with Mr. Canton in the cort at his last

100

examination Also I hearde all accordinge to Mr. Grens testymony above
written

per me Thomas Fisk   Jo. Coote

Signum Christoferi X Gray   Thomas Slaughter

This record was sent from Nyköping to Tobias Hume in England.
It is worth noting that the mention of 'the players apparrell' in the
record is additional evidence that an English company of players was
engaged at the Duke's court during these years.

The cause of the lawsuit appears from the documents to have been the
personal feud between Lennart Tuckertz and James Hill and the circumstance that Hill was suspected of having been a party to the death of his
step-father, Mr. Rudolph Scryvener, who was also in the service of Duke
Charles at Nyköping at this time. On April 6, 1600, Scryvener was
stabbed by a Scots mercenary after a quarrel and although Hill was not
directly responsible for his death, he was considered to have brought the
quarrel to a head, so the Duke decided to refer the case to the courts in
London.

Rudolph Scryvener was buried in Nyköping, the ceremony being
attended by Duke Charles, Princess Christine, Prince Gustavus Adolphus
and the Holstein ambassadors, Clement Gadendorff and Gerhard Stedingk, both of whom were members of the Duke of Holstein's Council,
Stedingk also being councillor to Duke Charles.[2] The obituary,[3] composed by the Superintendent of Strängnäs, Petrus Jonae, was forwarded
to Queen Elizabeth.

The clumsy pronouns in the record of the preliminary hearing in
Nyköping on May 4, 1600, make it difficult to be quite certain of the
origin of the quarrel but this does not affect the offence against the
players. John Caunton, John Nicolaj, and Thomas Fisk each affirm that
'myself hearde not of the words *stolen away*, but of *takinge away* their
apparrell, and yet stolen away, stoode upon the record of the cort wch
myself heard reade openly.' William Greene testifies that 'the sayd
Tucker did call him shellam player roge & tayler.'

Of the witnesses Johannes Nicolaj was Hill's companion ambassador

---

[1] Dom. SP XII/274, fol. 278 r; PRO.

[2] H X. 130. Cf. the instructions for an embassy from Holstein to Sweden February–May 1600, Landesarchiv Schleswig-Holstein, Schloß Gottorf, 238 Schleswig,
West Germany.

[3] SP 9–201–3, PRO.

in 1599.[1] Thomas Fisk, John Coote, and William Greene were all London merchants and Duke Charles's commissionary agents. William Greene was distantly related to Thomas Greene of 'Tu Quoque' reputation. Slaughter is more distinctive, and since acting runs in families, if this Thomas Slaughter was any relation of the Martin Slater or Slaughter who belonged to the Admiral's men 1594–97 and was in Scotland in 1591, he too may have been a player.

Concerning John Caunton, there is an entry in Henry Francklin's album:

Johannes Caunton Cantianus. Stockholm, December 27th 1599[2]

in which context it may be noted that the use of Cantianus for Kentishman was an academic trait. I have also found that a John Caunton studied at Oxford:

Caunton, John, of Kent, gent., *Univ. Coll.*, matric. 25 Oct., 1588, aged 15.[3]

A lawsuit between John Coote and Lennart Tuckertz was held at the Court of Records in Stockholm on July 16, 1600, as follows:

Den 16 julij närwarande teße effter:ne edle wälbårne, wälbördige herrer och gode män

G. Moritz Stenßon	Nils Larßoon.
G. Magnus Brahe	Laße Jacobßon.
Nils Biälche.	Gödche Finke.
Päär Ryningh	Matz Larßonn.
Jöns Vlfßonn	Hans Hanßonn

Kom för rätten Jahann Cut och klagade till enn engilsch adelßman Lenart benämpndh at hann icke allenest dagligenn dagz blifuer skält vtaf honom för enn skälm, vthann och der öfuer låter höra sigh at han will skära strupann af honom, begärede fördenschuldh Jahann Cut vtaf the gode herrer at hann måtte derföre tagas vthi tillbörligit straff här vpå beropade Jahann Kut sigh till witne Richert Ruff, Willm Niderwudd och Rütkert Känt.

Richert Ruff witnedhe på sinn edh at hann för 8 dagar sädhan på Norremalm hörde af Lenart at hann schälte / Jahan för enn järnhiertadh schälm. Rötchert Känt staddes intet till witne efter hann war hans afwundzmann.

Willm Niderwudd witnedhe på sinn edh, at Lenart hade sagt at hann will skära strupann af honom der till schälte hann honom för willinn vnd rogg, det ähr så mÿckit på swänscha, enn schälm som hafuer stådt widh kåkenn, och sade han at ther hittes intet wärre och slemmare ordh på engilscha.

---

[1] SP For. Sweden (95/1), fol. 101; PRO.

[2] Op. cit., fol. 18 r.

[3] Foster, *Alumni Oxonienses*, I, 251.

Här till swarade Lenart at i theres språk achtas int*et* så högt at denn ene skeller denn andre för en schälm. Män huadh de orden ahnlanga at hann schulle wille schära strupann af hono*m*, sade hann at the ähre så falne, får iagh min fot på främmande landh, då skall iagh schära strupann af digh för det du hafuer giordt migh emot. Spordes fördenschuldh Lenart till om hann wiste något schälmstycke medh Jahann Kut effter han hono*m* sådant beschylt hafwer? Der / till swarade Lenart 'at' han int*et* skälmstycke wet medh honom icke vthi det ringste.

Widare sade Lenart at Jahann Cut hafuer kommit alt detta pärlamente till wäge och ähr rätte orsakenn till at owänschap ähr vpkom*m*inn emellenn honom och hans la*n*dzmän, männ det hann skälte hono*m* för enn schälm det schedde vthi dryckenschap och wet int*et* annat m*ed* honom ähn det som ährligt wore.

Röchert Kent inlade copier vtaf några breff först ifrån Tobias Hiums i Danmark som hono*m* ähr sänt ifrånn Engillandh, en copie som lydde: at i Engillandh war en som giorde 2 barnn medh sinn eginn dotter, på denn tijdh tiänte Lenart dråtningenn i Engillannd lät så Lenart schrifua sigh et bref vthi dråtningenns nampn, och stal h. m:tz secret der vnder, och lydde brefuet at hann schulle examinere sakenn, drogh så åstadh och togh en summa penninger af honom som gerningenn giorde, och släpte ho/nom sinn koos, huarföre schulle Lenart Tuckertz wara dömder at hans både öronn schulle afschäras och skulle stå på kåkenn, sädhann blifua gißlat igenom landet.

Här till swarade Lenart, at om han hade något bedrifuit i Engillandh thet hade h f. n:de int*et* beställa medh och sade han widare, at huar h. f n:de antingenn täckes låta blifua honom här quar så länge at något beschedh här om kann komma ifrånn dråtningenn i Engilla*n*dh medh h. m:tz secret vnder då will hann gerna lijda der före. Täckes och h. f. n.de sända honom till Engillandh at stå der till suars will hann gärna wara lijdhachtigh.

Noch inlade Rötchert en copie af et annat breff som Johannes Kempter hafuer schrifuit Jahan Cut till dat. i Engillandh den 5 junij 1600. således lijdandes: "Thet ähr ingenn tuifuelßmål at Tobias Hiums schall nogsam bewis bekomma at Jacob Hilles / wederpart schall wara en schälm till det hogsta."

Männ på sidlijchtonne effter Lenart Tuckertz badh Jahann Cut högeligenn om wänschap, lät Jahan sin saak falla, blefue wänner och rächte huar annann handen.[1]

[1] 'On July 16 [1600] the following noble and most honourable gentelmen and knights were present: Count Maurice Stenßon, Count Magnus Brahe, Nils Bielke, Per Ryningh, Jöns Ulfßon, Nils Larßon, Laße Jacobßon, Gödche Finke, Matz Larßonn, Hans Hanßonn.

John Coote appeared before the Court and accused an English gentleman named Lennart of not only abusing him daily and saying that he is a rascal but also of threatening every day to cut his throat, wherefore John Coote requested of the most honourable gentlemen that Lennart be punished for this. Coote called as witnesses Ricard Raff, William Netherwood and Roger Kent.

Ricard Raff witnessed on oath that eight days ago in Norrmalm [in Stockholm]

The preliminary hearing in Nyköping on 4 May 1600 and this record from Stockholm on 16 July in the same year clearly indicate that the English colonies in Nyköping and Stockholm were divided into two camps for and against James Hill. Wild accusations are made against Hill and his antagonist Lennart Tuckertz, no doubt engendered by

he had heard Lennart abuse Coote, calling him an out-and-out [*lit.* iron-hard] rascal. Roger Kent was disqualified and not allowed to witness because he was envious of Lennart.

William Netherwood witnessed on oath that Lennart had said he would cut his throat. Furthermore, he abused him and called him a villain and rogue, which in Swedish is the same as a rascal who has been pilloried, and asserted that there is scarcely a worse or fouler word in English.

To this Lennart replied that in English it is of little account if one person calls another a rascal. But concerning the words that he would cut his throat, he said that they were uttered thus: If I get abroad I'll cut your throat for going against me. Thereupon Lennart was asked if he could remember any knavery with John Coote since he accused him of such. Whereupon Lennart replied that he did not know of the least knavery with John Coote.

Furthermore Lennart said that John Coote had occasioned all this argument and that it was he who was the real cause of the enmity that had arisen between himself and his countrymen, but that his calling him a rascal had occurred while they had been drinking and he knew nothing with him except that which was honourable.

Roger Kent submitted copies of some letters, first from Tobias Hume in Denmark that had been sent to Kent from England. One copy ran thus, that in England there was a person who had two children with his own daughter, at which time Lennart was in the Queen of England's service and he had written a letter in the Queen's name and stolen Her Majesty's seal thereunder, which letter ran that he was to investigate the matter, whereupon he departed and secured a sum of money from the man who had committed the deed and let him go free, for which Lennart Tuckertz would be sentenced to have both his ears cut off and to stand in the pillory, after which he would be whipped through the realm.

To which Lennart replied that if he had done anything in England, this was no concern of Duke Charles. Furthermore, he would prefer the Duke to let him remain in Sweden until a despatch arrived from the Queen of England with Her Majesty's seal, whereupon he would be prepared to take the consequences. Should the Duke consider it suitable to send him to England to stand trial there, he was willing to comply.

Roger also submitted a copy of another letter written by Johannes Kempter to John Coote and dated England, 5 June 1600, as follows: "There can be no doubt but that Tobias Hume will receive detailed information to the effect that James Hill's opponent is a great rascal."

But ultimately, after Lennart Tuckertz had expressly asked John Coote for his friendship, Coote withdrew his case, the two became friends and shook hands'; *Stockholms stads tänkeböcker från år 1592*, 3, 1600, p. 93.

envy over Hill's increasingly strong position with Duke Charles. Thus the preliminary hearing records that Hill is suspected of murdering his brother, Mr. Scryvener, of making homosexual advances to a boy on the journey from Finland and of stealing or appropriating costumes belonging to the English comedians. The hearing in Stockholm, on the other hand, seems to have been instigated by James Hill against Tuckertz. One of the witnesses on this occasion was the English comedian Richard Raph.

Some interesting information has also come to light concerning Tobias Hume, to whom the record of the preliminary hearing in Nyköping was addressed. A soldier and musician, he had the reputation of being an excellent performer on the viola da gamba and a composer of vocal and instrumental music. Hume served Duke Charles as a mercenary from 1598 to 1600[1] and the Public Record Office has a curious document—'The Humble Petition of Captayne Humes'[2]—giving a very brief account of his service with 'the kinge of Sweathen' and an offer to perform great deeds for England if he is sent to 'Mickleburgland' (Mecklenburg).

Some of his compositions are still extant. In 1605 he published:

The First Part of Ayres, French, Polish, and others together, some in Tabliture, and some in Pricke-Song.
With Pavines, Galliards and Almaines for the Viole de Gambo alone ... and some Songs to bee sung to the Viole ... containing 116 airs in tableture and five songs.

The title 'Musical Humors', sometimes applied to the publication of 1607, is printed at the top of every page of the 'First Part of Ayres ...'. In 1607 he published:

Captaine Hume's Poeticall Musicke principally made for two basse-viols yet so contrived that it may be plaied eight severall waies upon sundry instruments with much facilitie ... containing eighteen instrumental and four vocal pieces.

Hume lived to be a very old man and spent his last years, from 1629 to 1645, as a poor brother of the Charter House. In 1642 he presented a

[1] Hertig Karls räntekammare 1598; KA.
[2] Cal. State Papers Dom. Ch. 1. vol. 179, No. 7. Cf. Tobias Hume's works; Register of Charterhouse; Notes and Queries, 2nd ser. 7, p. 369; Add. MS 24489 (Hunter's Chorus Vatum); Jeffrey Pulver, A Biographical Dictionary of Old English Music, Kegan Paul, Trench, Trubner & Co., London 1927 (Tobias Hume); and Grove's Dict., 4, 404.

'True petition of Colonel Hume' to the House of Lords, offering his services against the Irish rebels. He afterwards printed this document and its contents show that he was labouring under a mental delusion. While at the Charter House he became increasingly depressed and the accounts of his service in Sweden grew more and more fanciful. His attempt to obtain an official commission in Mecklenburg may have been prompted by a desire to re-establish contact with James Hill, who was resident there for some time after his marriage to Elizabeth von Zeulen. Tobias Hume's claim to a colonel's rank may also have been inspired by Hill's promotion to a colonelcy in December 1600 at the hands of Duke Charles. It is a noteworthy coincidence that Hill's promotion is dated December 12, 1600 and that Tobias Hume (Engelske Tobius) received, not a military commission but 40 daler cash from Duke Charles three days later, on December 15.[1]

In this context it may also be mentioned that Tobias Hume made an entry in Henry Francklin's album, though without recording the place or date.[2]

Another matter connected with Tobias Hume is his address in London, to which the record of the preliminary hearing in Nyköping on May 4, 1600, was to be sent:

Tobias Humes at the signe of the boores head hard by Chepside Crosse at a Silkmans Cross shoop in his absence to inquir for one Edward Edgcoke at the same signe.

Concerning the Boar's head, Chambers maintains:

There appear to have been at least six city inns under the sign of The Boar's Head. The most famous was that on the south side of Great East-cheap in St. Michael's which seems to have been regarded in the middle of the seventeenth century as the traditional locality of the tavern scenes in Henry IV.[3]

Chambers thus assumes that all signs with The Boar's Head were to be found outside inns of this name, but this need not have been the case. During this period in London, and indeed in other European cities, signs were used quite regularly instead of street names and numbers. In any event, it is unlikely that anybody would have tried to act plays at a

---

[1] Riksregistraturen, Pars 2, 12.12.1600, fol. 363^r, and 15.12.1600, fol. 370^r.
[2] Op. cit. fol. 159^r.
[3] Chamb., *Eliz. Stage*, 2, 443 ff.

silk shop, though it is possible of course that in the present case the sign The Boar's Head referred to a large building with several entrances and that Tobias Hume had to be approached through the silk merchant's shop. The combination of a silkman's shop and The Boar's Head—suggesting the making of players' costumes—may in fact indicate some form of theatrical activity. According to the Marquis of Newcastle[1] we may assume that, at the Restoration, the Boar's Head, at which plays were acted, may have been either a house with a large hall, suitable for indoor performances, or an inn with a convenient garden. It is conceivable, however, that this was the case at The Boar's Head 'hard by Cheapside Crosse'. Can The Boar's Head at which Tobias Hume lived in 1600 have been an inn and theatre or connected in some other way with The Boar's Head Inn on the north side of Whitechapel Street in the parish of St Mary Matfellon or Whitechapel (outside Aldgate)?[2] It is not far from Whitechapel to Cheapside. Tobias Hume, like Philip Rosseter, was a musician closely connected with the world of the theatre and James Hill had been in touch with the stage of the period and the Elizabethan and Jacobean Companies on the Continent.

Little is known about The Boar's Head—theatre and inn alike—the Marquis of Newcastle being the only chronicler to definitely record its existence:

... Some Played att the Bores Heade & att the Curtain In the feildes & some att the Hope whiche Is the Beare Garden ...[3]

Otherwise the only contemporary record occurs in a letter to Edward Alleyn from his wife Joan on October 27, 1603, in which she writes:

... All the Companyes be Come hoame & well for ought we knowe, but that Browne of the Boares head is dead & dyed very pore he went not into the Country at all ...[4]

The latter source suggests that The Boar's Head served as a rendezvous for the Companies in the provinces and on the Continent.

Can some confirmation be derived from Tobias Hume's address in London—'at the signe of the boores head hard by Chepside Crosse ...'?

---

[1] William Cavendish, Marquis of Newcastle (1592–1676).

[2] Cf. Bentley, 6, 121–131.

[3] S. A. Strong, *Catalogue of Letters at Welbeck*, p. 226.

[4] R. A. Foakes & R. T. Rickert, *Henslowe's Diary*, p. 297.

These facts concerning The Boar's Head were available to Adams[1] and Chambers,[2] while further details—chiefly that The Boar's Head Inn was located in Whitechapel, as well as some information about the construction of the theatre—are to be found in more modern sources.[3]

The record of the preliminary hearing in Nyköping on May 4, 1600, and several letters from James Hill to Queen Elizabeth elicited a reply from The Privy Council in 1601. I quote:

> For as much as her Majesty hath perceived by your letters written both to herself and her Council that you have been maliciously used by one Tucker, who was recommended unto you by Sir W. Raleigh, the captain of her guard, and by some others, to do service in the wars between Poland and Sweden, and that he hath gone in the wars, between Poland and Sweden and that he hath gone about to touch you in your reputation here as a man not well esteemed by the state: ... (Draft, the last part in Cecil's hand).[4]

In the present context it is particularly interesting to find a further reference to Sir Walter Raleigh.

After their wedding, James Hill and Elizabeth von Zeulen resided in Hesse before settling in Mecklenburg. Hill maintained his connections with Sweden for a long time, writing[5] on March 18, 1608, to Nils Chesnecopherus, Charles IX's Chancellor, and mentioning his wife and son. He also relates for Chesnecopherus that he has come into an inheritance in England which, at the turn of 1607, he transferred to his brother for as long as he himself is obliged to live on the Continent, with the provision that should he die before returning home, then the brother would have to pay 3,000 daler to James Hill's son.

---

[1] J. Q. Adams, *Shakespearean Playhouses*, 1917, p. 17.

[2] Chamb., *Eliz. Stage*, 2, 443–445.

[3] Cf. C. J. Sisson, 'Mr. and Mrs Browne of the Boar's Head', *Life and Letters of Today*, 4 (1936), idem, 'The Red Bull Company and the Importunate Widow', *Shakespeare Survey* 7 (1954), pp. 57–68, and Leslie Hotson, *Shakespeare's Wooden O* (1959), pp. 92, 179, 235, 264–265, 268–270, 287–288 and 291 concerning The Boar's Head playhouse in Whitechapel, and pp. 14, 20 and 95 concerning The Boar's Head Tavern in Great Eastcheap. The findings of these two reseachers have been summarised and elaborated in Gerald Eades Bentley, *The Jacobean and Caroline Stage*, Vol. 1 (1941), p. 158, and Vol. 6 (1968), pp. 121–131, 133, 189 and 217.

[4] Cecil MSS, 11, 571.

[5] Letter 18.3.1608 from James Hill to Nils Chesnecopherus. 11. Brev till kanslitjänstemännen; Karl IX:s tid; RA.

Elizabeth von Zeulen also kept in touch with the court at Nyköping, as witness an entry in Duke Charles's diary in 1604:

kåm Berendt Mörner och Lisabet Syll ifrån Tyskland[1]

It therefore seems that another person of the same name took out the marriage licence for:

James Hill of St. Margaret, Westminster, gent., and Elizabeth Gifferson, of same, widow—at same. 1. Feb. 1607[–08][2]

It has been possible to follow James Hill's doings right up to 1618 after which year the documents give information of James Hill's widow and later up to 1700 of his sons and grandsons, some of them German landed proprietors in Mecklenburg and officers in the Polish army.[3] The more we learn of James Hill's career, however, the less are we inclined, as Thomas Cornewallis alias George Graye, Philip Bruggis, and John Howse have done, to believe that he was at any time 'traitor', 'shellom', 'roge', 'taylor', or 'taylor's apprentice' and though we lose sight of him as an actor there is compensation in the account of his adventures as ambassador and commander of 'brave regiments', which gives us in outline the portrait of one of the many enterprising Elizabethan gentlemen, who learned to put trust in Princes or in Queens.

[1] 'Came Berendt Mörner and Elizabeth von Zeulen from Germany'; op. cit. 9.9.1604, p. 157.

[2] Foster, *Marr. Lic.* 1521–1869 (James Hill).

[3] Acta feudorum specialia, Staatsarchiv Schwerin, Schwerin, East Germany, and Externa Kurland (Schwerin), Staatliches Archivlager Göttingen, Göttingen, West Germany. I quote 'Acta feudorum':

Lehngut Zickhusen

1609. Januar 23. Konsens über den von Heinrich Sperling zu Naudin an Obrist Jacob Hilles Ehefrau für 2.000 Reichstaler verpfändeten Bauernhof.

1618. Klage der Witwe Jacob Hills gegen Heinrich von Sperling zu Zickhusen. wegen der Zinsen auf die 2.000 Reichstaler.

CHAPTER 9

Other International Companies on the Continent at This Time

A natural question arising out of the visit of the English company of players to Nyköping during 1591 and 1592 is whether their repertoire included performances of comedies, histories and tragedies. Most Swedish historians consider that the company engaged by Duke Charles consisted entirely of musicians, and so far documentary evidence to show that acting was included on the programme has been lacking. Before going into this question further, it is necessary to review the activities of English companies on the Continent in the late sixteenth and early seventeenth centuries and also to review the Danish, French and Spanish declared accounts for the same period concerning certain occasions when English companies feature during the visits paid by foreign embassies to England.

As already mentioned, Michael Heberer von Bretten has left us a description of the festivities at Nyköping on the occasion of Duke Charles's wedding with the Princess Christine. This description contains the following much-quoted passage:

> ... und haben sich dabey auch Engelländische Comoedianten und Springer finden lassen / die ihrem Gebrauch nach zimliche Kurtzweil geübet und gemacht / auch warden Fechtschulen und andere Kurtzweilen gehalten / ...[1]

One of the first to draw attention to it was Dahlgren,[2] who adds in a note that these so-called English comedians probably belonged to one of the companies of players which were common in Germany at that time; these players, however, were Germans who had trained in the English arts, i.e. not only as players but also as swordsmen, rope-dancers, &c.

---

[1] '... in addition there had been engaged English comedians and tumblers who amused the spectators in the customary manner/at the same time there was also a display of fencing exercises and other entertainments ...'; *Aegyp. Serv.*, 626.

[2] Dahlgren, 5, note **.

This interpretation, which was first put forward by Ludwig Tieck[1] and the German historian of the theatre, Devrient,[2] was refuted by Cohn[3] in his original survey of the tours undertaken on the Continent by English companies of players from 1580 to 1630. German companies of strolling players on the English model did not appear until the middle of the seventeenth century.

Aber Wandertruppen mit deutschem Prinzipal, deutschen Mitgliedern und ernstlichem Bemühen um eine selbständigen Spielstil, der nicht ausschließlich durch Bearbeitungen aus fremden Litteraturen getragen wurde, wagten sich erst eine ganze Weile nach Abschluß des Westfälischen Friedens heraus.[4]

Several more detailed studies have been published since Cohn's time and these have been summarised by E. K. Chambers in *The Elizabethan Stage*, II, in the chapter on international companies.

The first known troupe of English players to visit the Netherlands probably came over with the Earl of Leicester, and gave an acrobatic show of *The Forces of Hercules* at Utrecht on the feast of St George, 23 April 1586. The presence of this company is noted in John Stow, *Annales*, as follows:

The three and twentieth of Aprill, the Earle of Leicester, Lieutenant gouernor, Generall of her Maiesties forces in the Low countries, of the vnited Prouinces making his residence at that time in Utricht, (a great and goodly Towne upon the frontiers of Holland) kept most honorably the feast of Saint George therein, the proceedings whereof beeing so Princely performed, to the honor of our nation, in the view of so many strangers, ...

... To be briefe, the feast ended, and tables voyded, there was dauncing, vau(l)ting and tumbling, with the forces of Hercules, which gave great delight to the strangers for they had not seene it before and thus they passed the time, til euensong, and then departed. At supper beeing all assembled againe, great was the feast, and plentifull the cheere: and after supper beganne the barriers, b(e)tweene challengers, and defendants, men of armes,

---

[1] Ludwig Tieck, *Alt-Englisches Theater*, Vorrede zum ersten Theil, X.

[2] Devrient, 1, 150.

[3] Cohn, 1, Historical Part.

[4] 'Strolling players with a German as first player, Germans as other players and a genuine ambition to achieve their own independent German style that was not inspired exclusively by foreign examples, first ventured out in their own country and on the Continent some while after the conclusion of the Peace of Westphalia in 1648'; Kindermann, *Theatergeschichte Europas*, 3, 391.

wherein the Earle of Essex behaved himselfe so valiantly that he gave all men great hope of his noble prowess in Armes.[1]

Leicester's Men included one Will who is referred to in a letter from Sir Philip Sidney to Sir Francis Walsingham, written from Utrecht on 24 March 1586. I quote:

I wrat yow a letter by will my lord of lester iesting plaier, enclosed in a letter to my wyfe, and I never had answer thereof, it contained something to my Lord of lester, and cownceil that sum way might be taken to stay my lady there. I since dyvers tymes have writt to know whither [you] had receaved them. But yow never answered me that point. I since fynd that the knave deliverd the letters to my Ladi of Lester.[2]

It is a fairly common opinion that this Will was William Kempe, whom we know to have been in Dunkerque (as Mr. Kemp, called Don Gulihelmo) a few months earlier, in November 1585.[3]

The basic modern works on the earliest appearances by English comedians at the Danish court of Frederick II are by V. C. Ravn and Johannes Bolte.[4] Both papers were based on archive research and they also served as a foundation for E. K. Chambers' comprehensive study of the English comedians' activities abroad in the period 1579–1630.[5]

In his *Apology for Actors* from 1612,[6] Thomas Heywood mentions, p. 40:

The King of Denmarke, father to him that now reigneth, entertained into his service a company of English comedians, commended unto him by

---

[1] Op. cit. (Ed. 1631), pp. 717 f. This account in Stow, *Annals*, is written by Sir William Segar, who in the capacity of Portcullis pursuivant, College of Arms, attended the splendid festival. Cf. *DNB*, 51, 197. Chambers, *El. Stage* 2, 90, 272, 550 and *W. Shp.* 1, 39, interprets the author as referring to the 'forces of Hercules' as the name of a play. Stow's description of the entertainment seems, however, to admit the interpretation that the 'forces of Hercules' was the name of a company specialising in acrobatics. Chambers (2, 272) mentions that this company 'had given a show, half dramatic, half acrobatic, of *The Forces of Hercules* at Utrecht on 23 April 1586' but there is nothing in Stow's (Segar's) account to indicate drama.

[2] MS Harleian, p. 138, code 287, art. 1; BM.

[3] MS Cottonian, Galba C. VIII. Cf. Chamb., *Eliz. Stage*, 3, 90.

[4] V. C. Ravn, 'Engelska Instrumentister vid det danske hof paa Shakespeares Tid', *For Idé og Virkelighed*, 1, 1870. Johannes Bolte, 'Englische Komoedianten in Dänemark und Schweden', *Shakespeare Jahrbuch*, 1888.

[5] E. K. Chambers, *The Elizabethan Stage*, Oxford 1923, vol. 2, chap. 14, International Companies, 3, English Players on the Continent, pp. 270–294.

[6] Chambers thought the treatise was probably written in 1607 and touched up in 1608. Cf. idem, *Eliz. Stage*, 2, 271 and 4, 250–254.

the honorable the Earle of Leicester: the Duke of Brunswicke and the Landgrave of Hessen retaine in their courts certaine of ours of the same quality ...

A thorough investigation of the Danish household accounts at the National Archives in Copenhagen has given the following result concerning the period 1579–1586:

I quote Chambers:

There were English *instrumentister* at the Danish Court in 1579–80, and again in 1586 George Bryan and Thomas Pope, later of the Chamberlain's, were there with three other English players together with William Kempe and his boy Daniel Jonns.[1]

It used to be thought that two different English companies were engaged in Denmark on two occasions about six years apart. Furthermore, the Elsinore city accounts for the year 21/12/1584–21/12/1585 suggest that a third English company appeard there in 1585:

Giffuett for, att lade ferdige the*tt* plannckewerck Emellom Lauritz schrifuers och raadhuss gordenn, som folck red neder, thennd tid the Enngelske lechtte i raadhus gordenn, iiij ß.[2]

In Chambers' opinion, this company may have been the same one that appeared in Leipzig on July 19, 1585:

5 Thaler den Englischen Spielleuten, so ufm Rathaus ihr Spiel mit Springen und allerlei Kurzweil getrieben.[3]

A further search in the Danish household accounts and other records has brought the following additional historical facts to light.

The earliest documentary evidence of an English company in Denmark dates from January 1579:

---

[1] *Ibid.*, 2, 272 f.

[2] 'Granted for repairs to the planking between Lorenzo the town-clerk's and the courtyard of the town hall, which the people tore down when the English played [lechtte] in the courtyard, 4 shillings'; Helsingör stads räkenskaper 21/12 1584–21/12 1585, 'Udgifft ... paa Raadhussett, The Bolige ther nedenn under, Och udi Raadhusgaarden'.

[3] '5 Thaler to the English players who performed a comedy at the town hall as well as acrobatics and all manner of entertainment;' Treasury Accounts of the city of Leipzig 1585; Cf. Chambers, *Eliz. Stage*, 2, 272 and footnote 1.

Artus Damler bleff anthagen aff Konn. Mai^{ett} for een Instrumentist 18 Januarij.[1]

Ibid., fol. 211ᵛ (cont. from fol. 211ʳ)

Skall haffue om aarett thill besoldningh ½^{st.} daler (i.e. 50 d). Ther aff giffuett hannum effther Konn: Maiett befallning for eett fierring aar thend 29. Martij thill Paaske.   XIIJ dʳ

Thisse effterschreffne Instrumentister finnge theris besoldning for
1 aar thill Paaske

X	dʳ	Thomas Sefeldt thennd 20 Maij
X	dʳ	Valentin Skeinn samme dag
X	dʳ	Anndreas Thiide samme dag
XXV	dʳ	Hanns Lauritzenn Organist paa Frederichsborge, thennd 20 Maij

Johann Krafftt, Johann Persenn och
Johann Kirckmann Instrumentister bleffue
anthagenn aff Konn: Maiett thill Crempe thennd 18 Januarij 1579. Skulle
haffue thill besoldning aarligenn sum
thennum XXX daller 1 hoffklaedningh[2]

Ibid., fol. 212ʳ

Och V daller thill kostpenndinge, finge the
22 Junij hŭar for iij Monneder, frann
thennd 18 Januarij thill Paaske nest forledenn som her effther fölger

viij	dallʳ	Johann Krafftt
viij	dallʳ	Johann Persenn
viij	dallʳ	Johann Kerckmann
xv	dallʳ	Thennd 13 Octobris giffuett Johann Persenn hanns besoldning for 1 aar fran

[1] 'Artus Damler engaged by His Majesty as an Instrumentalist from 18 January 1579. Fol. 211 r.'

[2] '(Entry on fol. 211 r continues:) To have annually as payment ½ daler (i.e. 50d). Of which he has been given on H.M.'s order for one quarter of a year on 29 March until Eastertide XIIJ daler. The following engaged Instrumentalists received for 1 year until Eastertide: X daler Thomas Sefeldt 20 May, X daler Valentin Skeinn same day, X daler Anndreas Thiide same day, XXV daler Hanns Lauritzenn, Organist at Fredriksborg, 20 May. Johann Krafft, Johann Persenn and Johann Kirckmann, Instrumentalists, were engaged by H.M. for Crempe, 18 January 1579. To have in remittance annually the sum of XXX daler, 1 court apparel. 1579. Fol. 211 v.'

		Paaske thill Michaelis.
xxv	dall^r	Thennd 14 Octobris giffuet Artus
		Damler hanns besoldning for ½ aar
		frann Paaske thill Michaelis[1]

Ibid., fol. 212^v
Thisse effterschreffne Instrumentister
finnge theris besoldning for ½ aar thill Michaelis i 1579.

xv	dall^r	Johann Krafftt thennd 15 decembris
xv	dall^r	Johann Kerckmann samme dag.
viij	dall^r	Thomas Bull bleff anthagenn
		Scti Hans dag skall haffue om aarett
		xxx dall^r fick for i fierinng aar thill
		Michaelis thennd 13 Decembris
x	dall^r	Valentinn Scheinn
x	dall^r	Anndreas Tiide
x	dall^r	Thomas Sefeldt[2]

The earliest known employment for English comedians at the Danish court was thus at the town of Crempe in Schleswig-Holstein, not far from the subsequent site of Gluckstadt, which was founded in 1616 on the right bank of the Elbe near its estuary. In the Middle Ages and until the founding of Gluckstadt, Crempe was a lively port. Frederick II of Denmark had a residence there.

The above engagements were renewed tor the years 1580–86 as follows:

År 1580. Fol. 170^r

Mathias Zoega, dannser	xl daller
Artus Damler	xxv daller
Johann Personn	xv daller
Johann Krafft	xv daller
Johann Kirckmann	xv daller
Thomas Bull	xv daller

---

[1] 'V daler for board, allowed on 22 June for iij Months, from 18 January to next Eastertide after this: viij daler Johann Krafftt, viij daler Johann Persenn, viij daler Johann Kerckmann. xv daler given on 13 October to Johann Persenn as his pay for 1 year from Easter until Michaelmas. xxv daler given on 14 October to Artus Damler for ½ year from Eastertide until Michaelmas. 1579. Fol. 212 r.'

[2] 'The following engaged Instrumentalists received their pay for ½ a year up to Michaelmas 1579: xv daler Johann Krafftt 15 December, xv daler Johann Kerckmann same day. viij daler Thomas Bull engaged—in that he is to have annually xxx daler, received for a quarter year up to Michaelmas on 13 December. x daler Valentinn Scheinn, x daler Anndreas Tiide, x daler Thomas Sefeldt. 1579. Fol. 212 v.'

115

Valentin Skeinn		x daller
Annders Tiide		x daller
Thomas Sefeldt		x daller[1]

År 1581. Fol 199ᵛ

Artus Damler		iii Rosenobele och
		xiii gamle Daller
Johann Personn		ii Rosen: vii dʳ
Johann Krafftt		ii Rosen: vii dʳ
Valentinn Scheinn		i Rosen: vi dʳ
Thomas Bull		ii Rosen: vii dʳ
Thomas Sefeldt		i Rosen: vi dʳ[2]

År 1582. Fol. 223ʳ

9 juni	Artus Damler	L daller
19 juni	Valentin Skeinn	xx daller
19 juni	Thomas Sefeldt	xx daller
19 juni	Johann Personn	xxx daller
19 juni	Thomas Bull	xxx daller
frann thendt 13 Ju- nij 81 thill paas- kedag 82 –19 juni	Anders Tiide	xxv daller
19 juni	Johan Krafft for 1 aar til paaske 82	xxx daller[3]

År 1583. Fol. 219ᵛ

Artur Damler	xxv daller
Johann Krafft	xv daller
Thomas Bull	xv daller
Thomas Sefeldt	x daller
Vallentinn Scheinn	x daller
Johann personn	xv daller

kom udj thiennisten igienn 13 Aprilis, skall haffue om aaritt 30 daller, lige som thilforenn, fick nu for 1 aar.

Thomas Warrinn aantagenn for eenn Instrumentist 10 Aprilis, skall haffue om aaritt till besoldning xv daller, fick for ½ aar viii daller[4]

---

[1] 'Mathias Zoëga, dancer, xl daler, &c. 1580. Fol. 170 r.'

[2] 'Artus Damler iii Rose nobles and xiii old daler, &c. 1581. Fol. 199 v.'

[3] '9 June Artus Damler L daler; ... Thomas Bull xxx daler, from 13 June 1581 until Easter Day 1582; 19 June Anders Tiide xxv daler; 19 June Johan Krafft for 1 year to Easter 1582 xxx daler. 1582. Fol. 223 r.'

[4] 'Artur Damler xxv daler, ... Johann Persson xv daler, entered service again on 13 April, is to have 30 daler annually, as before, received now for 1 year. Thomas Warrinn engaged as an Instrumentalist 10 April, to have annually xv daler, received for ½ a year viii daler. 1583. Fol. 219 v.'

116

Ibid., Fol 220[r]

Thenndt 12 Octobris giffuitt Andreas Tide Organiste hanns Besoldning for ½
aar frann paaske dag 83: och till Sti: Michels dag nest forledenn.[1]

År 1584. Fol. 234[v]

Artus Dambler	xxv daller
Johann Krafftt	xv daller
Thomas Bull	xv daller
Johann Personn	xv daller
Valentin Skeinn	x daller
Thomas Sefeldt	x daller
Thomas Warrinn	viii daller

Thend 8 Junij giffuett Anders Thide Organist hanns Besoldning for ½ aar
frann Michaelis 83 och thill Paaske dag 84.

Artus Dambler	xxv daller
Valentinn Skeinn	x daller
Thomas Sefeldt	x daller
Thomas Bull	xv daller
Johann Personn	xv daller
Thomas Warrinn	viii daller
Johann Krafftt for ½ aar frann Paaske dag 84	xviii daller

och thill Michaelis ther nest effther
xv daller. Sammeledes iii for eenn Maanetz
besoldning i frann Michaelis, och thill thennd
29 Octobris 84 hannd kom aff thienistenn er
thilsamens[2]

Ibid., fol. 235[r]
Andreas Thide Organista

Thennd 24. Decembris (1583) giffuet	xx daller

samme hanns Besoldning for ½ aar, frann Paaske dag
84 thill Michaelis i samme aar[3]

År 1585. fol. 269[v]
Instrumentister och organist

Andreas Tide Organist	xx daller

Thennd 29. Maij giffuett samme hans besoldning
for ½ aar fran Michaelis 84 och thill paaske dag 1585

[1] 'On 12 October gave Andreas Tide, Organist, his pay for ½ a year from Easter
Day 1583 until Michaelmas Day next. 1583. Fol. 220 r.'

[2] 'Artus Dambler xxv daler, ... Thomas Warrinn viii daler. On 8 June gave
Anders Thide, Organist, his pay for ½ a year from Michaelmas 1583 until Easter
Day 1584. Arthus Dambler ... Johann Krafft for ½ a year from Easter Day 1584—
xviii daler—until the following Michaelmas xv daler. The same iii for one month's
pay from Michaelmas until 29 October 1584 when he left service. 1584. Fol. 234 v.'

[3] 'Andreas Tide, Organist. On December 24 (1583) given xx daler as his pay for ½
a year from Easter Day 1584 until Michaelmas the same year. 1584. Fol. 235 r.'

117

Thisse effterschreffne Kon: Maiette Instrumentister
haffuer bekommet theris besolding for ½ aar frann
Scti Mickels dag 1584 och thill Paaske dag 1585
nest forledenn:

Artus Damler	25. Junij	xxv daller
Johann Personn	27. Junij	xv daller
Thomas Bull	27. Junij	xv daller
Thomas Sefeld	24. Junij	x daller
Valentin Skeinn	25. Junij	x daller
Thomas Warrin	28. Junij	viii daller

Thend 10. Novembris giffuett Simon Detre Instrumentist hanns besoldning for 10 Maaneder, iiij dage, fran thend 20. Maij nest forledenn hand er
först anthagen udi K. Maij: thienniste, och thill Scti Michels dag 85 hans
besoldning skall aarligen warre effth^r hans bestillings lijdelse xxx dall^r ...
xij dall^r iiij skilling.

Thend 1. Octobris giffuett Thomas Sefeld Instrumentist hans besoldning
for ½ aar frann Paaske dag 85 och thill Scti Michels dag i same aar nest
forlidenn ... x daller.[1]

The knowledge that an English company was in Frederick II's service in
1585 throws new light on the identity of the company that performed
outside the town hall in Elsinore. There is every reason to suppose that
during their stay at Kronborg Castle, Artus Damler et consortes obtained permission to give a performance for the general public.

År 1586. fol 274^r
Instrumentister och Organista.
Andreas Tide Organista   40 daller
    Thennd 17 Aprilis giffuett honnum hans besoldning for 1 aar, frann Paaske
dag 1585 och thill Paaske dag 1586 ... xl dall^r
    Effterschreffnne Kon: Maietts Instrumentister som bleffue forskickett med
Hendrick Rammell thill Engeland, finge theris besoldning for 1 aar, frann
Paaske dag 85 och thill Paaske dag 1586. 17 Aprilis.

---

[1] 'Instrumentalists and organist. Andreas Tide, Organist xx daler, given on 29
May as his remittance for ½ a year from Michaelmas 1584 until Easter Day 1585.
The following engaged Royal Instrumentalists have received their pay for ½ a year
from Michaelmas Day 1584 until Easter Day, 1585: Artus Dambler 25 June ...
Thomas Warrin 28 June viii daler. On 10 November Simon Detre, Instrumentalist
received his pay for 10 months, iiij days, from 20 May last, when he first entered
H.M. service, until Michaelmas Day 1585; his annual pay according to his contract
is to be xxx daler ... xij daler, iiij shillings. On 1 October Thomas Sefeld, Instrumentalist, received his pay for ½ a year from Easter Day 1585 until Michaelmas
Day in the same year ... x daler. 1585. Fol. 269 v.'

118

Artus Damler	L daller
Johann Personn	xxx daller
Thomas Bull	xxx daller

Simon Detre, Instrumentist, fick hans besolding for ¼ aar, frann Michaelis 85 och thill Paaske dag 86 ... xv daller

Valentin Scheinn Basun blaeser fick hanns besolding for 1 aar frann Paaske 85. Och thill Paaske dag 86. Och bleff honnum thette aar aff Kon: Maiett Naadigst forbedrett hans aars besoldning med x daller, ijdermere med hannd fick thilförenn.

Thomas Sefeldt for ½ aar frann Michaelis 85 och thill Paaske dag 86 ... x d^{rl}

Ibid., fol. 274^v

Thomas Warrinn for 1 aar frann Paaske dag 85 thill Paaske dag 86 ... -xv d^r

Effterschreffnne nogle aff Konn. Maij: Instrumentister haffuer bekommett theris besoldning for ½ aar frann Paaske och thill Scti Michels dag 86.

Artus Damler, 24. Octobris	xxv daller
Thomas Sefeldt, 2. Novembris	x daller
Valentin Skeinn, 12. Decembris	xv daller

Johann Personn fick hans besoldning for vij Monneder xx dage i frann Paaske dag 86 och thill thennd 18. Novembris wdj same aar hannd bleff affthackett, haffde om aaret thill besoldning xxx daller thendn 21 Nouembris ...   xix d^r v skilling st.

Simon Detre, Instrumentist, bleff och han affthackett samme thid. Och fick lige saa megett   xix d^r v skilling st.

Thomas Warrin, Instrumentist, bleff och saa affthackett samme thid och thilkom for vij Monneder xx dage, fran Paaske dag 1586 och thill thend 18 Novembris aff same aar som forschreffuet staar, haffde om aarett xv daller thill besoldning, fick ...   x d^r iij skilling st.[2]

---

[1] 'Instrumentalists and Organist. Andreas Tide, Organist, 40 daler. On 17 April gave him his pay for 1 year from Easter Day 1585 until Easter Day 1586 xl daler. The following engaged Royal Instrumentalists who have been sent with Henry Ramelius to England, received their pay for 1 year, from Easter Day 1585 until Easter Day 1586. 17 April. Artus Damler L daler, Johann Persenn xxx daler, Thomas Bull xxx daler. Simon Detre, Instrumentalist, received his pay for ½ a year, from Michaelmas 1585 until Easter Day 1586. Valentin Scheinn, bassoon player, received his pay for 1 year from Easter 1585 until Easter Day 1586. This year H.M. graciously increased his pay x daler, which he received in addition. Thomas Sefeldt for ½ a year from Michaelmas 1585 until Easter Day 1586 x daler. 1586. Fol. 274 r.'

[2] 'Thomas Warrinn for 1 year from Easter Day 1585 until Easter Day 1586 xv daler. The following engaged Royal Instrumentalists have received their remit-

Bertholomeus van Oesterreich instrumentist er anthagenn wdj thiennisten thend 17. Junij 86. Och er egenn affthackett thennd 18. Novembris wdj samme aar er v Monneder v dage. Skulle haffue om aarett thill besoldning **xxx** dall^r, fick nu thennd 21. Nouembris xiij d^r xiij skill. st.

Thomas Sefeldt Instrumentist bleff och saa affthackett thennd 18. Novembris 1586 thilkom hannum tha aff hans besoldning frann Michaelis 86 thill huilckenn thid hannd war so nistenn affbethallet effth^r som forshff^{tt} **staar** for i monnett xx dage haffde om aarett thill besoldning xx dall^r fick

iij d^r j ortt[1]

According to these accounts, Artus Damler, Johann Persenn and Thomas Bull accompanied Henry Ramelius's embassy to England in April–May 1586. Queen Elizabeth's recredential for Ramelius to Frederick II of Denmark is dated May 26, 1586, and on June 17 that year William Kempe, Thomas Stevens and others were engaged at the Danish court. Thus it is conceivable that the latter group accompanied Henry Ramelius on his return from England along with Artus Damler et consortes.

Concerning Thomas Bull, the last occasion on which he appears in the above accounts is on April 17, 1586, when in connection with Ramelius's embassy he received his remittance for the year from Easter Day 1585 to Easter Day 1586. This should not be taken as an indication that Bull remained in England after the embassy since there is evidence that in August 1586 he was in Elsinore, involved in the death of his compatriot Thomas Boltum. Bull admitted to having killed Boltum in a fit of jealousy, which is no doubt why he does not appear together with

tances for ½ a year from Easter until Michaelmas Day 1586: Artus Damler .... Johann Personn received his remittance for vij months xx days from Easter Day 1586 until 18 November in the same year and was released from service, his annual pay being xxx daler, on 21 November xix daler v shilling. Simon Detre, Instrumentalist, was also released from service at the same time and received an equal sum: xix daler v shilling. Thomas Warrin, Instrumentalist, was also released from service at the same time and received for vij months xx days, from Easter Day 1586 until 18 November that year as agreed, his annual pay being xv daler, given x daler iij shilling. 1586. Fol. 274 v.'

[1] 'Bartholomew the Austrian, Instrumentalist, engaged in service on 17 June 1586. Released again on 18 November that year, v months v days. Was to have an annual payment of xxx daler, now received 21 November xiij daler xiij shilling. Thomas Sefeldt, Instrumentalist, was also released from service on 18 November 1586. 1586. Fol. 275 r.'

the other instrumentalists who received payment for their services in November 1586.[1]

Henry Ramelius's embassy to England is mentioned in a letter from Leicester to Francis Walsingham, dated Hamersford,[2] May 6, 1586:

... I am sorry I had not knowledge enough to send you worde of the great embassage the kinge of Denmark doth send to her majestie, which, it is reported, is the greatest that euer went out of the last countrey; his expectation is great of her majesties forwardnes in their causes. I praie God he maie receave that comfort I wish ...[3]

Ramelius's reception in London was princely indeed. Accommodation was provided for him in a house known as Crosbie Place[4] and the following description is taken from Ramelius's letter to King Frederick, dated London, May 13th:

Durchleuchtigster grossmechtiger gnedigster Koning und herr, ess sein E. Kon. Ma:tt meine underthenigste gehorsame dienste mitt allem schuldigen fleiss und treuen zuvor. Gnedigster Koning und her, E. Kon. Ma:tt soll ich ihn unterthenigsten gehorsam nicht verhalten, dass wir mitt E. Kon. Ma:tt schiffen alhie in Engelandt nach gehabtem allerlei gutten und widrigen windt und wetter gotlob endlich den 6:ten dieses fur Grönwitz angekommen und ancker gefellet. Und obwol ich mich alsbaldt dieselbige stunde durch ein schreiben bei dem obristen secretario FRANCISCO WALSINGHAM, wie hie gebreuchlich, ahngegeben, auch die Kon. Ma:tt eben darauff gnedigst ahn mich geschicket, so bin ich doch den folgenden tagk allerhandt ursachen halben auffm schiff geplieben und den 8:ten, welchs wahr auff den sontagk Vocem jucunditatis, nach gehaltener predige und mittagessens zu landt in das losamendt, so von I. Kon. Ma:tt mir verordnet worden, in die statt Lunden gezogen. In den schiff haben I. Kon. Ma:t mich zu unterschietlichen mhalen durch furnheme hern besuchen, auch allerlei frische speise verehren, darnach mitt ahnsehliger auffwartung abholen und in das losamendt vergleitten lassen. Und konnen E. Kon. Ma:t nicht gleuben, was fur eine grosse menge leutte von allen seiten zu wasser und lande zugeschlagen, daruber solch ein drengen und getummel geworden, als ich nicht neulich gesehen hab. In meinem losamendt werde ich nebst meinen beihabenden junckern und allem andern gesinde, so ich zur auffwartung mitt zu lande genommen, gar stadtlich tractiret, und haben I. Kon. Ma:t alle dazu gehörende not-

---

[1] Helsingørs Tingbog 1583–86, (25 August 1586), fol. 156 v–158 r. Cf. Gunnar Sjögren, 'Thomas Bull and other "English Instrumentalists" in Denmark in the 1580s' Shakespeare Survey No. 22/1969, pp. 119–123.

[2] Probably a variant spelling of Amersfoort in the Netherlands, 12 miles east-north-east of Utrecht.

[3] Bruce, Leycester corr., pp. 259 f.

[4] Stow's Survey of London, I. 173.

turfft zu kuchen, keller und taffeln selbst ordentlich und ahnsehenlich bestellen lassen, also das daraus unter andern I. Kon. Ma:t ehrerbietliges und wolgewogenes gemudte jegen E. Kon. Ma:t gnugsam zu spuren ist. So viel aber meine audientz betriffet, hatt mhan mich biss auff gestern dato damit auffgehalten und solche gar höfflich endtschuldigt, dass mhan mich nicht ubereilen, sondern nach gehabter unlust der schiffardt mir einen tag oder 3 zu meiner ergetzung rhuhe hett lassen wollen. Ich aber halt es darfur, wie ich auch sonst erfahren, das mhan inmittelst etlige der furnembsten rethe ahnhero verschrieben hatt und sich dahero der verzug verursachet hab. Gestern nach mittage (wie hie der gebrauch sein sol) bin ich durch einen reichsradt, rittern des ordenes, und andere hern und vom adel in grosser ahnzahl zur audientz gefhuret worden nach Grönwitz, da mich ahn der porten des schlosses andere mhe furnheme hern reichsrathe und ritter des ordens entfangen und also hinauff in den shael zu I. Kon. Ma:t gefhuret, die mir, als ich hinauff gekommen, etwas entjegen gangen und von wegen E. Kon. Ma:t gar freundelichen entfangen, darnach ahn iren stuel zurucke getretten und mich stehendt gehöret, doselbst ich meine werbung, so viel E. Kon. Ma:tt mir zum ahnfang furzubrengen g:st. befholen und sich offent- lich zu thun schicken wollen, abgeleget. Darauff I. Kon. Ma:tt mich zu sich gezogen, das ich nebstderselben auff einen stuhl hab sitzen mussen, und haben I. Ma:tt da ahngefangen zu erzehlen, was von jugent auff, als sie nurt von 15 jharn gewesen, E. Kon. Ma:tt viel treu und bruderliger freundtschafft bewiesen, die sie nimmer vergessen kondte, deweil sie lebete. Dabei dan I. Kön. Ma:tt viel schertz und ernst durcheinandergemischet, welche ahn E. Kön. Ma:t zu danck zu schreiben, darnegst sich der grossen ehre und treue, so E. Kön. Ma:tt ihr mitt dieser schickung erweisen wollen, sere weitleufftig und zum högsten bedancket, insonderheit weil es zu dieser zeit geschehen wehre, daraus sie so viel mhe E. Kön. Ma:tt bestendige bruderlige liebe und treue zu erspuren hette. So viel aber sonsten meine werbung wegen der frids- handlung zwischen dem koning aus Hispanien und Ihrer Ma:tt belangen thette, muste sie zwar bekennen, das E. Kon. Ma:t vorhaben sehre christlich und rhumblich ahn ihm selbst, I. Ma:tt wolte aber nicht zweiffeln, wen E. Kon. Ma:tt wusten, was sie all fur verkleinerung, spott und schimpff von dem koninge von Hispanien erlitten, wie ehr nicht allein I. Ma:tt nach irer koniglichen cron und standt sondern auch nach leib und leben trachten lassen, und solchs offt und vielfaltigk, so wurden E. Kon. Ma:tt ire lange gedult und grosse torheit (wir Irer Ma:tt wordt gewesen), das sie es so lange gelitten, viel mhe dan dasjennige, was sie jetzo angefangen hette, beschul- digen. Fieng ahn, nach der lange alles, was ir bejegnet in etligen jahren, zu erzehlen. In summa der beschluss wahr, wan I. Ma:tt gleich frieden mitt Hispanien erlangeten, so wurden doch die Hispanier denselbigen halten so lange, bis sie ire gelegenheit ersiehen, das sie inen ohne gefhar brechen und ir desto besser hinwiederumb zusetzen kondten. Wass ich nun darauff underthenigst geantwortet, auss was ursachen E. Kon. Ma:t bewogen worden, diese friedshandlung furzuschlagen, wie christlich, treulich und bruderlich ess gemeinet, dabei der alten vertrege und bundtnussen, so zwischen Den- marcken, Engelandt, Hispanien och Franckreich auffgericht und bis dahero bestanden sein, gemeldet worden, darumb E. Kon. Ma:tt keinem teil kegen das ander heimlich oder offentlich einige tadtlige hulff oder befurderung thun kundten, ess wehren dan zuvor die alten bundtnussen cassiret und auffgekundet, welchs ohne gegebne gnugsame und vorgehabten reiffen radt nicht geschehen kondte. Inmittelst aber hetten E. Kon. Ma:tt der zu beden teilen tragenden verwandtnuss halben diesen christligen wegk der gutligen friedensunterhandlung auss wolmeinendem hertzen freuntlich und bruderlich vorgeschlagen etc. Solchs alles gnedigster Koning und herr, wehre viel zu lanck zu schreiben. Will davon, wen ich mitt Gottes gnediger hulff und verleihung wiederumb bei E. Kon. Ma:tt ahnlange, weitere ausfuhrlige underthenigste relation einbringen. Der abscheit aber fur dies mhal ist gewesen, weil die sache wichtig, woltens I. Ma:tt in ein geringes bedencken ziehen und mitt dem furderligsten etlige irer vertrauten furnembsten redte verordnen, die mitt mir weiter davon aus und in reden solten. Damitt Ire Ma:t iren g:sten abscheit von mir genommen. Im scheiden aber hab ich underthenigst ahngedeutet, dass ich sonsten noch andere sachen mitt I. Kon. Ma:t zu derselben g:sten wolgelegenheit zu reden in befehlich hette, darauff I. Ma:t geandtwortet, ob dis wol die erste unterredung gewesen, so solt es doch die leste nicht pleiben. Dabei ichs dan, insonderheit weil ess spete und fast umb 7 uhr auff den abendt wahr, unterthenigst bewenden lassen. Ess ist aber diesen tagk jemandt von rathen noch bei mir gewesen, jedoch ahndeutung geschehen, dass sie morgen zu mir kommen werden. Ich will so viel muglich ahnhalten und fleiss ahnwenden, das ich meine ahnbefohlene sachen mitt dem furderligsten verrichten und abfertigung erlangen muge. Im fall ich dan fur meinem abreisen mhe gelegenheit zu schreiben werde haben, will E. Kon. Ma:t, was weiter furleufft, underthenigst meiner pflicht nach vermelden. Sonsten lest mhan sich alhie nicht anderss vermercken, alss wen mhan zu den kriege einen grossen mudt und hoffnung hette und des könings von Hispanien geruhmte grosse gewalt und macht wenig achtete. Capitain Drake ist in Indien ungefehrlich mitt 50 schiffen, darunter aber die meisten kauffardt, jedoch wolgerustet und ausgestaffieret sein solten. Hie sein etlige hern und vom adel, die schone schiffe auff iren eigenen unkosten erbauen und ausgestaffiret haben, die wir zum teill auswendig im vorbeifahren hie auff dem strome hin und wider liegen gesehen haben, deren etlige wollen in Indien, etlige sonsten auff die Hispanier streuffen. Ess haben etlige fast alle ire wolfardt darin gesteckt. Und denselbigen, auch andern iresgleichen, wie ich vermercke, gefellt es nicht besonders, das von frieden geredet werdt. Ess hatt mir der reichsadmirall ahnbieten lassen, die koniglige schiffe, so hie noch liegen, sehen zu lassen. Hab noch nicht richtig erfahren konnen, wie viel schiffe von ohrloch in alles aus sein, dan es ungleich berichtet werdt. Die Kon. Ma:t alhie hatt mir austrucklich gesagt, sie furchte sich gar nichts fur den Hispanier, dan sie wisse das das wol gewis und eigentlich, das ehr keine armada ausrusten khan, darfur sie sich besorgen durffe etc. In Hollandt vor Grave sollen die Engelischen mitt den Spaniern einen starcken scharmutzel gehalten haben und viel vornhemer Hispanier, aber wenig Engelischen im lauff gebliben sein. Davon werden E. Kon. Ma:t bessere zeittung im Sunde haben. Und weil jetzo von hinnen ein schiff ablauffen will, das ich

123

nicht nie zu schreiben habe, so mus ichs auff dis mhal hiebei unterthenigst bewenden lassen. Will derohalben E. Kon. Ma:tt zusambt dem gantzen konigligen löbligen hausse nebst allen, so E. Kon. Ma:t lieb sein, in gnedigen schutz des getreuen barmhertzigen Gottes zu langem konigligen gesunden glucksehligen leben und regiment hiemit getreulich und mich E. Kon. Ma:tt zu allen gnaden und schuldigen getreuen gehorsamen diensten unterthenigst empfolen haben, mitt underthenigster bitt, E. Kon. Ma:t wollen m. g:ster koning und her sein und pleiben. Dat. Lunden in Engelandt den 13:ten maii anno 1586.

E. Kon. Ma:tt

underthenigster, getreuer und gehorsamer

diener, weil ich lebe,

Heinrich Ramell

m. propria

Dem durchlauchtigsten, grossmechtige hochgebornen fursten und herrn, herrn Friderichen dem andern, zu Dennmarcken, Norwegen, der Wenden und Gotten könige, hertzogen zu Schlesswig, HOLSTEIN, Stormarn und der Dietmarschen, graffen zu Oldenburg und Delmenhorst, meinem gnedigsten konig und herrn, underthenigst

Reg. Cronburgk am pffingstage
den 22 maii 1586.[1]

---

[1] 'Most High Puissant and Gracious King and Lord. My humble, loyal services remain with all diligence and faithfulness as previously at Your Majesty's command. Most Gracious King and Lord, I cannot refrain from relating that we arrived here in England with Your Majesty's ship after favourable and unfavourable winds and good and bad weather and finally on the 6th inst. (6 May 1586) anchored at Greenwich. Although immediately on anchoring I addressed myself through the Secretary of State, Francis Walsingham, as is customary here, to the Queen and Her Majesty thereupon sent Walsingham on board here, I nevertheless remained for several reasons on the ship during the following day (7 May) and did not disembark until 8th May, which was a Sunday, Vocem jucunditatis (5th Sunday after Easter), after divine service and dinner on board, to the dwelling in the City of London which had been assigned to us by Her Majesty. Several times Her Majesty visited us through prominent men and gave me and the crew sundry fresh foods and vegetables, after which we were fetched by a not inconsiderable retinue and conducted to the lodgings in London. Your Majesty cannot conceive the crowds by water and on land that joined us, thereby creating such a jostling and tumult as I have not experienced for many a day. At the dwelling I and my attendant retinue and other servants whom I had taken on land for service were most munificently regaled and Her Majesty had personally arranged for everything necessary in kitchen, cellar and table in plentiful quantity, from which one could deduce Her Majesty's great goodwill towards Your Majesty. Concerning my audience, until yesterday (May 12th) I have been delayed and in a courteous manner asked my pardon that I be not in a hurry but be left in peace three days for recreation after

the discomfiture of my sea voyage. I believe this to be because—as I have also learnt in another way—that meanwhile some of the foremost councillors have been summoned hither, thereby causing this delay.

Yesterday afternoon (as is the custom here) I was conducted to an audience at Greenwich by a Privy Councillor who was a Knight of the Garter and a large number of other noble gentlemen. At Greenwich at the gates of the palace I was received by other Privy Councillors and Knights of the Garter, who conducted me up to the chamber to Her Majesty The Queen, who, on my arrival, took a few steps towards me and out of consideration for Your Majesty received me with particular friendship. Thereafter the Queen retired a few steps to her throne and listened standing while I delivered my message in the manner graciously commanded me by Your Majesty. Thereafter the Queen brought me closer and had me sit upon a chair by Her Majesty's side; she then started to tell of the faithful brotherly friendship Your Majesty had shown her while she was still young, only fifteen years old, which she would never forget as long as she lived. In this the Queen mingled much jesting and solemnity, which would be conveyed in writing to Your Majesty, not least the great honour and faithfulness which Your Majesty desires to display to the Queen through this embassy, for which she expressed her gratitude at length and in great degree, particularly as it has taken place at this time, whereby the Queen to such a great extent had recognised Your Majesty's constant friendship and faithfulness.

Concerning my embassy in other respects, the peace negotiations between the King of Spain and Her Majesty, Her Majesty certainly admits that Your Majesty's doings are in themselves clearly marked by religiousness and also highly praiseworthy, but Her Majesty would not hesitate if Your Majesty knew what she has had to put up with in the form of disparagement, scoffing and scorning from the King of Spain, how he has coveted not only the Queen's royal status but also her life and limb, and this again and again, for then Your Majesty would hold the Queen responsible for her great patience and her great madness (as Her Majesty literally said) in putting up with all this for so long, more than that which she has now started. The Queen then started to relate all that she has experienced in recent years. The sum of which was that if the Queen were to make peace immediately with Spain, the Spaniards would simply only keep the peace until such time as the opportunity arose for them to break it again without danger and attack the Queen's England with greater force. In my humble reply to the question: for which reasons had Your Majesty seen fit to propose these peace negotiations, I mentioned first the Christian spirit, faithfulness and brotherhood in which this was meant and also referred to the long-standing treaties and alliances that had been concluded between Denmark, England, Spain and France and which are still in force. Your Majesty had in this context neither in secret nor publicly taken sides for or against either party. In such a case the old alliances would be dissolved and rescinded, which ought not to happen without holding careful and well-meaning mature council. Meanwhile, however, Your Majesty out of a well-meaning heart in friendship and brotherhood with family ties in both directions, had proposed this Christian path with peace negotiations in good faith. Much could be written on this matter. I shall, when with God's help and grace I return to Your Majesty, submit further detailed humble accounts in this matter. I took leave of Her Majesty on this occa-

125

sion. Thus as the matter was of great importance, Her Majesty however desired a brief respite for consideration and immediately appointed some of her confidential—and at the same time foremost—councillors, who would continue the discussion in this subject with me. In this manner Her Majesty graciously bid me farewell. In conjunction with my departure I had humbly intimated that I had been commissioned on this occasion to present other business to Her Majesty. The Queen then replied that while this was the first audience, it would certainly not be the last. I wished, however, particularly as it had grown late and the time was almost 7 in the afternoon, humbly to let this audience rest. However, this day a member of the Council came to me and gave me to understand that the Council would return to me on the morrow. I shall be perseverent and diligent as far as possible in order to perform the tasks entrusted to me to the best of my ability and finish my business. Should I have occasion to write before leaving, I shall dutifully and humbly relate what happens after this.

Otherwise there is nothing to note here except that people are of good courage and good hope and that they trouble themselves very little about the King of Spain's renowned and great realm and power. Captain Drake is in India with some fifty ships, of which most are merchantmen but nonetheless apparantly well e-quipped and well furnished. Here in England there are many gentlemen and nobles who with their own funds have built stately ships, which they have also fitted out themselves. Some of these were seen by us on the Thames as we journeyed to and from our own ship, others have accompanied Drake to India, while others again are patrolling the Spanish waters. Some of these gentlemen have invested their entire fortune in this shipbuilding. And these gentlemen, as well as others like them, are not overpleased as I have noticed when one speaks of peace. The Lord Admiral has invited me to go aboard the ships which lie at anchor. I have not been able to get reliable information as to how many English warships are available all told, as reports differ in this respect. The Queen expressly declared to me that she is not in the least afraid of the Spaniards, as she is fully convinced that Spain cannot fit out an armada worth her consideration &c. In the Dutch waters off Grave [Gravesend] it is said that the English have held a great sea battle with the Spanish, in which many prominent Spaniards have fallen but few Englishmen. Concerning this, Your Majesty will receive fuller information in The Sound. As a ship is about to depart, and as I have no more to write, this will humbly have to do for now. I therefore wish Your Majesty together with the Royal Family and all those close to Your Majesty's heart by the gracious protection of the merciful Lord a long and prosperous life and rule with a humble prayer that Your Majesty may be and remain my gracious King and Lord. Dated London, England, 13th May 1586.

Your Majesty's most humble, faithful and obedient servant, for as long as I live, Henry Ramelius, m. propria.

To the high, mighty, most noble prince and lord, Frederick II, King of Denmark, Norway, the Vandals and the Goths, Duke of Schleswig, Holstein, Stormarn and Dietmarschen, Count of Oldenburg and Delmenhorst, my most gracious King and Lord, most humbly.

Registered: Cronborg Castle, Whit Sunday, 22nd May 1586'; T.K.U.A., England 10; Danish RA.

This is the only letter by Henry Ramelius extant from May 1586 and it is hardly likely that he sent another before his departure from London on May 30. The best description of the entertainments provided during his stay is to be found in Holinshed's Chronicles:[1]

Henrie Ramelius ambassador out of Denmarke.

On sundaie the eight daie of Maie, an ambassador namelie Henrie Rame-lius, intituled Cancellarius Germanicus, arriued at the Tower of London. A gentleman he was of goodlie personage, somewhat corpulent and of san-guine complexion: verie eloquent likewise and learned not onelie in the knowledge of diuerse toongs, as Latine, French, Italian, and Germane; but also in diuerse sciences. He came in ambassage from Frederike the second of that name, king of Denmarke, vnto the queens maiestie of England, and arriuing (as you have heard) at the Tower, was honorablie receiued by the lord Cobham and other great estates; who conueied him from thense through Tower street, into bishops gate street, and so to a faire and large house called Crosbies place,[2] where he was lodged, and remained.

The Danish ambassador honorablie intertained.

The said Ramelius during the time of his tariance, had attendance doone him conuenient for his person both by water and by land: the queens maiesties barges and seruants imploied about him to and from London, the court then being at Greenewich; whither alwaies when he came, the nobilitie of England failed in no point of courtesie that might be shewed. Which he seemed (as he could no lesse) verie acceptablie to take. Now being in England and in the English court, he might (and no doubt did) marke the magnificence of hir maiestie, in all respects admirable.

The maiestie of the English court.

Whereof a notable president was giuen in Whitsunweek,[3] at what time the said ambassador, being at the court, was accompanied with certeine English lords to hir highnesse chapell, and placed not far from hir excellencie did heare diuine service so melodiouslie said and soong, both by voice and instruments of consort as a man halfe dead might thereby haue beene quick-ened.

Hewenlie musike in the queens chapell.

The gentlemen of the chapell with the rest of the quier bending themselves, both with skill and zeale, that daie to honor their prince according to their place. The bishop of Salisburie and others distinclie reading part of diuine seruice, and in presence of all the auditorie dooing such obeisance with knee

---

[1] Op. cit., 4, pp. 894 f.
[2] Cf. p. 121, footnote 4.
[3] Whit Sunday, 22nd May 1586 (stylo vetero).

127

and countenance, as the presence of so gratious a souereigne as they had in their eies did require.

The ambassador of Denmarke seeth the roiall seruice of the queene of England.

Now when this solemnitie was ended, hir maiestie departed and so did the ambassador attended upon and accompanied vnto the place appointed for dinner: where standing neere to a faire window fronting into the open court, he might (being in communication now with one, and then with another English lord, as the lord Charles Howard, lord admerall, the lord Cobham, lord warden of the cinque ports, &c:) behold the roiall seruice of hir maiestie, verie personable gentlemen thereto sorted, carrieng couered dishes, all of silver and gilt verie beautifull; themselues in veluet and silke sutable in each respect, and as decentlie made, so decentlie worne; the trumpet sounding, and the drum plaieng therevnto: a maruellous deligtsome thing to heare, and a passing gallant sight to behold.

Recreations and disports for prince and people.

When dinner was doone, the ambassador was made partaker of such courtlie recreations, as for that time were fit, wherewith he could not but be pleasantlie conceipted; considering that as euerie thing was doone with purpose to delight: so he with others must needs be accordinglie affected. And as the better sort had their conuenient disports, so were not the ordinarie people excluded from competent pleasure.

Bearebaiting described.

For vpon a greene verie spatious and large, where thousands might stand and behold with good contentsment, there bearebaiting and bulbaiting (tempered with other merie disports) were exhibited; whereat it can not be spoken of what pleasure the people tooke.

For it was a sport alone of these beasts, to see the beare with his pinke eies leering after his enimies, the nimblenesse and wait of the dog to take his aduantage, and the force and experience of the beare againe to auoid the assaults: if he were bitten in one place, how he would pinch in another to get free; and if he were once taken, then what shift with biting, clawing, roring, tugging, grasping, tumbling, and tossing he would worke to wind himselfe awaie; and when he was loose, to shake his eares with the blood and slauer about his phisnomie, was a pittance of good releefe.

Bulbaiting and an old ape on horse back.

The like pastime also of the bull, and the horsse with the ape on his backe did greatlie please the people, who standing round, some in a ring vpon the greene, other some aloft, and some below, had their eies full bent vpon the present spectacle, diuerse times expressing their inward conceived ioy and delight with shrill shouts and varietie of gesture.

This Crosbie was a knight see his gift to the citie of London.

Now the daie being far spent, and the sun in his declination, the pastimes ended, and the actors therein wearie; the ambassador withdrew to his lodging by barge to Crosbies place, where (no doubt) this daies solemnitie was thought vpon, and talked of; if not by him, yet by his traine, and perhaps (as like enough) of both.

The ambassador departeth home towards Denmarke.

Now after this, and manie other English courtesies elsewhere, verie bounti-fullie giuen and taken: the ambassador after the finishing of such affaires as he was put in trust withall, taking his leave both of court, citie, and countrie, returned towards Denmarke on the thirtith daie of Maie next following, whome we will leaue vpon his voiage, and touch other matters happening at home.

This account from Holinshed's Chronicles indicates that no play was performed for Henry Ramelius during his stay in London in May 1586. Leicester was presumably desirous of compensating for this and when Ramelius returned to Denmark at the end of May, a company of Leicester's Men was accredited to the Danish Court.

The Danish household accounts for August and September 1586 mention 'Wilhelm Kempe instrumentist' and a boy 'Daniell Jonns'. The entry runs as follows:

XXXVI dal. Wilhelm Kempe Instrumentist fich for II Maaneders Kost-pennche paa seg och I drenng wid naffn Daniell Jonns hannd haffde fortienntt fra thend 17 Junij hand kom wdj thienesten, och ther till I Maanett hannom skenngtis till afftog, er tilsamen 3 Maaneder, hver Maand 12 dal.[1]

This entry is immediately followed by:

	Thisse 5 instrumentister och
	springere
Thomas Stiwens	kome vdj thiensten 17
	junij, er fraa thendt tid
Jurgenn Brienn	och till thenne 8 maaned
	endis, som er thend 18 sep-
Thomas Koning	temb. — 3 monneder och 3 da-
	ge hver om monneden vj
Thomas Pape	daler. belöffver hver 18½ d.
	3 ß. er tilsammen 92½ d.

[1] '36 daler paid to William Kempe, *instrumentist*, for 2 months board for himself and a boy, by name Daniel Jonns, which sum he had earned from June 17 when he was engaged, theretill 1 month granted on his dismissal, in all 3 months, each month 12 daler'; Register på besoldning och kostpenge 22.1.1586–16.1.1587, fol. III v., Rentemesterregnskabet 1586, Danish RA.

Robert Persj 15 ß., som Thomas Stivens
annamett och quiteritt.[1]

These two Danish entries must surely be connected. Not only are they consecutive on the same document but also concerned with appointments from the same date, June 17, 1586.

In his *Apology for Actors* from 1612, Thomas Heywood mentions that the King of Denmark, i.e. the father of the reigning monarch, had engaged a company af English comedians upon Leicester's recommendation. This is probably a reference not only to William Kempe, Thomas Stephens and the others who performed in Denmark in 1586[2] but also to Artus Damler et consortes, who were engaged in Denmark 1579–86. After their engagement, this company proceeded to Christian I, Elector of Saxony and nephew of Frederick II. William Kempe and Daniel Jonns, on the other hand, appear to have gone on somewere else, since their names have not been found in any German records. There is, however, a letter of recommendation for an anonymous English instrumentalist in 'Ausländisches Register', 1586, in the Danish National Archives. This runs as follows:

'*Ahn den Graven von Lijcester.*
Cronenbürgh, den 26. August 1586.
Nachdem unß zeiger, so hiebevor in ewern dienst gewesen, neben anderen Englischen Instrumentisten ein zeitlang aufwertig gewesen und aber sich nunmehr wiederumb an euch seiner gescheffte halben zugegen entschlossen, alß haben wir ihme dieß unser gnedigst schreiben an euch mitgeben wollen, da ihr ohne denselben in ewere dienst nicht bestellen und aufnehmen werdet. Gesinnen wir auch hiermit gnedigst Ihr ihn wiederumb ahn unß kommen lassen wollett, Daran thut Ihr unß zu gnedigsten gefallen. In gnaden damit wir euch ohne daß gewogen, zuerkennen.'[3]

[1] 'These 5 instrumentalists and tumblers—Thomas Stephens, George Bryan, Thomas King, Thomas Pope, Robert Percy—were engaged from June 17 to September 18, 3 months and three days each, monthly 6 daler, 18½ daler 3 skilling, or in all 92½ daler 15 skilling, which Thomas Stephens received and acknowledged'; Register på besoldning och kostpenge 22.1.1586–16.1.1587, fol. 111 v. Rentemesterregnskabet 1586, Danish RA.

[2] Cf. Cohn, I, Historical part, XXIII.

[3] 'To the Earl of Leicester. Kronborg Castle, August 26th, 1586. Since the bearer of this letter, who was previously in Your service, together with other English Instrumentalists has been in Our service for some time and has now decided to place his services again at Your disposal, We have been graciously pleased to give him Our letter of recommendation to You, as without the same Your Grace cannot

It seems highly probable that this reference was written for William Kempe. The dates agree and there does not appear to be any other candidate. It was uncommon for letters of recommendation to be issued for foreign instrumentalists and the present document provides indirect evidence of how highly William Kempe was esteemed at Frederick II's court at Kronborg Castle. It also serves to verify Thomas Heywood's statement that the English instrumentalists were engaged in Denmark on the recommendation of Leicester.

The transfer of Thomas Stephens, George Bryan, Thomas King, Thomas Pope and Robert Percy from Denmark to Saxony was the result of a correspondence between the two monarchs which we still possess.[1] According to this, it was not until payment in the form of 100 daler per annum was offered that the Englishmen could be persuaded to venture forth to another unknown destination and a new language still further from their home. They left Denmark with a German interpreter on September 25, 1586, and shortly after their arrival at Weidenhayn (Waidheim) on October 16 they were ordered by the Elector Christian to accompany him to Berlin, where the Elector was to stay for a while. The Elector's own capital was Dresden, and the English players were engaged as members of the Elector's household. They were thus obliged to follow Christian I on his journeys and entertain him with music and tumbling on special occasions.[2] For this they were entitled, besides their payment, to board, free clothing and travelling expenses, as well as to lodging expenses of 40 thaler per man. The city records at Dresden give their names as Tomas Konigh, Tomas Stephan or Stephans, George Beyzandt, Tomas Papst and Rupert Persten. They left the Electoral court on July 17, 1587. It is clear from the records that this company performed music and tumbling, but it is quite likely that they were also players, since two of them, Thomas Pope and George Bryan, reappeared later among Strange's Men. These two are in the roll of actors for the *Seven deadly Sins* by Richard Tarlton (1585) and this was performed by Strange's Men around 1590.[3] They were subsequently members of the Chamberlain's

engage and receive him into Your service. We also wish to assure Your Grace thereby that We are graciously willing to let him return to Us anew. In this way Your Grace would graciously please Us'; Ausländisches Register, 1586, fol. 192 r; Danish RA.

[1] *Sh.-Jahrbuch* 1888, 104–6.

[2] Cf. Chambers, *Eliz. Stage*, 2, 272.

[3] *Henslowe's Diary*, 2, 304.

Company, together with Shakespeare, when this was reorganised in 1594, and they are among the actors listed in the First Folio edition of Shakespeare's dramas as 'The principall actors in all these plays'.

Thomas King was engaged as early as April 6, 1582, as

the Queen's Drum player in the place of Thomas Shingwell, deceased.

He held this post until his death, whereupon a special clothing allowance was granted on November 23, 1599, to John (or William) Gosson,

the Queen's drum player, in place of Thos. King, lately deceased.[1]

Richard Percy (Perce), an English musician, was engaged at Duke Charles's court at Nyköping in 1599–1600.[2] It could be that Richard and Robert Percy were members of the same family.

Professor Baldwin, however, maintains[3] that the company that was first in Denmark in 1586 and then in Saxony in 1586–87 was made up of musicians and tumblers only, since there is no evidence that performances were given of tragedies and comedies. On the other hand, several writers do not agree with Professor Baldwin here. Thus Professor Nungezer[4] terms these instrumentalists and tumblers 'actor-entertainers', implying that they were actors as well.

Following the death of Frederick II in 1588 there seem to have been no further companies of players from abroad at the Danish court before the occasion of Christian IV's coronation in 1596.

On the other hand,

Latinske og Danske Comoedier[5]

and other works were performed during the feast to celebrate the arrival on January 21, 1590, at Kronborg Castle of the newly wedded James VI of Scotland and Anne of Denmark, though this was most likely scholarly drama. According to Troels-Lund (*Dagligt Liv i Norden i det 16. Århundrede*), plays were also performed at Elsinore in the years

---

[1] Lord Chamberlain's records, L.C. 5/49, 203 and L.C. 9/75–88, PRO. Cal. of State Papers, Dom. Ser. 1598–1601, 346.

[2] H. XII. 69. Cf. Chambers, *Sir Henry Lee*, 205.

[3] Baldwin, *Organization and Personnel of the Shakespearean Company*, 73 ff.

[4] Nung., *Dict. of Act.*, 63 and 285.

[5] 'Latin and Danish Comedies'; Slange, 1, 33.

132

immediately after 1565. The man behind this was the headmaster of the Latin school there, Hans Christensen Sthen, and it was his pupils who gave the performances.[1] On the occasion of the wedding on April 19, 1590, at Kronborg between Henry-Julius of Brunswick-Luneburg and Elizabeth of Denmark, at which James VI and his queen were present, drama of different kinds was performed but here the players probably came with Henry-Julius from Wolfenbüttel.[2] It has not, however, been possible to confirm this from the Danish household accounts for 1588–90, though we know that Henry-Julius had five German trumpeters in his train, Josop Groß, Hanns Hertzberch, Jochum Sperhach, Balzar Labry and Jost Rattger.[3] According to the Danish accounts for 1589–90, the Danish King, who was not yet of age, had in his employ during 1590 a capellmeister named Bonaventura as well as instrumentalists, an organist, drummers, trumpeters and singers.[4] The same accounts also indicate that Queen Anne of Scotland had three Danish trumpeters in her train when she left for Scotland on April 21, 1590, their names being Willum Rytter, Hans Bagster and Giertt Giertzönn.[5]

During the years 1588–96, when Christian IV was still a minor,[6] interest in the theatre was not particularly great in Denmark. Christian was crowned on August 29, 1596, and his brothers-in-law, James VI of Scotland and Henry-Julius of Brunswick-Luneburg, were invited to attend, together with their wives. Although they were unable to accept the invitation, Henry-Julius despatched a company of comedians and acrobats to perform at the celebrations; the presence of this company is noted in the Danish household accounts:

Thend 20 Maij (1597) betaldis Michell Steen, borger wdj Kjøpnehauffn, for huis fortaering till wiinn, mad och øll, saa och ellers andenn omkostning, som er bleffuen giordt och opgangen wdj hans huus, aff hogborne førstis och herris, hertug Henrich Juliuszis aff Brunschuig och Lunneborgs, hans furstelige naadis comoedianten och springer, wore tillsamman 18 persohner, som aff hans furstelige naade herudj riged wore inndschickede, neste forgangen aar anno 1596, emod konn. maiets loffliige krønning och bleffue

[1] Troels-Lund, 7, 158 ff. and 168 ff.
[2] Chambers, *Eliz. Stage*, 2, 275.
[3] Rentemesterregnskabet 1.7.1589–1.5.1590, fol. 211 r, Danish RA.
[4] Rentemesterregnskabet 1.7.1589–1.5.1590., fol. 289 r–295 r, Danish RA.
[5] *Ibid.*, fol. 290 v.
[6] The Regency consisted of the King's Chancellor Niels Kaas, the Lord Admiral Peder Munch, Councillors Jørgen Rosencrantz and Hak Ulfstand, and the Treasurer Christoffer Valkendorff.

vdj hanns huus spiisede och vnnderholdett, paa XXVIII dagis tiid, vdj forschreffne aar, effther hoeszliggendis wnderschreffne zeeddels liudelsze ... 242½ kr.[1]

The Danish theatre historian, V. C. Ravn,[2] as well as several other writers, are of the opinion that this body of men was an English company of players. Troels-Lund, on the other hand, seems to be more to the point when he maintains[3] that, whether they were English or German, these players almost certainly performed plays written by Henry-Julius himself, e.g. *Susanna* and *Ehebrecherin*, which were printed in 1590–91 and 1594 respectively.

The Danish historian, Niels Slange, gives but a passing reference to these theatricals in connection with the coronation, so we know nothing about the language in which they were performed:

...; og saa snart Solen gik ned, begyndtes Comoedier, Dantz, Spil og Musik.[4]

Unquestionably, the man who did most to introduce and further the interests of the English players on the Continent was Robert Browne.[5] He made frequent journeys abroad, and between 1590 and 1620 spent considerable periods of time in Germany and elsewhere. Groups of players from England accompanied him at intervals, and some of these split up into independent companies. These 'Browne's men' are the 'Engländer' who became so well known and popular at the spring and autumn fairs at Frankfort, as well as in Holland, northern Germany and Denmark. Of course, Browne was not the only one to interest himself in these matters; there were several companies that had no connection with him. The activities of both these and Browne's on the Continent can be traced in the records from the period. There are many lacunæ, however,

---

¹ '20 May (1597) paid to Michell Steen, citizen of Copenhagen, for board with wine, food and ale and other necessities and lodging in his house of His Royal Highness Henry-Julius of Brunswick and Luneburg's "comoedianter och springer" in all 18 persons, who were sent to Denmark during His Majesty's Coronation 1596; 28 days according to the enclosed signed bill ... 242½ kronor'; Rentemesterregnskabet 1596–97, fol. 284 v–249 r; Danish RA.

² *For Idé og Virkelighed*, 1, 90.

³ Troels-Lund, 7, 181.

⁴ '...; and as soon as the sun had set, there commenced comedies, dancing, play and music'; op. cit., 1, 100.

⁵ Chambers, *Eliz. Stage*, 2, 273 ff., and Nung., *Dict. of Act.*, 60 ff.

and the absence of the players' names in the documents frequently makes it difficult to establish the details of their itineraries.

Robert Browne himself appears for the first time in 1583 as one of Worcester's Men in the company of Edward Alleyn. During 1589 the two of them—now probably as Admiral's Men—still shared a wardrobe with John Alleyn and Richard Jones.[1]

Browne's tours abroad began with a visit to Leyden on October 1590. The city accounts run as follows:

> Noch aen Robert Broun, Engelsman, ende zijne medehuelpers tsamen betaelt vijftien guldens, over gelijcke somme hem toegevoucht voor't verthoonen ende speelen van verscheyden comediën ende historiën, mitsgaeders 't doen van verscheyden sprongen, bij hem zoo voor Burgermeesteren als voor de gemeenten deser stede verthoont, blijckende bij de ordonnantie van daete den VII^{en} octobris anno 1590 ende quitantie overgeleevert; hier de voorsz ... XV gl.[2]

It is possible that this trip was little more than a reconnaissance, for in February 1592 he was getting ready for a new theatrical venture on the Continent. For this he received the following passport for himself, John Bradstreet, Thomas Sackville and Richard Jones from the Lord Admiral to the States-General of the Netherlands:

> Messieurs, comme les presents porteurs Robert Browne, Jehan Bradstriet, Thomas Saxfield, Richard Jones, avec leurs consorts, estants mes joueurs et serviteurs, ont deliberé de faire ung voyage en Allemagne, avec intention de passer par les païs de Zelande, Hollande et Frise, et allantz en leur dict voyage d'exercer leurs qualitez en faict de musique, agilitez et joeuz de commedies, tragedies et histoires, pour s'entretenir et fournir a leurs despenses en leur dict voyage. Cestes zont partant pour vous requerir monstrer et prester toute faveur en voz païs et jurisdictions, et leur octroyer en ma faveur vostre ample passeport soubz le seel des Estatz, afin que les Bourgmestres des villes estantz soubz voz jurisdictions, ne les empeschent en passant d'exercer leur dictes qualitez par tout. Enquoy faisant, je vous en demeureray a tous obligé, et me treuverez tres appareillé a me revencher de vostre cour-

---

[1] *Henslowe's Diary*, 2, 239.

[2] 'Paid to Robert Browne, Englishman, and to his fellows, in all fifteen guilders, for a like sum granted to him for having acted and performed divers comedies and histories besides having made divers leaps, performed by him both in the presence of the burgomasters and before the community of this city, as appears by the order dated October 7, 1590, receipt being delivered ... XV guilders.' Reeckeninghe van Jan Brouwer Jansz. Thresorier Ordinaris van 't jaer XV^c tnegentich. Leyden 1589(–90), fol. 463; and Ordonnantieboek B (Secret. arch. 1575–1851, No. 3734), fol. 97.

toisie en plus grand cas. De ma chambre a la court d'Angleterre ce Xᵉ jour
de Febvrier 1591.

Vostre tres affecsioné a vous
fayre plaisir et sarvis,
C. Howard[1]

It would appear that the Lord Admiral issued this passport in his
capacity as patron of the Lord Admiral's Men—'estants mes joueurs et
serviteurs'. The passport covered not only the four men named in it but
also 'leurs consorts', presumably the entire company of Lord Admiral's
Men.[2] Its date, 1591, was intended to cover 1591–92, which, translated
into modern terms, gives February 10, 1592,[3] as the date it was signed.
This agrees well with other historical data, since nothing is known about
Browne's travels abroad in 1591, whereas we still possess records from
1592 concerning this company.

The Lord Admiral's passport was thus issued six months after another
English company had left for Nyköping in August 1591 and only about
two months before Philip Kingman and Philip Gibson left in April 1592
to reinforce the players there.[4]

In 1592 Robert Browne and his company were in Arnhem with the
permission of Count Maurice of Orange-Nassau. The XIIth account (1592)
of the treasurer, Caerl van Gelders, has the following entry referring to
this visit:

Aen Robert Brŭyn, Johan Bradsdrat, Thomas Saxwiell, Richardŭs Jonas
und Everhart Sanß[5] Mŭisickerß und Hystorispeelderß alhier tot Arnhem mit

---

[1] van den Bergh, 41 f. According to the Algemeen Rijksarchief, 's-Gravenhage,
this passport no longer exists in the original. It existed when van den Bergh's
book was published in 1857 and up until about 1900, but disappeared sometime
between 1900 and 1920. For this reason it does not appear in *Resolutiën der Staten-
Generaal* by Dr. N. Japikse.

[2] Cf. Cohn XXVIII ff. and XXXII, footnote 1; Chambers, *Eliz. Stage*, 2, 274,
and Riewald, *New Light* ..., 71. Concerning the sense of the French word *consort*,
cf. Huguet, 2, 467.

[3] The passport was issued in England, where Lady Day, March 25, was generally
accepted as the beginning of a new year from the 12th until the middle of the 18th
century.

[4] Cf. Chapter 4.

[5] In his book *Arnhemsche Oudheden*, G. van Hasselt transcribes this name
Everhart Sauß. A comparison with the records shows that Sauß is probably Sanß.
Paleographically the letter *u* may be the letter *n*. Cf. Riewald, *New Light* ..., 7,
footnote 24.

patent van S.Ex:tie[1] gecomen sijnde die somme van twelff ponden haer bij
den heeren raeden und recckenmeesteren tot eene vereeringe toegelachtt &c.
Alß blict bij die ordinantie hier mit quitantie aevergelevertt. Dairomme alhier
dieselve ... XII £.[2]

Unfortunately, nothing is said about the exact dates of this engagement. Compared with the 15 guilders paid out in Leyden in 1590, the
£12 paid here would seem to indicate that either the company's stay
was shorter or else the company itself was smaller than it had been in
Leyden.[3]
On August 30, 1592, Robert Browne applied for permission to perform theatricals at the autumn fair at Frankfort,[4] and we are fortunate
in possessing an eye-witness account of the resultant performance.[5]
Balthasar Paumgartner the younger, a native of Nuremberg, was at the
fair on September 13, 1592, and described what he saw there in a letter
to his wife. Concerning the theatricals he writes:

> Die englischen Komödianten haben eine herrliche gute Musika und sind so
> perfekt mit Springen, Tanzen, dergleichen ich noch nie gehört, noch gesehen
> hab.[6]

This observation is of interest in connection with the doings of the
English company at Nyköping at this time. The accounts from both
places show that a much greater impression was made by the music and
the acrobatics than by the drama itself. Paumgartner also mentions
that the company, which consisted of ten to twelve persons, was

> ... köstlich herrlich und wohl gekleidet,[7]

and he adds that he hopes that these players will shortly visit Nuremberg, as in fact they did.

[1] Count Maurice of Orange-Nassau.

[2] 'Paid to Robert Browne, John Bradstreet, Thomas Sackville, Richard Jones
and Everhart Sanß, musicians and players of histories, who arrived at Arnhem with
a licence from his Excellency, £12 as actor's fee and honorarium granted by the
councillors and treasurers of the city of Arnhem &c. As appears by order delivered
here with a receipt. Therefore here the same ... £XII'; op. cit., 49.

[3] Guilders in Holland and ponden van XL groten vlerins in Gelderland were,
during the 16th century, equivalent and interchangeable coins. Koninklijk Kabinet
van Munten, Penningen en Gesneden Stenen, Zeestraat 71 b, 's-Gravenhage.

[4] Menzel, *Geschichte der Schauspielkunst in Frankfurt am Main*, 23.

[5] *Ibid.*, *Das alte Frankfurter Schauspielhaus*, 21.

[6] 'The English comedians have played an excellent good music and are so talented
in acrobatics and dancing that I have neither heard nor seen the like'; op. cit.

[7] '... expensively magnificent and well dressed'; op. cit.

There seems to be little doubt but that the Lord Admiral's passport and Paumgartner's letter both relate to the same company. Fynes Moryson's[1] observation of an English company at Frankfort during an autumn fair:

> having nether a Complete number of Actours, nor any good Apparell, nor any ornament of the Stage,

and Richard Jones's letter[2] to Edward Alleyn:[3]

> ... this it is, I am to go over beyond the seeas with Mr Browne and the company, but not by his meanes, for he is put to half a shaer, and to stay hear, for they ar all against his goinge. ...

are in fact both of uncertain date and mention the deficiencies in equip-ment etc. of the company concerned. They can thus hardly be connected with the performance by the Lord Admiral's Men at Frankfort in 1592 and must be attributed to some later occasion.[4]

At the time when the company was engaged in the summer of 1591 to journey to Nyköping, and even more so when Philip Kingman and Philip Gibson joined this company about May 1, 1592, the English travelling companies were fully organized for performances on the Continent with theatricals, music and acrobatics.

Michael Heberer von Bretten's eye-witness account of the performance by the English 'Comœdianten und Springer' in Nyköping in August 1592, compared with the same writer's description of the Italian Commedia dell'arte performed by amateurs at King Sigismund's wedding at Cracow in May the same year, certainly gives rise to doubts as to the kind of theatricals, if any, that were performed at Nyköping. What did von Bretten mean by

> die ihrem Gebrauch nach ziemliche Kurtzweil geübet und gemacht.[5]

Unquestionably this leaves the impression that the emphasis in the Nyköping performance, at least as von Bretten saw it, was more upon the music and the tumbling than upon the drama. Nevertheless, von Bretten does not use the expression 'Musiker und Springer' but rather

---

[1] Hughes, *Shakespeare's Europe*, 304.

[2] *Henslowe Papers*, 33.

[3] He married Joan Wordsworth, Philip Henslowe's step-daughter.

[4] Cf. Chambers, *Eliz. Stage*, 2, 287.

[5] '... which in the customary manner entertained the spectators.'

'Comoedianten und Springer', and this can scarcely refer to a company consisting entirely of musicians.

As has already been mentioned, Balthazar von Paumgartner was also more struck by the music and tumbling than by the drama when he saw an English company perform at Frankfort in 1592.

At this time John III had players at his court in Stockholm, and these were musicians. On one of the pay-bills in the Royal Wardrobe in 1594, issued shortly after John's death, we even find the entry *Musici eller Spellemän*. Again, in an account for 1591 in Stockholm Castle there is a list headed *Spelemän*, which has entries such as Casparutz Defabry, 'fiddler', Laurentz, 'harpist', and Franns Olsson, 'bassoonist'. This list ends with the names of a number of musicians without any note as to the instruments they played. However, both these lists and those of Duke Charles's Swedish musicians always contain information as to the instruments played by the leading musicians.

The English company at Nyköping was divided into six *Instrumentister* and six *Trommetter*, according to the household accounts for 1591. This division was most likely made already in England, since the two groups received different pay and different tasks in Sweden. It would also seem that they took with them a number of instruments from England, lutes, hautboys, &c. as well as trumpets and drums. The accounts have nothing to tell us about what the company did outside the field of music.

In James Hill's dispatches from Nyköping in January 1593, Johannes Huss (John Howse) is called 'the Duke's trumpeter', while Philip Bruggis (Brigges) is referred to as 'the Duke's Jester', and this in spite of the fact that both these two are in the group of trumpeters listed in the accounts for 1591.

Another factor that seems to indicate that *Instrumentister* were not simply musicians is that William Kempe is entered in the Danish household accounts as an *Instrumentist*. We know that Kempe was in fact an actor, a clown and a dancer who sometimes, it is true, played a small wind instrument while he danced.

An engagement that lasted thirteen months, moreover, was too long to have been entirely concerned with music and tumbling. Furthermore, it is known that at this time musicians and players in England had not yet become segregated into two distinct professions. Contemporary English documents distinguish between 'minstrels' and 'players'. Minstrels, or troubadours, at the end of the 16th century appeared singly

139

as a rule, moving from castle to castle, and relied on singing and instrumental music to gain them an entry. Players at that time usually appeared in companies of six or multiples of six, and could perform music, comedies, histories, tragedies and acrobatics.

It is interesting to note that Kingman's company of players from 1596 also consisted of twelve persons to begin with. For instance his travelling company, which visited Strasburg in that year, comprised twelve players, whereas the Nyköping company had six *Instrumentister* or players and six *Trommetter* or trumpeters. The latter company was prepared to entertain Duke Charles at dinner with music and tumbling, as well as to perform theatricals of some kind. There is also no doubt that they did so, albeit to a somewhat limited extent; the Duke was in fact in Nyköping for seven of the thirteen months of the company's engagement.

The company that left England for Nyköping in August 1591 was in many respects similar to the English company that performed in Denmark in August and September 1586, before proceeding to Saxony for an engagement there from October until July 1587. This latter company consisted of only five or, if William Kempe is included, six *Instrumentister*. The Nyköping company consisted of six *Instrumentister* and six *Trommetter* and thus in a way represented a transition to the company that performed at Strasburg in 1596 under Philip Kingman and that, as has already been mentioned, consisted of twelve players.

It should also be noted that von Bretten's description of the Nyköping company as 'Comoedianten und Springer' is used by the Danish treasurer for the eighteen persons sent by Prince Henry-Julius of Brunswick-Luneburg to Christian IV's coronation in 1596. The circumstance that Philip Kingman was in Cassel in 1594–95, where he was engaged by Landgrave Maurice of Hesse as a player and playwright and that he was subsequently leader of a company of players in Strasburg in 1596, when comedies and tragedies were performed, would seem to indicate that he was called to Nyköping in April 1592 in order to stimulate the theatrical life there with a view especially to the wedding celebrations to be held at the end of August. The entry in the wardrobe accounts for May 1, 1592, implies a new departure; Kingman is described neither as a player nor as an instrumentalist but as a *Timlare*, a less common title that on at least one occasion in the Swedish literature of the period can be connected with the idea of an actor.

It may be easier to understand the tasks performed by players, instrumentalists and trumpeters if we take a look at the declared accounts

140

for two subsequent Danish embassies to England, by Arild Huitfeld and Christian Barnekow in 1597 and by Henry Ramelius in 1605. The first of these embassies lasted from 12 August to 7 November and included the following items:

fol. 11 v	Giffŭet enn Engelsk Luttenist som lod sig hörre hos herrerna thil schienck		
(London)	... J engelod	(5/9	1597)
fol. 12 v	Giffŭet spillemennd wdi Enfeld som herrerne Lowe for theris praesentz, de lode sig hörre hos herrerne		
(Enfield)	... ij daller	(8/9	1597)
fol. 12 v	Giffŭet Dronningens Thrometter som		
(Enfield)	blaeste for herrerne		
	... xLiiij dr	(8/9	1597)
fol. 12 v	Giffŭet Raadzens Thrometer, som och Loed sig hörre hos herrerne		
(Enfield)	... xVi dr	(8/9	1597)
fol. 13 r	Giffŭet Dronningens thromslaer och		
(Enfield)	piber thil shienck ... X daller	(9/9	1597)
fol. 14 v	Giffŭet en aff Raadzens Thrometer		
(London)	thill skienck .... V dlr	(11/9	1597)
fol. 15 r	Giffuedt Nogle Spillemendt ßom lechte for herrerne om Morgenen		
(London)	... V dlr	(11/9	1597)
fol. 15 v	Giffuet en af Dronningens Musicanter thill skenck for noget hand forniedt herrerne mz		
(London)	... ij engelotter	(12/9	1597)
fol. 16 r	Giffuedt Nogle spillemendt, som lechte wden herrens Losementhe		
(London)	... j dlr	(13/9	1597)
fol. 22 v	Giffuedt Lundens stadz Instrumentister ßom legte for herrerne		
(London)	... X dlr	(19/9	1597)
fol. 23 r	Enn lutteniste thill skenck ßom legte for herrerne om afftenen		
(London)	... ij dlr	(19/9	1597)
fol. 28 v	Giffuet alle Lundens Instrumentister ßom lode thennom hörre hŭoes herrerne till skenck		
(London)	... X engelotter	(25/9	1597)
fol. 34 v	Giffuidt Medelburgs Instrumentister ßom legte for herrerne		
(Middelburgh)	... X dlr	(2/10	1597)
fol. 36 v	Giffuett Nogle Spillemend och Instru-		

	mentister — ßom legte for herrerne wdj Loßementhz	
(Rotterdam) fol. 37 v	... X dlr Giffuet en Thromsler och en piber thill skennck	(5/10 1597)
(The Hague) fol. 38 v	... j dlr Giffuet en Lutteniste ßom legte for herrerne	(6/10 1597)
(The Hague) fol. 40 r	... ij dlr Giffŭet Staternis (Leydens) Thrometter som bleste for herrerne paa herrernis affthoug thill shenck	(15/10 1597)
(Leyden) fol. 40 v	... X dlr Giffŭed Nogre Instrumentister som leegte for herrerne udj Harlum thill skenck	(17/10 1597)
(Harlem) fol. 42 v	... XIIIJ dlr Giffŭet Instrumentisterne och Musican- terne wdj Amsterdam som legte och sang for herrerne, ald den stunnd wy war der	(19/10 1597)
(Amsterdam) fol. 49 v	.... XX dlr Giffŭet Instrumentisterne wdj Ham- borge till skienck	(22/10 1597)
(Hamburg)	... XX dlr	(3/11 1597)[1]

[1] 'Granted an English Lutenist who 'let himself be heard' by the Embassy: 1 engelot, 5/9. Granted players at Enfield whom the Embassy praised for their presence; they 'let themselves be heard' by the Embassy: ij daler, 8/9. Granted the Queen's Trumpeters who blew for the Embassy: XLIIIJ daler, 8/9. Granted the Trumpeters of the Privy Council, who 'let themselves be heard' by the Embassy: XVI daler, 8/9. Granted the Queen's trumpeters and pipers: X daler, 9/9. Granted one of the Trumpeters of the Privy Council: V daler, 11/9. Granted Some Players who played for the Embassy in the morning: V daler, 11/9. Granted one of the Queen's Musicians for something with which he entertained the Embassy: ij engelots, 12/9. Granted Some players, who played by the Ambassador's lodgings: j daler, 13/9. Granted The City of London's Instrumentalists, who played for the Embassy: X daler, 19/9. Granted a lutenist who played for the Embassy in the evening: ij daler, 19/9. Granted all London's Instrumentalists, who 'let themselves be heard' by the Embassy: X engelots, 25/9. Granted Middelburgh's Instrumentalists, who played for the Embassy: X daler, 2/10. Granted some of Rotterdam's Players and Instrumentalists, who played for the Embassy at the lodgings: X daler, 5/10. Granted in The Hague a Trumpeter and a piper: j daler, 6/10. Granted in The Hague a Lutenist, who played for the Embassy: ij daler, 15/10. Granted the City of Leyden's Trumpeters, who blew for the Embassy on its departure: X daler, 17/10. Granted Some Instrumentalists, who played for the Embassy at Harlem: XIIIJ daler, 19/10. Granted the Instrumentalists and Musicians at Amsterdam who played and sang

Henry Ramelius's embassy, which lasted from 9 August to 6 November 1605, included the following items in the declared accounts:

fol. 4 r	Giffűed sex Thrommetter som bleste for Gesantens Lossemend till London (Lombard Street)		
(London)	... XI dlr	(2/9	1605)
fol. 4 v	Thend 3 Septembris. Giffűed Nogle Piberer och thromster som spillede for herrens loßemend (London)		
(London)	... ij dlr	(3/9	1605)[1]
fol. 7 r	Thend 9 septembris. Giffued Kongens (James I) Trommetter aff England som bleste till Windzor ther Gesanten blef opförtt fra Kircken och op paa slotted. Och Även Bleste for Loßementen till Lunden.		
(Windsor &c)	... XXX dlr	(9/9	1605)
	Rigenns Raadz Trommetter		
(London)	... j dalr	(9/9	1605)
	Giffued Nogle Trommetter och Instrumentister som ligte for Gesantens Loßemende		
(London)	Engelotter ... i	(9/9	1605)
	Giffued — 5 Kongens Instrumentister aff Engeland som ligte udenfor gesanthens Loßemendt till Rißmund		
(Richmond)	... X dalr	(20/9	1605)[2]

In these entries three different expressions are used in association with the *Instrumentister* and *Trommetter*: the *Trommetter* 'bleste' (blew);

for the Embassy, all the time we were there: XX daler, 22/10. Granted the Instrumentalists at Hamburg: XX daler, 3/11'; T.K.U.A., Speciel Del. Gesandtskabsregnskaber, 7 (Arild Huitfelds och Christian Barnekows Regnskab 1597).

[1] 'Granted six Trumpeters who blew at the Embassy's lodgings in London (Lombard Street): XI daler, 2/9 1605. Granted Some Pipers and trumpeters who played at the Embassy's lodgings (London): ij daler, 3/9.

[2] 'Granted the King of England (James I's) Trumpeters who played at Windsor where the Embassy proceeded from the Church to the castle. And also blew at the lodgings in London: XXX daler, 9/9. The Trumpeters of the Privy Council: j daler, 9/9. Granted Some Trumpeters and Instrumentalists who played at the Embassy's lodgings: i engelot, 9/9. Granted five of the King of England's Instrumentalists who played outside the Embassy's lodgings at Richmond: X daler, 20/9'; Footnotes 1 and 2 both T.K.U.A., Speciel Del Gesandtskabsregnskaber, 7 (Henry Ramelius's Accounts, 1605).

143

on one occasion when they performed together with 'Nogle Pibere' (some pipers) they 'spillede' (played); but when the *Instrumentister* performed alone or together with *Trommetter*, the usual term is 'ligte' or 'lechte' (played or performed). These embassies took place in the heyday of the Shakespearean period in England and some kind of drama was no doubt produced outside the ambassadors' lodgings in London, Enfield and Richmond.

Once the ensemble of 1591–92 in Nyköping, Sweden, had been reinforced by the arrival of Kingman and Gibson, the preparations for the performances in connection with the wedding celebrations on August 27–29 were started in earnest. The addition of these two probably also meant a reorganisation of the company, with more emphasis being placed upon the drama. Nevertheless, reading between the lines, it would seem that the theatrical efforts of the company were either not appreciated or else, on account of language difficulties, not understood by Duke Charles and his court in the same way as were the trumpeters and drummers, and the music and acrobatics. This would at least seem to be reason behind the fact that all the English trumpeters stayed behind in the Duke's service after October 5, 1592, when all the players except one left Nyköping. This may, of course, have been a matter of expense, since the players received the higher pay, but it does not seem likely that such an arrangement was dictated entirely by financial considerations.

After the majority of the English company had left Nyköping, the player and trumpeters left behind cannot have given any performances, as indeed is borne out by the accounts for the period. They were instead employed as musicians and acted as trumpeters (drummers) on board the Duke's warships and elsewhere. The trumpeters were also used as heralds, messengers, ceremonial guards and as extras. It should also be noted that among the trumpeters in the Nyköping company there was a boy, Nicholas King, who in accordance with the custom of the time could have been used in female parts. Four English trumpeters, John Howse, John and Robert Vaughan, and Philip Bruggis, either accompanied or preceded Duke Charles to Hegnetorp to meet his bride-to-be. They did not return to Nyköping until August 25, just before the wedding. Presumably Nicholas King and Richard Raph joined the instrumentalists or players during this period to take part in the rehearsals for the wedding celebrations.

In conclusion, it can be said that the following facts are known about the activities of the English company at Nyköping. The players certainly took part in the arrangements for Charles Sture's wedding on October 17, 1591, in the wedding ceremonies for a number of court officials on March 27–29, 1592, and in Duke Charles's wedding on August 28, 1592. It is highly probable that the company also performed on the occasion of Maurice Leijonhufvud's marriage to Amelia von Hatzfeld on September 3, 1592, when most of the guests at Duke Charles's wedding were also invited. Besides these occasions, it can be assumed that the company performed for the Duke's court on those days when they are accounted as having dined at the Duke's table. All these performances were at Nyköping and there is no record to show that the players performed anywhere else in Sweden during their stay. On the other hand, several trumpeters accompanied the Duke on his travels on different occasions, in particular in August 1592, when he went to meet Princess Christine of Holstein.

It is not known which plays were performed by the English company. We know from the warrant by which he was engaged at Hesse that Philip Kingman wrote several dramas there, and it is probable that he did the same at Nyköping. No such dramas by him are extant, presumably because they never appeared in print. In this connection it is worth noting, however, that the earliest German play with which English players on the Continent can be associated is *Elisa*, otherwise called *Edward III*, by Philip Waimer,[1] with a plot rather like that of the anonymous English play, *The Reign of King Edward the third*, printed in London 1596.[2] The German play, *Elisa*, was printed at Gdańsk in 1591, the year the English company arrived at Nyköping. Its title runs as follows:

Elisa. / Eine Newe vnd / lüstige Comoedia, Von / Eduardo dem Dritten / dieses Namens, Könige, in Engel-/landt, Undt Fraw Elisen / einer gebornen Gräffin von / Warwitz, Gestellet / Durch / Philippum Waimern von Dantzigk, B.R.D. Summum crede nefas, animam præferre pudori, / Et propter vitam, vivendi perdere causas.[3] / Gedruckt zu Dantzigk, durch / Jacobum Rhodum / 1591. / (Berlin, Danzig).

---

[1] Professor and D.Ph., Master of the High School of Gdańsk.

[2] Cf. C. F. Tucker Brooke, *The Shakespeare Apocrypha*, pp. 67–101.

[3] 'Deem it to be the summit of impiety to prefer existence to honour, and for the sake of life to sacrifice life's only end'; Juvenal, *Satires*, 8, 79–84.

The preface is dated Gdańsk, May 18, 1591. This date provides further evidence that the time was ripe for English companies to appear on the Continent. Moreover, at this time there was a lively political and cultural exchange between Sweden and Poland, so that it is not entirely outside the bounds of possibility that plays of some kind reached the English company at Nyköping from Gdańsk[1]

It should moreover be remembered that among the foremost guests from abroad at Duke Charles's wedding at Nyköping in August 1592 were the two counts, John and Christopher of East Friesland, the sons of Duke Charles's sister, Catherine Vasa. They had been in Italy[2] 1589/90 and in Poland[3] 1591/92. From Poland they went straight to Nyköping for the wedding, and were the first guests to arrive, in August 1592.[4] They remained in Sweden as the guests of Duke Charles until May 11, 1593, when, accompanied by Nicholas King,[5] the apprentice among the players, they embarked from Ny Lödöse (Gothenburg) for England with a letter of introduction from Duke Charles to Helena, Marchioness of Northampton.[6] For this latter leg of their journey, Count Edzard II of East Friesland had issued them with a passport to Queen Elizabeth dated May 9, 1593.[7] Elizabeth replied[8] in French on July 27, 1593, and began by emphasizing the family ties between the young counts and the royal house of Sweden:

... la lignée de leur mere du sang royal du roy tres illustre Gustavus de Suède,[9] auquel nous avons eu beaucoup d'obligation.[10]

The Queen also noted the good education and wisdom of her guests:

... faisants profession tant des lettres que des armes.[11]

[1] Cf. Johannes Bolte, *Das Danziger Theater im 16. und 17. Jahrhundert*, Bonn 1895, 22 ff., and Fredén, *Friedrich Menius*, 190 and 205 ff.

[2] Fürstliches Haus — Reisen; Niedersächsisches Staatsarchiv, Aurich/East Friesland.

[3] *Ibid.*

[4] *Aegyp. Serv.*, 616.

[5] Cf. p. 79.

[6] *Cal. Car. IX*, 82 f. and 88 f., and Hertig Karls registratur, fol. 104 v and 106 v, RA.

[7] SP 81/7, fol. 126 ff., PRO.

[8] *Ibid.*, fol. 152 f.

[9] Gustavus Vasa, the first national king of Sweden. Cf. Index.

[10] '... their mother's lineage with the blood royal of the renowned King Gustavus Vasa of Sweden, to whom We are much indebted'; op. cit.

[11] '... professionals both as men of letters and as officers'; op. cit.

In a letter[1] dated London, July 25, 1593, the two counts thank William Cecil, Lord Burghley, for the 'entertainment' at his family residence at Theobalds, Hertfordshire, the previous Sunday. Thus Counts John and Christopher of East Friesland, shortly after visiting Sweden in the early 1590's, were guests at the court of Queen Elizabeth and while there may quite possibly have come in contact with English literary circles.

It was Henry Francklin, Duke Charles's ambassador in England, who engaged the Elizabethan players in the summer of 1591 for service at the Duke's court at Nyköping. The company was not a body of strolling players who turned to Duke Charles as a possible source of patronage, and no evidence has been found to show that interest in the theatre at Nyköping had been influenced by the visits of English companies to Denmark and elsewhere.

One of the reasons for engaging this company was that Duke Charles was negotiating a second marriage. The wedding did not take place until the end of August 1592, however, so the Englishmen remained at Nyköping for thirteen months all told.

On the other hand, there is no doubt that the engagement of this company by Duke Charles was part of the overture to his acquiring an English wife, though in fact nothing came of these plans. The transactions concerning the company of players were proof of England's friendly relations with Duke Charles and Sweden, and may well have been intended to counter the trade in 'muskets, powder and shot' which England carried on with Russia in 1590 and 1591 during the latter's war against Sweden.

It has not been possible to say with certainty just how the company bound for Nyköping was recruited. It may be that Helena Northampton and Sir Walter Raleigh, together with William Dethick, Garter King of Arms, negotiated the engagement in London and Greenwich; on the other hand, Lord Thomas Burgh and his wife, Lady Frances Burgh, née Vaughan, may have helped Henry Francklin gather a full company from York, Herefordshire, Radnor and elsewhere in the provinces. In support of the first alternative are the facts that William Dethick was an ardent supporter of the theatre, that Francklin stayed a considerable time in London and Greenwich, and that the last entry from this journey in

[1] SP 81/7, fol. 149 f., PRO.

Francklin's album is dated July 20, 1591, in William Dethick's hand. However, one would expect in this case to find that the majority of the players had connections with London theatrical life and Queen Elizabeth's court, and this is not substantiated by the records. The biographical details, in fact, support the second alternative. Thus the leading player in the company, Philip Kingman, was a native of Herefordshire according to *Coryat's Crudities*, while John and Robert Vaughan, both of them trumpeters, were in all probability members of some branch of the Vaughan family residing in the Welsh marches. The Exchequer Depositions in the Public Record Office mention John and Robert Vaughan as being from Radnorshire in 1590–91. Lady Frances Burgh came from Sutton-on-Derwent, which was owned by the father, John Vaughan. He had removed to York as a member of the well-known family of Vaughan from Porthamal in Brecknock.

Duke Charles's agent in London, the merchant draper Thomas Fisk, subsequently transmitted payments to the families[1] of two of the players, but he does not appear to have had anything to do with the engagement of the company.

Thus the genealogical and other details would seem to indicate that the English company which visited Nyköping from 1591–92 was not drawn from the London theatres but rather from the provinces.

After the visit of the English company to Nyköping in 1591–92, an entertainment was given in February 1594 at Uppsala Castle on the occasion of Sigismund of Poland's coronation as King of Sweden. The records of the Swedish Parliament have an entry for February 12, 1594 (old style), which runs as follows:

Upå denne tisdag gaf konungen sigh tid att se et commediae, löije, ageret af the Välsche.[2]

and this is confirmed by an entry in Abraham Brahe's diary for the 11th of February (old style):

... Daghen ther effter hade kongen Hertigerne, och hertiginnerne till gääst bleff ta enn Comedia agerett på slottet.[3]

as well as by the Austrian notary in Queen Anne's suite who wrote:

---

[1] Cf. p. 75.

[2] 'Upon this Tuesday (Shrove Tuesday) the King took time to see a comedy performed by the Italians'; op. cit.

[3] '... The next day the King had the Dukes and the Duchesses as his guests at a party during which a comedy was performed at the Castle (in Uppsala)'; op. cit., 2.

Den 22 [new style] haben Ir Khön. M:t faßnacht gehalten undt seindt diesen tag fröhlich gewesen mit springen und tanzen wie auch auf den abent mit tragedien in wellscher sprach da dann Ir M:t engegen gewesen sambt dem ganczen frauenzimmer und hoffgesindt bis in die halbe nacht.[1]

while Olof von Dalin has the following to say of the coronation celebrations:

'Fet-tisdag d. 12. Febr. höll Konungen Fastlags-gästebud, som om aftonen skulle lyktas med en Italiensk Comedia[2] af en Salvator Fabriz: wid middagsmåltiden war hertigen tilstädes; men från skåde-spelet warnades han af Gref Hieronymus Strozzi, som fådt kunskap, at något stämplades mot hans lif.'[3]

A more detailed account of this plot against Duke Charles's life is to be found in *Exegesis Historica,* an anonymous defence of the 'Massacre of Linköping' of 1600 in which many of Sigismund's supporters in Sweden were summarily executed. Good reasons have been given for assuming that this defence was in fact written by Duke Charles himself with the help of Nils Chesnecopherus. The plot to murder the Duke during the coronation celebrations in February 1594 is recounted as follows:

'Imo vero non minus est exercrandum, quod Sigismundus Rex ipsa festivitate Coronationis, nefariam erga Patruum charissimum foverit mentem Vbsaliae, in S. C. aliquot vexilla Heudonum ex insidiis subordonare statuens, à quibus sceleratissime trucida-
retur, idque pro votis successisset, nisi quidam nomine Hyeronimus Strozi, S. C. has vita
insidias detexisset, prout eius confessio attestatur. Hoc autem dolo non succedente quan-
dam Comaediam per nonnullos Italos agendam insticuit larvatos, & nudis ensibus ac-

---

[1] 'On 22 February 1594 [new style] Their Majesties held a Shrove Tuesday feast; it was a joyous occasion with acrobatics and dancing, while in the evening there were tragedies in Italian, at which His Majesty was present as were all the ladies of the court and the court servants until far into the night'; op. cit.

[2] Michel Levassor, *Histoire de Louis XIII, roi de France,* ..., 1, 252.

[3] 'Shrove Tuesday, 12 February, the King held a Lenten Feast that was to be enlivened in the evening with an Italian Comedy by one Salvator Fabriz: the Duke was present at the dinner but was warned away from the play by Count Hieronymus Strozzi, who had learned of a plot against his life'; Swea Rikes Historia 3: 2, 295. Cf. Jacob Typotius, *Relatio historica de regno Sveciae et bellis civilibus atque externis* ..., 1606.

149

cinctos, quod raro auditum est quos inter erat Salvator quidam Fabriz, nominatus, co-
memorate Actor & Author Tragediae, quae diem & noctem integre tenuit, variis gesti-
culationibus intenta & occupata, Ille autem Salvator Fabriz. S. C. eam Tragediam
moliebatur, quae non multum deleclasset; Quamvis S. C. has stutorum & sicariorum ge-
sticulationes parviduceret, in quibus nec comparere voluit: Verum si illuc S. C. adve-
nisset (ut Regis Sigismundi & Consiliariorum opinio fuit) crudelissime trucidata fuisset; Quam nefariam machinationem Iacobus Typotius in sua Relatione Historica con-
firmat & attestatur, qui Pontificiae sector religionis erat & eo tempore Ubsaliae con-
stitutus, cui omnes Polonorum & Jesuitarium occultae molitiones probe fuerant perspectae.
Que etiam nefaria machinatio, infidis illis Consiliariis, qui postmodum Regem Sigismundum armata manu infestum in hoc Regnum deduxerunt, caussamque primariam
huic discordiae praebuerunt perniciosae explorata satis extitit, Ideo sese primo die & no-
cte, quilibet eorum latebras coniiciebat, ut si Tragaedia illa successum nacta fuisset spe-
ratum, innocentes à Justi viri sanguine existerent, quemadmodum suam deposuit Pi-
latus excusationem: Deus tamen Clementissimus eorum nefaria proposita, ex sua mise-
ricordia infinita impedivis, ut sperato frusstrarentur progressu.
Neque minus illud memoriae commendandum, quod porro in ipsa corona-tionis solen-
nitate usu venit Ubsaliae: Quippe si obiiceretur Illustrissimum Principem: tantospere gu-
bernationi Suecane Reipub. inhiasse è diametro contrarium evincet veritas. Quandoquidem maior pars Ordinum Regni, non semel, sed frequentissime S. C. proclamaverit
invitaveritque, ad Regni Diadema capessendem ingeminas.[1]

[1] 'Yes, indeed, and no less despicable is the manner in which King Sigismund during the actual coronation festivities in Uppsala hatched an infamous scheme against his beloved uncle, whereby he would send out some troops from his body-guard in secret against Duke Charles, by whom the Duke was to be murdered in the most terrible manner. And this would have happened as Sigismund planned had

When assessing this anonymous description it should be noted that *Exegesis historica* was printed in 1610—sixteen years after the imputed plot. Duke Charles does not mention the plot in his almanac. The period 8–12 February 1594 is summed up in a single word:

Kröningsfestligheter.[1]

Perhaps it was not until later that the Duke fully realized the danger that had threatened him during the coronation celebrations.

The name Salvator Fabriz is interesting in this context. Here we have one of the foremost fencing-masters of the day—both playwright and player—a man who served Sigismund III of Poland–Sweden as well as Christian IV of Denmark (from 1601 to 1607), besides publishing one of

not a certain Hieronymus Strozzi disclosed this scheme to Duke Charles, as his evidence witnesses. After the failure of this treacherous scheme, Sigismund decided to have a comedy performed by some Italian actors, masked and armed with drawn rapiers—the like of which one has seldom heard—among them one Salvator Fabriz, actor in and author of the above-mentioned tragedy, which was played unceasingly day and night, holding the audience enthralled and full of lively mimicry and expressive gestures. Salvator Fabriz endeavoured, however, in every way to perform this tragedy before Duke Charles, though the play would not have entertained him greatly. But Duke Charles set little story by the actions and gestures of such fools and assassins and did not whish to appear in public in such company. Had Duke Charles attended, as King Sigismund and his Councillors hoped, then the Duke would have been most cruelly murdered. This infamous strategem is verified and witnessed too by Jacobus Typotius in his historical account, for he was of the papal faith and at this time engaged in Uppsala and well acquainted with the doings of all the Poles and Jesuits.

The infamous murder plot was also known to the ill-renowned, false Councillors who subsequently brought King Sigismund here to Sweden with evil intent and accompanied by armed forces, which was the origin of the present civil war. Thus all these Councillors suddenly went into hiding on the first day and night in order that, if the tragedy took the turn for which they hoped, they would appear innocent of the just man's death in the same way as Pilate washed his hands. God's infinite charity thwarted their infamous intent, however, in keeping with His great mercy, so their hopes of success came to nought.

Similarly one should relate for posterity what took place during the actual coronation ceremony in Uppsala. For should one accuse the most illustrious Prince, Duke Charles, of having greatly aspired to government over the Swedish realm, the historical circumstances will refute this and prove the opposite. Since the majority of the Estates of the Realm not once but several times called upon and offered Duke Charles the royal crown during their sighs and lamentations. ...';
anon., *Exegesis Historica, non minus* ..., 1610, pp. 78 f. (114 f.).

[1] 'Coronation celebrations'; *Cal. Car. IX,* 96.

151

the first modern textbooks on fencing.[1] It is also conceivable that Fabriz helped to build up Christian IV's pro-Catholic attitude. At all events, the combination of the plot to murder Duke Charles during Sigismund's coronation in Uppsala in 1594 and the non-stop coronation spectacle featuring Salvator Fabriz in various fencing scenes tempts one to speculate whether accounts relayed from Sweden may have inspired Shakespeare to the duel with poisoned rapiers between Hamlet and Laertes.

A little more than a year after these coronation celebrations in Uppsala, a comedy was performed for Duke Charles at the Castle in Stockholm. An entry for the day in question—March 3, 1595—in Abraham Brahe's diary runs as follows:

Den 3 Martij. Ageredes een Comedia opå slottet för Hertigen i then stoore [Rijß-saalenn, oansett att Presterne myckett wore ther emott].[2]

In order to appreciate the historical circumstances surrounding this performance at Stockholm Castle it is necessary to consider some events which preceded it.

The following entry occurs in Duke Charles's almanac for 1594:

'December 9. [1594] föddes min sån Gustafwus Adolff, gudh alzmechtigh latte ware skett honom till låff, äre och pris och hans evige siels salighett och ås såsom föräldrerne äre till hugnett och gledie och föddes han emellom 7 och 8 åm morrenen. 14. afferdige iagh Jörren Classån och Erick Stake till Dennemarck och Holsten att biyde fadderer, gudh förlene ware sket i en godh stund och giffue dem lycke på resen, ...'[3]

In January 1595 a Swedish ambassador to Denmark arrived in Copenhagen and his reception is commented on as follows by the Danish historian Niels Slange in his book on Christian IV:

---

[1] De Lo Schermo overo scienza d'Arme. Di Salvatore Fabris. Capo dell'ordine del sette cori. Copenhagen at Henrico Waltkirch 1606. Cf. Index and Plate 7.

[2] 'March 3. A comedy was performed at the Castle for the Duke in the great Hall of State, regardless of the clergy being very much against it'; Abraham Brahes Tidebok. (Ed. by C. M. & Reinh. Stenbock.) P. A. Norstedt & Söners Förlag, Stockholm 1920, pp. VII & 11. In the extant text, which is a copy, the part reproduced in brackets here has been crossed out.

[3] 'December 9 [1594]. My son Gustavus Adolphus born, God Almighty grant him praise, honour and glory and salvation to his eternal soul, a comfort and joy to his parents, he was born between 7 and 8 in the morning. 14th. Sent Jörren Classån and Erick Stake to Denmark and Holstein to invite godparents, God grant it happened at a propitious time and give them good fortune on their journey, ...'; op. cit.

152

1595

Dend anden Nyt-Aars-Dag i dette Aar ankom til Kiøbenhafn Hertug Carls Gesandte fra Sverrig, Jørgen Clauson til Bibye, med et Følge af 4 unge Svenske Adel foruden andre Opvartere, for at indbyde Kongen til Fadder og Vidne over hans nyføde Prinzes Daab, som skulle forrettes den 9de Dag udi Blide-Maaned eller Februario. Printzen var fød Aaret tilførn udi Christ-Maaned eller Decembri. Gesandten blef med stor Aere imodtaget, saa at der var ingen Forskiael imellem hans og andre kronede Hoveders Gesandters Opførsel og Antagelse uden at da hand aflagde sit Vaerf og Aerinde, stod Kongen med sin Hat paa, men Gesandten stood aaben Hovedet, saa og at Kongen gik ikke videre imod ham end et Trin, da hand rakte ham sin Haand. Hand talte Svensk og Kongen svarede ham self paa Dansk. Christian Friis til Borr-Bye, som var af de Friiser, som føre de 3 sorte Egerne udi Skiold, og som da var øverst Secreterer og siden blef Canceller, blef strax udnaefnt til Gesandt til Sverrig, Kongens Person at føre og hans Staed vid Daaben at beklaede; da Printzen blef kaldt Gustaf Adolph, som siden blef en stor Konge over Sverrig og Seyer-Herre baade udi Lifland og Tydskland. ...[1]

In connection with the christening of Gustavus Adolphus, Olof von Dalin[2] mentions a horoscope for the young prince that had been cast by Tycho Brahe, the famous Danish astronomer and astrologist, who had predicted as early as 1571 that a prince would be born fairly soon in Scandinavia who would greatly influence events in the Scandinavian countries and in Germany. From the astrological point of view, Brahe found the birth of the prince at 8 a.m. on December 9, 1594, 'rather remarkable'.

---

[1] '1595. On the second day of the New Year there are arrived in Copenhagen Duke Charles's Ambassador from Sweden, Jörren Classån, and a retinue of four young Swedish Noblemen as well as other followers, to invite the King to be God-father and Witness at the christening of his newborn Prince, to be held on February 9th. The Prince was born last year in December. The Ambassador was received with great honour, so that there was no distinction between his presentation and acceptance and that of the ambassadors of other monarchs: while he declared his business and mission, the King stood with his hat on, but the Ambassador stood bareheaded, then the King did not go more than one step towards him when he extended his hand. He spoke Swedish and the King replied in Danish. Christian Friis of Borr-Bye, who belonged to the branch of the Friis's who bear the three black oaks in their coat-of-arms, and who was then Chief Secretary and subsequently became Chancellor, was appointed shortly afterwards Ambassador to Sweden, to represent the King's person and act for him at the christening; the Prince was named Gustavus Adolphus and later became a great king of Sweden, victorious both in Livonia and in Germany'; Slange, 1,82.

[2] Olof von Dalin, *Swea Rikes Historia* ..., 3: 2, 317 ff.

153

One of those who accompanied Christian Friis on his embassy to Stockholm was Sivert Grubbe, who comments in his diary on the composition of the embassy as follows:

Jeg tilligemed Jakob Rosenkrands, Eske Bilde den yngre og Erik Hardenberg bleve ham medgivne paa Rejsen, og det blev paa vor naadige Herres Wegne os paalagt at yde ham al skyldig Opmaerksomhed.[1]

Among these names it is worth noting that of Eske Bille. There is no evidence that Tycho Brahe visited Sweden in person at this time but his mother's maiden name was Berta Bille, so we may suppose that Brahe received inside information from his close relative Eske Bille concerning events in Stockholm early in 1595.

The ceremonies connected with this christening were noted by Abraham Brahe in his diary as follows:

Den 9 Feb [1595]: Giorde Hertigen sin sons Barnsööl vtij stockholm der till Christiern fris konung Christierns vtij danmarcks Sändebud Teslikest The Holstenische Commissier worde opledsagede opå Slottet. Ward och så Lindorm Bonde konungens i Polans Sendebud then komun hitt i Ricket till Hertigen och Rickezens Radh vtsent hade om Riligions och Regemens sacker att förhandla, vpfordrett och till gest Beden igenom greff Carll Sture och migh, Män han endtschyllade sigh och ville intett komme. ... Den 14 Feb (1595): Latt Hertigen Tractere sendingebuden i theres Herberge der och månge aff the Swensche Herrar och Ridderschap wore till städes, sedan droge sendebuden till upsala att besee det, ...[2]

The kitchen accounts show that in the week of March 3–8, 1595, the Nyköping court—Duke Charles, Charles Sture, Henry Francklyn, Dr.

[1] 'Myself together with Jakob Rosenkrands, Eske Bille the younger and Erik Hardenberg accompanied him (Christian Friis) on the journey, and we were instructed by our gracious Lord (Christian IV) to pay him (Duke Charles) all due attentions;' "Sivert Grubbes Dagbog", edited by Holger Fr. Rørdam in *Danske Magazin* 4.2.4., pp. 361–406, and 4.4.1., pp. 4–83.

[2] '9 February [1595]: Duke Charles celebrated in Stockholm the christening of his son. This ceremony was attended by the Danish ambassadors and the representatives from Holstein at the Castle in Stockholm. Lindorm Bonde, King Sigismund of Poland's ambassador, who had come to Sweden to negotiate with Duke Charles and the Council of the Realm concerning religion and the government of the realm, was also approached with an invitation to attend this celebration via Carl Sture and me. He asked to be excused, however, and explained that he was otherwise engaged ... '14 February [1595]: The Duke invited the ambassadors and representatives to dinner in their inn together with many of the Swedish Gentry and Nobility. Shortly afterwards the envoys journeyed to Uppsala to see that city.' Op. cit. p. 10. Cf. Hist. bibl. 2, 267.

Teofilus Homodeus, Maurice Stenßon Leijonhufvud, Lybert Kafern, James Hill and others—resided at Stockholm Castle.[1] March 3rd was a Monday in Lent and one researcher has claimed that the 'Comedia' was probably just a Lenten morality, i.e. a performance similar to those given in churches and other places with the approval of the clergy, the religious drama being mixed with burlesque humour.[2] Profane drama, on the other hand, was viewed with suspicion at this time by Lutheran and Catholic clergy alike, not only in Sweden but everywhere in the Christian world, so that one is inclined to believe that the performance which Abraham Brahe reports as being against the wishes of the clergy was quite simply what he writes—a comedy.

It is interesting to note that the Danish and Holstein embassies to the christening journeyed on 15 February 1595 to see the city of Uppsala, so that (although I have not been able to find any definite record of when they left for home) it is conceivable, considering the state of communications in those days, that both embassies were back in Stockholm on March 3rd and saw the 'Comedia' at the Castle there.

The christening of Prince Gustavus Adolphus on February 9th was more than a family occasion for the House of Vasa. It seems that the event was accompanied by considerable political activity in Duke Charles's Stockholm. Lindorm Bonde, the Polish delegate, declined an invitation to attend the ceremony but appears from Abraham Brahe's diary to have been in Stockholm on March 1st that year:

Den 1 Martij [1595] [War Cantzeleren Her Erich Sparre med migh hos lindorm Bonde till aftenmaltid].[3]

It seems therefore even more probable than in the case of the Danish and Holstein embassies that Lindorm Bonde as the representative of Poland, accompanied by Erik Sparre and Abraham Brahe, saw the

[1] Kungl. Hofförtärningen 1595; SA.

[2] Cf. Chambers, *Mediaeval Stage*, 2, 68–105 and 179–198.

[3] '1 March [1595]: The Chancellor, Eric Sparre, and I dined with Lindorm Bonde'; op. cit., p. 11. Concerning the significance of the brackets, see p. 152, n. 2. It seems that Abraham Brahe's diary was copied out with a view to publishing it, any entries that appeared inopportune being crossed out in this connection. The entry for March 1, 1595, has been entirely deleted, as has most of the entry for March 3rd; this suggests that approaches and attempts at a reconciliation between King Sigismund and Duke Charles were made as late as the early part of 1595. It is most unfortunate that we lack Duke Charles's own diary for the historic events of 1595 in Stockholm.

'Comedia' at Stockholm Castle on 3 March 1595. It has not been possible to establish the nationality of this company of players. From James Hill's presence at Stockholm Castle on this occasion it might be argued that the company was English but against this it must be noted that the Swedish Lutheran clergy, with their Calvinist leanings inspired by Duke Charles, do not appear to have protested on previous occasions against English and Scottish players with puritan leanings. At this time Duke Charles was desirous of a reconciliation with King Sigismund and the attendance of the letter's ambassador, Lindorm Bonde, together with notable Swedish Catholics, chiefly Abraham Brahe and Erik Sparre, coupled with the attitude of the Swedish clergy, may indicate that the performance at Stockholm Castle on March 3, 1595, was given by Catholic Poles from Lindorm Bonde's retinue. This at all events would make the Swedish clergy's reaction more understandable, considering the plot to murder Duke Charles a year earlier during Sigismund's coronation celebrations in Uppsala. The phrase in Abraham Brahe's diary is also worth noting—'a comedy was performed ... for the Duke'—hardly the wording one would expect if the company had been in the Duke's own service. Entertainments at Stockholm Castle came under the authority of Sigismund, who was still King of Poland–Sweden.

We know that theatricals were also performed when Duke Charles was crowned Charles IX of Sweden in Uppsala on 15 March 1607. The account of the coronation mentions Duke Joachim Carl of Brunswick and his court servants as the actors:

Om aftonen anrättades ett härligit gästbud tijt och alle Ständerne budne och therwid plägade woro. När måltiden wore öfverståndet, och borden wore alle utsijdes satte kom Hertig Joachim Carl af Brunsswijk med sine hoftienere alle förkläde och förmummede och anrättade ther i Stora Salen ett Skodespeel.[1]

---

[1] 'In the evening a splendid feast was arranged to which all the Estates were invited and entertained. When the meal was over and the tables all removed, Duke Joachim Carl of Brunswick came with his court servants all disguised and masked and performed a play in the Great Hall'; Kungl. Arkiv 6. Karl IX. Lefnadsförhållanden, testamenten m. m.; and K 17. Fasc. 'Konung Carl den IX[s] och drottnings kröningsprocess i Uppsala den 15 Mart. 1607.' Copies of these documents in 'Berättelse om Karl IX[s] kröning', L 500, Handskriftsavdelningen, UUB (a collection of manuscripts that comes from Elias Palmsköld and A. A. von Stiernman and has been donated to UUB by Olof von Celsius Jr.).

Charles IX's almanac tells us that Duke Joachim Carl of Brunswick arrived in Stockholm on 23 September 1606 and remained in Sweden as the guest of the King until 3 June 1608, when he sailed from Kalmar to return to Germany. Abraham Brahe, who was Duke Joachim Carl's guest in Stockholm on 16 November 1606, notes in his diary that news of the Duke's arrival in Stockholm came two days earlier, i.e. on 21 September. This diary also tells us that the Duke's servants (*tienere*) were involved in the murder of a Scottish nobleman, John Neave, on 27 August 1607 after a tavern brawl in Stockholm.[1] Although we know very little about these servants, a reply from Charles IX—dated Kopparberget 25 November 1607—to a letter from the Council of State concerning Neave's fate does mention some of their names:

'... de andre Niderwdd (Netherwood), Geristorff, Huge (Hughes) och hwadh de heete, ...'[2]

Judging from these names, some at least of Duke Joachim Carl's *tienere* were of English rather than German origin. The description of the entertainment after the coronation in 1607 indicates that this was not a professional company but a group of amateurs headed by Joachim Carl. In other words, a parallel to the performance given by noblemen in Cracow on 25 May 1592[3] and a forerunner of the productions undertaken later in the 18th century by Gustavus III of Sweden.[4]

Theatrical entertainment was also provided at the next coronation in Sweden, for Gustavus Adolphus on 12 October 1617.[5] William Portington, an Englishman engaged in Swedish service as an architect and builder, writes as follows in an undated letter to Sir Harbottle Grimston:

'On the thirde daie there was performed greate tilting and tournamentes with the barriours, but one amongst the rest having his beaver unbuckled received a hurte in the head.

On the 4th, 5th, and 6th daies 1, great banquitting, feasting, and revelling, The Duke van Saxee being there a stranger, daunced with the Queene.

A masque performed on the 7th daie at night. By the Skotts, Frenche and Swedons being in number 24. The order of it. A Tartar was sente into

[1] *Cal. Car. IX*, pp. 145, 151, 156, 157; and *Abraham Brahes Tidebok*, pp. 64, 72.

[2] '... the other Netherwood, Geristorff, Hughes and what they are called ...' RR 25.11.1607, fol. 216 v, RA.

[3] Cf. pp. 51–52.

[4] The van Suchtelen Papers (Documents concerning the Swedish Royal Family), Saltykov Library, Leningrad, U.S.S.R. (Microfilm KB, Stockholm).

[5] Kungl. Arkiv C, Gustaf II Adolfs lefnadsförhållanden m. m., RA.

the presence representing the majestick state of a kinge, who presenting a crowen and a scepter to his ma^{tie} delivered this Embassie: that there wer certen Tartarians that craud accesse into the presence, which was graunted with all honorable sufferance. The messenger returned delivered to the maskers the kings pleasure. The maskers were mounted, furnished with complet acutrimentes, all cladd in red and white tinssell, hattes and fethers sutable, everie horse carying in his frounte a plume of white fethers. Betweene the maskeers, 2 and 2, in rancke, rid a Tartar ca(-r-)ijng a burninge taper or a torche. Dismounting theimselves within the courte, they came upp into the presence, and instantly, upon a stande made after their severall homages doone to the kinge. The first twoo drewe the rest into the forme of a ringe, and, then doubling their files, and ranckes answereable to the true decorum of the warrs: They singled theimselves out againe. Standing 24 in the forme of a file: that doone some fell to dancinge, and some to dicing. After many exquisite and dilicate dances p(-er-)formed, and much money wounne and lost: The maskeers departed. After theim came in certen Ragged Satyrs Plaijing verie musicallie upon severall Instrumentes, and standing aloof before His Mtie in a rancke. Then appeared 22 Laplanders all clade in the skinnges of wilde deare, with the haire outwards according to the true habite and wearing of that cuntrie. They danc'd before His Mtie: but in such admirable fashion, like so many Antiques and soe variable, as caused the Kinge and all the honorable Spectators to laughe hartilie.'[1]

Here we have a completely different type of entertainment, reminiscent of Ben Jonson's Masques. Portington was in fact closely associated with Ben Jonson and Inigo Jones. Ben Jonson himself relates that it was Portington who arranged the wings for *The Masque of Beauty* (1608).[2] We also know that William Portington, The King's Master Carpenter, was 'an officer of the Board of Works', appointed during the reign of Elizabeth I on 20 August 1589, and that according to 'The Pell's Issue Rolls' for 19 May 1610 he received a salary of 'one shilling a day'. His visit to Sweden was not the only occasion on which he served abroad. In 1620, for instance, 'the King's Carpenter with many other carpenters and artificers went overseas to Guiana to help with the erection of wooden buildings at the Field of the Cloth of Guld'. This was only nine years before his death on 28 March 1629 at the age of 84.

It is interesting to note that Portington's description of the performance at the coronation of Gustavus Adolphus has certain points in common with the Harmonia scene from Ben Jonson's *Masque of Beauty*

[1] Gorhambury Mss. B. 136; Hertfordshire County Record Office, Hertford. (Publ. in Hist. Mss. Comm. 64th Report, 112 ff.)

[2] Cf. Chamb., *Eliz. Stage*, 1, 180 and 3, 380, and Herford & Simpson, *Ben Jonson*, 7, 188–190, and 10, 462.

which, as we have seen, had had scenery devised by Portington. Jonson's scene runs as follows:

225.   'Harmonia

A Personage, whose dressing had something of all the others, and had her robe painted full of *Figures*. Her head was compass'd with a crowne of *Gold*, hauing in it seuen jewels equally set. In her hand a *Lyra*, whereon
230. she rested.

This was the Ornament of the *Throne*. The ascent to which, consisting of sixe steps, was couered with a multitude of *Cupids* (chosen out of the best, and most ingenuous
youth of the *Kingdome*, noble, and others) that were the
235. *Torch-bearers*; and all armed, with *Bowes*, *Quiuers*, *Wings*,
and other *Ensignes of Loue*. On the sides of the *Throne* were curious, and elegant *Arbors* appointed: and behinde in the backe part of the Ile, a Groue, of growne trees laden with golden fruit, which other litle *Cupids* plucked, and
240. threw each at other, whilst on the ground *Leuerets* pick'd
vp the bruised apples, and left them halfe eaten. The ground-plat of the whole was a subtle indented *Maze*: And, in the two formost angles, were two *Fountaines*, that
ran continually, the one *Hebe's*, the other *Hedone's*: In
245. the *Arbors*, were plac'd the *Musicians*, who represented the
Shades of the olde *Poets*, and were attir'd in a *Priest*-like habit of *Crimson*, and *Purple*, with *Laurell* gyrlonds.
The colours of the *Masquers* were varied; the one halfe in *Orenge-tawny*, and *Siluer*: the other in *Sea-greene*, and
250. *Siluer*. The bodies and short skirts of *White*, and *Gold*, to both.
The habite, and dressing (for the fashion) was most curious, and so exceeding in riches, as the *Throne* whereon
they sat, seem'd to be a Mine of light, stroke from their
255. iewels, and their garments.
This *Thorne*, (as the whole Iland mou'd forward, on the water) had a circular motion of it owne, imitating that which were call *Motum mundi*, from the *East* to the *West*, or
the right to the left side. For so *Hom. Ilia. M.* vnderstands
260. by δεξιὰ, *Orientalia mundi*: by ἀριστερὰ, *Occidentalia*. The
steps, whereon the *Cupids* sate, had a motion contrary, with *Analogy, ad motum Planetarum*, from the *West* to the *East*: both which turned with their seurall lights. And with these three varied *Motions*, at once, the whole *Scene* shot
265. it selfe to the land.
Aboue which, the *Moone* was seene in a *Siluer* Chariot, drawne by *Virgins*, to ride in the clouds, and hold them greater light: with the *Signe Scorpio*, and the Character,
plac'd before her.

159

270. The order of this *Scene* was carefully, and ingeniously
dispos'd; and as happily put in act (for the Motions) by
the *Kings* Master Carpenter.[1] The Painters, I must needs
say, (not to belie them) lent small colour to any, to attribute
much of the spirit of these things to their pen'cills. But that
275. must not bee imputed a crime either to the inuention, or designe.
      Here the loud *Musique* ceas'd; and the *Musicians*, which were
placed in the *Arbors*, came forth through the *Mazes*, to the other Land:
singing this full *Song*, iterated
280. in the closes by two *Eccho's*, rising out of the Fountaines.'[2]

The English company in August 1591 presumably sailed direct from
London to Nyköping in an English ship. It is possible that they were
accompanied by Severine John and the two English gun-founders he
had engaged. The cargo consisted of cloth from Thomas Fisk, Duke
Charles's agent in England. It would seem that Severine John and his
two gun-founders disembarked at Elsinore, crossed to Helsingborg and
travelled overland to Gripsholm Castle, where they were on August 15,
1591. The English ship, after staying a while at Elsinore, probably proceeded to Nyköping with Henry Francklin and the English players and
the cargo of cloth. That Henry Francklin was also on board is confirmed
by the fact that, after a long absence, his name reappears in the kitchen
accounts in August 30, 1591, the day before the English company was
presented to the Duke.

No trace of the Nyköping company (1591) has been found either in
Professor Nungezer's *Dictionary of Actors* or in the extensive roll of musicians of different kinds from this period collected in Dr. de Lafontaine's
The King's Musick. Philip Kingman, who joined the company sometime
around May 1, 1592, does, however, appear to have become a prominent
actor among the English companies on the Continent and in London. He
had engagements in Hesse-Cassel with Robert Browne in 1594 and as
first player in Strasburg in 1596 and was in partnership with Philip
Rosseter and others as Porter's Hall patentee in 1615. While Kingman
was undoubtedly a contemporary of Shakespeare, the players engaged
in the summer of 1591 probably belonged to Shakespeare's immediate
predecessors, active in the years around 1590.

[1] William Portington.
[2] Herford & Simpson, *Ben Jonson*, 7, 188–190.

In view of Duke Charles's Calvinist sympathies, it seems justifiable to assume that the members of the English company may have had similar leanings and been the first Puritans from England to find a refuge in Sweden. That the company became thoroughly acquainted with Swedish life is illustrated by the number of its members who asked to have their period of engagement extended after October 5, 1592. Richard Havill and Richard Raph became completely Swedish and remained in Sweden for the rest of their lives.

There are certain indications that Duke Charles's ambassadors, Henry Francklin and Dr. Teofilus, may have been in contact with Oxford and the University Wits there during their stay in England in 1590–91. The Wits included John Lyly, Christopher Marlowe, George Peel, and Robert Greene at this time and as a curiosity it may perhaps be worth mentioning that the name John Lyly, an English captain, appears in Duke Charles's household accounts in a warrant from 1593 for 'Nederlendske Capitainer'. John Lyly was a not uncommon name at this time, however, and no conclusions can be drawn from what is probably only a coincidence.

Henry Francklin's engagement of Philip Kingman and Philip Gibson was probably effected at the same time as he contracted with the rest of the company. These two, who did not arrive at Nyköping until May 1592, probably accompanied a contingent of English mercenaries via the Netherlands and Emden.

The majority of the members of the company returned to England direct, and it would seem that the conveyance of the company to and from Nyköping was largely carried out in conjunction with the engagement of mercenaries from the Netherlands, England, Scotland, France and Germany by Duke Charles for the war against Russia (1589–95).

Any influence that the Nyköping company may have had upon early Swedish drama can be summed up as follows. In the first place, of the members of Duke Charles's court Dr. Teofilus Homodei seems to have been interested in the Elizabethan stage. He probably assisted Francklin in engaging the company in 1591, and while in Gdańsk from 1596 until 1629 he may have had a hand in arranging that several English companies appeared in that city, headquarters for Swedish Catholic migrants. One of the early writers of Swedish drama was Johannes Messenius the elder, who was a brother-in-law of Dr. Teofilus, having like him married a daughter of Arnold von Grothusen, the tutor of Sigismund of Poland. After his marriage Messenius stayed for a year (1607–8) with Dr. Teofilus in Gdańsk and his son, Arnold Messenius, was born in Teofilus's home.[1]

Messenius had come in contact with Jesuit school dramas during his own schooldays at the seminary at Braunsberg and his work has a certain originality too. Nevertheless, there may be something of the 'Elizabethan' in it as well, in its use of the chronicle play so popular during this period. Messenius's plays were written between 1611 and 1614 a few years after he arrived in Sweden.

Another early writer of Swedish drama was Magnus Olai Asteropherus, whose only extant play *Tisbe* appears to be more closely related to the Shakespearean period than is any other Swedish drama. Asteropherus studied abroad and was at Wittenberg in 1604. Apart from his activities as a priest he was also known as a physician. He learned the secrets of this latter profession from Petrus Magnus's book of herbs, a copy of which he received from Johannes Messenius.

Although the English company had no immediate effect on Swedish drama, the possibility remains that Dr. Homodei may have inspired his brother-in-law Messenius while they were both in Gdańsk; Asteropherus, perhaps indirectly, may also have had his attention drawn to English playwrights in this way.

The Englishman James Hill, who was attached to Duke Charles's court at Nyköping at various times in the 1590's, was unquestionably familiar with the English theatrical world of the time. He also seems to have been the chief intermediary in negotiations with Sir Walter Raleigh and the Elizabethan players who visited Nyköping during 1598–1600.

The importance of the visit by the English company to Nyköping in 1591–92 was clearly and more immediately noticeable in another sphere, namely the activities of English companies on the Continent shortly afterwards.

About the time of Duke Charles's wedding, William IV of Hesse-Cassel died[2] and was succeeded by the Landgrave Maurice (1592–1627). Maurice announced his conversion to Calvinism and displayed great interest in English theatrical life. The undated orders for Robert Browne and Philip Kingman can almost certainly be ascribed to the years 1594–95,

---

[1] Cf. p. 201.
[2] Cf. *Cal. Car. IX*, 6.10.1592, p. 81.

since two lutenists, probably members of a larger English company, were in Hesse at the end of 1594 and since Robert Browne was in London on business for the Landgrave in April 1595. Around the turn of the sixteenth century English companies were extremely active in Hesse. William IV's close kinship with Duke Charles and both his wives led to the Landgrave sending an embassy from Hesse to the Duke's wedding. At its head was John Louis von Harstall, who had previously been the young Count Maurice's chamberlain. On the death of his father, Maurice took von Harstall into his own service once more. One is therefore tempted to suppose that it was von Harstall who informed Maurice of the performances by the Elizabethan players during the wedding celebrations at Nyköping in 1592.

PLATE 1b. Duke Charles of Sudermania in 1592 by unknown artist.

PLATE 1a. Princess Christine of Holstein, Duke Charles's second duchess, later queen consort.

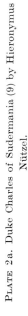

PLATE 2b. King Christian IV of Denmark 1592 (15 years old) by unknown artist.

PLATE 2a. Duke Charles of Sudermania (9) by Hieronymus Nützel.

The Lady Marchionesse of Northampton
Principall Mourner assisted by two
Buckhost Lord Tresuror and the Earle
of Notingham Lord Admirall.

Her trayne assisted by two
Countesses and S.r John
Stanhop Vice chamblaine

PLATE 3. Helena Northampton as First mourner at the funeral of Queen Elizabeth I in 1603.

PLATE 4. Henry Ramelius (Henric Ramel, Sr.) by Karel van Mander, Jr.

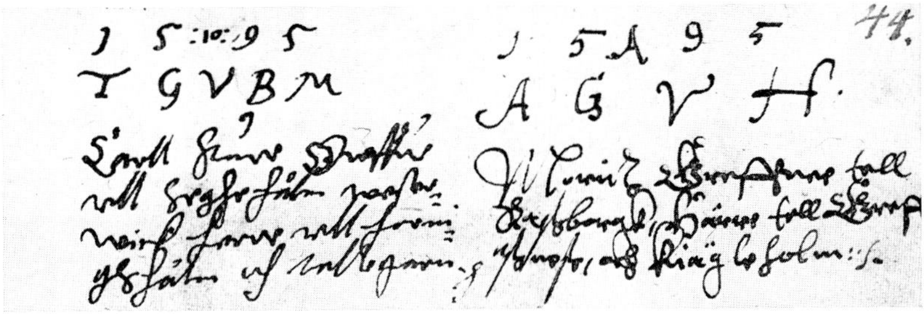

a b

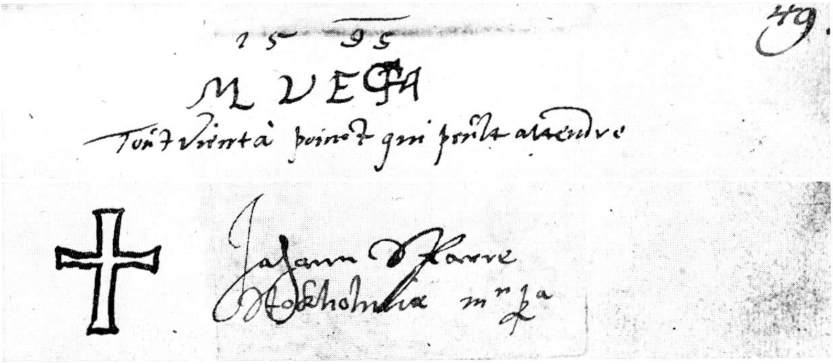

c

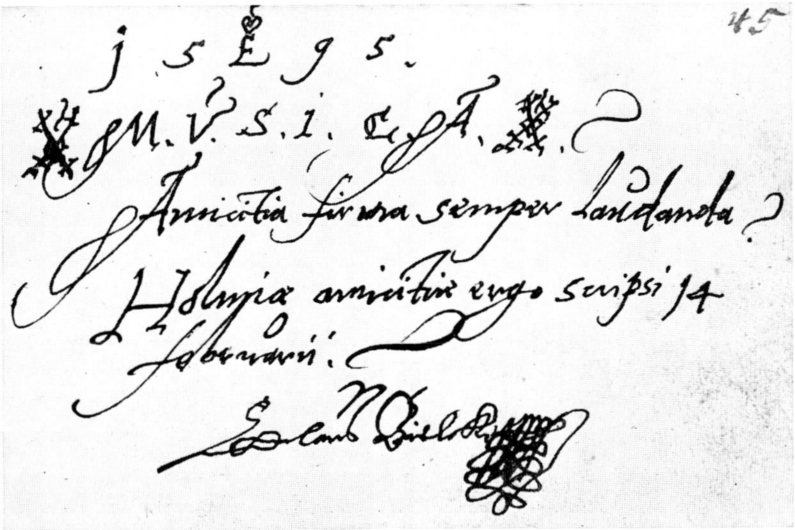

d

PLATE 5. a) Charles Sture. b) Maurice Leijonhufvud. c) John Sparre. d) Nils Bielke. Entries in Morten Bornholm's album, probably all February, 1595.

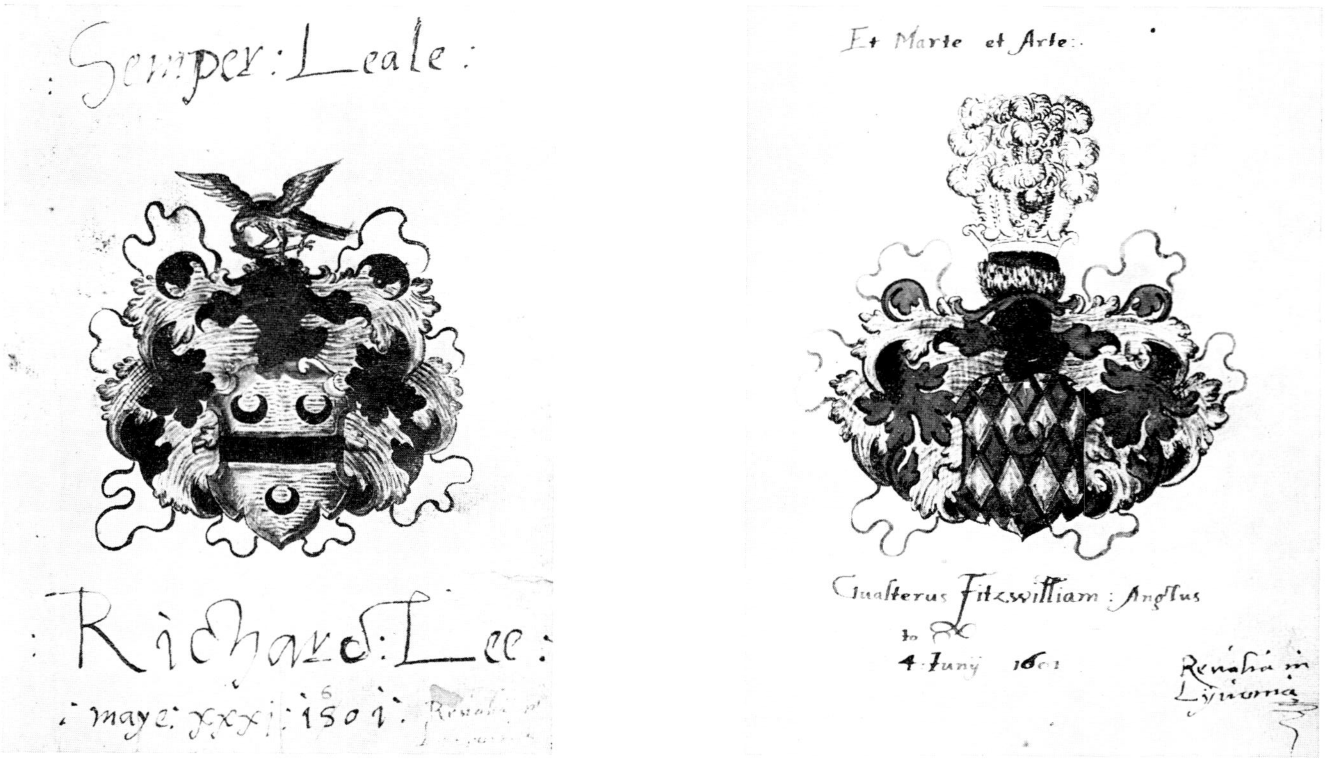

Et Marte et Arte.

Semper: Leale:

Richard: Lee:
: maye: xxij: 1601. Rivali...

Gualterus Fitzsvilliam : Anglius
4 Juny 1601

PLATE 6. Richard Lee and Walter Fitz-William in Henry Francklin's album, Tallinn, Esthonia, USSR, 1601.

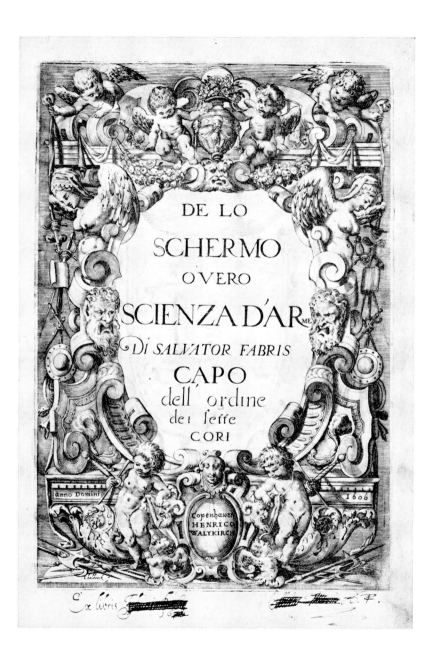

PLATE 7. Salvator Fabris's textbook on fencing, Copenhagen 1606.

PLATE 8. Ordinary Swedish male and female costumes 1592. Bourgeois.

PLATE 9. Swedish Laplanders 1592.

PLATE 10. Russian merchant and Russian foot-soldier from Moscow 1592.

5a. Count Charles Sture. Note in Morten Bornholm's album, fol 44^r, n.p. and n.d. 1595.

5b. Count Maurice Leijonhufvud. *Ibid.*

5c. Count John Sparre. *Ibid.*, fol 49^r, Stockholm, Sweden, n.d. 1595.

5d. Count Nils Bielke. *Ibid.*, fol 45^r, Stockholm, Sweden, February 14th, 1595.

All Rostgaard 28; The Royal Library, Copenhagen, Denmark.

Morten Bornholm, envoy to Sweden, was in the suite of the Danish Ambassador Christian Fries, during the christening of Prince Gustavus Adolphus February 9th, 1595. Entries in Morten Bornholm's album, probably all during his sojourn in Stockholm with Swedish noblemen.

6a. Sir Richard Lee. Entry in Henry Francklin's album, fol 2^r. Tallinn, Livonia, May 31st, 1601.

6b. Walter Fitz-William: Anglus. Entry in Henry Francklin's album, fol 26^r. Tallinn, Livonia, June 4th, 1601.

Uppsala University Library Department of Manuscripts, Uppsala, Sweden.

7. The title-page of Salvator Fabris, *De lo schermo overo scienza d'arme*; Henrico Waltkirch, Copenhagen 1606.

The Royal Library, Copenhagen, Denmark. There is also a copy at The British Museum, London W.C. 1, England.

8. Ordinary Swedish male and female costumes of the period. Bourgeois.

Drawing 1592 in Baron Augustin's von Moersperg und Beffort journal s.y. Artist unknown.

The Library of Sondershausen, East Germany, through the gracious medium of the German Shakespeare Society, Weimar.

9. Swedish Laplanders (huntsmen) 1592.

Not typical Laplanders of the present-day near-Mongolic type, hardly more than 5 feet high. May be ordinary Swedish Norrlanders, dressed in animal's skins.

Ibid.

10. A Russian merchant and a Russian foot-soldier from Moscow 1592.

Ibid.

Helena Northampton

One of the more outstanding ladies at the court of Elizabeth I was Helena Ulfsdotter Bååt (Snakenborg), who became the Marchioness of Northampton. She did a great deal towards developing and strengthening Anglo-Swedish relations at this time. In 1565 she accompanied Cecily Vasa to England and subsequently remained there as lady-in-waiting to Queen Elizabeth. She made swift progress in court circles and soon became First Lady of the Privy Chamber. When Elizabeth was buried in 1603, Helena Northampton was present in the capacity of 'First Mourner'.

Six years after her arrival in England, on April 29, 1571, at the age of 22, she married William Parr, Marquis of Northampton and brother of Catherine Parr, Henry VIII's sixth and final Queen Consort. When her mother was executed in 1536, Elizabeth I was only 3 years old and her childhood was a very lonely one. She was looked after by the subsequent queens of Henry VIII and by Catherine Parr in particular. Through her marriage to William Parr, Helena Northampton became closely related with the reigning house of Tudor. William Parr died in the home of Thomas Fisher in Warwick on October 28, 1571, just six months after his marriage to Helena, and was buried on December 5 at St Mary's Church, Warwick. Around 1577 Helena Northampton was married again, this time to Sir Thomas Gorges of Longford, but retained her title of Helena, Marchioness of Northampton. Between 1578–1589 she gave birth to eight children. Sir Thomas died in 1610, but Helena survived until April 1, 1635, when she was 86 years old. She was buried with her second husband in Salisbury Cathedral. According to her epitaph in the cathedral, she was persona grata with Queen Elizabeth 'on account of the shy charm which radiated from her entire person'.

On January 1, 1592, Edmund Spenser dedicated his *Daphnaida* to Helena Northampton and it is very probable that it was she who was personified as *Amoret* in the *Faerie Queene* (3.6.51–2). In the poem *Colin Clout's Come Home Again*, (508–515), dedicated to Sir Walter

Raleigh from Kilcolman in Ireland on December 27, 1591, Spenser praised her as *Mansilia* in the following words:

> No lesse praise worthie is Mansilia,
> Best known by bearing up great Cynthias traine:
> That same is she to whom Daphnaida
> Upon her neeces death I did complaine.
> She is the patterne of true womanhood,
> And only mirrhor of feminitie;
> Worthy next after Cynthia to tread,
> As she is next her in nobilitie.

Among the ladies from the court of Elizabeth who are mentioned in *Colin Clout's Come Home Again*, occur in particular the names of those who are mentioned in Spenser's earlier poems. Apart from Helena Northampton (Mansilia) and Elizabeth herself (Cynthia), there is Mary Herbert, Countess of Pembroke (Urania), Anne (Marie), Countess of Warwick (Theana), Margaret Clifford, Countess of Cumberland (Marian) and the three sisters, relatives of Edmund Spenser, Hunsdon, Dorset and Derby Spencer, the daughters of Sir John Spencer (Phyllis, Charyllis and Amaryllis). Stella is Penelope, Lady Rich, sister of Robert Devereux, Earl of Essex, Elizabeth's favourite. Sir Philip Sidney sang the praises of Lady Penelope in *Astrophel and Stella*, printed in 1591, and following the early death of Sir Philip Sidney in 1586, Edmund Spenser, who was a good friend of his, composed his splendid poem of homage *Astrophel* which was printed in 1596.

Mary Pembroke and Helena Northampton both held high positions in the court of Elizabeth I and, besides this, were neighbours at Salisbury. But the relations between these two women were not entirely without friction. The spirit of rivalry between them for the favours of the Queen emerges clearly from Sir Philip Sidney's *Arcadia*, where Longford Castle—Helena Northampton's home—is described as Amphialus' palace and Helena herself as Cecropia, Amphialus' mother.

The palace was described as being situated on a high cliff and regarded by all as inaccessible, partly because of its peculiar architecture, but chiefly on account of its natural position. This was in contrast to Longford Castle, which in reality had been built with great difficulty on the marshy bank of the river.

Cecropia—probably Sir Philip Sidney's most hateful character—was violent, ambitious and resentful by nature. Her threats were serious and as time went by they became worse and worse. Her violent

167

attacks were embellished by good promises. Cecropia's disgraceful out-
bursts developed gradually into complete despotism. She flogged her
innocent victims with canes, &c., &c.

But this portrayal of Helena Northampton is all too biased to be taken
seriously. It should be remembered that Sir Philip Sidney's *Arcadia*
was first published after his death by his sister, Mary Pembroke, who
was so unaware of the value of her brother's literary heritage that she
actually made changes and additions to his manuscripts without even
indicating where this had been done.

Particularly indicative of Helena Northampton's literary interests is
the dedication of *Daphnaida* by Edmund Spenser, dated January 1,
1592.[1] Sir Arthur Gorges of Longford, Helena Northampton's nephew
by marriage, married Lady Douglas Howard (daughter of Henry,
Viscount Byndon) in 1584. Lady Douglas Howard inherited one of the
largest fortunes of her time. In 1590, after only six years of married life,
Lady Douglas died, leaving a one-year-old daughter, Ambrosia. *Daphnaida* was written as an homage to the deceased Lady Douglas and at
the same time Spenser interpreted the great sorrow of Sir Arthur, her
husband.

There emerges from Spenser's dedication to Helena Northampton
the great devotion which Lady Douglas Howard bore for Helena, who
was regarded as the First Lady, not only by title but also in the eyes of
the generation of women which was growing up at that time.

The dedication is as follows:

Daphnaida
An Elegy

Upon the Death of the noble and vertuous Douglas Howard, Daughter and
Heire of Henry Lord Howard, Viscount Byndon, and Wife of Arthur Gorges, Esquier.

To the Right Honourable, and Vertuos Lady, Helena Marchioness of
Northampton.

I have the rather presumed humbly to offer unto Your Honour the
Dedication of this little Poem: for that the Noble and Vertuous Gentlewoman
of whom it is written, was, by match, near allied, and in Affection greatly
devoted unto Your Ladyship. The Occasion why I wrote the same, was as
well the great good Fame which I heard of Her Deceased, as the particular
Goodwill which I bear unto her Husband, Master Arthur Gorges, a Lover of
Learning and Vertue; whose House, as your Ladiship by Marriage hath ho-
noured, so do I find the name of them by many notable Records, to be of

---

[1] Presumably 1591. Cf. *Edm. Sp. Var. ed.*, 7, 435 ff.

great Antiquity in this Realm; and such as have ever borne themselves with honourable Reputation to the World, and unspotted Loyalty to their Prince and Country: Besides, so lineally are they descended from the Howards, as that the Lady Anne Howard, eldest Daughter to John Duke of Norfolke, was Wife to Sir Edmund, Mother to Sir Edward, and Grandmother to Sir William and Sir Thomas Gorges Knights. And therefore I do assure myself that no due Honour done to the White Lyon, but will be most grateful to Your Ladyship; whose Husband and Children do so nearly participate with the Blood of that Noble Family. So in all Duty I recommend this Pamphlet, and the good Acceptance thereof, to your honourable Favour and Protection. London this first of
January, 1591.

Your Honour's humbly ever,
Ed. Spenser[1]

A tree may help to clarify the kinship of persons concerned. Their names are in italics.

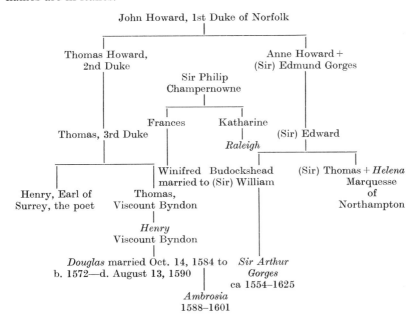

Sir Arthur Gorges and Sir Walter Raleigh were thus first cousins,[2] had been childhood friends in Devon and had studied together at Oxford.

[1] Cf. *The Works of Mr. Edmund Spenser*, edited by John Hughes, London 1715, 5, 1316 ff.

[2] W. Sh.sp., *Third Variorum*, 1821, 2, 245–8, and Edm. Sp., *Var. Ed.*, 7, 435.

Helena Northampton was their aunt. Edmund Spenser was a good friend of Sir Walter Raleigh and the Gorges family, while Raleigh was frequently a guest at Longford Castle. In his *Apothegms New and Old*[1] Francis Bacon writes the following about Helena Northampton as a hostess at Longford:

> There was a Lady of the West country, that gave great entertainment at her house to most of the gallant gentlemen thereabout, and amongst others, Sir Walter Raleigh was one. This Lady, though otherwise a stately dame, was a notable good housewife, and in the morning betimes she called to one of her maids that looked to the service and asked: 'Is the piggy served?' Sir Walter's chamber was fast by the Lady's so as he heard her. A little before dinner the Lady came down in great state into the great chamber, which was full of gentlemen; and as soon as Sir Walter Raleigh set eyes upon her: 'Madam (saith he) is the piggy served?' The Lady answered: 'You know best whether you have had your breakfast.'

Any possible tinge of acidity which may be thought to accompany the repartee would surely have vanished beneath the witchery of Mansilia's gentle smile.

The Snakenborgs were a branch of the ancient Swedish family of Bååt; they were closely associated with the royal house of Vasa and it is evident that from Queen Elizabeth's court Helena Northampton followed the destiny of the Vasas with great interest. In 1594 Henry Francklin married Constantia Eriksdotter, Eric XIV's second daughter with Agda Persdotter.[2] Constantia was 34 when she married and it is fairly clear from the passport for his journey to England in 1591[3] that Henry Francklin and she had known each other for some years before they married. In the summer of 1591 Henry Francklin had been in contact with William Dethick,[4] Garter King-of-Arms, from whom he received the Grant of Arms on June 2, 1592,[5] presumably on account of his forthcoming marriage.

At the same time as the English players were engaged at the Court of Duke Charles at Nyköping, a very lively correspondence began between Helena Northampton and the Duke, and gifts and suchlike were ex-

---

[1] *Works of Francis Bacon*, 7, 165. Cf. Bradford, *Helena Northampton*, 207.
[2] Cf. pp. 210 and 213.
[3] Cf. pp. 22 f.
[4] Henric Francklyns stambok, fol. 52 v.
[5] Cf. pp. 27 and 210.

changed. Duke Charles also assisted Helena Northampton at this time in transferring to England her inheritance from her mother.[1]

Through her marriage with William Parr, Helena Northampton began to sympathize with the Puritan circles in England at this time. William Parr was one of the people who was on good terms with the Swedish ambassador, Nils Gyllenstierna, and he was also in favour of Eric XIV's courtship of Queen Elizabeth in 1561. It is also probable that, being resident in Warwickshire and through her family ties with the Throckmortons, Helena Northampton came into contact with the Puritan advocates who signed themselves 'Martin Marprelate'. William Parr was also interested in the theatre and during the 1550's, possibly longer, he had his own group of players, known as 'The Marquis of Northampton's Company'.[2]

As a result of her second marriage, to Sir Thomas Gorges of Longford, Helena Northampton—as is quite evident from Spenser's dedication to *Daphnaida*—began to associate closely with the literary group which included Edmund Spenser and Sir Walter Raleigh. In view of this it is reasonable to assume that Helena Northampton was also very familiar with the theatrical life of the time—a fact to which her position as First Lady of the Privy Chamber must have contributed considerably.

Both she and her second husband, Sir Thomas Gorges, contributed a great deal to Anglo-Swedish relations. Sometime after their marriage Sir Thomas was appointed ambassador and was an emissary to Sweden in 1582.[3] At this time there was no permanent English ambassador in Sweden and there were many problems in Anglo-Swedish relations which needed both diplomatic skill and discretion if they were to be solved to the satisfaction of both sides. Through his marriage Sir Thomas was in close contact with Swedish conditions and furthermore there was no doubt that he was greatly liked by the Vasas. In 1569 John III had succeeded Eric XIV and he soon made it clear that he was disinclined to take over his brother's debts. He stated categorically that it was not his intention to repay the large loan of £12,000 which had been granted to Eric XIV at the time of his courtship of Elizabeth I. This sum had been handed over to Sweden's London ambassador Nils Gyllenstierna by Sir

---

[1] Cf. pp. 32 f. [2] John T. Murray, *English Dramatic Companies 1558–1642*, 2, 90.
   [3] Passport in Cal. S.P. For. 1582, May–December, p. 230, and recredentials by John III and Queen Catharina in Uppsala on 28 July 1582 as well as by Duke Charles in Nyköping on 6 August 1582. Cf. SP 95/1, fol 14 v ff. and this book p. 178, last §.

Lionel Ducket and John Dymock. At the same time Cecily Vasa had borrowed £1000 from the same sources. The situation was further complicated since John III had imprisoned John Dymock and kept him locked up for more than five years because the latter had 'submitted to His Majesty some malicious letters'. The negotiations around these affairs were extremely prolonged and during the reign of John III they led to no positive results whatsoever. But, on the other hand, Duke Charles felt it his duty to repay the loan which had been arranged in 1571 by William Parr on behalf of Catherine Jagiello during the latter's visit to England. This repayment was not made before 1591, however, in connection with the appointment of the English players to Duke Charles's court in Nyköping. The Duke's willingness to repay this debt indicates that he was desirous of obtaining Helena Northampton's connivance in preventing the export of English arms to Archangel.

The first mention of Dr. Teofilus Homodei in Swedish archives is made in the Royal Wardrobe on August 1, 1582, about the time when Helena Northampton was visiting Sweden. It is thus not unlikely that Dr. Teofilus arrived in Sweden with the same suite[1] which brought Sir Thomas Gorges and Helena Northampton to Sweden, particularly in view of the fact that Dr. Teofilus was quickly accredited to John III and then to Duke Charles.

Helena Northampton's sister, Catherine Ulfsdotter Snakenborg-Bååt, was married to Baron Philip Bonde in 1580. In 1604 she was a lady of the bedchamber in Nyköping and Stockholm to Duke Charles's second wife, subsequently Queen Christine the elder. This too was of great importance to Anglo–Swedish relations at this period. All this time the two sisters had been corresponding with each other.[2]

There is a record from as late as 22 July 1607, when James I ruled in England and Duke Charles had become Charles IX of Sweden, showing that the latter was still in touch with Helena Northampton. He thanks her for all her services in England and for her great interest in her native land. It is also clear that the two exchanged gifts.[3]

---

[1] Bradford, *Helena Northampton*, pp. 80 ff. It is intriguing to speculate on the identity of the 'Walter' in an entry in Duke Charles's almanac for June 18, 1582, during Helena Northampton's sojourn in Sweden:

'18. — — — samme dagh kåm Walter igen.'

[Walter came again the same day].

Could it have been Sir Walter Raleigh with Helena Northampton's suite?

[2] *Ibid.*   [3] Riksregistraturen 22.7.1607, RA.

Teofilus Homodei D.M.

The Homodei family (Omodei, Amidei), which is of ancient lineage, comes from Milan. It was represented among the senators of the city council there as early as the 10th century; branches have been traced to Rimini, Sicily, Piedmont, Novara and Valtellina.[1] The Sicilian offshoot became extremely wealthy and received large estates such as Vallelonga, Monterosso, li Milgi, Iancarano, Iandigalgano, Falconieri and Maletto, the saltworks at Reda, Baranio, Cantarella and Cianciana, and the tunny fishery at Trapani. Its members also held high office in the city administration of Palermo. Members of the Valtellina branch have been traced in Tirano, Sernio and Grosotto, from whence it spread later to the canton of Tessin in Switzerland. The various branches each had a coat of arms; while these are fundamentally the same, they differ sufficiently for them to be clearly distinguishable. Dr. Teofilus Homodei's coat of arms is known to us only from a seal on his letter of farewell to Duke Charles, dated Örebro May 11, 1596. This seal bears the same arms as those of the Tessin branch of the family. Since we know (see below) that Dr. Teofilus belonged to the Valtellina branch, the similarity of these coats of arms confirms that these two offshoots belonged to one and the same branch of the Homodei family.[2]

The oldest existing biography of Dr. Teofilus is included in Ludovico von Hammen's work, *Vitae Medicorum Gedanensum*, which was written in 1679 after the death of Teofilus. The manuscript which we now have was preserved by von Hammen's biographer and is only a copy of an eighteenth-century copy. von Hammen gives the following data on Teofilus Homodei:

---

[1] Guasco, *Dizionario Feudale* ..., I, 492, II, 631, 684, 1105 and III, 1259. De Crescenzi, *Anfiteatro Romano* ..., 225. Imhoff, *Genealogiæ* ..., 58 and index. Di Crollalanza, *Dizionario Storico* ... Di Casalgerardo, *Il Nobiliario di Sicilia*, II, 21. *Rivista dell Collegio Araldico* 1921, 16. Lienhard-Riva, *Armoriale Ticinese*, 306.

[2] Cf. Brev till Hertig Karl, Kungl. arkiv 15, and Lienhard-Riva, *Armoriale Ticinese*, 306.

Natus A.C. 1550. Tirani Vulturenorum Rhaetiae¹ inferioris oppido Parentibus Nobilibus.²

Thus Dr. Teofilus Homodei, who belonged to the Valtellina branch of this noble family, was born in 1550 in the vicinity of Tirano in the southern Rhaetian alps. The family castle was at Sernio, which lay about half way between Sondrio and Grosotto. A letter to Duke Charles dated February 19, 1586,³ is signed Theophilus Homodeus Rhaetus, thus confirming von Hammen's claim that Dr. Teofilus was in fact from Valtellina, which at this time belonged to Switzerland.⁴ Other members of this noble Valtellina-family of Tirano were Antonio Homodei and Joh. Antonio Galeazzo Homodei. Antonio H. was 1522 captain of Robustelli's Regiment during the invasion of Munstertal. Joh. Antonio Galeazzo H. supported the preparations for the Massacre of Valtellina in the year 1620-21.⁵

There is also a commoner family called Homodei (Omodei) and it is from this family that the patron saint of Tirano, St Mario Omodei, originates.⁶ In 1504 the Holy Virgin is reputed to have appeared before Mario Omodei and a chapel has been built on the spot in Tirano where this is purported to have happened. Even to this day there is in Tirano an annual harvest feast in memory of Saint Mario Omodei on September 23.⁷

It has not been possible to establish any connection between the noble and commoner families of Homodei (Omodei). Nevertheless there prob-

---

¹ Tirani Vulturenorum Rhaetiae, i.e. a Rhaetian from Tirano in Valtellina. In G. Toepke's student registers for Heidelberg the index entry Veltlin, Valtellina has the following alternative versions: Vulturenus Rhetus, Rheto-Vulturenus, Vultureno-Rhetus and Volturens-Rhoetus. According to the same registers (II, p. 537), Daniel Paravicinus, Volturens-Rhaetus, and Barthol. Paravicinus, Curia-Rhaetus, entered Heidelberg on 11 September 1660. Cf. also p. 163 in the same volume concerning Johannes Baptista Homodei, who in the register for Bâle University is designated 'Nobilis Rhaetus ex Vulturena' and 'Tiranensis Rhaetus'.

² Ludovico von Hammen, 49.

³ Brev till hertig Karl, RA.

⁴ During the Middle Ages Valtellina was a part of Lombardy. From 1512 to 1797 it belonged to Switzerland as a part of Les Grisons. Dr. Teofilus was thus Swiss and had Rhaeto-Romance as his mother tongue, *Schweizer Lexikon*, 7, 795. Cf. also the letter from Dr. Teofilus to Ture Bielke 3.1.1597 (Skoklostersamlingen Avd. II in fol. Miscellana, vol. 1, RA).

⁵ Heinrich Türler &c., *Historisch-Biographisches Lexikon der Schweiz*, IV, 286.

⁶ *Enciclopedia Italiana*, vol. XXXIII, 912, and Quadrio, *Storia memorabile ...*, Ch. III.

⁷ Quadrio, *Storia memorabile ...*, Milano 1753.

174

ably once was some connection between these two families with the same name and from the same district, however long ago this may have been.

The first record of Dr. Homodei's medical studies comes from the University in Bâle, which he attended according to the register during the years 1572–73.[1] This makes him a contemporary of many persons who fled from the Massacre of St. Bartholomew in Paris.[2]

Ludovico von Hammen had the following to say concerning Dr. Teofilus's further training as a doctor of medicine:

> Promotus in Art. et Medicinae D. Valentiae in Delphinatu Galliae sub Carolo de Lebron, Valentiae ac Diensis Diaeceseos Episcopo A.C. 1576, 20 April.[3]

Hence Dr. Homodei studied medicine at the University of Valence in southern France, where he, on April 20, 1576, was given his doctorate in the presence of the Bishop of Valence, Charles de Lébéron, nephew of the previous bishop there, Jean de Montluc.

Jean de Montluc[4] of the d'Artagnan-Montesquiou family was born in 1508 and was the brother of Blaise de Montluc, Marshall of France. Jean was a Dominican monk when, impressed by his attractive manner and his addiction to new ideas, Queen Margaret of Navarre (d'Angoulême) took him with her to her court in Paris. He soon found favour with Francis I and Henry II and a diplomatic career was opened to him. Altogether Jean de Montluc was an emissary to no less than sixteen different countries, including Ireland, Poland, Italy, England, Scotland, Germany and Constantinople. He made himself indispensable to Catherine of Medici and it was not long before all the French court's diplomatic business of a confidential nature passed through his hands. In 1573 he had great success in Poland where the parliament, assembled to elect a king, was so charmed by his eloquence that it gave its vote to Henri Valois, who in the following year became Henry III of France.

Jean de Montluc was very tolerant of Calvinism and saved many a Calvinist from the death sentence. It was accepted in the Paris court that Jean de Montluc preached 'tantôt à la catholique, tantôt à la huguenote'.

---

[1] Wackernagel, 2, 215.
[2] Cf. *ibid.* and *Les Refugiées à Bâle*, passim.
[3] Ludovico von Hammen, 49 f.
[4] Perrier, 73 ff.

In recognition of his services he had been named Bishop of Valence as early as 1553, although he did not actually take up office until 1558.

In due course his lenient attitude towards Calvinism became known in Rome and he was excommunicated for heresy by Pope Pius IV following a report from the alderman of Valence in 1560,[1] shortly before the Colloquy of Poissy in 1561. The French court intervened, however, and the sentence of excommunication was never carried out. Jean de Montluc retired from his office as Bishop of Valence in 1575, i.e. shortly after his embassy to Poland (1572–73), though at his death in Toulouse on April 15, 1579, he still held the bishopric officially. His nephew Charles de Lébéron was acting Bishop during the period 1575–79 and received the office officially in 1580.

Charles de Lébéron, as Abbé in St. Ruf, was made a doctor 'in utroque jure' at the University of Valence on June 6, 1573, in the presence of Jacques Cujas and Claude Rogier,[2] and he had also been with Jean de Montluc in 1573 at the parliamentary election of the king of Poland.[3]

Teofilus Homodei had taken his medical degree shortly after Jean de Montluc had retired from his bishop's office and the post of Diocesan Superintendent of the University of Valence. Presumably Charles de Lébéron took over his duties as bishop in Valence at the same time as Homodei began his medical studies there. Students at the University of Valence during the period when Homodei was there were presumably interested in Jean de Montluc.

Valence was the first town in France to embrace Calvinism wholeheartedly. As early as 1560 the local administration was Calvinistic and this was to a considerable extent a result of Jean de Montluc's attitude. Later during the Reformation Valence was the scene of many bloody disputes between the Catholics and the Calvinists. After the Massacre of St. Bartholemew on August 24, 1572, the situation became extremely critical for the Valence authorities. The principal lecturer in law at the University from 1567–75 was the famous specialist on Roman law, Jacques Cujas. In 1570 Cujas asked the well-known philologist Joseph Scaliger to come to Valence. Cujas was himself not officially a Calvinist but he was a very strong sympathizer and it was because of this that he was just able in 1572 to save the lives of the two Calvinists, Joseph

[1] *Dictionaire de Théologie Catholique*, 10, 2394.

[2] Nadal, 273.

[3] de Noailles, 1, 95.

Scaliger and the lecturer in civil law, Ennemond Bonnefoy. Scaliger fled with all haste to Geneva, where between 1572 and 1574 he held the chair of philosophy.

The man who inspired the lecturers at the Faculty of Medicine at the University of Valence and who influenced Homodei during his studies there was probably the famous physician Laurent Joubert,[1] born in Valence on December 6, 1529. Joubert, who became known and appreciated throughout Europe, had studied at the University of Montpellier where he graduated as a doctor of medicine on July 5, 1558.[2] He subsequently studied in Paris, Turin, Padua and Ferrara. From 1561 to 1567 he was lecturer in medicine at the University of Valence, after which he moved back to Montpellier. In 1573 he became Chancellor of the University of Montpellier and Physician-in-ordinary to Henry III and the King of Navarre. He died in 1583. His most important works are his translation of Guillaume Rondelet's *Histoire entière des poissons* (1558) and his own papers, *La peste* (1567), *Erreurs populaires au fait de la medicine et regime de santé* (1578), *Seconde partie des erreurs populaires* (1579), *Pharmacopée* (1579) and, posthumously, *La Grande Chirurgie de Guy de Chantiac restitue par Joubert* (1598). After his studies in Italy Joubert came into opposition with the prevailing classical medical doctrines which had been founded by Galen. Joubert argued that nature herself was the best healer and that medicines derived from the world of plants would stimulate the body to foster its own resistance to disease.

It is true that Joubert had in fact left the University of Valence when Homodei began studying there, but the distance between Montpellier and Valence was not great and, because he had family relations in the latter town, it is probable that Joubert was often there visiting. Furthermore Laurent Joubert's brother, François, was an examinations official at Valence university during Homodei's time.

There are lists for the periods 1566–75[3] and 1583–86[4] (but not for the intervening years) of those students who graduated as doctors of medicine from the University of Valence. It was in the intervening period that Dr. Teofilus graduated. The lecturers at the Faculty of Medicine in 1574–75[3] were François de Quercy and Louis de Quercy and in 1583[4] François de Quercy and Benoit Merula.

[1] Nadal, 82.
[2] Gouron, 116.
[3] Valence, D 17.
[4] *Ibid.*, D 18.

It is not known exactly when Homodei began studying in Valence, but probably at the latest it was 1574–75. It will be noticed in the earlier and later student registers of the University of Valence that, as a result of the infiltration of Calvinists into university circles, the Faculty of Theology there was but little frequented. It was only on the odd occasion that a doctor's degree was conferred 'in sacratissima theologia', while at the same time over 300 students graduated in law and became doctors 'in utroque jure', 'in utroque jure canonico et civili' or 'in jure civili tantum'. A lesser number of students graduated in philosophy and medicine, 'in artibus philosophiae et medicinae' and very occasionally in medicine alone, 'in medicinae'. In the biographies by Ludovico von Hammen[1] and Sacklén[2] it is stated that Dr. Teofilus graduated as 'Promotus in Art. et Medicinae D.', and 'Artis Medicae Doctor' respectively, which implies that Dr. Homodei graduated both in medicine and philosophy.

There is no information available concerning Dr. Homodei's activities or whereabouts between the year of his graduation[3] (1576) and his arrival in Sweden in 1582. Communications between Valence and Holland and England were fairly lively at this time, however, and it is very probable that Teofilus came to Sweden by this route. The first mention of Dr. Teofilus in Sweden is in His Majesty's (John III's) Royal Wardrobe,[4] dated August 1, 1582. This is a receipt in Latin for various items of materials supplied from the wardrobe store. In the 'Account Book' there is also an entry as follows, dated 1582:

Dr. Theophilus hafver bekommit efter K. Mts bref 21 aug. 1582
Peningar . . . . 75 daler[5]

It is thus quite evident that upon his arrival in Sweden Teofilus was first in the service of John III.

In the summer of 1582, as has already been mentioned, both Sir Thomas Gorges of Longford and Helena Northampton visited Sweden,[6] and it is probable that Dr. Teofilus travelled with them. This would also

---

[1] Ludovico von Hammen, 49.

[2] Sacklén, I, 319.

[3] Nadal, 9, and Appendix; Perrier, 75 ff.

[4] K. klädkammaren 1582, vol. 37:4 (Siffredh Olssons uthgifft), fol. 50 r, SA.

[5] 'Doctor Teofilus has received according to His Majesty's letter of August 21, 1582: the sum of ... 75 daler';

[6] SP 95/1, fol. 14 r ff., PRO. Cf. p. 171, last §.

explain the claims made by Werwing and Sacklén to the effect that Dr. Teofilus was of English birth.[1]

On October 11, 1583, Dr. Teofilus received a warrant from Duke Charles according to which his appointment was to run from Michaelmas the previous year. His salary was fixed at 300 daler, equal to that of a chamberlain, and also included '4 loads of grain and 4 oxen'. The appointment also entitled him to '2 servants with clothing allowance for 11 daler and free victuals for a third servant'.[2] An undated letter of recommendation relating to Dr. Teofilus's appointment with Duke Charles was sent to the Duke's Latin secretary by Teofilus's brother, Vincentus.[3] In view of the date of the above-mentioned letter of appointment it might be reasonable to date this letter of recommandation a few months earlier, i.e. during the summer of 1583.

Letters were issued on 5 May and 3 July 1584 from John III to Hogenschild Bielke concerning 'Dr. Teofilus Homodei's outstanding salary' and 'Dr. Teofilus Homodei's supply of grain', while the Lord High Chancellor, Per Brahe, was ordered on 29 March 1586 'to help Dr. Teofilus to his outstanding salary'.[4] Dr. Teofilus never moved to Nyköping, residing in Stockholm throughout his stay in Sweden (1582–96).

During his first period of service as physician-in-ordinary to the Nyköping court Dr. Teofilus was much patronized in his professional capacity by Duke Charles and his wife, the Duchess Mary. This fact emerges from a letter from the doctor to the Duke dated Kalmar, February 19, 1586.[5] In this letter he first expresses his gratitude for all the kindness and consideration which has been extended to him and then goes on to beg of the Duke not to regard it as failure of duty or neglect that he has not been present with the Duke as had been agreed. The reason was that when he arrived in Nyköping His Grace had already left and nobody knew where he had gone. Meanwhile, however, he—the doctor—had taken with him for Her Grace as much 'Centaurea minoris'[6] and 'Melissa'[7] as was to be had from the apothecaries in Stockholm. He then mentions that he has received a letter from his brothers, wherein they inform him

[1] Werwing, 1, 102; Sacklén, 1, 319.

[2] Beställningsregister 1579–89, KA.

[3] Kungl. arkiv. Brev till hovmän m. fl., K355, RA.

[4] Riksregistraturen (Johan III), fol. 140 r and 144 r/1584, and fol. 54 r/1586.

[5] Kungl. arkiv; Prinsars och prinsessors arkiv; Brev till hertig Karl; K343, RA.

[6] Gentiana Centaurium L.

[7] The seed of heartsease.

that they will be coming to Stockholm in March 'with a considerable store of silk and various other goods'. Dr. Teofilus goes on to say that he hopes it will be possible for him within a couple of weeks to visit the Duke as promised. He concludes,

Ser: ^{mae} Cels:^{nis} V^{rae}

humillimus servitor

Theophilus Homodeus Rhaetus[1]

After the death of the Duchess Mary of the Palatinate in 1589 Dr. Homodei was used less by Duke Charles in his professional capacity and more in the capacity of ambassador and grand merchant. In a letter to Count Ture Bielke on January 3, 1597,[2] i.e. shortly after the arrival of Dr. Homodei in Gdańsk, the latter complains that before his departure for his new appointment he was held in Stockholm and accused of having tried to poison the Duke nine years previously. This, if true, would explain the Duke's unwillingness to continue to rely on Teofilus as his physician-in-ordinary.

In 1589 the shadow of the Swedish–Russian war (1589–1595) began to descend over the country. Rearmament was urgent, since measures had to be taken against the Russian attacks on Kolahus and Petsamo and other districts on the Arctic front. Furthermore in February 1590 the Russians retook Iwangorod near Narva on the Baltic front. In July 1589 John III and Sigismund met at Tallinn, presumably to establish a Swedish–Polish alliance against Russia. After Sigismund's return from Tallinn to Poland in 1590, parliament assembled in Warsaw. According to Werwing,[3] Duke Charles had sent Dr. Teofilus, 'an English doctor of medicine', as his ambassador to this parliament assembly. Dr. Homodei conducted himself very stubbornly in this office and his attitude provoked many people, especially the enemies of Duke Charles. Werwing particularly pointed out that Teofilus's behaviour here 'gave even His Brother (John III) occasion to think somewhat angrily about him (the Duke)'. As a result of Dr. Teofilus's representation in Warsaw the planned alliance between the two kings in Tallinn in 1589 failed to materialize.

The claims of Werwing and Sacklén that in the summer of 1591 Dr.

---

[1] 'Your Grace's most humble servant Theophilus Homodeus, Rhaetus'; op. cit.

[2] Skoklostersamlingen Avd. II in fol. Miscellana, vol. 1, RA.

[3] Werwing, 1, 102 f.

Teofilus was in Poland are hardly correct. At this time Teofilus and Henry Francklin were both in England engaged in recruiting mercenaries, purchasing cloth and arranging for the employment of the English players, &c. The Polish parliament met in the summer of 1590 and at this time John III's councillors Eric Ribbing and John Gyllenstierna were in Warsaw amongst other places.[1] According to the kitchen accounts for 1589–90[2] Dr. Teofilus, having left Sweden on April 29, 1590, returned to the court of Duke Charles in Nyköping on August 27, 1590, and was thus probably in Warsaw during these intervening months. Francklin, on the other hand, was busy in the summer of 1590 with, *inter alia*, the purchase of four Turkish horses[3] for the Duke. At this time he was serving Sigismund in Poland.[4]

The reason why John III and Sigismund were displeased with Dr. Teofilus on this occasion was probably because the latter, on behalf of Duke Charles, had begun to pursue another form of Swedish foreign policy, partly by collaborating with Samuel Laski and Geronimo Strozzi[5] in Poland.

During 1587–88 several dispatches were sent from Duke Charles to various authorities in Denmark concerning the passage of certain ships through the Sound, certain trade agreements, &c., all of them questions to be settled by Dr. Teofilus Homodei.[6]

During 1589 Duke Charles also became interested in the idea of trading with Spain. The Spanish fleet had to be rebuilt following the 'Armada Summer' of the previous year. Duke Charles decided to try exporting Swedish timber for the masts and general construction of the new Spanish ships, and with this aim in view he appointed Dr. Teofilus his ambassador. As early as the beginning of 1589 it would seem that these plans were beginning to be well formulated.

The following notes are to be found in the Duke's records for 1589:

---

[1] Henric Francklyns stambok, fol. 134 v.

[2] Kungl. Hofförtärningen 1589–90, SA.

[3] Cf. p. 209.

[4] Cotton MSS, Vespasian, Fr III, 137, BM. Cf. p. 209.

[5] Cf. Chapter 3.

[6] 'Message to the King of Denmark &c. about/Dr. Teofilus Homodei, Nyköping 16.10.1587; message to Christopher Valkendorff/about the brother of Dr. Teofilus, Marieholm 14.3.1588; message/about Dr. Teofilus to Axel Gyllenstierna, governor of Copenhagen. Örebro 8.5.1588; message/about Dr Teofilus Homodei to Niels Kaas, Örebro 20.6.1588'; All in Hertig Karls registratur, RA.

Till Thomas Klinch, borgare i Stockholm, om 698½ daler, som han D. Theophilo Homodej &c. ... lefrere skall. Datum Marieholm den 17 Februari 1589.[1]

A similar unspecified sum appears in the Duke's treasury accounts for 1589[2] under the main heading 'Court salary' and the sub-heading 'Chamberlains':

Doctor Theophilus — 697 daler.

For March 28, 1589, the Duke's almanac reads:

drog Libertt Kåber[3] och D(octor) Teofulus ... sin kos.[4]

After this Teofilus is not mentioned again in the 1589 almanac and since the Duke's almanacs for 1590 and 1591 are missing no more information for these years concerning Dr Teofilus can be derived from this source.

Among Duke Charles's letters for 1590 there is one noted as follows:

Creditifsbref för D Theophilo Homodeo till Rijksens Rådh i Danmark. Stockholm 14 Martij 1590.[5]

Next to this has been inserted:

Tenkiezedel hwad som ... hertig Karl hafwer befalet sin tienere D. Teophilo Homodeo att andrage hoos Regeringen i Danmark. Actum Stockholm 15 Martij 1590.[6]

From this memorandum it is clear that the Duke had some 22,000 daler in Lubeck and that he did not wish to risk transporting this sum by sea, but desired instead to have it transferred by road to the Swedish border via Denmark. This indicates that the Duke, probably through his agent in Amsterdam, William IJsbrandtz Kieft, had concluded a large deal in Swedish timber with Spain and that IJsbrantz had negotiated payment to Duke Charles through his subagent in Lubeck.

[1] 'To Thomas Klinch, burgher in Stockholm, 698½ daler for delivery to Dr. Teofilus Homodei &c. Dated Marieholm, February 17, 1589'; Hertig Karls registratur 1589, fol. 31, RA.

[2] Hertig Karls Memorials Register 1590–91, fol. 5 v, KA.

[3] Cf. Chapters 1 and 5.

[4] 'Lubert Kaver and Dr. Teofilus went their way.' Op. cit., 62.

[5] 'Letter of credit for Dr. Teofilus to the Regency in Denmark. Stockholm, March 14, 1590'; Hertig Karls registratur 1590, fol. 24 v, RA.

[6] 'Memorandum concerning what Duke Charles has ordered his servant Dr. Teofilus to relate to the Regency in Denmark. Stockholm, March 15, 1590'; *ibid.*

A merchant fleet was equipped in Emden for the 'Spanish Venture', according to several instructions in December 1589 for Severine John &c., &c.[1] In the autumn of 1587 the Duke had delivered two fully equipped naval vessels to England.[2] Then in the autumn of 1589 Elizabeth I had given the Duke permission to use these two ships for his 'Spanish Venture'.[3] One of the ships which took part in this voyage, *Elephanten*, was carrying a valuable cargo of masts when she sprang a leak off the coast of France in the beginning of 1590. She was driven across the channel to Dartmouth and wrecked in Lyme Bay on the Devonshire coast. A large part of the cargo of masts was seized by the coastal people, chiefly those in the Isle of Wight. As a result of this, Dr. Teofilus wrote to Queen Elizabeth on behalf of Duke Charles. The original of this letter is preserved in the British Museum and there is a copy in the same hand preserved in the Swedish National Archives.[4] The language in the original is diplomatic, but the tone of the copy which was passed to Duke Charles is so brusque as to be almost rude. This affair was ultimately settled to Sweden's advantage. By an Act of the Privy Council dated March 15, 1590, any person finding these masts was ordered to return them to Dr. Teofilus, Severine John or another such specified person.[5] But the matter of returning or compensating for the masts was not yet settled. Dr. Teofilus had long negotiations with Sir George Carey, afterwards Lord Hunsdon, governor of the Isle of Wight, concerning the return of the greater part of the masts, which had floated ashore at Cowe's Castle.

According to Duke Charles's diary a letter of introduction to his sister, Catherine, Countess of East Friesland, and the following passport were issued for Dr. Teofilus to visit England:

1590, October 1

Till furstinnan aff Ostfrijsland om doct. Theophili reesa til Engeland och hŭadh kunskaper der höres. Nyköping.

Paß för doctor Theophilo till Engeland. Nyköping.[6]

---

[1] Hertig Karls registratur 1589, fol. 121 v ff., RA.

[2] SP 95/1, fol. 20 and 25, PRO. Cf. p. 13, last §.

[3] Acts Priv. Counc. XX, 350 ff.

[4] Landsdowne MSS, No. 108, BM, and, Anglica, Förhandlingar 1559–1632, RA.

[5] Acts Priv. Counc. XX, 350 f.

[6] 'October 1st, 1590. To the Countess of East Friesland about Dr. Teofilus's journey to England and what happens there. Nyköping. Passport for Dr. Teofilus to England. Nyköping'; Hertig Karls diarium 1566–92, RA.

This entry was made after Dr. Teofilus's sojourn in Warsaw and shortly before Duke Charles left for John III's court in Uppsala on October 24. The passport does not seem to have been preserved in any Swedish archive and neither can it be found anywhere in England. The letter of introduction, on the other hand, exists in a copy in the records of Duke Charles.[1] Dr. Teofilus left Sweden for England in the beginning of October 1590 and he seems to have taken the route via Emden and the Netherlands. Expenses for this journey are registered as follows:

Doctor Theophilus Homodei på en resa
ifrå Nyköp. in åth Engelandh, 1 8^{bris} 90
Ung^{sch} gyllen . . . . 30 st^r
Pening^r . . . . 20 dal^{r2}

Dr. Teofilus arrived in England about March 15 and stayed until the middle of July in the same year.[3] This indicates that his stay in Emden and the Netherlands between times was fairly long. Severine John[4] remained in England from July 1, 1590, to the end of July 1591 to assist Teofilus with the problems relating to the foundering of the *Elephanten*. Apart from the question of the return of the masts, there was also an enquiry in Dartmouth,[5] and the matter of the plundering of the ship by her crew, the negotiations in London with the Admiralty[6] and so on. Most of the Admiralty negotiations were conducted through the Admiralty lawyer, Dr. Julius Caesar, who received a sum of money for his services. Severine John's bill for this is as follows:

Åhr förähredht Doctor Julius Cæsar
Judex wttij Admiralitetedh till Lundenn
Penning^r . . . . 4 p^d sterling, samt
Åhr giffwitt Juditz Dörewachtere
Penning^r . . . . 1 skelling.[7]

---

[1] Hertig Karls registratur 1589–90, fol. 140 v, RA.

[2] 'Dr. Teofilus on a journey from Nyköping to England, October 1, 1590: Hungarian ducats 30, Coin 20 daler'; Hertig Karls räntekammare, Håkan Larsson m. fl. 1590–97, fasc. 1, 32 v, KA.

[3] Söffring Jönssons räkning från en resa i England 1590–91, fol. 11 r and 15 v, KA.

[4] Cf. pp. 27 and 34.

[5] Söffring Jönssons räkning från en resa i England 1590–91, fol. 5 v, KA; Hertig Karls diarium 15.8.1591, RA.

[6] Söffring Jönssons räkning från en resa i England 1590–91, fol. 9 v, KA.

[7] 'Presented to Dr. Julius Caesar, Lawyer at the Admiralty in London, coins ... £4. Tips to Dr. Caesar's porter, coins ... 1 sh.'; *ibid.*, fol. 9 v f.

A paragraph in Dr. Teofilus's accounts for his stay in England states:

Hafuer dochtoren uthlagdt på den engelske reesen såsom hans rechning förmäler, riiksdaler .... 252 stycker.[1]

It would thus seem that during his 'English journey' Dr. Teofilus had heavy duties and among other things had to advance £20 to Severine John.[2]

It is not possible to discover in detail what Dr. Teofilus was doing in England in 1590–91. But it is known that he studied the political situation, estimated the extent of war material deliveries to Russia, via the North Cape and Archangel,[3] collaborated with Severine John on the *Elephanten*[4] negotiations and submitted a report to Duke Charles on this affair,[5] and also looked into the opportunities for recruiting mercenaries in England and Scotland for Duke Charles's campaign against Russia. It was probably in connection with these activities that Dr. Teofilus and Henry Francklin came into contact with the English theatrical world and witnessed the final phase of the 'Martin Marprelate Controversy'.[6] In Duke Charles's household accounts it appears in connection with the payment of the 'Netherland Captains' that a list of Scots and Englishmen were also receiving remuneration. The head of this contingent was the Scottish captain of cavalry, Henry Leal. It would seem that the Scots and Englishmen who volunteered to serve with Duke Charles's army at this time were not sufficient to make up the mercenary force which was required. Because of this, Dr. Teofilus turned to the Netherlands and it was from here that the majority of the mercenary officers were recruited.

Dr. Teofilus's lack of success in recruiting sufficient numbers of mercenaries in England was probably due to the fact that at this time an expeditionary force was being mustered to be sent to France under the Earl of Essex,[7] while 1000 men had already been recruited on behalf of

---

[1] 'The doctor's expenses on his English journey as his accounts show, riksdaler ... 252'; Dochtor Theophili Reckning 1.6.1590–30.11.1591 in 'avräkningsboken 1589–91', fol. 189 v, KA.

[2] Söffring Jönssons räkning från en resa i England 1590–91, fol. 3 r, KA.

[3] Hertig Karls registratur 1591, fol. 132 v f., RA.

[4] Lansd. MS 67, No. 108 and Add. MS 36744, BM. Cf. Söffring Jönssons räkning från en resa i England 1590–91, fol. 11 r ff., KA.

[5] SP 95/1, 16.8.1591, fol. 56 r, PRO.

[6] Harrison, *Elizabethan Plays and Players*, 35 ff.

[7] On June 24, 1591, while Dr. Teofilus and Henry Francklin were in England, the preliminary documents were drawn up for enlisting this force. Acts Pr. Counc., vol. XXI.

Poland.[1] Teofilus left England in the middle of July[2] and arrived back in Sweden in the beginning of August 1591,[3] whereupon he immediately submitted a report to Duke Charles on the transport of war materials from England to Russia. As a result of this report the Duke despatched an official protest to Elizabeth I on August 16[4] and also the letter to Helena Northampton, dated August 10, 1591,[5] mentioned previously. A number of 'Netherland Captains', who had been recruited through the efforts of Dr. Teofilus, arrived in Nyköping in the autumn of 1591.[6] Dr. Homodei returned to Sweden early in November 1591 and appears to have received part of his annual remuneration:

'Doctor Theophilus Homodeus hafuer bekommitt på sinn besoldning aff Tullen i Stockholm therpå hanns zedell gifuenn thenn 10 Novembris Anno 91 Penning   120 Dal[r7]

Sometime afterwards preparations were made for an embassy to the Netherlands, according to a letter of introduction dated January 15, 1592,[8] and Dr. Teofilus left Nyköping on the 19th of the same month.[9] The Swedish military archives contain the accounts for this mission:

Doctor Theophili Reckningh för the penningar han haffuer uthlagdt till at ahntage fremmende Krigzfolk på Cronones wegne i Sverige Anno Dni 1592.

These records, which amount to an almost complete diary, give a full report on the doctor's activities during his stay of at least fourteen months in the Netherlands.[10] The first entry of interest runs as follows:

[1] SP 88/1, fol. 165 ff.
[2] Söffring Jönssons räkning från en resa i England 1590–91, fol. 15 v, KA.
[3] Kungl. Hofförtärningen 1591–92, SA.
[4] SP 95/1, fol. 56 r f.
[5] Cf. p. 33, last §.
[6] Hertig Karls räntekammare, Strödda handlingar 2, 1591, KA.
[7] 'Dr. Teofilus Homodei has received his pay from the customs in Stockholm, as witness his bill signed 10 November 1591. Coins: 120 daler'; Hertig Karls räntekammare 1588–92, fasc. 3, Cronones sampt Köpmens leffueeringh som rechnas Min n: förste och herre i betalningh, fol. 9 r.
[8] RASG No. 6528, DNA.
[9] Cal. Car. IX, 73.
[10] 'Doctor Teofilus's account for the money which he has laid out for the purpose of recruiting foreign soldiers on behalf of the Swedish Crown, Anno Domini 1592'; Militieräkningar 1592, Nr 14, fol. 247–275, Krigsarkivet.

'*Förähringer*

... Then 27 Martij förähredt Grefue Mauritz tienere drabanter och lackere som någre gånger folgde Doctoren ifrå hofuet till hans härbärge om aftonen. Carlsgijlden   5 Rdr 15 stiber.'[1]

It is probable that at this time the Lord Admiral's Men with Robert Browne as first player were also at Count Maurice's court. Their passport is dated 15 February 1592 and the company appeared in Arnhem shortly afterwards by permission of Count Maurice.[2] It is thus conceivable that while at The Hague, Dr. Teofilus had an opportunity of seeing one of the company's performances.

On April 6, 1592, Dr. Teofilus was received by the assembly of the States-General and submitted his letter of introduction and a request to recruit Netherlands mercenaries. On the very next day the reply of the States-General, which had been drawn up by Jan van Oldenbarnevelt after instructions by the Prince of Orange and Count Willem Lodewijk, was ready.[3] Here again Dr. Teofilus managed his representations clumsily, so much so that the Danish envoy to the Netherlands developed the suspicion that the Swedish plans for recruiting in the Netherlands were not intended to provide troops to fight Russia but were for the purpose of upsetting Norwegian–Russian communications and trade in the northern Arctic waters. As a result of these suspicions a note of protest was sent to the States-General authorities by the Danish regency in Copenhagen on May 9, 1592.[4] Consequently the decision to permit the recruiting of mercenaries by the Swedes was limited by various conditions. A guarantee had to be given that the mercenaries would only be used against the Russians, officers and men belonging to the Netherlands army could not be recruited, a list of the names of all Netherlands recruited mercenaries was to be submitted to the States-General for perusal and approval and a description of the weapons which these mercenaries

[1] '*Gifts*. Given March 27th (1592) by Dr. Teofilus to Count Maurice's (of Orange-Nassau) servants, halberdiers and footmen who at several times in the evening accompanied Dr. T. from the Court (at the Hague) to his inn'; Militieräkningar nr 14/1592, fol. 273, Krigsarkivet. Cf. The same entry occurs in 'Diplomaträkenskaper, vol. 5, (1570–93), fasc. 10; Doctor Theophili och Gerdt Jostings opbörd på Nederlendske Reesenn, fol. 7 r.'

[2] Cf. pp. 135 ff.

[3] RASG 6528 (original draft with alterations by Jan van Oldenbarnevelt), DNA.

[4] RASG 5897, DNA.

were taking with them should also be submitted to the States-General. A list of the weapons involved was duly sent in and this exists today in the National Archives in The Hague.[1] On May 29, 1592,[2] the States-General despatched a letter to Nieasius de Sille in Amsterdam, the Dutch envoy to both England and Denmark, requesting him to remind Dr. Teofilus of the required lists of Netherlands mercenaries in Swedish service. But it seems that no such list was forthcoming. On the other hand, there exists in the Swedish National Archives[3] a list of 37 mercenaries, engaged in secret, over and above the 150–200 who were admitted to being in service. This list is dated July 7 and has no year. On June 8, 1592,[4] the States-General received the above-mentioned protest note from the Danish regency but it was set aside the next day,[5] when the conditions were put forward for the Swedish raising of mercenaries in the Netherlands.

As early as the beginning of 1591 Dr. Teofilus had been in contact with the Dutch champion of freedom in the Spanish war, Willem van Bloys Treslong[6], and requested him to become the commander of the Netherlands mercenary regiment in Sweden. Treslong accepted the offer and made energetic and successful efforts to carry through the recruiting campaign.[7] A large number of recruits joined up[8] and were billeted at field camps in Emden, seat of the court of Count Edzard II of East Friesland and his wife Catherine Vasa, sister of Duke Charles. The recruited regiment was not moved directly from the field camps to the Baltic front at Iwangorod-Narva, but travelled instead via Sweden. The route taken was either from one of the German Baltic ports (Lubeck or Rostock) by water to Nyköping, or else from Emden to Ny Lödöse (Gothenburg) and thence to Nyköping. The regiment was moved in a series of small contingents, each commanded by a captain. The contingents which went via Ny Lödöse were billeted in various camps in Sweden before being sent on to Narva. There were various camps or assembly points

---

[1] RASG 1.7.1592, DNA. Cf. Militieräkningar nr 14/1592, fol. 271 r, Krigsarkivet.
[2] RASG 4696, DNA.
:Hollandica 1598–1611, fasc. 1, RA.
[4] RASG 5897, DNA.
[5] *Ibid.*
[6] Vaderlandsch Woordenboek, vol. 28, 269 ff.; Biografisch Woordenboek, I, 295; Nieuw Nederlandsch Biographisch Woordenboek, VI, col. 121–123.
[7] Hollandica 1598–1611, fasc. 1; Het Staatsche Leger, II, 197 ff.
[8] Res. S.G. 8.6.1592, DNA.

in Norrköping, Söderköping and Arboga[1] and the contingents which came across the Baltic from the German ports were put ashore at Nyköping before being moved on to the Baltic front. The entire regiment was required to swear allegiance to Duke Charles before leaving Sweden.[2]

Dr. Teofilus mentions in his bill[3] the foremost officers in the recruited regiment as follows:

(1) Willam van Bloys Treslong, Colonel.
(2) Carolus Lucz A' Sweveselio, Lt.-Col.
(3) Carolus van Hartim
(4) Abraham van Bloys Treslong, Captain
(5) Gotfridt van Bockolt, Captain
(6) Isembert de Soisson, Captain
(7) Jacob de Rode, Captain
(8) Claus van Dicke und Harlem, Captain
(9) Zacharias De Foß, Captain
(10) Gierhart Felingh, Captain
(11) Johan de la Gardie, Captain
(12) David Olifant, Scottish captain
(13) Albrecht Nolman
(14) Abraham Jungh, Scottish captain
(15) Arent Knopp, Captain
(16) Carolus Cabeliau, Captain
(17) Wilhelm Cratel, French firemaster

On the way back from Nyköping after being present at the wedding of Duke Charles, Michael Heberer von Bretten, on September 6, 1592, met a contingent of foreign mercenaries near Söderköping. He describes them as follows:

Des folgenden Tags / zogen wir durch Saurcöpping / ein Stadt / dieser Landsart nach gantz unbeschlossen. Underwegen begegnet uns / auff ein paar Hundert Soldaten zu Fuß / so für Hertzog Carln / In Niderlandt waren geworben und angenommen / darunter allerhandt Gesindlein / von Frantzosen / Wallonen / Niderländern und etlichen Hochteutschen.[4]

This description confirms that through the efforts of Willem van Bloys Treslong *et alios*, Frenchmen, Walloons, Dutchmen and some Germans had been conscripted. The Scots and the few Englishmen who

[1] Hertig Karls registratur 1592, fol. 152 r, 159 v, &c., RA.

[2] Johan III:s riksregistratur 1591, fol. 78 v, RA.

[3] Militieräkningar nr 14/1592, fol. 250 r ff., Krigsarkivet.

[4] 'Next day / we passed through Söderköping / a town / that as is customary in this country, was entirely open. On the road we met a couple of hundred mercenaries on foot, who had been enlisted and engaged in the Netherlands on behalf of Duke Charles. There were various nationalities among these soldiers, namely Frenchmen, Walloons, Dutchmen and some High Germans'; *Aegyp. Serv.*, 633.

had been recruited at an earlier date were not with this relatively late contingent, having left Emden and arrived in Sweden earlier in the year. Thus the recruiting areas for mercenaries in the Swedish army were Picardy in northern France, Belgium, Holland, England, Scotland and Germany.

The recruited regiment, which had originally been intended for service on the Arctic front[1] was used chiefly for laying siege to Iwangorod in the vicinity of Narva. Soon after they had arrived on the Baltic front there arose 'dissension among the Netherlands soldiers'.[2] The reasons for this seem to have been the lack of Swedish currency, a supply service that did not always function satisfactorily,[3] and the relative isolation of this theatre of war. Even though the mercenaries from the Netherlands were good soldiers, the physical and mental strains were harder than those they were used to, what with the long sea voyage to Sweden, the long march across the country, a further sea voyage and then the prolonged siege with its attendant disease and so on.[4] In October 1592 the siege was broken off. As early as September 22 the Dutch mercenary captains Isembert de Soissons and Godefroy van Bockholt had requested to be released from service with Duke Charles[5] and on October 30 the Netherlands mercenaries returned to Nyköping. Duke Charles recorded this in his almanac as follows:

30 kåm ten förste snö medh nordenweder och derupå stark fråst, samme dagh fick iagh wette, att tett Närlenske kri(g)sfålck war kåmmett tillbake igen och intett utrettett, brefven förde Jörren enspenner.[6]

The mercenary regiment was taken back to Emden in 1592–93 and in the spring of 1593 mutiny broke out and severe disturbances and plundering followed. Duke Charles informed the States-General of this.[7]

But despite all the setbacks the Duke continued to recruit mercenaries

[1] Hertig Karls registratur den 29 februari 1592, fol. 63 r, RA.

[2] *Ibid.*, september–oktober, several letters, RA.

[3] Hertig Karls registratur 1592, juli–augusti, several letters to the supply officers in Söderköping and Norrköping, RA.

[4] *Ibid.*, september–oktober, several letters, RA.

[5] *Cal. Car. IX*, 81.

[6] '30th. Came the first snow with north winds and thereupon strong frost, the same day I learned that the Dutch soldiers had come back again without anything having been accomplished, the dispatch was carried by George'; *ibid.*

[7] Letter from Duke Charles 29.12.1592 received by the States-General 1.9.1593 (Resolutiën der Staten-Generaal VIII: 53, No. 4698), DNA.

throughout 1592. Captain Isembert de Soissons, who was released from Swedish service on September 22, 1592, was apparently duly re-enlisted, since the Duke's almanac for June 5, 1593, reads:

... kåm Capiten Sånso från Lifland.[1]

A promissory note in the Amsterdam trust department, dated Nyköping August 23, 1593, by which Willem IJsbrandtz's son, Gerrit Willemsz Kieft,[2] acknowledges a debt of 292 riksdaler to Captain Godefroy van Bockholt, which debt shall be paid by the debtor's father[3] within three months, indicates that von Bockholt was in Swedish service at the same time as de Soisons.

Money had been advanced to Willem van Bloys Treslong personally for recruiting mercenaries and to this end he had also taken out loans from Dutch private bankers. Three promissory notes were signed[4] by Dr. Teofilus and were drawn upon on the guarantee of Willem van Bloys Treslong, two to Brun die Feyter in The Hague for 4000 and 6000 gulden on May 23 and December 7, 1592, respectively, and one to Johan Bovertz (Jan Gerritsz), burgher, in Dordrecht for 2000 gulden on June 4, 1592.[5] There was an annual interest of 12 per cent on all of these promissory notes. When these debts were not paid, Treslong was held responsible and ordered by the 'Hof van Holland' to redeem the promissory notes, since Sweden had failed to pay her debts.[6] On December 16, 1592, Dr. Teofilus left Amsterdam without having been able to redeem his debts there. After stopping for some time in Emden the doctor returned to Nyköping on March 1, 1593[7].

Due to the financial complications, Willem van Bloys Treslong had been unable to leave the Netherlands.[8] Through the mediation of Philip

[1] 'Captain Soisons came from Livonia'; op. cit., 89 f.

[2] The father of Willem Gerritsz Kieft, the fifth governor of the 'New Netherlands' (1638–1645), i.e. during the first years of the Swedish colony 'New Sweden'. Cf. the record of baptisms at the Oude Kerk, Amsterdam, and the Dict. Am. Biogr., 10, 370 f.

[3] Notariële archieven (Gemeentelijke archiefdienst van Amsterdam) No. 32, fol. 216, May 25, 1594.

[4] Hollandica 1598–1611, fasc. 1, RA; Het Staatsche Leger, II, 197 ff.

[5] Ibid.

[6] Vreede, 15, with reference to P. Bor. It has not been possible to find any record of the proceedings in the archives of the Hof van Holland. In all probability, however, Bor's information is accurate.

[7] Cal. Car. IX, 87.

[8] Hertig Karls räntekammare, Strödda handlingar 2, 1591, KA.

of Nassau the command of the mercenary regiment was handed over to Lt.-Col. Carolus Lucz A' Sweveselio,[1] who at the same time was relieved of his post in the Dutch regular army. A' Sweveselio was in the service of Duke Charles from September 1592 until the beginning of June 1593, when, according to the following note, he left Sweden:

Tärepening^r på resor: 4 junj $\overline{93}$. It^m Hans v. Kiöpenhaffn Ensp^{nr} medh Hern aff Sueuensell åth Nylöse .... 1 Dall^{r2}

'Gifts 1593' in Duke Charles's household accounts contains the following:

Skenchte H.F.N. Caroli lux v. Sueuensel öf^{r}ste Lutinants tiener för en förgyltt spetz som han bahr til H.F.N. och hans Herre hade H.F.N. förährett, 22 Maij $\overline{93}$. Slagne Dal .... 2 str.[3]

Thus, despite the obvious failure of the Netherlands mercenary troops, van Sueuenseel left Sweden, probably in June 1593, with the thanks of Duke Charles. A note in Henry Francklin's album by van Sueuenseel indicates that the latter was executed. Francklin himself added to this note the words: 'Gnad Dir Gott. Bist geköpft worden'.[4] The execution of van Sueuenseel must have taken place at a later date, meanwhile, probably in the Netherlands.

According to the 'Calendaria Caroli IX' the Duke wrote on November 18, 1593:

kåm Dochtor Teofulus till migh på broen medh heftige ord, deruppå och suar.[5]

Seen against the background of the above-mentioned loan transactions, it should be fairly obvious what this trouble was about.

In the same diary the Duke wrote the following in December:

[1] *Ibid.*

[2] 'Travelling expenses: June 4, 1593. Item Hans v. Kiöpenhaffn, rider, accompanied Lt.-Col. van Svevensel to Nylödöse [Gothenburg] ... 1 Daler'; *ibid.*, 1593–95, fasc. 8 (Håkan Larsson 1593) under the heading 'Tärepening^r på resor'.

[3] 'Presented His Royal Highness Lt.-Col. Charles van Svevensel's servant for a golden arrow he carried to His Royal Highness, and his patron had presented to His Royal Highness, Daler ... 2'; *ibid.*, under the heading 'Skänckning^r Anno &c. $\overline{93}$'.

[4] 'God be merciful unto Thee. Beheaded'; op. cit., fol. 152 v.

[5] 'On the bridge met Dr. Teofilus, who spoke angrily to me, whereupon I answered him'; op. cit. 93.

3 kåm D(octor) Teofulus med G(eronimus) Stråssi från Ståckhålm. 5 war åm natten en sådan stårm såsom iagh aldrig haffuer hörtt, gudh ware ås nådigh och barmhertigh. 9 kåm Viting från Ståckhålm, samme dagh kåm Geronimus Strossi och fick matt medh migh ...[1]

It looks as if Geronimus Strozzi tried to mediate between the Duke and Dr. Teofilus. As result of the round-table conversation at Nyköping on December 9, 1593, only three days later Duke Charles granted Dr. Teofilus certain tithe rights in Kumla.[2] But in view of the extent of the credit business in Amsterdam and Dordrecht it is not likely that these tithes would make it possible for Teofilus to pay back all the loans in question.

In 1594 Dr. Teofilus was in the Netherlands again and still unable to redeem the promissory notes.[3] On March 28, 1594, Treslong wrote and informed the Duke[4] that Teofilus had again left the Netherlands without having settled the debts and he urged the Duke to show some gratitude for what he, Treslong, had done for Sweden and to relieve him of the responsibility of the notes. Shortly after this Treslong died at Noordwijk (some 7 miles north of Leyden)[5] and the promissory note responsibilities fell on to the shoulders of his son, Casparus van Bloys Treslong. Thirty-three years later, in 1625, letters were still coming from The Hague[6] reminding King Gustavus Adolphus of Sweden of the still outstanding debt.

At the same time as Teofilus was making his arrangements directly with Treslong and various others, other sums of money were being paid out by Duke Charles to his commissioner in Amsterdam, Willem IJs-brandtz Kieft, for mercenary troops.[7] The treasury records thus show the following accounts:

Willem Issbrandsson i Amsterdam haffuer leffuereratt Doctor Theophilus till underhold och soldaters ophåld och mångas geld sampt till andre utgifter

---

[1] '3rd. Came Dr. Teofilus with Geronimus Strozzi from Stockholm. 5th. There was at night such a storm as I have never heard, may God be merciful and gentle to us. 9th. Came Viting from Stockholm, the same day came Geronimus Strozzi and dined with me ...'; op. cit. 94.
[2] Hertig Karls registratur 1593, fol. 236 v, RA.
[3] Hollandica 1598–1611, fasc. 1, RA.
[4] *Ibid.*
[5] De Navorscher 1856, 300.
[6] Hollandica 1598–1611, fasc. 1, RA.
[7] A member of the well-known family in Amsterdam. Cf. Index.

anno 92, slagne daler 300 och Carlsgylden 5229 på tre resor samt försträckt på 8 kopparstycken (i pant) 1500 slagne daler.[1]

The above account, which is exclusively concerned with expenses for foreign mercenaries, was apparently not paid, but only handed over to the Lord Treasurer at the Court in Stockholm. In the Swedish National Archives there is also a collection of 15 letters[2] from Willem IJsbrandtz to Duke Charles covering the period 15.4.1593–17.8.1594. The last of these letters is signed by IJsbrantz's widow, Erm Bertolomeusdochter, exactly a month after her husband's death on July 17, 1594. The letters all contain obsequious references to the outstanding debts and the precariousness of Willem IJsbrandtz's position as a result of these. The widow informs the Duke that she does not think she will be able to keep the estate together, what with her young children and the great demands that are being made of her.

The reason why these sums of money, all of which were connected with the acquisition of mercenary troops under the command of Treslong, were not repaid seems to have been that Duke Charles considered that this was the concern of John III, who had authorized him to recruit the mercenaries for the Swedish Crown.[3] John III died on November 21, 1592, and Sigismund did not feel himself obliged to pay his father's debts in the Calvinist Netherlands. At the beginning of his reign John III had refused to repay Eric XIV's debts arising out of the latter's English negotiations.[4] Shortly after the death of John III, in connection with the loan transactions and debts of Treslong, we encounter Willem IJsbrandtz Kieft, another of Duke Charles's economic negotiators. It is an odd coincidence that both Willem van Bloys Treslong[5] and Willem IJsbrandtz Kieft[6] died on the same day, July 17, 1594. It is interesting to speculate whether the news of the definite break between Duke Charles and Sigis-

---

[1] 'William IJsbrantz in Amsterdam has delivered to Dr. Teofilus for his own upkeep and the upkeep of the soldiers, and his debts to many persons and other items 1592, 300 daler and 5229 Carlsgylden for three journeys and has advanced him 1500 daler against 8 copper pieces as security'; Hertig Karls räntekammare, Räkningar med diverse personer 1589–1596, KA.

[2] Skrivelser till hertig Karl, K343 (fasc. 'Brev från Willem Issbrandsson'), RA.

[3] Johan III:s registratur (riksregistraturen) den 13 december 1591, RA.

[4] Ingvar Andersson, *Erik XIV:s engelska underhandlingar*.

[5] De Navorscher 1856, 300.

[6] Skrivelser till hertig Karl, K343, (fasc. 'Brev från Willem Issbrandsson', Amsterdam den 17 aug. 1594), RA.

mund reached them both at the same time, whereupon it became quite evident that John III's debts to Holland were not going to be repaid at all. It is also an historic fact that shortly after the death of John III, when the Netherlands loan transactions were brought out for examination with Treslong and Kieft, the Royal Chancellor Nils Gyllenstierna was reminded of another unpaid loan, £10,000, which had been borrowed on account of Eric XIV's approaches to Elizabeth I in 1561–62 from the English banker John Dymock. In singularly irritable terms Gyllenstierna replied to the German merchant adventurer, Georg Erhardt, that he personally felt no inclination to repay the debt, which had been made originally on behalf of the Swedish Crown.[1]

As late as September 3, 1595, Duke Charles issued an 'open letter'[2] to Dr. Teofilus, whereby the latter's annual salary of 300 daler was replaced by the income in kind from several farms in Uppland. In 1595 Dr. Teofilus made a private visit to Italy[3] lasting about four months.

During his period in Stockholm Teofilus had met Arnold von Grothusen, Sigismund's Catholic tutor. As a result of his acquaintance with von Grothusen, after the death of John III in 1592, the doctor supported Sigismund's party in Sweden, and this must have further complicated his relations with Duke Charles.

Towards the end of his Swedish visit the doctor was consulted by a number of persons from the country who had fallen ill. One of these was Princess Elizabeth of Mecklenburg, Duke Charles's sister. I quote the Duke's register concerning his answer to the Princess on June 12, 1595:

Såsom E^{rs} K^{tt} derhoos förmeller sigh wara någedt siukeligh blefwen och fördenskuldh begärer, att D. Theophilus medh Apotekaren motte blifwe till E^{rs} K^{tt} send, Szå hafwer Wij fasth ogerne förnummedt att E^{rs} K^{tt} medh någen suagheet skulle ware beladd. Och hade Wij gerne sendt Doctoren till E^{rs} K^{tt}. Men Wij hade sielwe thenne tiden lathitt Oss Curere, och fördenskuldh hafwe Wij honom än her till icke kunnedt miste. Doch der så är, att E.K. honom ändeligen begärer och behöfwer eller och will hafue Simon Apotekare till sigh wele Wij een thee till E^{rs} K^{tt} förskickie når Wij få förnimme E^{r} K^{ts} mening derom.[4]

[1] Tysk registratur 1592–93, fol. 25 r ff., RA, and F. Ödberg, *Tidsbilder ur 1500-talets Svenska häjder*, pp. 43–110.

[2] Hertig Karls registratur 1595, fol. 254 v, RA.

[3] Kungl. Arkiv, vol. 18, Hertig Karl. Handl. rörande hovhållning m. m. 3, K 351, RA.

[4] 'Inasmuch as that Your Highness relates that You have become somewhat indisposed and therefore request that Dr. Teofilus with the Apothecary might

It seems therefore that Duke Charles regarded Dr. Teofilus as his physician-in-ordinary as late as in June 1595. The Princess's entreaties through her brother also bear witness to Dr. Teofilus's excellent international reputation as a physician.

Another person who consulted Teofilus was Count Abraham Brahe, who wrote in his diary in 1596:

Utij Januarij Månatt war iagh illa siuck ock lott Curere Migh aff Doctor Theophilo på Rydboholm.[1]

At this time Abraham Brahe belonged to Sigismund's party. He was present at the court and among other things he assisted Eric Sparre in making an inventory of the government offices in March 1596. In March 1598 he left for Poland and then accompanied Sigismund on the latter's second Swedish journey and it was not until October 29, 1598, that he addressed an apology to Duke Charles.[2] Brahe's consultation of Dr. Teofilus at this time is thus to a certain extent a confirmation of the latter's loyal feelings towards Sigismund.

After Homodei's return from his visit to Italy his Swedish engagement began to draw to a close. He seems to have stopped on the way back at Kumla in Närke where he had been granted tithes[3] by Duke Charles and wrote his letter of resignation to the Duke from Örebro on May 11, 1596,[4] thanking him at the same time for the payment of his entire salary. This has been interpreted by some researchers as implying that the Duke and Dr. Teofilus parted as friends,[5] although this is scarcely likely. The Örebro letter was probably written chiefly in order that the doctor might be given permission to leave Sweden, but despite this his departure was a complicated matter.[6]

be sent to Your Highness, so have We albeit unwillingly understood that Your Highness is afflicted with some ailment. And we had willingly sent the Doctor to Your Highness. But We Ourselves at that time were undergoing a cure and therefore could not dispense with him. However, if Your Highness nonetheless requests and needs or wishes to have Simon the Apothecary sent to You, We will dispatch him to Your Highness when We have heard Your Highness's opinion'; Riksregistraturen (Hertig Karls diarium), Pars I, 12 June 1595, fol. 176 r.

[1] 'In the month of January I was very ill and had myself cured by Dr. Teofilus at Rydboholm'; *Abraham Brahes tidebok*, 20 and 'Rättelser'.

[2] *SBL*, 5, 673 ff.

[3] Cf. p. 193, 2nd §.

[4] Brev till hertig Karl. Kungl. arkiv 15, RA.

[5] Kockum, 170 f.

[6] Cf. p. 197, 2nd and 3rd §§.

In the summer of 1596 Dr. Teofilus moved to Gdańsk, where he became the Municipal physician in 1607. In about 1604 he married Anne, daughter of Arnold von Grothusen, who had died in 1599, and four of Dr. Teofilus's children are registered as being baptized in St. Peter's Church, Gdańsk, between 1606 and 1611. The eldest son, also named Teofilus, was admitted to Gdańsk High School in August 1612[1] and died probably in 1620.[2]

According to a letter from Arnold von Grothusen's brother-in-law, Nils Rasch, to Johan Tidiksson Bultius on 14 December 1596, it seems that Dr. Teofilus had a lot of trouble before his departure from Stockholm. I quote:

'Doctorem Theophilum Homodeum suo principi, quod eius actiones non probaret, iamdudum valedixisse, arbitror te intellexisse. Is a Duce ex navi per vim retractus, cum minis e maledictionibus postremo dimissus est Inde cum uxore gravide Gedanum se contulit.'[3]

The parish registers of the City of Gdańsk give no indication of when the Doctor's marriage to Anne von Grothusen took place but the references in this letter and the years of the children's baptisms (1606–11) have caused Schwarz to wonder whether the doctor had perhaps been married before. At all events, considering that the eldest son entered Gdańsk High School in 1612, he cannot have been born much later than 1596–98.

None of Dr. Teofilus's correspondence in Gdańsk has been preserved. According to Ludovico von Hammen's 'Vitae medicorum Gedanensium', there exists only one anecdote from Teofilus's time there:

Lepidam de ipso Historiam vulgo narrant,
nimirum ereptis ipsi furto aliquot centum
aureis post aliquot menses invenisse prope
musaei januam schedulam, quae et locum
indicabat, ubi nunc cum foenore nummi aurei

---

[1] The Register (Catalogus discipulorum) of Gdańsk High School.

[2] Schwarz, 32.

[3] 'You presumably know that Dr. Teofilus left his Prince, Duke Charles, long ago as he did not approve of his actions. On this account he was forcibly extracted from the ship by the Duke but was ultimately released and sent on his way under threats and calumnies. He then made for Gdańsk together with his wife, who was pregnant'; Kanslitjänstemännens koncept och mottagna skrivelser, 10, Sigismunds tid, RA.

depositi et gratias pro praestito agebat
beneficio.[1]

Dr. Teofilus died in 1629. The burial register for Marienkirche 1604–85, which served for all the parishes in this city, has the following entry:

1629. 29 Jun. H. Theophilij Homodeus ins 80 Jar
M. Doct.   G.M.[2]

His wife Anne, née von Grothusen, died fifteen years later and the same register has the entry:

1644. 20 Julij Theophilij Homodej witt. 66 Jahr
X fl. beij N° 249[3]

One of Dr. Teofilus's brothers, Jacobo Homodei, was a silk merchant[4] and spent quite a long time in Sweden with the doctor, among other things selling large quantities of silk in connection with the furnishing of Nyköping Castle.

The first delivery of this silk is mentioned in a letter from the doctor to Duke Charles, dated 19 February 1586, stating that the silk was expected to arrive in the following month.[5] Even though Jacobo was the merchant, John III and Duke Charles did their business in this field with the doctor and it was to him that the cash payments were made. Thus for the first delivery to the Duke, Teofilus received 79 daler in payment[6] and on September 10, 1586, John III asked Sparre to receive

... vad aff Doctor Homodeus wij låtit anamma till wårt egit behoff någre stycken sammet och siden huilka belöper sigh till niehundrede och sjuttio daler ...[7]

---

[1] 'A delightful story is told of him, to the effect that he had a number of gold coins stolen from him. A few months later, however, he discovered a note near the museum door telling him where the money and the interest could be found and thanking him for the blessed loan'; op. cit.

[2] '29.6.1629. Mr. Teofilus Homodeus, M.D., † in his 80th year'; op. cit., No. 249.' G.M. = Graue Mönche, i.e. a Franciscan monk. In this case it indicates that Dr. Teofilus was given a Catholic burial in the Church of the Holy Trinity close by the Franciscan monastery in Gdańsk.

[3] '20.7.1644. Teofilus Homodeus's widow. † 66 years old. Buried next to No. 249'; op. cit.

[4] Cal. Car. IX, 10.11.1589, p. 69.

[5] Cf. p. 179, last §.

[6] Hertig Karls räntekammarböcker, KA.

[7] 'that which of Dr. Teofilus we have been pleased to receive for our own needs some pieces of velvet and silk which amount to nine hundred and seventy daler ...'; Johan III:s registratur 1586, fol. 162 v–163 r, RA.

The bailiff of Westmanland was to pay this bill. It seems, however, that the full sum was not paid until February 25, 1587, when Anders Larsson was ordered by John III to pay from copper profits the outstanding debt, which by this time amounted to 1700 daler. The passage in the letter to Anders Larsson runs:

... att tu aff kopperwinsten steller för[ne] Doctor Theophilus medh thett förste tillfridhz att wij aff honom herom icke offtere motte bliffue bekymbrede ...[1]

The following year there must have been a new delivery of silk goods to Sweden, because on August 1, 1588, five people, one of whom was the Stockholm-resident Venetian merchant, Johan Baptista Pelerini, complained to the Gdańsk authorities over the affreightment arrangements by the brothers Theophilus and Giacomo (Jacobo) de Omedais of the *Morianen*, a vessel which at this point was in Copenhagen.[2]

There was yet another delivery to Nyköping at the end of 1589 when the Duke noted in his almanac:

... kåm D(octor) Teophulus bror med någre siden waror.[3]

On January 10, 1592, during the Swedish–Russian war, Jacobo Homodei made a large delivery of various types of goods,[4] both on behalf of the Duke and the Crown. This delivery included silk, velvet, satin, beaver-skin hats, 670 barrels of grain and so on, to a value of 8609 daler, of which the Duke's part was worth 3517 daler.

Jacobo Homodei spent long periods in Stockholm and was able to adapt himself to Swedish conditions better than his brother, chiefly due to the fact, in all probability, that he stuck fast to his Calvinist beliefs. In the earlier mentioned letter[5] dated Gdańsk, January 3, 1597, from Dr. Teofilus to Ture Bielke, Teofilus seemed to be uneasy about his brother's fate in Sweden, even though Jacobo was managing perfectly well. When the Duke's chancellor, Nils Chesnecopherus, in July 1602

---

[1] '... that you of the copper profits as soon as possible make good to Dr. Teofilus so that We shall not be troubled by him any more for these expenses'; Johan III:s registratur 1587, fol. 64 r, RA.

[2] *Danz. Inv.*, 778.

[3] 'came Dr. Teofilus's brother with some silken goods'; *Cal. Car. IX*, 10.11.1589, 69.

[4] Hertig Karls, räntekammare, räkningar med diverse personer 1586–95, KA.

[5] Skoklostersamlingen, Avd. II in folio, Miscellana, vol. 1, RA. Cf. this appendix, p. 180.

'through remarkable favour and grace' became the owner of the von Grothusen family estates, an exception was made of 'the stone house which was purchased by Jacob Homodej with his own money.'[1] Jacobo had three sons, Vincentus, Caesare and Johannes Baptista. Vincentus became a silk merchant like his father.[2] Caesare became a judge of the City of Stockholm on May 12, 1595,[3] taking the oath at the Court of Records. Johannes Baptista studied medicine at the University of Bâle in Switzerland and was awarded his doctorate on 12 December, 1598. The entry in the university register runs as follows:

'Johannes Baptista Homodaeus, Nobilis Rhaetus ex Vulturena ... 1598, 12.XII., dr. med. (Jo. B. Homodaeus, Tiranensis Rhaetus).[4]

He subsequently became a municipal physician in Elbląg[5] and drowned on 24 July, 1628, while crossing the Vistula near Frisches Haff on his way to attend King Gustavus Adolphus, who had a bullet wound in his shoulder, at the headquarters in Dirschaw.[6] Johannes Baptista had been recommended to the King by the field padre, John Bothvidius. A son of Johannes Baptista, Jacob Homodei,[7] was entered on the lists of the University of Groningen in 1633, having previously studied in Uppsala and Oxford. He had matriculated at Uppsala on 21 July, 1628, as

'Jacobus Homodei Elbingens. Ex. Germ.'[8]

A notice about him in *Elbinga Literata* runs as follows:

'Jac. Homodaei, Joh. Babtistae, Nobilis Rhaeti, Medicinae D. ejusdemque Practici & Physici Elbing. a. 1628 insperato in Habo submersi filius, itidem Medicinae in patria Practicus & Physicus celebris, Groeningae studiis incumbens sub Joh. Freytagio de Paradoxis & erroribus novae Sectae Sennertio-Paracelsicae, disputationem edidit in 8.s. anno.'[9]

[1] Reduktionskollegiets aktsamling nr 8, KA.
[2] Hertig Karls räntekammare. Strödda handlingar 2/1593, KA.
[3] *Stockholms stads tänkeböcker 1592–95*, 312.
[4] *Matrikel der Universität Basel*, 2/469.
[5] *Elbinga Literata*, 128.
[6] *Hoppe*, 3, 266.
[7] *PHT*, 1927.
[8] *Ibid.*
[9] 'Jacobus Homodaei was the son of Johannes Babtista Homodaei, a Rhaetian nobleman, Doctor of Medicine and Municipal doctor in Elbląg, who in 1628 accidentally drowned in Frisches Haff. Jacobus Homodaei also became a Municipal doctor in his native town Elbląg. While studying at Groningen under Johannes Freytag he defended a thesis on 'The new Sennertio-Paracelsian sect's paradoxes and delusions'; *Elbinga Literata*, 128.

While living in Gdańsk, Dr. Teofilus met Johannes Messenius the elder, who in 1607 married Lucie von Grothusen, younger sister of the doctor's wife Anne. As Messenius was born while his mother's first husband was still alive, he was the child of an illegal marriage according to canon law (though not according to contemporary Swedish law) and on 13 January, 1607, shortly before he married Lucie von Grothusen, a papal licence was granted for him to became a Catholic priest (he had completed his studies at the Jesuit seminary in Braunsberg in 1603):

'humillime supplicat S.S.D.N., ut secum quoad ordines sacros promoveri possit super quacunque irregularitate praemissorum occasione contracta, clementer sua S^tas dispensare dignetur.'[1]

His marriage naturally put an end to the idea of becoming a priest. The long interval between the completion of Messenius's studies in Braunsberg and the granting of a papal licence may help to explain his many lengthy tours in the years 1603–07. Johannes Messenius stayed in Teofilus's home in Gdańsk in 1607–8 with his wife and it was here that his eldest son, Arnold Messenius, was born.[2]

There is not much available information concerning the relations between Teofilus and Messenius, but it is quite possible that Messenius's long stay in the Teofilus household may have been of considerable importance to his development as a playwright.

In 1626, when Messenius was making his will while imprisoned in Kajaneborg,[3] he was critical of Dr. Teofilus. Messenius considered that as the son-in-law of Arnold von Grothusen he had been extremely ill-treated. Dr. Teofilus, on the other hand, had received a great deal of value from the home of his wife's parents, including a dowry of 600 German daler, silver and copper pots, silver dishes, hock glasses, cushions and bolsters. While writing an historical thesis in Kajaneborg, Messenius revealed particular irritation over the fact that the doctor had acquired his wife's parents' valuable library—estimated by Messenius to be worth at least 300 Carlsgyllen—for a mere 80 gyllen.[4]

---

[1] '[Johannes Messenius] most humbly entreats His Holiness that, should it be possible to extend the holy ordinations of priests, His Holiness in His mercy may free him from every conceivable ecclesiastical obstacle that he [Messenius] may have incurred as a result of the above'; Fondo Borghese 2, 234, fol. 140; Archivo Segreto; The Vatican.

[2] Cf, p. 162.

[3] Messenius, *En lithen wnderwijssningh*.

[4] Cf. Schück, *Johannes Messenius*.

Before Dr. Teofilus moved from Sweden to Gdańsk in 1596 there were only occasional visits by English theatrical groups to this town, but when the doctor took up his post as city physician these visits became considerably more frequent. John Green's company[1] in particular performed in several towns in Poland and eastern Germany, e.g. in Gdańsk and Elbląg in 1607, in Gdańsk in 1615 and in Gdańsk and Rostock in 1619.

Trade between England, on the one hand, and the Hanseatic League, Poland and Russia, on the other, via the German Baltic ports, was very lively at this time,[2] and there was even an English Puritan colony actually residing in Elbląg.[3] But these circumstances alone do not explain entirely why the English theatrical groups made their way as far east as to Gdańsk. There must have been some driving force here and in view of the fact that Dr. Teofilus was resident in Gdańsk, and remembering his wide contact with the English theatrical world of that time, it is by no means unlikely that it was his influence and encouragement that brought them there.

[1] Chamb., *Eliz. Stage*, 2, 281 ff.

[2] Ingvar Andersson, *Hamlet-dramats nordiska miljö*, 148; Nina Bang, *Sundstulls-räkenskaperna*, 1: 5 and 2: 4.

[3] S. P. Poland, 88/1, fol. 159 r, PRO (Sir Christopher Parkin's Journal, 1591–92).

Henry Francklin

Henry Francklin was probably born about 1550. According to the records,[1] 'his father was an Englishman Roland Francklijn and his mother Dorotea Patavin, otherwise called Dorotea Ellmont (Ellmout) and by von Schantz[2] entitled Princess'.

It would seem to be correct that his father was English and that his name was Roland Francklijn. From Hungary in 1584 the young Henry Francklin reports in his album that during one of his journeys he discovered his father's signature in a prayer book:

> In this Herr Balthazar De Battianis prayerbook
> I found my father's name thus Rowlandus Francklijnus
> Anglus. Date Roan in Frans:
> 20 Maij Anno 1542.[3]

The following record from the time of Henry VIII concerns Henry Francklin's father and grandfather:

Hugo ffrankelyn de Hospicio dn̄i (domini) regis et Roulandus ffrankelyn
    filius & heres p(re)d(ic)ti Hugonis coram eodem dn̄o (domino) rege in Cancellaria
sua p(er)sonalit(r) constituti recognoverunt se et eorum utrumque per se
    debere Nicho(-lao) Sheperd civi & bruer London & Will(elm-)o Pomfrett civi
& ffysshemonger London viginti libros sterling solvend(as) eisdem Nicho(lao),
    & Will(elm)o aut suo certo attorn(o) exec(utoribus) vel assign(atis) suis in
festo Natalis domini pro(ximo) futuro. Et nisi fecerint concesserunt, quod
    dicta pecunia levetur de terris et catallis suis ad opus & usum prefatorum
Nich(ola)i & Will(elm)i exec(-utorum) vel assign(-atorum) suorum ubicumque
    inventa fuerint infra regnum Angliae. T(-este) R(-ege) apud Westmona
(sterium) XXXI die Januarii anno regni
sui tricesimo quarto (1543).

---

[1] *Elg.*, II, 817.

[2] C. L. von Schantz, *Adliga släkten Frankelin*, nr 48.

[3] Op. cit., fol. 8 v.

In the margin:

Recognitio pro Sheperd & Pomfrett.[1]

This implies that Hugo Francklin, Henry's grandfather, was employed at the court of Henry VIII. The date, 31 January, 1543, is interesting inasmuch as it indicates that Hugo Francklin probably entered the service of Henry VIII after the Catholic Queen Catherine Howard's execution on Tower Hill on February 13, 1542, and shortly before Catherine Parr became Queen of England following the wedding at Hampton Court on July 12, 1543, when Protestantism was becoming prevalent at the court. It should also be observed that the interval of time between Roland Francklin's entry in De Battiani's prayer book and the date of the above-mentioned promissory note is relatively short (20.5.1542–31.1.1543). In view of the political development in England it can be assumed that the Francklin family was in the service of Henry VIII from 1542–1547, but that in connection with the anti-Reformation movement of the catholics following the death in 1553 of Edward VI, when Philip and Mary were in power in England, they had to leave the court and probably flee the country, unable to return again until the accession of Elizabeth I in November 1558. Otherwise it is a fact that Roland Francklyn was back again in England shortly after the coronation of Queen Elizabeth I. The following record from the Elizabethan period is preserved to our time:

Regina Omnib(-u-)s ad quos & Salutem. Sciatis q(-uo-)d cum Roulandus
ffrankelein Gene(-ro-)sus alias dict(-u-)s
Rolandus ffrancklen de London Generosus nup(-er) in Cur(-ia) n(-ostr-)a
coram Antonio Broune et sociis suis
nup(-er) Justic(-iariis) Nostris de Banco p(-er) br(-ev-)e n(-ost-)r(-u-)m
implicasset Thomam Busshe nup(-e-)r de London gentilman

---

[1] 'Hugo ffrankelyn of the Royal Household and Roland ffrankelyn, son & heir of the aforesaid Hugo, in the King's presence in his Chancellery, have made a personal recognition that they each owe Nicholas Sheperd, citizen & Brewer of London, & William Pomfrett, citizen & fishmonger of London, twenty pounds sterling payable to the said Nicholas & William, or their settled attorney, executors & assigns, on next Christmas day. And in case they do not pay, they have agreed that the said sum shall be levied on their lands and chattels for the use of the aforesaid Nicholas and William their executors or assigns, wherever they may be found within the realm of England. Witness the King at Westminster, on 31st day of January in the thirty-fourth year of his reign [i.e. 1543]. In the margin: Recognition for Sheperd and Pomfrett'; Close Rolls 34 Henry VIII; Ref. C. 54/431; PRO.

alias d(-i-)c(-tu-)m Thomam Busshe de London Gen(-er-)osum de debito quadraginta ££S, quod idem
Rolandus a pr(-e)fato Thoma exigit ac idem Thomas p(-ro) eo q(-uo-)d non venit coram p(-re-)fat(-is) nup(-er)
Justic(-iariis) p(-re-)fato Rolando se(-cun-)d(-u-)m legem et consuetudinem regni n(-ost-)ri Angli(-ae) inde responsu(-ru-)s in exigend(-o),
posit(-us) fuisset in hustengo n(-ost-)ro London, ad utlagandum et ea occa-
(-sio-)ne postmodum utlagatus sicut
p(-er) tenorem Recordi et p(-ro-)cessus utlagari p(-re-)dicte quem coram nob(-is) in Cancellaria n(-ost-)ra venire fecimus
plene liquet. Iamque idem Thomas se redd(-er-)it prisone n(-ost-)re de fflete occasione p(-re-)dict(-a) et in eadem moret(-u-)r
sicut dilectus et fidelis n(-ost-)er Jacobus Dyer miles capitularis Justiciarius noster de Banco predicto nos in Cancellaria
ad mandatum n(-os-)t(ru-)m certificavit. Nos pietate moti p(er)donavim-
(-u-)s eidem Thome utlagiam p(-re-)dictam et
firmam pacem nostram ei inde concedim(-u-)s, ita tamen q(-uo-)d stet rect(-u-)s in Cur(-ia) n(-ost-)ra, si p(-re-)dictus
Rolandus versus eum loqui voluerit de debito supradicto. In cuius rei &.
T(-este) R(-egina) apud Westmonasterium XI die ffebruarii (3 Eliz./1561/).

In the margin:

De perdonatione utlagarie pro T.Busshe.[1]

[1] 'The Queen ... To all, &., Greeting. Be it known that whereas Roland Franck-lyn, Esq., otherwise called Roland Francklyn of London, Esq., recently in our Court, in the presence of Anthony Browne and his associates, recently our Justices of the Bench summoned by our writ Thomas Busshe, lately of London, gentleman, otherwise known as Thomas Busshe of London, gentleman, for a debt of forty pounds which the same Roland demanded of the aforesaid Thomas, and the same Thomas, because he did not appear before the aforesaid recent Justices, there to answer the aforesaid Roland according to the law and custom of our Kingdom of England, as required. He was posted on our hustings of London as an outlaw, and as so outlawed in conformity with the law and trial of the aforesaid outlaw whom we summoned to our presence in our Chancellery as is manifest. The same Thomas was to give himself up in our prison of the Fleet on the aforesaid occasion and remain there. So our beloved and faithful James Dyer, our Chief Justice of the aforesaid Bench in Chancery, certified according to our order. We, moved by pity, have pardoned the outlawry of the said Thomas and granted him our assured reconcilation in such a way, however, that he may take his trial in our Court, if the aforesaid Roland should wish to enter a claim against him for the aforesaid debt. In which, &c., Witness the Queen, at Westminster, on the 11th day of February 3 Eliz. I [1561]'. In the margin: 'Of the pardoning of the outlawry of T. Busshe'; Ref C. 66/965, no. 31; P.R.O. Patent Rolls 3 Eliz. I, vol. II, 1560–63, p. 54.

C. L. von Schantz has the following about family No. 48 (Franckelin):

... af Rijssk familie H. Hindrich Rolandsson till Odensförs och Bocksjöholm, Kongl. legat ifrån Engeland till Sverige, blef här öfwerste och naturaliserad bland adeln ...[1]

In a note in Erik Falck's album, dated Vienna, 20 June 1583, Henry Francklin writes:

I Joye to heive this roote of gentries
for I am sprunge of such antiquity.[2]

Of all the available information on Francklin, this note by his own hand would seem the most reliable. His roots were in the English gentry. This is confirmed by the court record cited above, dated Westminster, 11 February 1561, where we find the expression

... Rolandus ffrancklen de London Generosus ...[3]

as well as by the following extract from a record drawn up at the College of Arms on 2 June 1592 in connection with the renovation of Franklin's coat of arms, where he is referred to as

... Henricus Francklyn natione Anglus filius Rowlandi Francklyn Generosi ...[4]

There does not appear to have been any Russian blood in the Francklin pedigree. von Schantz's claim that Francklin became a Swedish colonel is borne out to a certain extant by the College of Arms, where it is stated that before the Grant by William Dethick on May 20, 1592, he was in military service and that he belonged to a very old London family.[5]

Dorotea Patavin, otherwise known as Ellmont, cannot be localized. The names Patavin and Ellmont (Ellmout) in the pedigrees of the Swedish House of Nobility apparently are corruptions. von Schantz's claim that Dorotea Patavin was of princely origin probably came from Palmskiöld (1719). In the Palmskiöld collection at Uppsala, under Koskull,[6] we find:

[1] 'of Russian family H. Hindrich Rolandsson Frankelin to Odensfors and Bocksjöholm, Royal envoy from England to Sweden, where he became a colonel and was naturalized among the Nobility, ...'; *Genealogisk Matrikel*, Släktböcker och genealogiska samlingar, vol. 95, 203, RA.

[2] Op. cit., fol. 246.

[3] '... Roland Francklin of London, Gentleman ...'; op. cit.

[4] '... Henry Francklin, Englishman, son of Roland Francklin, Gentleman ...'; op. cit.

[5] Cf. pp. 28–29, and Patent Rolls 3 Eliz. I; Ref. C. 66/965, no. 31.

[6] Henry Francklin's daughter, Mary Catherine, was married to Baron Andrew Koskull.

Dorotea Patavin, en furstes dotter uti Engeland.[1]

The Stiernman Records state, concerning Dorotea Patavin:

Dorotea Patavin, den andra kalla Ellmout.[2]

After a careful perusal of the Francklin album with some 300 names between 1582–1610 and some 80 coats of arms, particularly those concerned with the English journey of 1591, one cannot help but wonder whether or not a relative of his had added his name. But unfortunately the album is not complete. It seems as if some of the pages were discarded during the unskilled bookbinding at the beginning of the 19th century, while other pages have been mutilated to such an extant that the notes have been made illegible or have even disappeared altogether. Of those names that do exist there are none that are of a character such as can be assigned with certainty to the Francklin family. The first name[3] from the English journey is Thomas Petevine, June 2, 1591. It is just possible that the Patavin of the Swedish pedigrees is a corruption of Petevine. It has not been possible to discover any data on this Thomas Petevine which might confirm his relationship with Henry Francklin.

It is also worth considering Henry Francklin's custom of getting his friends to enter their names in his album. The use of such albums derives from the German universities and was current from about 1550 to about 1800. The custom was rather unfamiliar outside Germany and when one comes across it in England, Holland and the Scandinavian countries, the album almost always belongs to someone who picked up the habit while studying at a German university. Judging from several notes in Francklin's album, it appears that he had a fairly good knowledge of German. At certain times when he has expressed himself violently it almost seems as if German were his native tongue. During one of his journeys he met an Englishman in Tallinn in 1600 and he writes:

Thomas Forster[4] in Revell
the 31 day of December Ann: 1600.

This note has been crossed out in his own hand and the words *ehrlos, forlogen, schellm*[5] added. At any time when he discovered that someone

---

[1] 'Dorotea Patavin, daughter of an English prince'; op. cit.
[2] 'Dorotea Patavin, otherwise called Ellmout'; op. cit.
[3] Op. cit. fol. 22 r.
[4] *Ibid.*, fol. 85 v.
[5] 'dishonourable, lying, scoundrel'; op. cit.

whose autograph was in his album had died, he added the words in German *Gnad Dir Gott*.[1] It is thus not unlikely that Henry Francklin was educated at some kind of German school or university.

Concerning Henry Francklin's coat of arms, it can be noted that before his grant was renewed in 1592, the coat was a simple one with a lion rampant but that after the renewal the coat was divided, the lion (representing his father's family) occupying the lower field and the imperial eagle flanked by two royal crowns (representing his mother's pedigree) the upper. The latter field is described in the grant of renewal thus:

... In superiori autem Ceruleo Aquilam aliis utrinque distentis inter duas regum coronas auro gemmisque micantes ...[2]

During Elizabeth I's reign it seems as if Henry Francklin served in either the English or else a foreign army, from which he subsequently requested release in connection with his move to Sweden. The College of Arms[3] register states as follows of him at the time of the renewal of his Grant of arms in 1592:

Quod cum Henricus Francklyn natione Anglus filius Rowlandi Francklyn generosi Qui extraque regionem iam *diu felicissime belligeri peragratione et*[4] perlustratione non mediocri sua cum Laude perfunctus ...

Maiorum suorum insignia ab antiqua familia et Stirpis sua prosapia derivata (testimonium) a nobis sub dyplomata nostrorum (accipere) *exemplicavi* obnixe dudum (postularit) *postulaverit*.[5]

It was in about 1579 that Henry Francklin served Duke Charles for the first time. The first mention of his name appears to be in Duke Charles's accounts in 1580, when "Henrich Engelskman" received a costume from the royal wardrobe.[6] Another record from the same year shows that Francklin had performed certain services for the Duke:

---

[1] 'God be merciful unto Thee.'

[2] 'In the upper blue field: no less than the imperial eagle on gold flanked by two royal crowns of gold and precious stones.'

[3] Vinc. Old Gr. fol. 518, 530 and 537, Coll. of Arms.

[4] The words in italics do not occur in fol. 537.

[5] 'Henry Francklin, Englishman, son of Roland Francklin, Gentleman, has for a long time served abroad with great distinction in military campaigns. ...

The coat of arms of his ancestors, a very old family, I have now exemplified below the under Grant, which for a long time he has requested to receive'; op. cit.

The words in brackets have been crossed out in the document and the words in italics substituted.

[6] Register på Hoffmantaledh som Clädninger skule bekoṁa pro anno &c. 80. Bunt 35. Kungl. klädkammaren 1580; SA.

'Hendrich Engelskman till K.M: medh Bref then andre Noŭemb. Peninger — 2 Daler. Annen gång till K.M: den 23 Noŭemb. Peninger — 3 Daler.'[1]

According to a letter from the Duke to Sigismund, dated Gripsholm, June 21, 1581,[2] Henry Francklin had been given a recommendation from the Duke for service in Sigismund's court. While it cannot be established just how soon he was appointed, it seems from Anne Vasa's letter of introduction for him to Queen Elizabeth on 17 December 1590[3] that Francklin had been in Sigismund's service for several years by then. His second engagement at Duke Charles's court in Nyköping started at Michaelmas in 1589.[4]

Judging from his album, Francklin travelled a great deal during the 1580's. In 1583 he met Erik Falck in Vienna.[5] Francklin visited Vienna on two subsequent occasions, in 1585 and 1586. During the 1580's he was also twice in Constantinople, from May 1587 until February 1588 and from January to October 1589. Since he had been there before, Duke Charles decided to send him to Constantinople a third time in 1590 to purchase four Turkish horses.[6] At the same time he was appointed a chamberlain in the Duke's service. For some reason this third journey to Constantinople was never carried out; he went to Warsaw in this year to be present at the assembly of the Polish parliament and it may be that he was thus too busy to find time to get there. According to his album Francklin was in Poland from April to August 1590 and during this time he met (April 4) King John III's councillors, Eric Ribbing and John Gyllenstierna,[7] as well as (May 2) the secretary of John III and Sigismund, Nicholas Rasch.[8] Probably because of this he was delayed in Warsaw. The Turkish horses were never purchased, but instead during this journey Francklin bought a Hungarian horse in Lemberg for the Duke.[9] According to the album, Francklin was in Lemberg on July

[1] 'Henry Englishman to His Majesty with letters 2 November (1580). Cash — 2 Daler. Yet again to His Majesty 23 November (1580). Cash — 3 Daler'; Täre-penninger, fol. 16 v, Kungl. Hofförtärningen; SA.

[2] Hertig Karls registratur 1581, fol. 45 r, RA.

[3] Cotton MSS, Vespasian F III, 137, BM.

[4] Hertig Karls räntekammare 1589–92, fasc. 4, fol. 18 r; KA.

[5] Erik Falck's album, fol. 246, and op. cit., fol. 49 v.

[6] Hertig Karls föreskrift till konung Sigismund den 9.1.1590. Hertig Karls registratur 1590, RA.

[7] Op. cit., fol. 134 v.

[8] Op. cit., fol. 70 r.

[9] Hertig Karls räntekammare 1590–92, fasc. 4, fol. 17 v–21 v, KA. Cf. Chapter 1.

14, 1590, when a Frenchman called Carolus Cortesius Gallus[1] entered his name.

In the autumn of 1590 Francklin was at Uppsala where Anne Vasa issued a passport for him on December 17 to Elizabeth I. At the turn of the year (1590–91) he was at Nyköping and on January 23 Duke Charles also issued a passport for him to go to England to 'buy cloth' and another, on February 1, to Queen Elizabeth. A report on the subsequent journey to England has been made elsewhere.[2]

It is worth mentioning meanwhile that Henry Francklin met William Dethick, Garter King-of-Arms, at this time,[3] probably because Francklin wanted to renew his grant of arms. Such a renewal was in fact arranged, in London, a letter to this effect being issued by the College of Arms on May 20, 1592, signed by William Dethick.[4] In appearance and layout it is reminiscent of the draft dockets of the grant of arms which in 1596 and 1599 were issued for John Shakespeare, William Shakespeare's father. These, too, were both signed by William Dethick.[5]

The reason why Francklin wished to get the Grant by Dethick was probably his forthcoming marriage with Constantia Eriksdotter, the illegitimate daughter of Eric XIV. The marriage took place in 1594 but these two had known each other for a long time before this and had agreed upon marriage as early as 1590–91 in connection with Henry Francklin's journey to England.[6] After Eric XIV had been deposed and imprisoned, Constantia spent several years at Duke Charles's castle at Nyköping as a lady-in-waiting to Catherine Vasa.[7] When she married Francklin, she received two parishes[8] in the district of Boberg, Ostrogothia, and also Bocksjöholm, a small estate in the district of Vadsbo in north Westrogothia.[9]

In 1592 Duke Charles sent Henry Francklin on a journey up to the Arctic Ocean as far as the western shore of the White Sea, and issued instructions to this effect to Sven Pedersson Bagge,[10] who had commanded

---

[1] Op. cit., fol. 76 v.

[2] Cf. pp. 15–32

[3] Henric Francklyns stambok, fol. 52 v.

[4] Vinc. Old Gr., fol. 518, 530 and 537, College of Arms.

[5] C. W. Scott-Giles, *Shakespeare's Heraldry*, 36 ff.

[6] Ms Additional 36774, fol. 17 r, BM. Cf. pp. 22–24.

[7] Duke Charles's daughter by his first marriage.

[8] Sandbergska samlingen, KA.

[9] *Ibid.*

[10] Hertig Karls registratur 1592, fol. 136 r and v, RA.

a successful expedition against the Russians in this northern theatre of war in 1591. The commander-in-chief in the Arctic theatre 1590–92 was Sven Bagge's father, Peder Bagge. Soon after the Duke had issued these instructions on June 16, 1592, Francklin began to make preparations for his trip and according to the household accounts, received a sum of money from the Duke for this purpose. He was still in Stockholm on July 16 but must have left soon afterwards since on July 26 the vicar of Kemi, Laurentius Henrici, entered his name in Francklin's album.[1] Kemi was to be the starting point of the expedition. During the sea voyage there from Stockholm some of the provisions were spoiled and there is an entry in Hans Christofferson's accounts to show that on 30 July 1592 Francklin had this loss made good to him at the storehouse in Kemi:

Hindrich   Bekienies iag Hindrich Frannchleinn att
Franchlein   haffue anamatt aff Erlig och Förståndig
              Hanns Christåffuerson I denne stadh att
              min Fettalie wartt Fördärfuatt Påå Siönn
              som iagh Bekom ifrånn StochHållm thz
              Effterskrene Parseller ... Deß till Wißo
              Under mith Signeet Dat^m Kime (Kemi)
              thenn 30 Jullij Anno 92.[2]

Francklin was accompanied by two servants and a chamberlain, Jöran Woritz, who signed himself Georgius Wogesserius after the following entry in Francklin's album:

Haec in sua memoria scribebat Georgius Wogesserius in Mare Album in Russia 20 Augustij Ann salutis 1592.
a Gießensis.[3]

Francklin and his company followed the Kemi river northwards. The military operations in 1592 proved considerably less extensive than in 1591. There was a minor encounter between the Swedish and Russian forces at Suma but as the Russians had strengthened their positions and

[1] Op. cit., fol. 161 v.
[2] 'I, Henry Francklin, certify to having received from honest and understanding Hans Christofferson in this town—after the provisions which I had with me from Stockholm had been spoiled at sea—the items listed below. ... Thereunto I affix my seal at Kemi on 30 July 1592'; Provianträkenskaper för Norrbotten 1592–93, fasc. Hans Christoffersons Rechenschap för Proviant uti Kimmehampn (Kemi); KA.
[3] 'This in his memory wrote Georgius Wogesserius on the White Sea in Russia. Giesen, August 20th, 1592'; op. cit., fol. 111 r.

generally reinforced their defences, the Swedish campaign in North Bothnia in 1592 was in effect a complete failure. Francklin returned from his expedition to the White Sea on about 1 September 1592. In order to reach the Gulf of Bothnia as quickly as possible, he travelled some parts of the route at least by 'rapids boat' down various Finnish rivers to Uleåborg. Three boatmen were paid by him after the various river voyages in Uleåborg on 20 September 1592:

Hen =   Till Hinrich Franchlin Hertig Carls hofiunckare till — 3 Forskarar
rich   ther på hans quittens giffuinn then 20 Septembris Anno &c. 92.[1]
Franck =
lin

On 28 September Francklin was the guest of the vicar of Torneå, Eskillus Andreae.[2] We know that while Francklin was in Uleåborg, Peder Bagge and a company of fifteen secured provisions there on 24 September for their journey home.[3] It is thus conceivable that the two travelled in company from Finland to Sweden until they reached Gävle or thereabouts. Peder Bagge was back in his home district—Söderby in the parish of Örtomta, Ostrogothia—early in 1593.[4]

Francklin was as far south as Uppsala by 25 October.[5] It was probably during this journey that the Vicar of Tierp made an undated entry in his album.[6]

On October 29, 1592, Francklin reported on his trip in the north to John III. The King's secretary, Olof Sverkersson, received a letter[7] to the effect that the Russian garrison in Kollansso had been strengthened and that nothing had been done. According to Duke Charles's almanac, on November 7, 1592:

[1] 'To Henry Francklin, Duke Charles's chamberlain, for 3 'rapids boatmen' on his receipt granted 30 September 1592.' Proviranträkenskaper för Norrbotten 1592–93, fasc. 'Gabriell Tomesons Räckenschap för Uleåå Proviant från 17 Juni Anno &c. 92 till ijterste Septembris Anno &c. 1593'; KA. A *forskar* or *forskarl* was a ferryman who plied the swift-running, boulder-strewn rivers.
[2] Henric Francklins stambok, fol. 161 r.
[3] Finska fogderäkenskaperna för Uleåborg 1592; No. 4795, fol. 33; Finlands Riksarkiv, Helsinki.
[4] *SBL*, 2, 571.
[5] There is an entry in Francklin's album by the mayor of Uppsala, Bengt Håkansson, with this date, fol. 163 v.
[6] Op. cit., fol. 163 v.
[7] Hertig Karls registratur 29.10.1592, fol. 230 v, RA.

kåm Hinrick Frankelin igen ...[1]

After his return to Nyköping preparations began for the wedding and when this had taken place Francklin and his wife Constantia settled down at Bocksjöholm where, according to the album, there were a number of guests from abroad between 1595 and about 1610.

Unlike Teofilus Homodei, Henry Francklin was always on good terms with Duke Charles and remained completely loyal to him. This is illustrated by the fact that Francklin was one of the signatories of the Riksdag decrees in Arboga (1597) and Vadstena (1598).[2] During the summer of 1599 Francklin was also marshal of Sigismund's Polish legation to Duke Charles in Stockholm.[3] Earlier that year, on February 8 in fact, Francklin had been visited at Bocksjöholm by William Greene and his associate John Bland. Greene was Thomas Fisk's successor as Duke Charles's agent in England.[4] In 1601 Francklin was at Tallinn, in Esthonia, where Duke Charles had his headquarters during the war against the Poles. With the Duke were his Duchess and their son Gustavus Adolphus, while their second son, Charles Philip, was born at Tallinn and christened there in May 1601, with the English ambassador Sir Richard Lee as Queen Elizabeth's deputy. Besides Francklin, those present at Tallinn on this occasion included James Hill. Sir Richard Lee was there in the course of his embassy to Russia, which lasted from June 1600 until July 1601 and will be considered briefly here.[5]

Francis Cherry, a leading man in The Muscovy Company, had returned to England in March 1599 with letters from Boris Godunoff to Queen Elizabeth that called for an English embassy to Russia, particularly in view of the threat to Anglo–Russian trade inherent in the alarming development of relationships between Sweden, Russia and Poland. Czar Boris suspected that England was allying with Russia's enemies on both sides. His own ally, Duke Charles of Sweden, was at war with Poland over the Livonian question and King Sigismund of Poland had recently commandeered some English warships in the Baltic for service in the Polish fleet. Boris had heard that Elizabeth had 'ministred aide

[1] 'Henry Francklin returned ...'; *Cal. Car. IX*, 82.
[2] Reproduced in *Svenska riksdagsakter*, III, 2, page 1903, and IV, page 692 (Nos. 241 and 242).
[3] *Hist. handl.* 23, 346 ff.
[4] Henric Francklyns stambok, fol. 143 r.
[5] H. XI. 207, 264; XII. 233; *SPD.* 12/281; and *Fugger²*, No. 714. Cf. Chamb., *Sir Henry Lee*, 177–180, 203–206, and 224–227.

unto Sigismundus, King of Poland, against Duke Charles of Sweden' and asked her, therefore, 'to certify Us in what sorte You furthre the Kinge of Poland, against the said Duke, with men, munitions, and money', for he wished her 'not to support anie of those with men, munitions, and money which profess themselves enimies of such princes as are under Our mightie Government, or are confederated, and live instantly in leage and amitie with Us'. In the South, Boris suspected that the establishment of Anglo–Turkish trade connections in Constantinople implied English support for the Turks during their campaign against Hungary.[1]

Furthermore, the Swedish embassy led by James Hill to Queen Elizabeth in May–June 1599 called for an English embassy in return to Duke Charles.[2]

After numerous, lengthy negotiations, Sir Richard Lee was ultimately appointed on 25 March 1600 to head an embassy. Sir Richard was chosen chiefly on account of representations by The Muscovy Company, which paid for the lion's share of the costs of the mission. Sir Richard's instructions for the embassy, dated 1 June 1600, were couched in fairly general terms, though they stipulated that the return journey would pass through Swedish territory, whereupon conciliatory letters from Queen Elizabeth were to be handed over to Duke Charles.[3] The embassy departed for Russia on about 13 June 1600 and after 'a long and miserable journey by sea' reached Archangel on 30 July 1600, where Sir Richard took to his bed with a serious bout of influenza. He sent a report to Cecil via The Muscovy Company's representative in Archangel, John Mericke, who also carried a letter from Czar Boris to England.[4]

Sir Richard appears to have been well received in Russia, although a later English ambassador reports that he made a name for himself in Moscow as a strict observer of etiquette. Little is known, however, concerning his doings in Russia. When the embassy left, Czar Boris presented—as a gift to Queen Elizabeth—a coat made from the wool of the legendary Scythian Lamb, receiving in exchange a pestle and mortar made from a huge agate, which was presented to the Czar by the physician to the English embassy.

The embassy's land route home went through Esthonia, where Sir

---

[1] H. IX. 112, 344, 430, and J. P. Collier, (ed.), *The Egerton papers*, pp, 288–292.
[2] Cf. Ch. 8.
[3] H. IX. 116, X. 169, 175; *SPD*. 12/274, and *Cotton MS. Nero*, B. VIII, fol. 32.
[4] H. X. 180, and 275.

Richard Lee—as already mentioned—met Duke Charles of Sweden in Tallinn. The latter tried to persuade Sir Richard to sell him the Czar's gift to Queen Elizabeth, which he had coveted for a long time, but the coat accompanied the embassy back to England. It is interesting to note, however, that a suit of armour belonging to Sir Richard is still preserved at the Royal Armoury in Stockholm and is listed in the first inventory of the Armoury, drawn up in 1671. We have no information to show how this armour came to be in Sweden but it does not seem unreasonable to suppose that Sir Richard gave it to Duke Charles in order to be able to keep Boris's coat for Queen Elizabeth.[1]

While the English ambassador was in Tallinn, the Swedish forces under Karl Karlsson Gyllenhielm were heavily defeated at Kokenhusen in southern Livonia on 17 May 1601. A great deal of political activity took place during Lee's stay in Tallinn. Duke Charles's correspondence included letters to Queen Elizabeth and the Privy Council with a proposal that the union with Poland be renounced and the Duke proclaimed king of Sweden. No reply to this proposal has been found in the Duke's archives or elsewhere. Judging from the time factor, the Czar's letter to Queen Elizabeth, and so on, Russia had no objection to a dissolution of the union between Sweden and Poland. Sir Richard departed from Tallinn, probably on a Swedish ship, for Lubeck, where he arrived at the end of June 1601.[2]

The English embassy to Russia was observed by Fugger's agent in Hamburg, whose report runs as follows:

'Auß Hamburg von 6. julii A:o &c. 1601.
Ain ennglischer amp:tor, welcher von der konigin auß Enng:dt nach der Moscau zum selben groß furstenn abgesanndt und inn 13 monat schon auß gewest, ist dise wochen uber Lubeckh von Revel mit 60 persohnen alhero kommen.[3]

---

[1] H. XI. 207, 264; XII. 233; *SPD.* 26/281; Smythe, *Voiage and Entertainment*, 1605, E. 1. The myth of the legendary Lamb of Scythia or Tartary, also called the Barometz from a Tartar word for lamb, was well known in the Middle Ages. Cf. Chamb., *Sir Henry Lee*, p. 226.

[2] Willan, *The Early History of the Russia Company*, 1553–1603, pp. 235 f.; H. XI. 207; Fugger², No. 714; and Riksregistraturen Reval May 28th, 1601, pp. 98 v– 100 r.

[3] 'From Hamburg, 6 July 1601. An English ambassador who was sent by the Queen of England to Moscow to the Czar there and who returned via Lubeck after spending thirteen months in Russia, has arrived here with a total of 60 persons'; Fugger², No. 714.

Henry Francklin appears to have accompanied the party to Lubeck, since Joannes Petreus Stockholmensis[1] made an entry in his album there on 20 June 1601. Whether Francklin continued all the way to England is not clear but at least the possibility is not ruled out by his album, as the next entry is not until 1 August 1602, when an Englishman called William Crofton of London entered his name during a stay in Stockholm.[2]

After Queen Elizabeth's death in January 1603 and the coronation of James I in July 1604, Duke Charles (now Charles IX of Sweden) wrote from Stockholm Castle on 28 August 1604 to thank Sir Richard Lee for all the assistance and favour he had shown to Henry Francklin, who had recently been sent on a mission to England. This suggests that Francklin was in England again in 1604, no doubt to establish contact with the new regime on behalf of the Swedish monarch. Once again there is no conflicting evidence in Francklin's album. Two entries by Englishmen in Stockholm, Thomas Davis and Eduardus Baynbrigg Anglus[3], on 17 June and 24 July 1604 respectively are followed by three entries, probably during a journey, without any place name: Johannes Richter Oppaw., Med. Dr., on 20 November, Maurice Jörenßån thill Diwlle on 22 December and Valentinus Snowe on 31 December 1604.[4] Although the album has no entries specifically from England during Francklin's journeys in 1601 and 1604, there are several entries by Englishmen without any date or place name that may well be from these years.

Following the death of Boris Godunoff on 13 April 1605, Charles IX was anxious to know how relationships between Sweden, Russia and Poland would develop. He therefore entrusted Henry Francklin with the task of establishing contact with Dmitry, the pretender to the Russian throne. Francklin's album has an intriguing entry, with no date or place name, 'Demetrius Iwanozijk Velsberg' with the arms of Demetrius above.[5] Perhaps this was the false Dmitry? Several documents[6] are listed as having been issued in connection with Francklin's journey,

---

[1] Henry Francklin's album, fol. 153 r.

[2] *Ibid.*, fol. 110 r.

[3] *Ibid.*, fol. 78 v and 110 r.

[4] *Ibid.*, fol. 95 v, 17 v and 109 v.

[5] *Ibid.*, fol, 42 r.

[6] Riksregistraturen 28.11.1605, fol. 247 v; 11.12.1605, fol. 258 r; 14.12.1605; fol. 259 v; 13.2.1606, fol. 39 r; 20.2.1606, fol. 51 r; 2.3.1606, fol. 71 r; 12.3.1606, fol. 90 v; 30.3.1606, fol. 111 r; 2.5.1606, fol. 199 v; 18.6.1606, fol. 224 v; 22.6.1606, fol. 232 v; 10.7.1606, fol. Suppl. 15 v; and 5.12.1606, fol. Suppl. 123 r.

including one on 18 June 1606, 'Till Henric Francklyn om Dmitri och dhe Tatterske Furstarne'.[1]

The prominent people Francklin met towards the end of his life included the well-known Calvinist, John Forbes, leader of the Scottish Presbyterians. Forbes was banished in the course of the Presbyterians' struggle with James I of England and arrived in Sweden in 1608, probably in the company of his brother, who was serving as an officer in the Swedish army.

Duke Charles's diary contains an entry, probably on John Forbes's brother, dated January 15, 1608:

kåm en skotz kapiten ved namn Forbus, then fulde Wolter Skåtte.[2]

Francklin's album has the following entry:

Johannes Forbesius, cutharisius scotus. 1608 6/9 Stockholm.[3]

On 17 November 1608 John Forbes participated in an academic disputation arranged in Uppsala by Duke Charles, defending a number of Calvinist theses against Archbishop Olaus Martini. In his ecclesiastical history,[4] J. Baazius, who was biased in favour of the Uppsala theologians, reports that Forbes was unable to vindicate himself on several occa-sions. Baazius's phrase has become proverbial:

Ad haec Forbesius nihil.[5]

Francklin made his last journey to the Continent in 1610, when he visited Gdańsk. During this visit he met the Englishman Rudiger Flodd and made the following entry in his album:

Rudiger Flud Englischer Dem Landsmann
Heinrich Fraencklin seinem lieben Andenken in
Danzigk zu Eren dis Schreiben Den X Aprilis Anno MDCX.[6]

---

[1] 'To Henry Francklin concerning Dmitry and the Tartar Princes'; Riksregistra-turen 18.6.1606; RA.

[2] 'Came a Scottish captain called (Arthur) Forbes, who followed Walter Scott'; op. cit., 154; Cf. *DNB*, 19, 401 f. (John Forbes).

[3] John Forbes, Presbyterian Scotsman. Stockholm, September 6th, 1608. Op. cit., fol. 28 r.

[4] J. Baazius, *Inventarium ecclesiae Suecanae* (1642). Cf. *SBL*, 2, 515 ff.

[5] 'To this Forbes had no rejoinder'; *ibid.*

[6] 'This entry is dedicated faithfully to my countryman, Henry Francklin, in dear remembrance, Gdańsk, April 10th, 1610. Rudiger Flud, Englishman'; op. cit., fol. 166 r. Cf. Catalogus discipulorum qui in Gymnasio hoc investi fuerunt cum in pos-

Francklin died on 4 May 1610, shortly after returning from this journey, and was buried in Undenäs church.[1] It is of course conceivable that he was ill beforehand and undertook the trip to Gdańsk for the purpose of consulting his good friend the municipal physician, Teofilus Homodei, D.M.

sesseonem manoris Scholastici Jacobo Fabricio Rector, cum M. Petro Lassio Prorectore immitterentur. Woj. Archivum Panstwowe w Gdansku; Poland. Sign. 300/42/93, fol. 156 v: 'Rudigerus Flodde, Dantiscanus imm. 1596'.

[1] In Vadsbo parish, Westrogothia, Sweden.

THE END

SOURCES

Manuscripts

RIKSARKIVET. Fack, S-100 26 Stockholm 34, Sweden.
Pergamentsamlingen. 18.10.1591.
Johan III:s registratur (Riksregistraturen) 1579–1592. 15 vols.
Riksregistraturen (Sigismund III and Charles IX) 1593–1609.
Hertig Karls registratur 1589–92.
Tysk registratur 1592–93.
Hertig Karls diarium 1566–92.
Anglica V:
    Engelska beskickningars memorial och noter 1591–1692.
Anglica VII:
    Diplomatica, Strödda handlingar. Vol 531 (Förhandlingar 1559–1632).
Germanica E. VII:
    Förhandlingar med Ost-Friesland.
Skrivelser till hertig Karl:
    Brev från Willem IJßbrandsson. K 343.
Kungl Arkiv:
    Hertig Karl av Södermanland m. fl. Handlingar rörande politiska och
    personliga förhållanden. K 348.
    Hertig Karls hovhållning m. m. Torneringar i Nyköping 1584–1602. K
    349.
    Hertig Karl. Handlingar rörande hertigens hövhållning m. m. K 351.
    Brev till ståthållare m. fl. K 353.
    Brev till hovmän m. fl. K 355.
Enskilda Arkiv:
    Arkivfragment.
Kanslitjänstemännens koncept och mottagna skrivelser:
    11. Karl IX:s tid.
    12. Sigismunds tid.
Svenska sändebuds skrivelser till Kongl. Maj:t:
    Hollandica 1592–1611
Riksdagsacta.
Avskriftsamlingar efter 1520:
    Jöran Knutsson Posses kopiebok 1593–1598.
Krönikor från 1500- och 1600-talen.
Strödda historiska handlingar:
    14. Handlingar angående Sigismunds första resa till Sverige 1593–94
    samt regeringens ordnande.
    15. Handlingar angående åtskilliga Sigismunds anhängare.

Schantz, C. L. von, Genealogisk matrikel, släktböcker och genealogiska samlingar. Vol. 95: 203.

Skoklostersamlingen.

Erik Brahes chifferkalendarium, Skoklostersamlingen, E 8925 and E 8917 Erik Sparres samling 1.

Three letters from Constantia Eriksdotter Francklin to the Chancellor Axel Oxenstierna 1644, 1645 and 1646.

Folke Wernstedt's Register

Kammararkivet (Department of Riksarkivet).

Hertig Karls räntekammare 1589–92, 1590–95 and 1593–97.

Håkan Larssons räkenskaper 1591.

Hindrich Hinderssons räkenskaper 1592.

Hertig Karls räntekammare. Strödda handlingar I–II:

Likvidationer 1592–93. Band 91:12,

Likvidationer 1604–05. Band 91:17, and

Likvidationer 1612–14. Band 91:18.

Hertig Karls räntekammarböcker. Räkningar med diverse personer 1586–95.

Diplomaträkenskaper 1570–93;

Söffring Jönssons räkning från en resa i England 1590–91.

Ludbert Kavers räkning från en resa i Tyskland 1591–92, and

Räkenskaper angående dr Theophili Homodei beskickning till Neder-länderna 1591–92.

Proviant- och andra räkenskaper 1590–93.

Södermanlands landskapsbok för år 1649. Södermanlands landskapshand-lingar.

Messenius, J., Sr., 1626. En Lithen Underwijssning, Kajaneborg, Finland. Reduktionskollegiets aktsamling nr 8.

Sandbergska samlingen:

Om introducerade adliga ätten Båt; FF 9872–9914,

Introducerade adliga ätten Frankelin; FF 10527–10550, and

Ulf Hindriksson och Sigfrid Engelsman till Fyllingerum, FF 20593–20603.

Slottsarkivet (Department of Riksarkivet).

K. Klädkammaren 1591–1602.

K. Hofförtärningen 1589–1603.

KUNGL. KRIGSARKIVET. Fack, S-104 50 Stockholm 80, Sweden.

Militieräkningar 1592:

Nr 14. Doctor Theophili Rechningh för the penninger han haffuer uth-lagdt till at ahntage fremmendhe Krigsfolk på Cronones wegne i Sverige A° D^{ni} 92.

Diverse enskilda arkiv. Viggo Keys samling.

KUNGL. BIBLIOTEKET, Department of Manuscripts, Box 50 39, S-102 41 Stockholm 5, Sweden.

Hertig Karls reseräkning avseende utgifter på resan från Sverige till Heidel-berg och tillbaka 1577–78. No. D. 583. (Removed 1854 from the Palace of Drottningholm, cat. no. 3). Probably in Ludbert Kaver's hand.

Peringskiöld, J. P., 1710–20. Monumenta Sueo-Gothica.
D 337:8 and 15 Johannis Messenii Scondia Illustrata. Tomus 8 and 15.
Index.
D 345:1 Johannis Messenii Shedae.
D 597 Axel Lewenhaupt, *Historisk berättelse.*
LUNDS UNIVERSITETSBIBLIOTEK, Department of Manuscripts, S-223 62 Lund,
Sweden.
The De la Gardie papers.
UPPSALA UNIVERSITETSBIBLIOTEK, Department of manuscripts, S-751 10
Uppsala, Sweden.
Historia Svecana. Acta Varia 1563–1611.
Hampus R. Huldt's papers. E 159.
The Palmskiöld papers. Diarium Sueo-Gothicum. (Palmsk. 189).
Stiernman's register.
Svecia illustris.
Henry Francklin's album 1583–1610.
KUNGL. VITTERHETS-, HISTORIE- OCH ANTIKVITETSAKADEMIENS ARKIV, S-
114 55 Stockholm, Sweden.
Säves reseberättelse för år 1862.
NORDISKA MUSEETS ARKIV, S-115 21 Stockholm, Sweden.
Theel, J. G., Anteckningar rörande Kongl. hofven 1526–1624.
UMEÅ LÄROVERK, Fack, S-901 01 Umeå 1, Sweden.
Erik Falck's album 1582.
RIGSARKIVET, Rigsdagsgården 9, København K, Denmark.
The almanacs of King Frederick II of Denmark during the 1580ies (1583,
1584, 1586 and 1587), Kongehuset.
Tydske Kancelliets Udenrigske Afdeling. Speciel Del:
England 10 och Sachsen 11. Letters from the Elector Christian I of
Saxony to King Frederick II of Denmark: 1585 2.7. and 5.12; 1586
25.1., 12.2., 7.4., 25.5., 28.5., 18.6., 22.6., 9.7., 26.8., 1.9., 8.9., 12.9.,
24.9., 19.10., 28.10., 3.11., 14.1., 18.1., and 15.12; and 1587 10.2.,
7.4., 29.4., 22.5., 22.5. (once more), 9.6., 13.6., &c.
England 10. Akter vedrørende Henric Ramels sendelse till England 1586;
(Credentials by King Frederick II 19.4. 1586; recredentials by Queen
Elizabeth I 26.5. 1586).
Scotland 2. Correspondance between the Danish and Scotch Royal Fami-
lies. Letters from James VI (1579–1602) and Queen Anne (1591–
1603).
Sweden 33. Sten Brahe's and Nicolaus Theophilus' Embassy to Nyköping,
Sweden (1592)
Gesandtskabsregnskaber 7. Declared accounts from Arild Huitfeld's and
Christian Barnekow's Embassy to England (1597); Christian Friis
Embassy to England (1603); and Henry Ramelius's Embassy to Eng-
land (1605).
Ausländisches Register Nr 43, 5.1. 1586–29.3. 1588 with drafts of letters
from King Frederick II to the Elector Christian I of Saxony and from
the same King to Robert Dudley, Earl of Leicester.

Rentemesterregnskabet 1579, 1580–85, 1586–87, 1589–90 and 1596–97.

Toldregnskaber fra Øresundstolden 1591–93.

DET KONGELIGE BIBLIOTEK, Department of Manuscripts, Christians Brygge 8, København K; Denmark.

En kort och riktig relationsskriffuelse om Den Kongelige Engelsche Reigze aar 1606. Rostg. 68, 4° (afskr. NKS 995, 4°).

(King Christian IV^s English journey June 12th–August 22nd 1606). Another relation of this journey in Thott 1624, 4°.

Carl IX:s (of Sweden) Historie. Thott 4°. No 2181.

LANDSARKIVET FOR SJAELLAND M. M., Jagtvej 10, København N, Denmark.

Helsingør bys regnskab 21.12. 1584–21.12. 1585.

Helsingør Tingbog 1581–82 and 1583–86.

ALGEMEEN RIJKSARCHIEF, Bleijenburg 7, 's-Gravenhage, Holland.

Nineteen letters (27 pages) during the period 6.7. 1593–6.7. 1594 by Willem van Blois Treslong in his capacity of Dutch chief forester to his secretary at the Hague, Jan van Muyden (Nuyen). Inv. No 115, Houstvesterij van Holland en Westfriesland.

GEMEENTELIJKE ARCHIEFDIENST VAN AMSTERDAM, Amsteldijk 67, Amsterdam-Z, Holland.

Notariële archiefen.

The baptismal register of Oude Kerk, Amsterdam.

RIJKSARCHIEF IN GELDERLAND, Arnhem, Holland.

The treasurer Caerl van Gelder's XIIth account (1592).

GEMEENTE-ARCHIEF LEIDEN, Boisotkade 2 A, Leiden, Holland.

Ordonnantieboek B (Secret. arch. 1575–1851, No. 3734). Reeckeninghe van Jan Brouwer Jansz; Thresorier Ordinarie van't jaer XV' tnegentich (1589–90).

PUBLIC RECORD OFFICE, Chancery Lane, London, W.C. 2, England.

State Papers Holland, Poland and Sweden. (Nos. 84, 88 and 95.)

State Papers Domestic Series. (No. XII/274.)

State Papers 9–201–3.

Close Rolls 34 Henry VIII (1543). (Ref. C. 54/431.)

Patent Rolls 3 Elizabeth I (1561). (Ref. C.66/965, m. 31.)

Lord Chamberlain's Records 1582–1599; vols. 28–41 and 811.

London Port Books 1589–1624.

BRITISH MUSEUM, Department of Manuscripts, Museum Street, London, W.C. 1, England.

Mss. Additional Cottonian, Harleian, Lansdowne, Royal & King's, Sloane & Stowe.

Ms Egerton 1994.

The Caesar papers. (Sir Julius Caesar 1558–1636.) Mss Additional 4190, 5664, 6038, 9045, 10.038, 10.113, 11.405, 11.406, 11.574, 12.495–12.507, 14.027, 14.313, 15.235, 34.324, 36.111, 36.113, 36.767, 36,969, 36.970, 38.170 and in Mss Lansdowne 123–174, 706, 768, and 784.

Ms Additional 36774. A small collection once belonging to the Carew family for Crewcombe Court, Somerset. Drafts of letters in Latin from Queen Elizabeth I to foreign princes, King John III and Duke

Charles of Sweden &c. and private persons, with other official documents, April 1st 1591 to March 15th 1592, probably by John Wolley, the Queen's Secretary of the Latin tongue. Several documents in favour of Henry Francklin.

Scholarium Etonens ovatio; 'Franckline', contributor to verses addressed to Queen Elizabeth at Eton in 1563. King's Mss; 12 A XXX, fol 13 and 56.

Johannes Cellarius' Album amicorum (1599–1606); Ms Additional 27.579.

SOMERSET HOUSE, The Literary Department, Probate Registry, Strand, London, W.C. 2, England.

Testament by Henry Francklyn, Windsor, May 18, 1575. No. 1575-P-CC, Pyckering, fol 22.

THE BODLEIAN LIBRARY, Oxford, England.

Ms. Ashmole 1763, fol 47. Letter from Czar Boris Godunov to Queen Elizabeth I 1602.

HERTFORDSHIRE COUNTY RECORD OFFICE, County Hall, Hertford, Herts., England.

Undated letter from William Portington to Sir Harbottle Grimston: 'Newes out of Suethland: or the Coronation of the young prince, Gustavus Adolphus, very honourably celebrated at Upsalia, an University in Suethland, written by a gentleman and a traveller.' Gorhambury Mss. VIII. B. 136. (Publ. Hist. Mss. Comm. 64th Report, pp. 112 ff.)

KENT ARCHIVES OFFICE, Kent, England.

Testaments by John ffrankeleen of Chart, June 17th 1618, James ffrancklyn of Maidstone, September 18th, 1618, and Henry ffranklyn, Sandwich, May 3rd 1631. No. PRC 31/18, 32/43/25 and 31/97, respectively.

COLLEGE OF ARMS, Queen Victoria Street, London, E.C. 4, England.

Henry Francklin's renewal of his grant of arms 1592. Signum: Vinc. Old Gr., fol 518, 530 and 537.

Herald's Visitation Books (unpublished). Some of the Visitation books are published in the publications of the Harleian Society.

Dethick's Grants.

SOCIETY OF GENEALOGISTS, 37, Harrington Gardens, London, S.W. 7, England.

The Library and the Card Index of the Society.

THE FOLGER SHAKESPEARE LIBRARY, 20003 Washington D.C., USA.

Theodoricus von Bewernest's Album amicorum (1590–1605); No. V.A. 325.

HENRY E. HUNTINGTON LIBRARY & ART GALLERY, San Marino, 91108 California, USA.

Francis Segar's Album amicorum (1599–1611); No. H.M. 743.

ISTITUTO GENEALOGICO ITALIANO, Ufficio Araldico, Via Benedetto Castelli 19, Firenze, Italy.

The Library and the Card Index of the Society.

ARCHIVIO SEGRETO DELLA SANTA SEDE, The Vatican, Rome, Italy.

Fondo Borghese 2.

ARCHIWUM GLOWNE, Dluga 7, Warszawa, Poland.

The Radziwill Collection.

BIBLIOTEKA NARODOWA, Plac Krasinskich 5, Warszawa, Poland.
Dr. Teofilus Homodei, the judge Walter van Holten and the merchant
Jan Luchsen give in 1600 evidence before the court of records at the
city of Gdańsk in the case against Jan Bernard Bonifacio, Marquis
d'Oria, Ms 837.

WOJEWODZKIE ARCHIWUM PANSTWOWE W GDANSKU, Gdańsk, Poland.
Rep. 300:9:50. Acta et Epistola Internuntiorum.
W. Behrings Nachlaß. Transcripts of the album amicorum of Samuel
Meienreis Elbingensis Borussus (1600–1602) and of the Gentleman
Hans von Bodeck (1597–1609).
The baptismal register of S:t Petri Kirche, Gdańsk.

BIBLIOTEKA PAN W GDAŃSKU, Gdańsk, Poland.
Hammen, L. von, 1697. Vitae Medicorum Gedanensium, Gdańsk. (The
copy of the Schlieff collection, furnished with marginal notes by
Schlieff.)
Seyleri, G. D., 1742, Elbinga litterata, Elbląg. (The copy of the Schlieff
collection, furnished with marginal notes by Schlieff.)

BIBLIOTHÈQUE NATIONALE, 58, rue de Richelieu, Paris IIième, France.
Album amicorum of Johann Lange of Liegnitz in Silesia (1592–1620);
The Stroelin collection. Rothschild No. 3370 (2522 f).

THE MUNICIPAL RECORD OFFICE OF THE CITY OF STRASBURG, Strasburg,
France.
Straßburger Rathsprotokolle.

ARCHIVES DE LA DRÔME, rue André-Lacroix, Valence, France.
Les archives de l'Université de Valence, Serie D (Registres de receptions
de docteurs au XVIe siècle, la période 1566–1575, D 17, et 1583–86,
D 18).

ARCHIVO GENERAL DE SIMANCAS, Valladolid, Spain.
Secretaria de Estado, Capitulaciones con la casa de Austria y papeles de
las negociones de Alemania, Sajovia, Polonia, Prussia y Hamburgo
1493–1796.
Las Pensiones. (Declared accounts from the Spanish Embassies to England 1603 to 1606.)

STAATLICHES ARCHIVLAGER, Göttingen, Germany/West.
Letters dated 4.10. 1596 from Princess Elizabeth of Mecklenburg, née
Vasa, to Helena Northampton, and Mr. Rudolph Scryvener in Eng-
land. Paket 348 der Auswärtigen Akten des Staatsarchivs Schwerin.

HESS. STAATSARCHIV MARBURG, Friedrichsplatz 15, 355 Marburg/Lahn,
Germany/West.
Aktenbestand 4 für Schweden (No. 54) and other references compiled by
Dr. Papritz and Dr. Franz.
Bestallungen Comoedianten, and 4 (4 b and f) England 1594–95, Urkun-
denbestand.
Several letters from James Hill and his family c. 1610–27.

LANDESARCHIV SCHLESWIG-HOLSTEIN, Schloß Gottorf, Schleswig, Germany/
West.

Nachrichten von der Vermählung Herzog Carls zu Sudermanland mit der Holteinischen-Gottorfischen Princesse Christinen 1592.

NIEDERSÄCHSISCHES STAATSARCHIV, v. Iheringstr. 17, (23) Aurich, Germany/West.

Die Heirat zwischen Herzog Karl von Södermanland und Fräulein Christine zu Schleswig-Holstein. 1 volume.

Schriftwechsel mit Schweden (4 letters 1587, 1590, 1591, and 1596, respectively); Rep. 4Bj f 1563.

Wicht, E. F. von, c. 1610 (The copy in Aurich a transcript 1734), Annales Frisiae. (A manuscript concerning the history of East Friesland from the mediæval time to the year 1601.) StA. Aurich: Rep. 241, Nr A 26.

GERSDORFF-WEICHA'SCHE STIFTUNGSBIBLIOTHEK ZU BAUTZEN, Stadt- und Kreisbibliothek Bautzen, Schloßstraße 10, Bautzen, DDR, Germany/East.

Diarium des Erich Laßota von Steblow. (No. 49.)

DIE BIBLIOTHEK SONDERSHAUSEN, Schloß, Sondershausen, DDR, Germany/East.

Die Moersperger Handschrift, A° 1592.

OESTERREICHISCHES STAATSARCHIV, Minoritenplatz 1, Vienna I, Austria.

Familienakten Kart. 24, 25 and Die Handschrift Böhm-Supplement 8.

Familienkorrespondenz A 32 and A 34.

Letters to the Emperor Rudolph II from the Archduchess Mary and the Archduke Ernest, dated 27.9. 1591 and 28.9. 1591, respectively.

Letter to the Archduchess Mary from the Emperor Rudolph II, dated 14.12. 1591.

FINLANDS RIKSARKIV, Helsinki, Finland.

Acta historica 1592–1599.

Acta Suecia V.

Fogderäkenskaperna c. 1590–c.1610.

THE SALTYKOV–SHCHEDRIN LIBRARY, Leningrad, USSR.

The van Suchtelen papers.

Furthermore c. 50 albums (Album amicorum) consulted.

Published manuscripts

(Arber, E., 1875–94), Transcripts of the Registers of the Stationers' Company 1553–1640, 1–5. Birmingham: privately printed.

(Almquist, H., 1910), Handlingar rörande mötet i Reval, Konung Sigismunds resor till Sverige 1593–94 och 1598 samt polska legationen 1599. *In* Historiska Handlingar 23. Stockholm: Norstedt.

(Bang, N., 1922), Tabeller over Skibsfart ... gennem Øresund 1497–1600, 1–2. Copenhagen: Gyldendal.

(Bergius, B., 1759), Konung Carl den IX:s rimchrönika ... jämte bilagor. Stockholm: Hesselberg.

(Bruce, J., 1844), Correspondence of Robert Dudley, Earl of Leycester, during his government of the Low countres in the years 1585 and 1586. The Camden Society Reprint No. 27. London.

Calendar, 1862–1932, of Letters and Papers, Foreign and Domestic, of the Reign of Henry VIII, preserved in the Public Record Office, the British Museum, and elsewhere in England, 1–21. London: Longman.

Calendar, 1830–52, during the Reign of Henry VIII, 1–11. London: Longman.

Calendar, 1909, of State Papers, Foreign affaires, May–December 1582. London: Longman.

Calendar, 1892–99, of Letters and State Papers relating to English Affairs, preserved principally in the Archives of Simancas. London: Stationery Office.

Calendar, 1883–1940, of the Manuscripts of the Most Hon. the Marquis of Salisbury preserved at Hatfield House, 1–18 and Index 1–2. London: Stationery Office.

Colección de Documentos Inéditos para la Historia de Espana, 1–112. Madrid: Calero & C.

(Dasent, J. R., 1900), Acts of the Privy Councel of England. New Series. Vols. 20–21, A.D. 1590–91 and 1591–92. London: Stationery Office.

De la Gardieska archivet, 1831–43. Vols. 1–20. Lund: Lundberg.

(Eraso, F. di, 1578–79), Depescher från det spanska sändebudet till Sverige, Francisco di Eraso. In Historisk tidskrift 1886. Stockholm: Norstedt.

(Foakes, R. A. & Rickert, R. T., 1961), Henslowe's Diary. Cambridge: University Press.

(Foerstemann, C. E., 1841), Album Academiae Vitebergensis, Ab A. Ch. MD II usque ad A. MD LX. Leipzig: Tauchnitz.

(Foster, J., 1891–92), Alumni Oxonienses, Early Series 1500–1714, 1–4. Oxford: Parker.

(Foster, J., 1887), London Marriage Licenses 1521–1869. London: Quaritch.

(Foster, J., 1889), Register of the Admissions to Gray's Inn 1521–1889. London: Privately printed.

(Frederick II of Denmark), Kong Frederick II's Kalenderoptegnelser fra Aarene 1583, 1584 og 1587. Danish Historisk Tidskrift 4, 3, 538 ff. Copenhagen.

Fugger. Cf. Klarwill, V. von.

(Grauers, S.), 1923, Nya Lödöse tänkeböcker. Göteborg: Elanders.

(Green, M. A. E., 1869), Calendar of State Papers Domestic Series of the Reign of Elizabeth I. London: Stationery Office.

(Halliwell, J. A., 1842), Private diary of Dr. John Dee. The Camden Society Reprints No. 19. London.

(Harleian Society), The Publications of the Harleian Society (Visitation and Register Sections), 1869– in progress. London: Granville W. G. Leveson-Gower, &c.

(Harrison, G. B., 1938), The Elizabethan Journals. Being a Record of Those Things most talked of during the years 1591–1603. London: Routledge.

(Hasso, A. G. & Kroman, E., 1962), Tyske Kancelli, II; Tyske Kancellis udenrigske afdeling till 1770. Copenhagen: Munksgaard.

(Hildebrand, E., 1877–1910,) Svenska riksdagsakter 1:1, 2:1–2, and 3: 1–3. Stockholm: Norstedt.

(Japikse, N., 1923–25), Resolutiën der Staten—Generaal, 7–8. s'-Gravenhage: Nijhoff.

(Klarwill, V. von, 1926), The Fugger News-letters. Second Series. Being a further Selection from the Fugger papers specially referring to Queen Elizabeth I and matters relating to England during the years 1568–1605. London: John Lane.

(Lincoln's Inn, 1896), The Records of the Honorable Society of Lincoln's Inn: Admissions 1420–1893 and Chapel Registers, 1–2. London: Lincoln's Inn.

(Lewenhaupt, A., 1903), Calendaria Caroli IX. Stockholm: 'Föreningen för Bokhandtverk.' This edition has reference to Duke Charles's (King Charles IX) almanacs or calendars in the Swedish National Archives (Riksarkivet). The almanacs have been bound together in two plain bindings made of blue cardboard, the first one consisting of the almanacs for the period 1581–97, of which the years 1587, 1590, 1591 and 1595 are missing, and the second one covering the years 1604–1609. Unfortunately the almanacs for the important transition years in between are not preserved to our time.

Die Matrikel der Universität Königsberg in Pr., 1–3. Leipzig: Duncker & Humbolt.

Notes & Queries, Ser. 1–13:1, 1849–1923; Vol. 146–198, 1924–53; N.S. Vol. 1, 1954 — in progress. London.

Rikskansleren Axel Oxenstiernas skrifter och brevväxling, 1888–1969 in progress, Stockholm: Norstedt.

(Public Record Office, No. 2, 1893), List and Index of Declared Accounts from the Pipe Office and the Audit Office. London: Stationery Office.

(Public Record Office No. 9, 1898), List of Sheriffs for England and Wales from the earliest times to A.D. 1831, compiled from documents in the Public Record Office. London: Stationery Office.

(Raa, F. J. G. ten & Bas, F. de, 1913), Het Staatsche Leger 1588–1609, 1–2. Breda: De Koninklijke Militaire Academie.

(Municipal Record Office of London, 1828), Analytical index to the series of records known as the Remembrancia. Preserved among the archives of the city of London. A.D. 1579–1664. London: Francis.

Transactions of the Royal Historical Society, N.S., Vol 12/1898. London.

(Schottin, R., 1866), Tagebuch des Erich Lassota von Steblau. Nach einer Handschrift der von Gersdorff-Weicha'schen Bibliothek zu Bautzen herausgegeben und mit Einleitung und Bemerkungen begleitet. Halle: Barthel.

Stationers' Register. Cf. Arber (Published manuscripts).

(Stenbock, C. M. & R., 1920), Abraham Brahes Tidebok. Stockholm: Norstedt.

(Stiernman, A. A. von, 1728), Alla riksdagars och mötens beslut, 1.

(Stockholms stad, 1953), Stockholms Stads Tänkeböcker från år 1592, 3, 1600, Stockholm: Norstedt.

(Theiner, A., 1842), La Suède et le Saint Siège (1569–1611), 1–3, Paris: Debécourt.

Aa, A. J. van der, 1852, Biografisch Woordenboek. Haarlem: Brederode.

Aakjær, S., 1936, Maal, Vægt og taxter i Danmark. *In* Nordisk Kultur, No. 30. Stockholm: Bonniers.

Adam, K., 1887, Das Reisestammbuch des D. Abr. Plato von 1607 bis 1616. *In* Zeitschrift für Kulturgeschichte, 1. Nuremberg.

Ahnlund, N., 1917, En furstlig brudfärd. *In* Ord och Bild. Stockholm: Wahlström & Widstrand.

Ahnlund, N., 1918, Stormaktstidens gryning. Stockholm: Gebers.

Allgemeine deutsche Biographie, 1880 and 1883, Vols. 11 and 17. Leipzig: Duncker & Humblot.

Almquist, J. A., 1917–23, Den civila lokalförvaltningen i Sverige 1523–1630, 1–4. Stockholm: Riksarkivet.

Almquist, J. A., 1931–47, Frälsegodsen i Sverige under storhetstiden, 1: 1–3: 2. Stockholm: Norstedt.

Almquist, H., 1910, Ett bidrag till markgrefvinnan Cecilias biografi. *In* Personhistorisk tidskrift. Stockholm: Norstedt.

Almquist, J. A., 1960, Herrgårdarna i Sverige under reformationstiden (1523–1611). Stockholm: Norstedt.

Almquist, J. E., 1954, Lagsagor och domsagor i Sverige. Stockholm: Stockholm University.

Almquist, J. E., 1955, Lagmän och Häradshövdingar i Sverige. Stockholm: Stockholm University.

Alvensleben, U. von, 1955, Die Lutetsburger Chronik: Geschichte eines friesischen Häuptlingsgeschlecht. Norden: Braams.

Andersson, I., 1935, Erik XIV:s engelska underhandlingar. Studier i svensk diplomati och handelspolitik. *In* Skrifter utgivna av Vetenskapssocieteten i Lund. Lund: Gleerup.

Andersson, I., 1943, Om Hamletdramats nordiska miljö. *In* Svenskt och europeiskt femtonhundratal: Fynd, forskningar och essäer. Lund: Gleerup.

Andersson, I., 1951, Erik XIV. A Biography. 4th ed. Stockholm: Wahlström & Widstrand.

Andersson, J., 1875, Om Riksdagen i Stockholm 1605. Linköping: Ridderstad.

Anderson, M. S., 1958, Britain's Discovery of Russia 1553–1815. London: Macmillan.

Anthoni, E., 1934, En relation om händelserna i Finland 1599 och Arnold J. Messenii Commentaria. *In* Historisk tidskrift för Finland. Helsinki: Mercator.

Anthoni, E., 1935, Till avvecklingen av konflikten mellan hertig Karl och Finland, 1. Helsinki: Mercator.

Arnell, S., 1951, Karin Månsdotter. Tolv kapitel om en drottning och hennes tid. Stockholm: Wahlström & Widstrand.

Baazius, J., 1642, Inventarium ecclesiae Sveogothorum. Lincopiae: Günther.

Bacon, F., cf. Spedding et al.

Baldwin, T. W., 1927, The Organization and Personnel of the Shakespearean Company. Princeton: University of Illinois Press.

Barkman, B. C:son, 1937–66, Kungl. Svea livgardes historia, 1–2, 3: 1–2, 4. Stockholm: Victor Pettersson.

Bauer, H., 1929, Alt-Elbinger Stammbücher in der Stadtbücherei. *In* Elbinger Jahrbuch, No. 8. Elbing: Saunier (Peicher).

Beijer, A., 1928, Recueil de plusieurs fragments des premières comedies italiennes qui été representées en France sous le Règne de Henri III. Recueil dit de Fossard conservé au Musée National de Stockholm. Paris: Duchartre et van Buggenhoudt.

Bentley, G. E., 1941–68, The Jacobean and Caroline Stage, Dramatic Companies and Plays, 1–7. Oxford: Clarendon.

Bergh, L. Ph. C. van den, 1857, 's-Gravenhagsche Bijzonderheden. 's-Gravenhage: Nijhoff.

Bergman, E. W., 1876, Handlingar rörande söndringen mellan hertig Carl och rådsherrarna 1594–1600. *In* Historiskt bibliotek 2, 255–354. Stockholm: Klemmings.

Bernegg, F. S., 1856, Geschichte der Kriege und Unruhen von welchen die drei Bunde in Hohenrätien von 1618 bis 1645 heimgesucht wurden. Chur.

Bethell, S. L., 1950, Shakespeare's Actors. *In* The Review of English Studies, N.S., 1, 3. Oxford: Clarendon.

Biaudet, H., 1906, Le Saint–Siège et la Suède durant la seconde moitié du XVI:e siecle. Thesis. . . Helsinki. Paris: Plon.

Biographie universelle, ancienne et moderne, 1811–1862, 1–85. Paris: Michaud.

Biographie universelle, ancienne et moderne, 1854–1865, 1–45. Nouvelle ed. Paris: Firmin, Didot.

Block, H., 1918, Karl IX som teolog och religiös personlighet. Studier öfver utvecklingen af hans åskådning. Lund: Gleerups.

Boderie, de la, 1750, Ambassades de Monsieur de la Boderie en Angleterre. Sous le Règne de Henri IV & la Minorité de Louis XIII depuis les années 1606 jusqu'en 1611, 1–5. Paris.

Boerge, V., 1937, Strindberg und Shakespeare. *In* Shakespeare Jahrbuch 73, 142–149. Weimar: Boehlau.

Boëthius, S. J., 1877, Om Svenska högadeln under Konung Sigismunds regering, 1. Stockholm: Norstedt.

Bogon, K., 1901, Die Stammbuchsammlung in der Stadtbibliothek zu Königsberg. *In* Vierteljahrsschrift für Wappen-, Siegel- und Familienkunde, No. 29. Berlin: Herold.

Bohrn, E., 1937, Nyköping. Svenska fornminnesplatser. Vägledningar utgivna genom Kungl. Vitt., Hist. och Antikvitets Akademien, No. 28. Stockholm: Wahlström & Widstrand.

Bohrn, E., 1941, Nyköpings Renässansslott och Herkules Mida. (Thesis.) Stockholm: Victor Pettersson.

Bolte, J., 1888, Englische Comoedianten in Dänemark und Schweden. *In* Jahrbuch der Deutschen Shakespeare-Gesellschaft 23, 99–108. Weimar: Huschke.

Bradford, Ch. A., 1936, Helena, Marchioness of Northampton. London: Allen & Unwin.

Bring, S. E., 1950, Itineraria Svecana. Descriptive catalogue of foreigners' journeys to Sweden from the Mediaeval time to 1950. Stockholm: Almqvist & Wiksell.

Broomé, B., 1960, Ätten Posses historia. 2. 1500–1625. Stockholm: Norstedt.

Brooke, C. F. T., 1908, The Shakespeare Apocrypha. Oxford: Clarendon.

Brun, F. de, 1923, Alfabetisk förteckning över svenska studenter vid inoch utländska universitet i gamla tider, 1, No. 3. (Typewritten.) Stockholm: Holmiana & alia.

Burenstam, C. J. R., 1871, Förteckning på handskrifter rörande Sveriges historia, befintliga i kejserliga 'Haus- Hof- und Staatsarchiv, Wien'. 's-Gravenhage: Smits.

Burgh, A. H. H. van der, 1886, Gezantschappen door Zweden en Nederland wederzijds afgevaardigd gedurende de jaren 1592–1795. 's-Gravenhage: Nijhoff.

Burman, O., 1910, Itinerarium för Torne och Kemi lappmarker 1598. In Handlingar och uppsatser angående finska lappmarken och lapparna, 1. Helsinki: Finska litteratursällskapet.

Camden, W., 1615, 1625 respectively, Annales, 1–2. London: Waterson &c.

Casalgerardo, A. M. di, 1912–15, Il nobiliario di Sicilia, compilato sui documenti esistenti negli Archivo di Stato notarili e dell'Ordine di Malta, e su tutte le fonti ufficiali, 1–2 Palermo: Reber.

Caselius, J., 1590, Nuptijs Herois Henrici Ivlii Gwelfii & Heroinae Elizabethae Cimbricae Trikopeion. Helmstedt: Iacobus Lucius.

Catholy, E., 1961, Das Fastnachtspiel des Spätmittelalters. In Hermaea N.F. 8. Tübingen: Max Niemayer.

Chambers, E. K., 1923, The Elizabethan Stage, 1–4 (Index cf. White). Oxford: Clarendon.

Chambers, E. K., 1930, William Shakespeare, 1–2 (Index cf. White). Oxford: Clarendon.

Chambers, E. K., 1936, Sir Henry Lee. An Elizabethan Portrait. Oxford: Clarendon.

Chambers, E. K., 1946, Sources for a Biography of Shakespeare. Oxford: Clarendon.

Chassant, A. & Tausin, H., 1878, Dictionnaire des Devises historiques et heraldiques. Paris: Dumoulin.

Cheyney, E. P., 1914 and 1926, A History of England from the defeat of the Armada to the death of Elizabeth I, 1–2. London: Longman.

Chopard, A., 1939–40, Genève et les Anglais (XVIe à XVIIIe siècle). In Bulletin de la Société d'Histoire et d'Archéologie de Genève, 7. Genève: Jullien.

Clark, A., 1887, Register of the University of Oxford, 2 (1571–1622), Part 2. Oxford: Clarendon.

Cohn, A., 1865 (1967), Shakespeare in Germany in the XVIth and XVIIth Centuries. Wiesbaden: Sändig.

Cohn, A., 1886, Englische Komödianten in Köln (1592–1656). *in* Jahrbuch der Deutsche Shakespeare-Gesellschaft *21*, 245–276. Weimar: Huschke.

Cokayne and The Complete Peerage. Cf. Gibbs.

Crescenzi, G. P. De, 1647, Anfiteatro romano, nel quale . . . si rappresenta la nobilità delle famiglie antichi e nouve della regia citta di Milano, 2nd ed. Milano: Visconti.

Crollalanza, G. di, 1886–90, Dizionario storico–blasonico delle famiglie nobili italiane estinte e fiorenti, 1–3. & App. Pisa: Giornale araldico.

Crueger, J., 1887, Englische Comoedianten in Straßburg im Elsaß. *In* Archiv für Literaturgeschichte *1*, 113. Leipzig: Teubner.

Dahlgren, F. A., 1866, Förteckning öfver svenska skådespel uppförda på Stockholms Theatrar 1737–1863. Stockholm: Norstedt.

Dahlgren, F. A., 1914–16, Glossarium öfver föråldrade eller ovanliga ord i svenska språket från och med 1500-talets andra årtionde. Lund: Gleerups.

Dalin, O. von, 1747–1762, Swea Rikes Historia 1–3: 1–2. Stockholm: Grefing.

Danielsson, B., 1955 and 1963, respectively, John Hart's Works, 1–2. Stockholm and Uppsala: Almqvist & Wiksell.

Dansk Biografisk Leksikon, 1933–44, 1–27. Copenhagen: Schultz.

Danske Magazin, 1751, Vol. 5. Copenhagen: Gyldendal.

Davidsson, A., 1968, Några stamböcker i Lunds universitetsbibliotek. *In* Nordisk Tidskrift för Bok- och biblioteksväsen, *55*, 33–58. Uppsala: Almqvist & Wiksell.

Davidsson, A., 1969, 'In pereginatione litteraria'. Kring några stamböcker i Stifts- och landsbiblioteket i Linköping. *In* Annales Academiae Regiae Scientiarum Upsaliensis. Uppsala: Almqvist & Wiksell.

De Navorscher. Cf. Muller, F.

Descampes, P., 1922, Dictionnaire de geographie ancienne et moderne. Berlin: Altman.

Devrient, E., 1848–74 Geschichte der deutschen Schauspielkunst, 1–4. Leipzig: Weber.

Dictionary of American Biography, 1928–58, 1–20, with supplements 1 and 2. London and New York: Oxford University Press.

Dictionary of National Biography, 1885–1912, 1–67. London: Elders.

Dictionnaire de Théologie catholique, 1909–50, 1–15. Paris: Letouzey & Ané.

Dielitz, J., 1888, Die Wahl- und Denkspruche, Feldgeschrei, Losungen. Frankfort on the Main: Rommel.

Dubrowsky, 1963, Catalogue of Letters and other papers of European scientists and writers of the XVIth–XVIIIth centuries now preserved in the Dubrowsky Collection. Leningrad: Saltykov–Shchdrin.

Duncker, A., 1886, Landgraf Moritz von Hessen und die Englischen Komödianten. *In* Deutsche Rundschau, *48*. Berlin: Gebrueder Paetel.

Edwards, E., 1868, The Life of Sir Walter Raleigh. Together with His Letters. London: Macmillan.

Ekholm, E., 1767–69, Den Swenska Fatburen, 1–9. Stockholm: Hesselberg.

Elgenstierna, G., 1925–36, Den introducerade svenska adelns ättartavlor med tillägg och rättelser, 1–9. Stockholm: Norstedt.

Enciclopedia Italiana, 1937–40, 1–35. Rome: Istituto della Enciclopedia Italiana.

Engelbrecht, Brennecke, Uhlendorff & Shaefer, 1959, Theater in Kassel. Cassel: Bärenreiter.

Engelbrecht, C., 1958, Die Kasseler Hofkapelle im 17. Jahrhundert. *In* Hessische Forschungen 3. Cassel: Bärenreiter.

Erich, A., 1597, Ausführliche und warhafte Beschreibung des . . . Herrn Christians, des Vierdten, dieses Namens, Dennemarck, Norwegen . . . Königes . . . Krönung. Copenhagen: Waldkirch.

Erich, A., 1598, Klarlige oc visse Beskriffuelse om den Stormectige, Hoybaarne Forstis oc Herris, Herr Christians den Fierdis . . . Kongelige Kroning . . . udi Kiøbenhaffn den 29 Augusti Anno 1596. Copenhagen: Waldkirch.

Esselborn, E., 1945. Das Geschlecht Cirksena. (Typewritten.) Aurich: Niedersächsisches Staatsarchiv.

Eton, 1943, The Eton College Register 1441–1698, 1–2. Eton: Ballantyne.

Exegesis Historica, 1610, non minus aeqvas, qvam graves commemorans cavsas, qvibus amplissimi ordines Regni Sueciae preuocati, Sigismundum Tertium, Regem Poloniae, eiusque progeniem vniuersam; in omnem aeuitatem, Suecano exuerant Diademate; & omnem (que nomine iurisiurandi ac unionis haereditariae obstricti tenebantur) obedientiam illi prorsus renunciantes. . . . Cum gratia, & priuilegio potentissimi Regis Sueonum. Stockholmiae: Ex Molybdographia Gutterviciana. (There is also a copy at the Royal Library, Stockholm 5, Dep. of Rare Books.)

Fabris, S., 1606, De Lo Schermo overo scienza d'Arme. Copenhagen: Henrico Waldkirch.

Falck, A. E., 1935, Nyköpings teater. Nyköping: Österbergs.

Faegerskioeld, C., 1966, Vasa-namnet och Carl Carlsson Gyllenhielm. *In* Personhistorisk Tidskrift. Stockholm: Norstedt.

Fischer, J. F., 1959, Die Englischen Komödianten in Salzburg. *In* Mitteilungen der Gesellschaft für Salzburgs Landeskunde, 99. Salzburg.

Flemming, W., 1936, Die beiden Bühnen in den Dramen des Herzogs Heinrich-Julius von Braunschweig-Lüneburg. *In* Lebendiges Erbe.

Fredén, G., 1939, Friedrich Menius und das Repertoire der Englischen Komödianten in Deutschland. (Thesis.) Stockholm: Palmers. (Reviews of this theses by L. M. Price, 1942, The Germanic Review No. 17; H. Knudsen, 1941, Geistige Arbeit No. 8; and St. Lindroth, 1941, Lychnos 1941.)

Freytag von Loringhoven, F. & Isenburg, Wilhelm Karl von, 1953–58, Stammtafeln zur Geschichte der Europäischen Staaten, 1–4. 2. ed. Marburg: Stargardt.

Friedenthal, R., 1922, Herzog Heinrich-Julius von Braunschweig als Dramatiker, 1–2. (Thesis.) Munich.

Friis, A., 1927, Alderman Cockayne's Project and the Cloth Trade. (Thesis.) Copenhagen and London: Munksgaard and Milford, respectively.

Friis, F. R., 1894, Et par optegnelser om Uraniborg. Copenhagen.

232

Fuerstenau, M., 1861, Zur Geschichte der Musik und des Theaters am Hofe zu Dresden, 1–2. Dresden: Kuntze.

Gibbs, 1910–59, The Complete Peerage of England, Scotland, Ireland. Great Britain, and the United Kingdom, Extant, Extinct or Dormant by George Edward Cokayne, new edition revised and much enlarged, edited by the Hon. Vicary Gibbs, 1–13. From 3 with the assistance of H. Arthur Doubleday; 13 edited by H. A. Doubleday and Lord Howard de Walden. London: St. Catherine.

Glarbo, H., 1956, Danske i England. Copenhagen: Munksgaard.

Goldmann, K. H., 1956, Der Poppenreuther Pfarrer Erhard Christoph Bezzel (1727–1801) und seine Stammbücher. *In* Mitteilungen des Vereins für Geschichte der Stadt Nürnberg, No. 47. Nuremberg: Selbstverlag.

Gollmert, L. & Schwerin, W. and L. von, 1875–1928, Geschichte des Geschlechts von Schwerin, 1–3, and supplements 1–3. Berlin and Goerlitz: Mitscher & Roestell.

Gouron, M., 1957, Matricule de l'Université de Montpellier (1503–1599). Genève: Droz.

Granqvist, P. M., 1924, Gustaf Vasas avkomlingar inom och utom Sverige. Norrtälje: Ehrengren.

Granstedt, E., 1943, Carl Carlsson Gyllenhielm och Vasa-huset. *In* Personhistorisk Tidskrift. Stockholm: Norstedt.

Greenlaw, E., Osgood, C. G., Padelford, F. M. & Heffner, R., assisted by Mason, D. E., 1932–57, The works of Edmund Spenser. A Variorum Edition: The Faerie Queene, 1–6: The Minor Poems, 1–2; The Prose Works and Index. Baltimore: John Hopkins.

Grindley, A., 1863–65, Rudolph II. Prague.

Guasco, F., 1911, Dizionario feudale degli antichi Stati Sardi e della Lombardia dell'epoca carolingia ai nostri tempi. Pinerolo: Societa' Storica Subalpina.

Hahr, A., 1908, Ur en schlesisk adelsmans dagbok i Sverige på 1500-talet. *In* Ord och bild. Stockholm: Wahlström & Widstrand.

Hamel, J., 1854, England and Russia, comprising the Voyages of J. Tradescant the elder, Sir H. Willoughby, R. Chancellor, Nelson, and others to the White Sea, &c. London: Bentley.

Hammerich, A., 1892, Musiken ved Christian den Fjerdes Hof. Et Bidrag till dansk Musikhistorie. Copenhagen: Wilh. Hansen.

Hampe, T., 1900, Die Entwicklung des Theaterwesens in Nürnberg von der zweiten Hälfte des XV. Jahrhunderts bis 1806. Nuremberg: Schrag.

Hansen, R., 1917, Bidrag till Finlands historia, 1 (in progress).

Harlow, V. T., 1928, The Discovery of the large and beutiful Empire of Guiana by Sir Walter Raleigh. London: Argonaut.

Harrison, G. B., 1956, Elizabethan Plays and Players. Ann Arbor: The University of Michigan Press.

Hart, S., 1959, The Prehistory of the New Netherland Company. Amsterdam: City of Amsterdam Press.

Hasselt, G. van, 1803, Arnhemsche Oudheden, 1. Arnhem: J. H. Moeleman Jr.

Hasted, E., 1778, 1782, 1790 and 1799, respectively, The History of the County of Kent, 1–4. Canterbury: Simmons & Kirkley.

Heberer, M. von Bretten, 1610, Aegyptiaca Servitus. Heidelberg: Voegelin.

Hechth, H., 1929, Thomas Platters des juengeren Englandfahrt im Jahre 1599. Halle/Saale: Niemayer.

Hennessy, G., 1898, Novum repertorium ecclesiasticum parochiale Londinense, or London Diocesan Clergy Succession from earliest time to the year 1898. London: Swan.

Hermansson, Å., 1962, Karl IX och ständerna. Tronfrågan och författningsutvecklingen i Sverige 1598–1611. In Studia historica Upsaliensia, 7. Uppsala: Almqvist & Wiksell.

Herz, E., 1903, Englische Schauspieler und Englisches Schauspiel zur Zeit Shakespeares in Deutschland. Hamburg and Leipzig: Litzmann.

Heywood, T., 1612?, An Apology for Actors. Containing three briefe Treatises. 1. Their Antiquity. 2. Their ancient Dignity. 3. The true use of theirs Quality. Reprinted by William Cartwright as The Actors Vindication (N.D. but according to Douce 1658) and in 1841 (Sh. Soc.). Summary in E. K. Chambers, The Elizabethan Stage, Oxford 1923, 4, 250 ff.

Hildebrand, E., 1889, Vasa-namnet och Vasa-vapnet. In Svenska autografsällskapets tidskrift. Stockholm: Norstedt.

Historisk Tidskrift, 1881, (in progress). Stockholm: Norstedt.

Historiskt bibliotek, 1875–1880, 1–7. Stockholm: Klemmings and Norstedts.

Hodges, C. W., 1953, The Globe Restored. A Study of the Elizabethan Theatre. London: Ernest Benn, Ltd.

Holinshed, R., 1577 and 1587, respectively, The Chronicles of England, Scotland, and Ireland, 1 ed., 1–2, illustrated, and 2 ed. enlarged, without illustrations. London: J. Harrison.

Holland, W. L., 1855, Die Schauspiele des Herzogs Heinrich Julius von Braunschweig nach alten Drucken und Handschriften. In Bibliothek des Literarischen Vereins in Stuttgart, No. 36. Stuttgart: Selbtsverlag.

Holm, I., 1969, Drama på scen. Stockholm: Bonniers.

Hoppe, I., 1887, Geschichte des ersten schwedisch–polnischen Krieges in Preußen. Leipzig: Duncker & Humblot.

Hotson, L., 1925, The death of Christopher Marlowe. London: Nonesuch.

Hotson, L., 1960, The Wooden O. London: Hart-Davis.

Hughes, C., 1903, Shakespeare's Europe. Unpublished chapters of Fynes Moryson's Itinerary. Being a survey of the condition of Europe at the end of the 16th century. With an introduction and an account of Fynes Moryson's career. London: Sherratt & Hughes.

Hughes, J. (Editor), 1715, The works of Mr. Edmund Spenser. London: Fonson.

Huguet, E., 1925–67 (in progress), Dictionnaire de la langue française du seizième siècle, 1–7. Paris: Didier.

Huldt, H. R., 1923, Afskrifter av i Vatikan-biblioteket förekommande handskrifter beträffande Sverige.

Ilsøe, H., 1963, Udlændinges rejser i Danmark indtil år 1700. En bibliografisk fortegnelse. Copenhagen: Rosenkilde og Bagger.

Imhoff, J. W., 1710, Genealogia viginti illustrium in Italia familiarum in tres classes secundum totidem Italiae ... ; accedunt in fine de genealogia et insignibus familae de Mediolano Vicecomitum &c., Amstelodami. (Le famiglie contenute nell'opera sono le suguenti: Cibo, Farnese, Pico della Mirandola, Biraghi, Omodei, Sfondrati, Ferreri, DelGuidice, Trivulzi, Medici, Conti Guidi, Piccolomini, Salviati, Strozzi, Colonna, Pignatelli, Sanseverini, Gambacorti, Ruffo, Orsini. Milano: Visconti.)

Indebetou, H. O., 1874, Nyköpings-Minnen, 1–3. Nyköping: Kullbergs.

Ingman (Ivalo), S., 1894, Kaarlo IX-nen jäämeren politickka (Charles IX's Arctic policy). (Thesis.) Helsinki: Päivälehden, Kirjgpainossa.

Jacobowsky, C. V., 1927 and 1936, Svenska studenter i Oxford c. 1620–1740. *In* Personhistorisk tidskrift. Stockholm: Riksarkivet.

Johnsen, O. A., 1923, Finnmarkens politiske historie. *In* Videnskapsselskapets Skrifter 2, Hist-, Filos. Klasse, 1922, No. 3. Oslo: Dybwad.

Jonge, J. K. J. de, 1855, Inlichtingen omtrent de staatkundige betrekkingen tuschen Nederland en Zweden in de jaren 1592–1609. Breda.

Jonge, J. K. J. de, 1862, De Opkomst van het Nederlandsch Gezag in Oost-Indie, 1595–1610, 1. 's-Gravenhage: Nijhoff. Reprint of Abraham Cabeliau's journal from the trading voyage to Guiana December 3rd 1597, to the end of December, 1598, in the foregoing book 1, 49–51 and 153–160. The trip was unsuccessful. The heaps of gold (Eldorado) believed to be in Guiana were not located. Duke Charles of Sweden and Sir Walter Raleigh were both involved in this trading voyage.

Jupp, E. B., 1848, Historical Account of the Company of Carpenters, 2nd ed. by W. W. Pocock, 1887. London: Pickering & Chatto.

Karlsson, K. H., 1901, Knut H:son Hand. *In* Personhistorisk tidskrift. Stockholm: Norstedt.

Kaufmann, J., 1905, Über Danzigs Sanitäts- und Medizinalwesen im XVI. und XVII. Jahrhundert. *In* Mitteilungen des Westpreußischen Geschichtsvereins, 4. 1. 11. Gdańsk: Saunier.

Keil, R. & R., 1893, Die Deutschen Stammbücher. Berlin: Grote'sche.

Kernkamp, G. W., 1905, Verslag van een onderzoek in Zweden, Noorwegen en Denemarken naar Archivalia, belangrijk voor de Geschiednis van Nederland. 's-Gravenhage: van Stockum.

Kernkamp, G. W., 1909, Baltische Archivalia, belangrirk voor de Geschiedenis van Nederlandh in Stockholm, Kopenhagen, en de duitsche oostzeesteden. 's-Gravenhage: Nijhoff.

Kindermann, H., 1959, Theatergeschichte Europas, 3. Salzburg: Müller.

Klopp, O., 1854–58, Geschichte Ostfrieslands, 1–3. Hannover: Ruempler.

Kockum, A., 1949, Läkare och apotekare vid Gustaf Vasas och hans söners hov. Stockholm: Gebers.

Koennecke, G., 1887/88, Neue Beiträge zur Geschichte der Englischen Komoedianten. *In* Zeitschrift für vergleichende Literaturgeschichte und Renaissance-Literatur, N.F., No. 1. Berlin: Haack.

Kok, J., 1780–95, Vaderlandsch Woordenboek, 1–35; 1–18 by Kok, 19–35 by Fokke. Suppl. 1797–99, 1–3. Amsterdam: Allart.

Krauß, R., 1898, Die Englischen Comoedianten im heutigen Wuertemberg. *In* Würtembergische Vierteljahrshefte für Landesgeschichte, N.F., No. 7. Stuttgart: Kohlhammer.

Laffleur, P. de Kermaingant, 1886, L'Ambassade de France en Angleterre sous Henry IV. Mission de Jean de Thumery, Sieur de Boissise (1598–1602). Paris: Didot.

Lafontaine, H. C. de, 1909, The King's Musick. London: Novello.

Lagerbielke, L., 1913–15, Nyköpingshus, 1–2. Stockholm: Hökerbergs.

Lagerbielke, L., 1930, Nyköpingshus genom seklerna. Nyköping: Södermanlands tidning.

Landberg, G., 1927, Cecilia. *In* SBL 7, 719. Stockholm: Bonniers.

Latham, A. M. C., 1959, Sir Walter Raleigh's Instructions to His Son. *In* Elizabethan and Jacobean Studies. Presented to Frank Percy Wilson in honour of his seventieth birthday. Edited by Herbert Davis and Helen Gardner. Oxford: Clarendon.

Lea, K. M., 1931, English Players at the Swedish Court. *In* Modern Language Review, No. 26, 1, 76–80. London: Modern Humanities Research Association.

Levassor, M., 1700–11 and 1750, Histoire de Louis XIII, roi de France, . . ., 1–10, (20 vols.). Amsterdam: Pierre Brunel.

Lidell, H., 1935, Studier i Johannes Messenius dramer. (Thesis.) Uppsala.

Lienhard-Riva, A., 1945, Armoriale ticinese. Lausanne: Imprimeries Réunies S. A.

Ludewig, F. A., 1833, Heinrich Julius, Herzog zu Braunschweig und Luneburg. Ein biographischer Versuch. Wolfenbüttel.

Lundkvist, S., 1965, Review of Hermansson, Å., Karl IX och ständerna. *In* Historisk Tidskrift 85, 2, 129–152. Stockholm: Norstedt.

Lundstroem, E., 1749, D.D. Dissertatio Gradualis, De Sudermannia, 2. Upsaliae.

McKerrow, R. B., 1910, A Dictionary of Printers and Booksellers in England, Scotland and Ireland and of Foreign Printers of English Books 1557–1640. London: Blades, East & Blades.

Marshall, G. W., 1903, The Genealogist's Guide. Guildford: Billing & Sons.

Meißner, J., 1884, Die Englischen Komoedianten in Oesterreich. *In* Jahrbuch der Deutschen Shakespeare-Gesellschaft *19*, 113–154. Weimar: Huschke.

Meißner, J., 1884, Die Englischen Comoedianten in Oesterreich. Wien. (Review of this book by A. Cohn. *In* Jahrbuch der Deutschen Shakespeare-Gesellschaft *19*, 311–313.) Weimar: Huschke.

Mentzel, E., 1882, Geschichte der Schauspielkunst in Frankfurt am Main von Ihren Anfängen bis zur Eröffnung des Städtischen Komoedienhauses. Ein Beitrag zur Deutschen Kultur- und Theatergeschichte. *In* Archiv für Frankfurts Geschichte und Kunst, N.F. 9. Frankfort on the Main: Voelcker.

Mentzel, E., 1902, Das alte Frankfurter Schauspielhaus und seine Vorgeschichte. Frankfort on the Main: Ritter & Loening.

Merick, Sir J., 1602, Report of Sir J. Merick's Mission to India. *In* The Gentleman's Magazine, 9/1824. London: Nichols.

Messenius, J., Scondia illustrata, Tomus 15.

Meyer, C. F., 1902, Englische Komödianten am Hofe des Herzogs Philipp-Julius von Pommern-Wolgast. *In* Jahrbuch der Deutschen Shakespeare-Gesellschaft *38*, 196–211. Weimar: Langenscheidt.

Meyersson, Å., 1939, Adligt nöje. Tornering och ringränning under äldre Vasa-tid. *In* Fataburen. Stockholm: Nordiska Museet.

Meyersson, Å., 1940, Hertig Johans (III) och Erik XIV:s engelska rustningar. *In* Livrustkammaren 2, 1, 1. Stockholm: Victor Pettersson.

Moes, E. W., 1887, Joannes Cabeljauw. *In* Oud-Holland 5. Amsterdam: Binger.

Mollerus, H., 1565, Ad illustrissimum principem ac dominum, Christopherum, Sacrii imperii Romani marchionem in Baden &c., et ad serenissimam conjugem ejus D. Ceciliam natam in Regia apud Suedos familia, gratulatio musarum Gedanensium. (A copy at the Royal Library, Copenhagen; Dep. of Rare Books.)

Morgan, E. D. & Coote, C. H., 1886, Early voyages and travels to Russia and Persia. *In* Hakluyt Society *72* and *73*. London.

Moritz, 1897, Die Bibliothek des Prinzen Moritz von Oranien. *In* Oud-Holland, 15. Amsterdam: Binger.

Morrison, P. G., 1950, Index to 'A short title catalogue of books, &c.'. Charlottesville: University of Virginia.

Moryson, F., 1617, An Itinerary written by Fynes Moryson, Gent., First in the Latine Tongue, and then translated by him into English (containing his ten years' travel through the twelve dominions of Germany, Bohmerland, Switzerland, Netherland, Denmark, Poland, Italy, Turkey, France, England, Scotland, and Ireland). London: J. Beale.

Muller, F., De Navorscher, 1851 (in progress). Amsterdam: Ipenbuur & van Seldam. (Periodical for heraldry and genealogy.)

Murray, J. T., 1910, 1–2, English Dramatic Companies 1558–1642. London: Constable & Co.

Nadal, 1861, Histoire de l'Université de Valence. Valence: Marc Aurel.

Nichols, J., 1823, reprint 1965, The Progresses and Public Processions of Queen Elizabeth I, 2nd ed., 1–3. London: Nichols.

Nichols, J., 1828, The Progresses, Processions and Magnificent Festivities of King James the First, 1–4. London: Nichols.

Nicoll, A., 1948, The Development of the Theatre, &c., 3rd ed. revised and enlarged. London: Harrap.

Nicoll, A., 1949, World Drama from Aeschylos to Anouilh. London: Harrap.

Nieuw Nederlandsch Biografisch Woordenboek, 1911–37, 1–10. Leiden: Sijthoff's.

Noailles, E. H. C. de, 1878, Henri de Valois et la Pologne en 1572, 2nd ed., 1–2. Paris: Calmann Lévy.

Norlind, T. & Trobäck, E., 1926, Kungl. Hovkapellets historia 1526–1926. Stockholm: Wahlström & Widstrand.

Nungezer, E., 1929, A Dictionary of Actors. New Haven: Yale.

Oedberg, J. F., 1896, Om prinsessan Cecilia Vasa, markgrefvinna af Baden-Rodemachern. Stockholm: Fritze.

Oedberg, J. F., 1896, Tidsbilder ur 1550-talets svenska häfder. Stockholm: Fritze.

Oedberg, J. F. 1897, Om stämplingarna mot Konung Johan III. Stockholm: Fritze.

Oedberg, J. F., 1903, Om vestgöta-adelsmannen Tord Bonde till Stensholmen och hans tid, 1550-1628. *In* Vestergötlands fornminnesförenings tidskrift, 2, 2, 12, 16–78. Mariestad och Stockholm: Fritze.

Ohlson, N. G., 1941, Hertig Sigismunds tukto- och läromästare. Stockholm: Westerberg.

Ohlson, N. G., 1945, Livmedikus och storköpman. Kalmar: privately printed.

Palme, S. U., 1938, En politisk giftermålshandel. *In* Personhistorisk tidskrift. Stockholm: Norstedt.

Palme, S. U., 1938, Två källor rörande händelserna i Finland 1599. *In* Finsk Historisk Tidskrift. Helsinki: Mercator.

Paludan, J., 1880–81, Om Dramaets Udvikling i Danmark mellem Skolekomedien og Holberg. *In* Dansk historisk tidskrift, 5. Række, 2. bind. Copenhagen: Gyldendal.

Pemberton, W. 1913, Elizabeth Blount and Henry VIII. London: Nash.

Perrier, J., 1887, Histoire des Evêques de Valence. Monaco.

Personhistorisk Tidskrift, 1898 (in progress). Editor 1971: Birgitta Lager, D.Ph. Stockholm: Norstedt.

Personne, N., 1913, Svenska teatern under Gustavianska tidehvarfvet. Stockholm: Wahlström & Widstrand.

Petersen, C. S., 1914–16, Rejser i Danmark indtil Fredrik IV:s død. *In* Fortid og Nutid, 1. Copenhagen: Lybecker.

Pfeilsticker, W., 1957, Neues Würtembergisches Dienerbuch, *1*. Stuttgart: Cotta.

Pfutzenreuter, W., 1936, Herzog Heinrich-Julius von Braunschweig-Luneburg und der norddeutschen Späthumanismus (Thesis). Munster.

Picot, E., 1884, 1887, 1893, 1912 and 1920, respectively, Catalogue des livres composant la bibliothèque de feu M. le Baron James de Rothschild, 1–5. Paris: Damascène Morgand, Libraire.

Platen, M. von, 1951, Främlingar i forna tiders Stockholm. *In* Stockholm 1252–1952. Stockholm: Frick.

Pocock, W. W., cf. Jupp, E. B.

Pollard, A.W., 1894, Sir Edward Kelly. *In* Lives of Twelve Bad Men. London: Unwin.

Pollard, A. W. & Redgrave, G. R., 1926, A short Title Catalogue of Books Printed in England, Scotland and Ireland and of English books Printed Abroad 1475–1640. London: Bibliographical Society.

Pulver, J., 1927, A Biographical Dictionary of Old English Music. London: Kegan Paul, Trench, Trubner & Co., Ltd.

Quadrio, F. S., 1755–56, Dissertazioni critico-storiche intorno alla rezia di qua dalle alpi, oggi detta Valtellina, 1–3. Milano: nella stamperia della societa' Palatina.

Quadrio, G. M., 1753, Storia Memorabile della prodigiosa apparizione di Maria S. S. in Tirano ecc. Milano mella stamperia della societa' Palatina.

Ravn, V. C., 1870, Engelske Instrumentister ved det danske hof paa Shakespeares Tid. *In* For Idé og Virkelighed, *1/1870.* Copenhagen: Steen.

Reaney, P. H., 1958, A Dictionary of British Surnames. London: Routledge & Kegan Paul.

Refugiés à Bâle, 1892, Quelques refugiés de la Saint-Barthélémy à Bâle. Extrait de la Matricule du Recteur de l'Université de Bâle 1572–73. *In* Bulletin historique et littéraire de la Société de l'Histoire du Protestantisme français, *41.* Paris.

Reimers, H., 1925, Ostfriesland bis zum Aussterben seines Fürstenhauses. Bremen: Friesen-Verlag.

Riewald, J. G., 1959, Some Later Elizabethan and Early stuart Actors and Musicians. *In* English Studies, 40, 1. Amsterdam: Swets & Zeitlinger.

Riewald, J. G., 1960, New Light on the English Actors in the Netherlands, *c.* 1590 – *c.* 1660. *In* English Studies, *41,* 2. Amsterdam: Swets & Zeitlinger.

Rivista del collegio araldico, 1903. Milano: Tip. dell'Unione Cooperative.

Roerdam, H. F., (Ed), 1873 and 1878, respectively, Sivert Grubbes Dagbog. *In* Danske Magazin, *4,* 2, 361–406 and *4,* 4, 4–83. Copenhagen: Gyldendal.

Rosenheim, M., 1910, The Album Amicorum. *In* Archaeologia. Oxford: Society of Antiquaries.

Roth, Fritz, 1959–, Restlose Auswertungen von Leichen predigten und Personalschriften für genelaogische und kulturhistorische Zwecke, 1– in progress, Boppard, Rhein: Fritz Roth. Selbstverlag.

Round, J. H., 1911, The King's sergeants & officers of state with their coronation services. London: Nisbet.

Ruhe, H., 1938, Chronik der Stadt Krempe. Glueckstadt: Augustin.

Ruhnke, M., 1963, Beiträge zu einer Geschichte der deutschen Hofmusikkollegien im 16. Jahrhundert. Berlin: Merselburger.

Sacklén, J. F., 1822–24 and 1835, respectively, Sveriges läkarehistoria, 1–3 and supplement. Nyköping: Winge.

Sacklén, J. F., 1833, Sveriges Apotekarehistoria ifrån Konung Gustaf I:s till närvarande tid. Nyköping: Winge.

Salis R., S., 1953, In Salis di Valtellina e il loro palazzo in Tirano. Chur.

Salis R., S., 1959, Tirano di ieri — Saggi storici. Chur.

Sallander, H., 1967, Nicolaus Olai Scarensis och hans stambok från åren 1604–1628. *In* Kungl. Humanistiska Vetenskaps-Samfundets i Uppsala Årsbok 1965–66. Uppsala: Almqvist & Wiksell.

Samse, H., 1950, Die Zentralverwaltung in den südwelfischen Landen vom 15. bis 17. Jahrhundert. *In* Quellen und Darstellungen zur Geschichte Niedersachsen, 49. Hildesheim: Lax.

Sargent, R. M., 1935, At the Court of Queen Elizabeth I. The Life and Lyrics of Sir Edward Dyer. London and New York: Oxford University Press.

Sattler, C., 1891, Reichsfreiherr Dodo zu Inn- und Knyphausen, Königl. Schwedischer Feldmarschall. Seine Lebensgeschichte. Norden: Soltau.

Schantz, C. L. von, 1727, Then Svenska matrikeln eller förteckning på Sveriges rikes ridderskap och adel åhr 1727. Stockholm.

Schlegel, B. & Klingspor, C. A., 1875, Den med sköldebref förlänade men ej å riddarhuset introducerade svenska adelns ättartaflor. Stockholm: Norstedt.

Schlegel, A. W. von & Tieck, L., 1839–40, Shakespeare's dramatische Werke, 1–12, Berlin: Reimer.

Schloßberger, A., 1865, Hans Jakob Breunings von Buchenbach. Relation über seine Sendung nach England im Jahr 1595. Bibliothek des literarischen Vereins in Stuttgart, 81. Stuttgart: Selbstverlag.

Schneider, L., 1891, Shakespeare in den Niederlanden. *In* Jahrbuch der Deutschen Shakespeare-Gesellschaft *26*, 26–42. Weimar: Huschke.

Schnell, I., 1941, En furste far genom sitt rike. *In* Sörmlandsbygden. Nyköping: Oesterberg.

Schoeldström, B., 1889, Seuerling och hans Comoedie-troupp. Ett blad ur Svenska Landsortsteaterns historia. Stockholm: Gebers.

Schroeder, J. H., 1847, William Parr. Uppsala: Leffler & Sebell.

Schueck, H., 1892, Englische Comoedianten in Skandinavien. *In* Skandinavisches Archiv. Lund: Gleerup.

Schueck, H., 1902, En scen i Hamlet. *In* Ur gamla papper, 5, 9 ff. Stockholm: Gebers.

Schueck, H., 1920, Johannes Messenius. Stockholm: Norstedt.

Schwab, H., 1899, Der Dialog in den Schauspielen des Herzogs Heinrich-Julius von Braunschweig. Troppau.

Schwarz, F., 1939, Danziger Ärzte im XVI.–XVIII. Jahrhundert. *In* Danziger familiengeschichtliche Beiträge, 4. Gdańsk: Danziger Verlagsges.

Schweizer lexikon, 1945–48, 1–7. Zürich: Encyclios-Verlag.

Scott-Giles, C. W., 1950, Shakespeare's Heraldry. London: Dent & Sons.

Scott, H., 1926, Fasti Ecclesiae Scoticanae, 2nd ed. Edinburgh: Oliver & Boyd.

Scott, W. R., 1910–12, The Constitution and finance of English, Scottish and Irish joint-stock companies to 1720. Cambridge: University Press.

(Shakespeare, W., 1821), The Plays and Poems of William Shakespeare with the corrections and illustrations of various commentators comprehending a life of the poet and an enlarged history of the stage by the late Edmond Malone, published by James Boswell, 1–21. London: Baldwin.

Sibbern, N. P., 1716, Bibliotheca historica Dano-Norvegica sive de scriptoribus rerum Dano-Norvegicarum commentarius historico literarius. Hamburg and Leipzig: Liebezeit.

Sigismund, 1594, Acta coronationis. Konung Sigismundi . . . Krönings Handling I Upsala / then 19. Februarij Anno MDXCIV. Stockholm: Gutterwitz.

Simon, P., 1911, Danziger Inventar 1531–91. Munich and Leipzig.

Sjoegren, G., 1969, Thomas Bull and other 'English Instrumentalists' in Denmark in the 1580s. *In* Shakespeare Survey *22*, pp. 119–123. Cambridge: University Press.

Slange, N., 1749, Kong Christian IV:s historie, 1–4. Copenhagen: H. M. The King's Printing House.

Sleumer, A., 1926, Kirchenlateinisches Wörterbuch. Limburg: Steffen.

Smith, S. B., 1883, Studier paa det gamle danske skuespils omraade. Copenhagen: Gyldendal.

Soedersteen, H., 1916, Askersunds landsförsamlings kyrka. Askersund: Holmberg.

Sokól, S., 1959, Medycyna w Gdańsku w Dobie odrozenia. Wróclaw and Warszawa: Polska Akademia Nauk.

Spedding, J., Ellis, R. L. & Heath, D. D., 1857–74: The Works of Francis Bacon, 1–14. London: Longman.

Sprinchorn, C., 1885, Om Sveriges förbindelser med Nederländerna från äldsta tider till år 1614. In Historisk Tidskrift, No. 6. Stockholm: Norstedt.

Stackelberg, F. von, 1937, Genealogisches Handbuch der baltischen Ritterschaften. Vol. Livonia, 2, 10. Goerlitz: Starke (Kretschmer).

Steckzén, B., 1958, A Guide to the Materials for Swedish Historical Research in Great Britain. Publications by Kungl. Krigsarkivet, No. 5. Stockholm: Norstedt.

Stenbock, C. M., 1912, Erik XIV:s almanacksanteckningar, hans dagböcker, ritningar och musiknoter i urval utgifna genom Personhistoriska samfundet. Stockholm: Fritze (Norstedt).

Stow, J., 1631, Annales or a Generale Chronicle of England from Brute until the present yeare of Christ 1580. London: Meighen.

Stow, J., 1603 (1908), Survey of London, 2nd ed. Oxford: Clarendon.

Strieder, F. W., 1785, Grundlage zu einer Hessischen Gelehrten- und Schriftstellergeschichte. Cassel: Luckhart.

Strindberg, A., 1908, Hamlet, ett minnesblad på årsdagen den 26 november (1908) tillägnadt Intima Teatern. Stockholm: Björck & Börjesson.

Strong, S. A., 1903, Catalogue of letters at Welbeck. London: John Murray.

Sundler, J., 1735, D.D. Dissertatio Academica de Nycopia Metropoli Sudermanniae. (Thesis.) Upsaliae: Literis Wernerianis.

Svensk uppslagsbok, 1947–55, 2nd ed., vols. 1–32. Malmö: Norden.

Svenska Akademien, 1898 (in progress), Ordbok över svenska språket. Lund: Gleerups. Also in certain cases the editor's records for the foregoing work.

Svenskt biografiskt lexikon, 1918– (in progress). Stockholm: Bonniers.

Tardel, H., 1926, Zur bremischen Theatergeschichte (1563–1763). In Bremisches Jahrbuch, 30. Bremen: Winter.

Tawaststjerna, W., 1918–20 and 1929, respectively. Pohjoismaiden viisikolmattavuotinen sota, 1–2. In Historiallisia Tutkimuksia 1 and 9. Helsinki: Julkaissut Suomen Historiallinen Seura.

Tayler, A. & H., 1937, The House of Forbes. Aberdeen: Third Spalding Club.

Thordemann, B., 1949, Porträtt av en svartkonstnär. In Nordisk Numismatisk Årsskrift 1949. Copenhagen: Langkjær.

Tieck, L., 1811, Alt-Englisches Theater 1–2. Berlin: Realschulbuchhandlung.

Tieck, L., 1817, Deutsches Theater, 1–2. Berlin: Realschulbuchhandlung.

Tieck, L., 1823–29, Shakespeare's Vorschule, 1–2. Leipzig: Brockhaus.

Tieck, L., 1836, Vier Schauspiele von Shakespeare. Berlin: Cotta'schen.

Tittman, J., 1880, Die Schauspiele der Englischen Komoedianten in Deutschland. In Deutsche Dichter des 16. Jahrhundert. Leipzig: Brockhaus.

Toijer, D., 1930, Sverige och Sigismund 1598–1600 (Thesis): Stockholm: Westerberg.

Tolstoy, G., 1875, The first forty years of intercourse between England and Russia, 1553–1593. S:t Petersburg.

Troels-Lund, T., 1903–04, Dagligt Liv i Norden i det 16. Aarhundrede, 1–14. Copenhagen: Gyldendal.

Troili, G. K., 1876, Ur Handelns och Sjöfartens häfder. Göteborg: GHT.

Tuerler, H., Godet, M. and Attinger, V., 1921–34, Historisch-Biographisches Lexikon der Schweiz, 1–7 with supplement 1. Neuenburg: H. B. L. S.

Tunberg, S., 1918 and 1922, Riksrådet Erik Brahes chifferkalendarium, 1–2. In Personhistorisk tidskrift. Stockholm: Riksarkivet.

Typotius, J., 1606, Relatio historica de regno Sueciae et bellis civilibus atque externis, n.p. (There is also a copy at the Royal Library, Stockholm 5, Dep. of Rare books.)

Uppsala universitets årsskrifter, 1915–17, Äldre svenska biografier, 1–6. Uppsala: Almqvist & Wiksell.

(Victoria), 1900 (in progress), The Victoria History of the Counties of England, ed. by H. Arthur Doubleday, William Page and L. F. Salzman. London: Archibald Constable.

Vreede, G. W., 1841–44, Nederland en Zweden in staatkundige betrekkingen van Gustaaf Wasa tot Gustaaf Adolf (1523–1618), 1–2. Utrecht: Monde.

Waaranen, J. E., 1863–66, Handlingar upplysande Finlands historia under Karl IX:s tid, 1–3. In Samling af urkunder rörande Finlands historia. Helsinki: Finska Litteratur-Sällskapets tryckeri.

Wackernagel, H. G., 1951, 1956 and 1962, Die Matrikel der Universität Basel, 1–3 (in progress). Bâle: Universitätsbibliothek.

Wagner, A. R., 1952, The Records and Collections of the College of Arms. London: Burke's Peerage.

Wagner, A. R., 1960, English Genealogy. Oxford: Clarendon.

Werwing, J., 1746, Konung Sigismunds och Carl IX:s historier, nu utgifna af And. Ant. von Stiernman, 1–2. Stockholm: Grefing.

Westling, G. O. F., 1883, Hertig Karls furstendöme under åren 1568–1592. (Thesis.) Sundsvall: Boktryckeriaktiebolaget.

White, B., 1934, An Index to The Elizabethan Stage and William Shakespeare: A Study of Facts and Problems by Sir Edmund Chambers. Oxford: Shakesperare Association.

Whitmore, J. B., 1953, A Genealogical Guide (an Index to British Pedigrees in continuation of Marshall's Genealogist's Guide, 1903). London: Walford.

Wiarda, T. D., 1797, Ostfriesische Geschichte, 1–11, 2nd. ed. Aurich: Winter.

Wieselgren, H., 1900, Markgrefvinnan Cecilia, Gustaf Vasas skönaste dotter. In I gamla dagar och i våra. Småskrift. Stockholm: Beijer.

Wigert, V., 1920. Erik XIV. Historisk-psykiatrisk studie. Stockholm: Gebers.

Willan, T. S., 1953, The Muscovy Merchants of 1555. Manchester: University Press.

Willan, T. S., 1956, The Early History of the Russian Company 1553–1603. Manchester: University Press.

Wilson, F. P., 1945, Elizabethan and Jacobean. Oxford: Clarendon.

Wilson, F. P., 1953, Marlowe and the early Shakespeare. Oxford: Clarendon.
Wilson, F. P., 1955, The Elizabethan Theatre. *In* Neophilologus. Lecture delivered in the University College, Amsterdam. Groningen and Djakarta: Wolters.
Wilson, F. P., 1956, More Records from the Remembrancia of the City of London. *In* Malone Society Collections IV, pp. 55–65. Oxford: Clarendon.
Winter, P., 1958. Beiträge zur Musikpflege am Neuburger Hof 1569–1614. *In* Neuburger Kollektanenblatt *3*. Neuburg/Donau: Heitmatverein.
Wrangel, F. W., 1888, Tullgarn (Svenska kungsgårdar, 1). Stockholm: Norstedt.
Wuelcker, R. P., 1879, Englische Schauspieler in Kassel. *In* Jahrbuch der Deutschen Shakespeare-Gesellschaft. *14*, 360–361. Weimar: Huschke.
Zbylitowski, A., 1597 (1843), Droga do Szwecyey, namoznieysyego w polnocnych karinach pana. Zygmunta III polskiego y szweckiego krolá, odprawiona w roku 1594. New edition: Biblioteka starozytna pisarzy polskich. Cracow & Warszawa: Wyd. K. W. Wojcicki T 2.
Zettersten, A., 1890, Svenska flottans historia, 1, 1522–1634. Stockholm: Seligmann.

INDEX

of persons with some biographical notes

A

'Admiral's Men'. 102, 135, 136, 138, 187

Agnes (1578–1627). Princess of Holstein, sister of Christine, Duke Charles's second wife. 65

von Ahlefelt, Henry (Heinrich) of Satrupholm. Represented John Adolphus, the reigning Duke of Holstein, at Duke Charles's second wedding; cf. Kneschke, *Deutsches Adels-Lexicon*, 1, 25, 1859, and Roth, *Leichenpredigten*, 4, Personenregister. 63, 65, 66

Allem (Allen?), Rubrich (Robert?). Draper. Collaborated with Thomas Fisk (Duke Charles's agent in England). 26, 27

Alleyn, Edward (1566–1626). Player and founder of Dulwich College. Cf. *DNB*, 327 ff. and Nung., *Dict. of Actors*, 4 ff. 107, 135, 138

Alleyn, John (1556–96). English player. Cf. Nung., *Dict. of Actors*, 11. 135

Amaryllis, pseudonym for Alice Spencer, Lady Strange, later Countess of Derby. Daughter of Sir John Spencer and closely related to Edmund Spenser. 167

Amoret, probably pseudonym for Helena Northampton in Edmund Spenser's *Faerie Queene*. 166

Andræ, Eskillus. Vicar of Torneå, northwest Finland. Entry in Henry Francklin's album 28.9.1592. 212

Anne (1574–1619). Princess of Denmark. Sister of Christian IV. Queen of Scotland 1590 and of England 1604, *m.*, James VI of Scotland 1589. Entry 1590 in the album of Theodoricus Bewernest (1590–1605), Nr V. A. 325, fol 2, The Folger Shakespeare Library, 20003 Washington, D.C., USA. 57, 69, 132, 133

Anne (1573–1598). Princess of Hapsburg, daughter of Charles of Steiermark (1540–1590) and Mary, née princess of Bavaria (1551–1608). Queen of Poland and Sweden, *m.*, Sigismund III, King of Poland & c. (q.v.), 1592. 37, 51, 83, 148

Anne (1575–1610). Princess of Holstein. Sister of Christine, Duke Charles's second wife, *m.*, 1598, Enno III, reigning Count of East Friesland 1599–1625 after his father's, Edzard II, death. 65

Anne Jagiello (1524–96). Queen of Poland 1575–86. Sister of Catherine J. (q.v.), *m.*, 1575, Stephan Báthory (q.v.). 14, 85

Anne Mary (1575–1643). Princess of the Electoral Palatinate. 68

Anne Vasa (1568–1425). Princess of Sweden, daughter of King John III and Catherine Jagiello. Sister of Sigismund, King of Poland & c. Cf. *SBL*, 2, 22 ff. 14, 15, 19, 21, 51, 52, 209, 210

Asteropherus Arbogensis, Magnus Olai (1575–1647). Swedish playwright. Ordained 1603. Headmaster of the High School of Arboga in central Sweden. Vicar of Västerfärnebo nearby 1614, m., (2) Margaret Johansdotter d. 1648. Entry 6.7.1631 in the album of Jac. Gutræus Scotus, Nr I, g. 12, fol. 188ʳ, KB. Cf. *SBL*, 2, 406 ff. 162

B

Baazius the elder, Joannes (Jöns) (1583–1649). Ecclesiastical politician and scholar. Studied at Uppsala, Wittenberg and Gießen. Finally Bishop of Växjö in 1647. Author of "Inventarium ecclesiæ Sveogothorum", 1642, a history of the Swedish church commissioned by Queen Christina's guardians. Cf. *SUB* 2, 1017 f and *SBL*, 77 (Forbes). 217

Bacon, Francis (1561–1626). 1st Baron Verulam and Viscount St Albans. Lord Chancellor. Philosopher. Author. Son of Sir Nicholas Bacon, Lord Keeper, by his second wife Ann, second daughter of Sir Anthony Cooke and sister of the wife of Sir William Cecil (q.v.). Cf. *DNB*, 2, 328 ff. 170

Bagge, Jakob (James) the younger (d. c. 1611). Governor of Stockholm Castle. 87

Bagge, Peder (Per) (fl. 1556–1599). Commander-in-chief in North Finland 1590–92 with headquarters in Uleåborg. 211, 212

Bagge, Sven Pedersson. Commanded an expeditionary force to the White Sea in 1591. 210

Bagster, Hans. Danish trumpeter. Accompanied Queen Anne to Scotland, 21.4.1590. Engaged again in Denmark 1597. Naval trumpeter 1598. Trumpeter at the Danish Court 1600. Engages 5 English trumpeters. Last mentioned in the Danish Household accounts July 1601. Cf., Hammerich, Index, Nr 18. 133

Baner of Djursholm, Gustaf Axelsson (1547–1600). Swedish Councillor of state. Beheaded at Linköping 1600, m., 8.10.1581 Christine Sture (q.v.) Cf. *SBL*, 2, 647 ff. 46ⁿ

Barnekow, Christian. Danish Ambassador to England in 1597. 141

Báthory. See Stephen Báthory.

Baynbrigg, Eduardus. Englishman. 216

de Battiani, Balthazar. (fl. 1540). Entry 1584, Nymethuyvar, Hungary, in the album of Henry Francklin, fol 8ᵛ, UUB, when Henry F. located his father's signature in de Battiani's prayerbook. 203, 204

Bengtsson, Nils. Treasurer at Nyköping Castle. 96

von Berlepsch, Christopher (c. 1555–before 1616). Gentleman-in-waiting at the court of Hesse-Marburg 1588. Represented Landgrave Louis of Hesse-Marburg and Landgrave George of Hesse-Darmstadt at Nyköping 1592. 67

Bertilßen, Andrew (Anders). Pilot. 40, 41ⁿ

Bertolomeusdochter, Erm (fl. 1590–95). Widow of Willem IJsbrantz Kieft of Amsterdam (q.v.). 194

Bestenböstel, Otto von; Master of the Royal Household. 63

Beysandt, George. See Bryan.

Bielke, Gunilla. See Gunilla.

Bielke, Hogenskild (1538–1605). Baron Bielke of Läckö, Councillor of state, Lord High Steward. Beheaded 1605, m., Anne Sture (1541–1595) (q.v.) Cf. *SBL*, 4, 197 ff. 46ⁿ, 179

Bielke, Nils. Count. 102, 103ⁿ, 165. Cf. Plate 5 d.

Bielke of Nynäs, Ture Nilsson (1548–1600). Member of the Treasury Board. Lord Treasurer. Beheaded in Linköping 1600, m., Margaret (Sigrid) Sture. Cf. *SBL*, 4, 210 ff. 46ⁿ, 84, 180, 199

245

Bilde (Bille), Berta. Tycho Brahe's mother. 154

Bilde (Bille), Eske, Jr. Envoy in the Danish Embassy to Stockholm 1595. 154

Bilefelt, Laurentius. Fl. 1591–92. Helena Northampton's secretary, entry in Henry Francklin's album 16.4.1592. 33

Blancke, George (Jorge). Member of a noble family from Meißen in Germany, gentleman-in-waiting to Duke Charles, Swedish ambassador to Hesse June 1592. Cf. Erich Lassotas diary 149. 59, 71

Bland, John. English draper and merchant adventurer. Collaborated with William Greene (q.v.). Entry in Henry Francklin's album 8.2.1599. Cf. Astrid Fries, *Alderman Cockayne*, 172. 213

Blewet, Ricardus. See Bluett.

von Blois Treslong. See Treslong.

Blount, Elizabeth (c. 1502–c.1539–40). Dowager Baroness Tailboys, Lady-in-waiting to Queen Catherine of England 1512–14, mistress of Henry VIII, *m.*, (1) Gilbert Tailboys of Kyme, Lincolnshire, d. 1530; (2) Edward Clinton, later Earl of Lincoln. Cf. *Compl. Peer.* 7, 692, footnote (a); 10, 829 f., and 12, 1, 602, footnote (i); and Childe-Pemberton, *Eliz. Blount & Henry VIII*, passim. 30

Blount, Sir John. 30

Blount, William, Lord Mountjoy. 44

van Bloys Treslong. See Treslong.

Bluett, Arthur (b. 1591). Son of Richard Bluett and Mary Chichester? 44

Bluett, Dorothy, daughter of William Blount, Lord Mountjoy. Mother of Richard Bluett? 44

Bluett, John, of Greenham, Somerset, father of Richard Bluett? 44

Bluett, Mary, née Chichester, *m.*, Richard Bluett, (q.v.), c. 1590? 44

Bluett [Blueth, Blewet, Blij], Richard

[Richardus, Ricard], (c. 1550–1615). English player at Nyköping 1591–92, *m.*, Mary Chichester c. 1590? Cf. *Alumni Oxonienses, 1500–1714*, Vol. I., Early Series, 142. 42, 44–46, 73–75, 78

Bluett, Sir Roger, of Holcombe Rogus, Devon. Grandfather of Richard Bluett? 44

van Bockholt, Godefroy, Dutch captain from Amsterdam. Entered Swedish service 1592 and 1593. Cf. *Het Staatsche Leger*, 199. 189, 190, 191

Bolte, Lorentz. 64

Boltum, Thomas. Englishman. 120

Bona Sforza (1493–1557). Daughter of Gian Galeazzo Sforza, *m.*, Sigismund I of Poland in 1517. Queen of Poland 1517–48. Retired as Queen Dowager to Italy. 14

Bonaventura (Borchgrevinck), Melchior (d. 1632). Danish capellmeister in the service of Frederick II. Later engaged by the regency government and by Christian IV, 1596 organ-grinder, 1599 to Italy, 1600 organ-grinder at the Danish court, 1618 capellmeister. Cf. Hammerich, Index. 133

Bonde, Carin, née Ulfsdotter Snakenborg Bååt, wife of Philip Bonde (q.v.), daughter of state councillor Ulf Henriksson Snakenborg Bååt and Agneta Knutsdotter Lillie of Ökna, sister of Helena Northampton, chief lady-in-waiting to Princess Christine, Duke Charles's second wife in 1604. 172

Bonde, Lindorm Nilsson (Lilliehöök), catholic. King Sigismund III's chamberlain. 154–156

Bonde, Philip. Son of John Bonde and Märta Posse, Duke Charles's councillor and marshall, one of the five witnesses to the Duke's betrothal with Mary of the Palatinate, *m.*, Carin Bååt (see above). 172

Bonnefoy, Ennemond (1536–1574). Lecturer in civil law at the University of Valence. 177

Boris Godunov (1551–1605). Appointed Russian Secretary of state by Ivan the Terrible. Guardian of the insane Czar Fyodor. Czar of Russia 1598–1605. 'The Imperor of Russia'. 25, 85, 213, 214, 215, 216

Bothvidius, John (1575–1635). Court chaplain to Gustavus Adolphus 1616. Created bishop of Linköping in the same year. 200

von Boventer (Båuenter), Daniel; court chamberlain in the service of Duke Charles at Nyköping Castle; courier between Elsinore and Segersjö 1–7.8 1592; cf. Hertig Karls räntekammare 1590–97, fasc. 5, Haakon Larsson 1591, fol 19v, KA. 61

Bovertz, Johan (Jan Gerritsz). Citizen of Dordrecht. Private banker. 191

Bradshaw, Alexander. Thomas Bradshaw's brother, published the latter's *The Shepherd's Starre*, 1591. 31

Bradshaw, Thomas. Wrote *The Shepherd's Starre*, 1591; his patron was Thomas, Lord Burgh. Cf. *DNB*, 6, 182. 31, 32

Bradstreet (Braidstrass), John. English player on the Continent. Entry 24 March, 1606, in the album of Johannes Cellarius. *MS. Additional 25579*, fol 82^r, BM. Cf. Nung., *Dict. of Actors*, 56, and Cohn, *Sh.sp. in Germ.* XXXV. 135, 136

Brahe, Abraham (1569–1630). Court chamberlain 1602, later Councillor of state. Cf. *SBL*, 5, 673 ff. 148, 152, 154–157, 196

Brahe, Eric (1552–1614). Count. Chamberlain to the young Prince Sigismund c. 1575. To King John III c. 1581. Swedish envoy to England and Scotland 1583. In Sigismund's suite to the Royal Election at Cracow 1587. Converted to Roman Catholicism 1591. Reconciled to Duke Charles

1598. One of the aldermen in the great trial against Ture and Nicolas Bielke 1600. Left Sweden in 1600. Author of Eric Brahe's ciphercalendars 1592–1601 and 1602–1607, now preserved in the 'Skoklostersamlingen', E 8925 and 8917, resp., RA, *m.*, 1582 Elizabeth of Brunswick-Luneburg. Cf. *SBL*, 5, 658 ff. 33

Brahe, Gustavus (1558–1615). Brother of Eric B., Count of Visingsborg. Chamberlain to King Sigismund III of Poland. Returned from Sweden to Poland in 1598. Cf. *SBL*, 5, 660 ff. 37

Brahe, Magnus; Count. 102, 103^n

Brahe, Per (1520–1590). Count. Lord High Chancellor. 179

Brahe, Sten of Knudstrup (1547–1620). Danish councillor of state. As chamberlain-in-waiting in the suite of Princess Anne of Denmark to Norway for her marriage in 1589 with King James VI of Scotland. Danish ambassador to Duke Charles's second marriage at Nyköping 26–28 August 1592. 66^n, 98

Brahe, Tycho (1546–1601). Danish astronomer and author. 153, 154

Bremer, Johan 64

Brienn, Jurgenn. See Bryan.

Briggis, Philip. See Bruggis.

Brockmann, Ludwig. German shoemaker of Cassel. Provided lodging for two English lutenists c. 1594. 55

Brocktorff, Detleff. Noble boy in the suite of Princess Christine of Holstein to the marriage in Nyköping August 26th, 1592. 64

Brouwer, Jan Jansz. Treasurer of the city of Leyden. 135^n

Browne, Anthony. Englishman. 204, 205^n

Browne, Robert. English player, was with Edward Alleyn (q.v.) in Worcester's company in 1583. In 1590 at

Leyden, and 1592 he began his foreign tours when he obtained a passport for himself and Lord Admiral's company. He and the company toured Germany with a repertory of English plays in 1592–93, c. 1594–99, 1601–07, 1618–20. Cf. Nung., *Dict. of Actors*, 60 ff., and, Cohn, *Sh.sp. in Germ.*, XXVII, and XXX ff. 53–57, 134–138, 160, 162, 163, 187

Bruck (Buick), Matthew (Matteus). English player at Nyköping 1591–92. 42, 73, 74, 78

Bruggiss (Briggis), Philip (Philpuss trumetere). English trumpeter at Nyköping 1591–93. 42, 45, 49, 60, 71, 73–75, 78, 79, 93, 94, 109, 139, 144

Brunswick, Duke of. See Henry-Julius, Duke of Brunswick-Luneburg.

Bryan (Brienn, Beyzandt), George (Jurgenn). English player. Engaged in Denmark 1586 and in Saxony 1586–87. In England one of Strange's Men 1590 and of Chamberlain's Company 1594. Named in William Shakespeare's First Folio 1623. Cf. Chamb., *Eliz. Stage*, 2, 271 ff., Cohn, *Sh.sp. in Germ.*, XXIII, XXV, XXVII and LXXVI, and Nung., *Dict. of Actors*, 63 ff. 113, 129–131

Buckhurst, Lord. See Sackville, Thomas.

Bull, Thomas. English player in Denmark 24.6.1579–17.4.1586. Returned to England 18.4.–30.5.1586 in the suite of Henry Ramelius. Involved in a lawsuit Elsinore 2.8.1586 for murdering his countryman Thomas Boltum out of jealousy. Executed in Denmark. Cf. *Helsingør Tingbog* 25.8.1586 and *Shakespeare Survey* 22/69, 119–124. 115–120

Bultius, John Tidiksson (c. 1558–c. 1609). Secretary of state in Poland. Accompanied Sigismund to the Royal Election in Poland 1587. Cf. *SBL*, 6, 670 ff. 17, 197

Buntmacker, Hans. 64

Burgh, Lady Frances. See Vaughan.

Burgh, Thomas (1555–1597). Lord Burgh de Gaynesboro 1567–97. Governor of ten Briel, Holland 1586/87–97. K.G. 1593. Entry in Henry Francklin's album 4.7.1591, *m.*, Frances Vaughan (q.v.). Cf. *Compl. Peer.*, 2, 424. 27–29, 31, 44, 147

Burgh, William (c. 1523–1584). Father of Thomas, Lord Burgh, *m.*, Catherine Clinton, daughter of Edward, Duke of Lincoln (q.v.) and Elizabeth, Dowager Baroness Tailboys (q.v.), daughter of Sir John Blount. 29, 30

Burghley, Lord. See Cecil, William.

Busshe, Thomas. Citizen of London. 204, 205

Byndon. See Howard.

Bååt, Carin Snakenborg. See Bonde, Carin.

Bååt, Helena Snakenborg. See Northampton, Helena.

C

Cabeliau, Abraham (1571–1645); Merchant of Amsterdam; removed 1607 to Sweden (Gothenburg); in Swedish service. Cf. *SBL*, 7, pp. 199 ff. 235

Cabeliau, Karl (Karel, Carolus or Charles) of Dagom and Mullem (d. 1597). Dutch captain from Flanders, entered Swedish service 1592, killed 1597 in a cavalry engagement at Turnhout, *m.*, Anne Sersanders, who had formerly been a nun, she was left with four children, the youngest of whom was born after his father's death. Cf. *Res. Staat. Gen.*, 8, 264; 9, 505, and *De Navorscher*, 4, 348 f., 8, 267 f. For the generalogy of the C. family cf. *Oud-Holland*, 5 (1887), 44. 189

Cadman, Thomas. 69[n]

Cæsar, Sir Julius (1558–1636); judge; was of Italian extraction; lawyer at the Admirality, London, in 1584;

Master of Requests 1600; Chancellor and Under-Treasurer of the Exchequer 1606; Master of the Rolls 1614. Cf *DNB*, 9, 204 ff. 184

Camden, William (1551–1623). English antiquary and historian. Clarenceux Herald, College of Arms. Entry Conington, England, 12 September, 1603, in the album of Johann Haan, medical student of Wurzburg, Germany; M.S. Additional 19.828, fol. 34; B.M. 98

Canton, John. See Caunton, John.

Cardoini, Camillo (1542–1623). Italian Calvinist belonging to a noble family from Naples; removed 1598 to Switzerland, burgher of the city of Geneva s.y., his own album amicorum now at the Harvard University Library, Cambridge, Mass. USA, Sumner 84. The album begins 1608 and is continued after Camillo Cardoini's death by Edwin C. (c. 1630–50) and John C. (c. 1660). No album of the international type, more a guestbook. Cf. André Chopard, 'Genève et les Anglais [XVIᵉ à XVIIIᵉ siecle]' in *Bulletin de la Société d'Histoire et d'Archéologie de Genève* 7, 1939–40, pp. 175–280 and Heinrich Türler & c., *Historisch-Biographisches Lexikon der Schweiz*, 2, 493. Entries in Henry Francklin's album, London 9.7.1591, UUB; in Francis Segar's album, Geneva 27.7.1602, H.M. 743 Henry E. Huntington Library, San Marino, California 91108 USA; in Wolfgang Rhumar's album, fol 323ᵛ, Geneva 22.11.1602, NKS 389ʰ 8°, Danish KB; in Abraham Plato's album, fol 80, 8°, Geneva 23.9.1608, L.Sb., 168, Frankfort on the Main/Germany, cf. Zeitschrift f. Kulturgeschichte I (1894), p. 287; in Nic. Ritterhusius' album, fol 119ᵛ–120ʳ, Geneva 8.3.1620, Mill. III, 522, 8°, Stadtbibliothek Nuremberg/Ger-

many; and in Joh. Diest's album, fol 174, Geneva 31.8.1621, L.Sb. 163, Frankfort on the Main/Germany. 27

Carey or Carew, Sir George (1547–1603). 2nd Baron Hunsdon 1596. Captain-general of the Isle of Wight 1582, Lord Chamberlain of the Household 1596–97. 183

Carey or Carew, Sir Henry (1524–1596). 1st Baron Hunsdon. K.G. Privy Councillor. The nephew of Anne Boleyn. 94ⁿ

Carl. See Charles

Carlsson, Joen, of Mem and Sjösa. Charles Sture's father-in-law. 46

Casimir. See John Casimir.

Catharine. See Catherine.

Catherine of Aragon (1485–1536). Henry VIII's first Queen Consort. 30

Catherine of East Friesland (1539–1610). Daughter of Gustavus Vasa and Margaret Leijonhufvud. Sister of Duke Charles, *m.*, Edzard II of East Friesland (q.v.) in 1559. 146, 183, 188

Catherine of Hapsburg (1576–1595). Sister of Anne of Hapsburg (q.v.). 37

Catherine Howard (1521/22–1542). Henry VIII's fifth Queen Consort. Executed on Tower Hill 13.2.1542. 204

Catherine Jagiello (1526–1583). Queen of Sweden 1569–83, *m.*, Duke John of Finland, later King John III of Sweden 1562. 14, 85, 172

Catherine de Medici (1519–1589). Daughter of Lorenzo de M. and Madeleine de la Tour d'Auvergne, Queen of France 1547–1559, *m.*, Prince Henry, later King Henry II of France, in 1533. 175

Catherine Parr (1512–1548). Henry VIII's sixth and last Queen Consort. 32, 166, 204

Catherine Stenbock (1535–1621). Gustavus Vasa's third and final Queen

Consort. Daughter of Gustavus Olaf-
son Stenbock and Bridget Leijonhufvud. Duke Charles's stepmother.
66, 68

Catherine Vasa (1584–1638). Daughter
of Duke Charles and his first wife
Mary of the Palatinate. 14, 67, 210

Caunton of Kent, John (b. c. 1573).
Alumni Oxonienses: 'John Caunton
of Kent, Gent., University College.
Matric. 25th Oct. 1588, aged 15.
Perhaps of the Middle Temple'. Inns
of Court Register: 'August 1, 1598,
John Caunton, late of New Inn,
Gent, son and heir of Thomas Caunton of Nonnynton, Kent, Gent'. Re-
corder and witness in Nyköping,
Sweden, in the case of James Hill,
May 4, 1600. Entry in Henry Francklin's album: 'Johannes Caunton Cantianus. Stockholm, December 27th,
1599'. 100–102

Cecil, Sir Robert (1520–1598). Secretary
of State. Privy councillor. 94n

Cecil, William (1520–1598). 1st Baron
Burghley. Lord High Treasurer,
Privy councillor. Queen Elizabeth's
most trusted adviser. 34, 78, 92,
93, 108, 147, 214

Cecily Vasa (1540–1627). Daughter of
King Gustavus Vasa of Sweden and
Margaret Leijonhufvud. Sister of
Duke Charles, *m.*, Landgrave Christo-
pher of Baden in 1564. 32, 166, 172

Cecropia. Pseudonym for Helena Northampton (q.v.) in Sir Philip Sidney's
Arcadia. 167, 168

Charles (1550–1611). Duke of Sudermania, Neriche and Vermelandt, later
King Charles IX of Sweden. 13–15,
19, 21–28n, 32–50, 52–54, 59–61, 65–
83, 86–90, 92–99, 101–106, 108–110,
132, 139, 140, 144–157, 160–164,
170–174, 179–186, 188–196, 198, 199,
208–217. Cf. Plates 1b and 2a.

Charles Philip (1601–1622). Brother of
Gustavus II Adolphus. 213

Charleton, Ham. Englishman. Entry in
Henry Francklin's album, London
5.7.1591. 27

Charyllis. Pseudonym for Dorset (Anne)
Spencer, Lady Compton and Moun-
tegle, daughter of Sir John Spencer
and a relation of Edmund Spenser.
167

Cherry, Sir Francis. Member of the
Muscovy Company. 213

Chesnecopherus, Nils (1574–1622). D.
Law. Duke Charles's secretary of
state. '*Doctor Nils*'. Cf. *SBL*, 8, 426 ff.
108, 149, 199

Chichester, Mary. 44

Christian I (1560–1591). Electoral
Prince of Saxony 1586. 130, 131

Christian IV (1577–1648). King of
Denmark 1588–1648, Regency 1588–
1596. 62, 68, 80, 97, 132–134, 140,
151–154, 181n. Cf. Plate 2b.

Christine (1543–1604). Duchess of Holstein-Gottorp, née Princess of Hesse.
Mother of Duke Charles's second wife.
35 38, 39, 60–65, 70, 71.

Christine (1573–1625). Princess of Holstein-Gottorp. Duchess, later Queen
of Sweden. Became Duke Charles's
second wife in 1592. 14, 19, 35, 36,
38, 39, 59, 60, 62, 63, 65, 67, 68, 101,
110, 145, 157, 164, 172, 213. Cf.
Plate 1a.

Christoffersson, Hans (fl. 1592); Pay-
master. 211

Christopher (Christoffer). Holstein trumpeter. 64, 65

Christopher (1569–1636). Count of East
Friesland. Son of Edzard II (q.v.) and
Catherine Vasa (q.v.). Nephew of
Duke Charles (q.v.). Converted together with his brother John (q.v.)
to Catholicism. The two brothers
Christopher and John performed
in 1592–93 a journey to Sweden.
Guest at Duke Charles's second marriage with Princess Christine of Holstein (q.v.) August 26–28, 1592. In

May 1593 to England with a letter of introduction from Duke Charles to Helena, Marchioness of Northampton [cf. Riksregistraturen (Duke Charles's) 2.5.1593, fol 104ᵛ]. After that engaged as officer in the French army, later in the Spanish army. Cf. *Cal. Car. IX*, 82 f. and 88 f., and von Wicht, *Annales Frisiae*, § 1592. 66, 67, 79, 146, 147

Clammers Junge (Clammer's Boy); Holstein trumpeter. 64, 65

Clifford, Margaret (c. 1560–1616). Countess of Cumberland (*Marian* in Edmund Spenser's *Colin Clout's come home again*), m., George Clifford, Third Earl of Cumberland, 1577. 167

Classon, Jöran (Jörren, George), Stjernsköld of Biby. Secretary of State. 152, 153

Clinton, Bridget, m., Robert Dymoke. 30

Clinton, Catherine, m., William, Lord Burgh (q.v.). 30

Clinton, Edward (1512–1585). Earl of Lincoln, m., Elizabeth Blount. 30

Clinton, Margaret, m., Charles, Lord Willoughby. 30

Cobham, William Brooke, 7ᵗʰ Lord Chamberlain. 127, 128

Cooper, William. See Coper.

Coote (Kuth), John (fl. 1590–1618). Englishman. Merchant draper. Assisted Duke Charles's agent in England, Thomas Fisk. Can be traced in the Swedish Household accounts until 1614, Likvidationer Ser. 91: 18, 'The Britaniskes Rechningh', 1612–14. Cf. Astrid Friis, *Alderman Cockayne*—passim. 26, 75, 76, 81, 94, 101–104

Coper (Cooper, Kupertt), William (Willam, Willuin). English player at Nyköping 1591–92. Cf. *Alumni Oxonienses, 1500–1714, Vol. I, Early Series.*

325. 42, 44, 45, 49, 54, 73, 74, 78

Cornelißen, Herman. Dutch merchant shipmaster from Hull. 40

Cornwallis, Thomas. See Graye, Christopher.

Cortesius Gallus, Carolus. French officer. Had a hand in the purchase of 'a Turkish horse' for Duke Charles. Entry in Henry Francklin's album Lemberg 14.7.1590. 210

Coryat, Thomas (c. 1577–1617). Traveller, wit, member of the Mermaid Tavern circle and author of *Coryat's Crudities*. 57

Cowell, John (1554–1611). D. Law at Cambridge. Left Eton College 1570 for King's College, Cambridge, where he taught civil law in 1594. Elected in 1594 Regius professor of civil law at Cambridge. Entry in Henry Francklin's album 19.7.1591. Cf. *DNB*, 12, 375. 27, 28

Cratel, Wilhelm (Guillaume). French firemaster. 54, 189

Crofton of London, William. 216

Cujas, Jacques (1522–1590). Headmaster of the Univeristy of Valence, specialist in Roman law. 176

Cumberland. See Clifford.

Cynthia. Pseudonym for Queen Elizabeth I in Edmund Spenser's *Daphnaida* and *Colin Clout's come home again*. 167

D

Damler, Artus. English player. Engaged in Denmark 18.1.1579–24.10.1586. Returned for a short time to England in the suite of Henry Ramelius April–May 1586. 114–120, 130

Davis, Thomas. Englishman. 216

von der Decken, Herman. 64

von der Decken, Volradt. Master of the Royal Household. 64

Defabry, Casparutz. Musician (fiddler)

39, 68, 69, 98–101, 103, 104, 108, 120–126, 146–148, 158, 164, 166, 167, 170, 171, 183, 186, 195, 204, 208–210, 213–216.

Elizabeth of Brunswick-Luneburg (1573–1625). Princess of Denmark. Sister of Christian IV, *m.*, Duke Henry-Julius of Brunswick-Luneburg in 1590. 133

Elizabeth of Mecklenburg (1549–1597). Princess of Vasa. Sister of Duke Charles, *m.*, Christopher of Mecklenburg. 35–37, 93^n, 95, 195, 196

Elizabeth, The Lady (1596–1662). Daughter of King James I and Anne of Denmark, best known as Elizabeth, Queen of Bohemia. Married Frederic V, Elector Palatine of the Rhine, who on November 4th, 1619, was crowned King of Bohemia. A company under her patronage received a patent on April 27th, 1611. Entry 1614 in the album of Sir Thomas Cuming of Scotland, MS Additional 17083, fol 6, B.M. 57

Ellmont (Ellmout), Dorotea. See Francklyn, Dorotea.

Erhardt, Georg (fl. 1593). German merchant-adventurer. 195

Eric XIV (1533–1577). King of Sweden 1560–68. 13, 88, 91, 170, 171, 194, 195, 210

Erichßon, Palne, Rosenstråle (d. 1596). Captain of horse and quartermaster of Ostrogothia. Cf. Hildebrand, *Släktforskning*, 38. 33

Erichßon, Simon. Treasurer at Duke Charles's Court at Nyköping. 43

Eriksdotter, Constantia. See Francklin.

Eriksson, Jörgen, Ulfsparre (1544–1612). Governor of Westrogothia and Fort Elfsborg. Councillor of state. 64

Ernest of Hapsburg (1553–1595). Archduke. Governor of Hungaria. 37

Ernest Louis (1539–17.6.1592). Duke of Pomerania. 68

Essex. See Devereux, Robert.

F

Fabricius, Jacobus. Master of the High School, Gdańsk. 218^n

Fabris, Salvator. Italian playwright, player and fencing-master. In King Sigismund III's suite at his Coronation in Uppsala 1594. Engaged 1601–1607 as fencing-master by King Christian IV of Denmark. Cf. Anon., *Exegesis historica*, Stockholm 1610, 115; *Meddelelser fra Rentekammerarkivet*, 1872, 199; O. Sperling, *Selvbiografi*, 1885, and H. Ehrencron-Müller, *Dansk Forfatterlexikon*, 3, 10.

Bibliography: Salvator Fabris, *De lo schermo overo scienza d'arme*, Copenhagen 1606; Copies of this book at 'Det Kongelige Bibliotek', Copenhagen, and 'The British Museum'. London, W.C.1.; idem, *Della vera practica & scienza d'armi libri due*, 2. edit., Padua 1624. Fol.; and, idem, *Italiänische Fechtkunst, d. i. Gründeliche und auszfürliche Unterrichtung von dem Fechten, in unsere algemeyne Hochteutsche Sprache vertolmetschet*. Leiden 1619. Fol. — 149–152, 165. Cf. Plate 7.

Falck, Erik (c. 1554–c. 1607). Catholic. King John III's favourite. During the 1580's ambassador to Austria and Turkey. Later to the Vatican and Spain. Knight of the Order of the Holy Sepulchre in Jerusalem. Erik Falck's album preserved at the library of the High school of Umeå, Sweden. 206, 209

Felingh, Gierhart. Dutch captain. Entered Swedish service 1592. 189

Felingh (Vheling) Zacharias. D. Law. Councillor. Belonged to a branch of the Westphalian Felingh-family, who during the end of the XVIth Century removed to Lubeck. In Danish service c. 1563–1572. Engaged by Duke

as Cornwallis, involved in dispute with James Hill. 93, 95, 101, 109

Green, John (fl. 1606–1627). English player. Performed in Germany and elsewhere on the Continent. 202

Greene, Robert (c. 1560–1592). English playwright and one of the 'University Wits'. 161

Greene, Thomas (d. 1640). William Shakespeare's 'cousin'. 102

Greene, William. Citizen and merchant draper of London. In the late 1590's succeeded Thomas Fisk as Duke Charles's agent in England. Entry in Henry Francklin's album 8.2.1599. Cf. Astrid Friis, *Alderman Cockayne* 84. 100–102, 213

Grimston, Sir Harbottle. 157

Groos, Thomas. Author of one of the prefaces to Thomas Bradshaw, *The Shepherd's Starre*, 1591. 32

Groß, Joseph. German trumpeter. Accompanied Duke Henry-Julius of Brunswick-Luneburg to Kronborg Castle in 1590. 133

von Grothusen, Anne (c. 1578–1644). Daughter of Arnold von Grothusen, King Sigismund's tutor, m., Dr. Teofilo Homodei (q.v.). 197, 198, 201

von Grothusen, Arnold. King Sigismund's tutor. 162, 195, 197, 201

von Grothusen, Lucie. Sister of Anne, m., Johannes Messenius Sr. 201

Grubbe, Sivert. Envoy in the Danish Embassy to Stockholm 1595. 154

Guildenstern. One of *Dramatis personae* in William Shakespeare's *Hamlet*. Courtier at Kronborg Castle, Elsinore, Denmark. 91

Gunilla Bielke (1568–1597). Second wife of King John III of Sweden. Queen of Sweden 1585–1592. 15, 66

Gustavus Vasa (c. 1496–1560). King of Sweden 1523–1560. 13, 66, 88, 146

Gustavus II Adolphus (1594–1632). King of Sweden 1611–1632.

82, 95, 101, 152–155, 157, 158, 165, 193, 200, 213

Gustavus (Gustaf) [1574–1597]. Duke of Saxony-Lauenburg. Son of Duke Charles's sister Sophia. 47, 157

Gustavus III (1746–1792). King of Sweden 1771–1792. 157

Gyllenhielm, Karl Karlsson (1574–1650). Son of Duke Charles and Catherine Nilsdotter. Baron. Soldier and state official. 47, 215

Gyllenstierna, Axel (c. 1542–1603). Danish secretary of state. Governor of Norway. Cf. *DBL* 8, 488 ff., och *NBL* 5, 133 f. 181[n]

Gyllenstierna, John (1569–1617). Swedish councillor to King John III. 181, 209

Gyllenstierna, Nils (1526–1601). Ambassador from King Eric XIV of Sweden to England. Lord Treasurer. Secretary of State. 83, 86, 88–91, 171, 195

H

Haakonsson (Håkansson), Bengt; mayor of the city of Uppsala, Sweden; entry in Henry Francklyn's album 25.10. 1592; UUB. 212[n]

Haard (Hård), Olaf Larsson (1555–1630). Accompanied Duke Charles on a journey to the Palatinate in 1577. Chamberlain to Duke Charles 1587. Governor of Jönköping Castle &c. 1600. Cf. *Elg* 3, 717 f. Tab. 7. 59

Haas, Jochim (John). Merchant draper of Warsaw, Poland. King Sigismund III's agent. 17, 18, 21

Hafre. See Havill.

Hamlet. One of *Dramatis personae* in William Shakespeare's *Hamlet*. 90, 91, 152

von Hammen, Ludovico (1652–1689). Studied medicine at Leyden and Montpellier. Physician of the city of Gdańsk and physician-in-ordinary to John Sobiesky. Author of the medical history, *Vitae Medicorum Gedanensum* 1679. 173, 175, 178, 197

von Han, Hans Bischoff (fl. 1590–1593). Draper from Silesia. 88

Hans. Trumpeter-apprentice. 54

Hansson, Hans. 102, 103[n]

Hardenberg, Erik. Envoy in the Danish Embassy to Stockholm 1595. 154

Harrison, John (fl. 1600–1601). Publisher in London. 57[n]

von Harstall, John Louis (Hans Ludwig) (1550–c. 1617). Hessian chamberlain. Governor of Werra Castle in Hesse. Represented Landgrave William of Hesse-Cassel at Duke Charles's wedding at Nyköping, Sweden, 1592. 67, 71, 163

von Hartim, Carolus (Charles de Hartaing or de Herating). Dutch captain. Entered Swedish service in 1592. Member of a noble family from Hainault that, having been converted to the reformed faith, left Walloon and settled in North Holland, where Daniel von Havtim received Heemskerk Castle, which he renamed Marquette. Cf. *Res. Stat.-Gen.*, 6, 1588–89, 94, 96, 366, 367, 372, 375, 389, 435, 449 and 453, and *Het Staatsche Leger*, 2, 199 and 301. 189

Hastings, Lady Mary. Daughter of Henry, Earl of Huntingdon. 24

von Hatzfeld, Amelia. Lady-in-waiting to Mary of the Palatinate, Duke Charles's first wife; *m.*, Maurice Leijonhufvud in 1592. Cf. *Cal. Car. IX*, 69 and 80. 69, 145

Hauell. See Havill.

Havill (Hauell, Havell, Hafre, Hefre), Richard (Ricard) [d. in Sweden c. 1616]. English player in Nyköping 1591/92. Remained in the service of Duke Charles (later Kings Charles IX) and Gustavus II Adolphus to his death. 42, 45, 54, 71, 73, 74, 77–79, 82, 161

Heberer, Michaël (d. c. 1612). Born in Bretten, the Low Palatinate, his mother Philip Melanchton's niece; Palatine ambassador (secretary); student of Heidelberg and Neuhausen near Worms; while a student at Heidelberg tutor 1579–1582 of the young Swedish Baron Eric Bielke (1564–c. 1592); traveller and adventurer; author; cf. *Biographie Universelle*, 67, 10 f, and *idem*, nouv. éd., 19, 13; and *Allgemeine Deutsche Biographie*, 11, 197 f. 50, 51, 66–70, 76, 110, 138, 140, 189

Hefre. See Havill.

van Heile, Petrus, Belga. Diplomatic agent of London in Swedish and Danish service. Entries in Henry Francklin's album dated London 13.6. 1591 and in that of Ian Isaac van den Brugge, dated Draxholm in Denmark 8.7.1599. Helped Niels Krag during his Danish embassy to England 1598–1599. Two original letters 16.6.1598 respectively London 23.9.1598 preserved in 'De la Gardieska arkivet', LUB, and several letters (c. 60 pp.) 'Vedr. Petrus van Heile's Hverv i England (1592; 1594 and 1597–98)', Danish RA. 27

Heneage, Sir Thomas (d. 1595). Vice-chamberlain of Queen Elizabeth's Household. Privy Councillor. 92, 93, 94, 94[n]

Henrici, Laurentius. Vicar of Kemi. Entry in Henry Francklin's album 26.7.1592. 211

Henry II (1519–1559). King of France 1547–1559. Second son of Francis I. 175

Henry III Valois (1551–1589). King of Poland 1573–74. King of France 1574–1589. Third son of Henry II and Catherine de Medici. 85, 175, 177.

Henry IV. Play by William Shakespeare. 106

Henry VIII (1491–1547). King of Eng-

I

Larsson, Haakon (Håkan). Treasurer at Nyköping Castle. 21^n, 26^n, 41^n, 42^n, 47^n, 53, 61^n, 73, 79^n, 184^n, 192^n

Larsson, Matz. 102

Larsson, Nils. 102

Laski, Samuel. Polish nobleman. Hieronymus (Geronimus) Strozzi his legate to Duke Charles in 1591. Polish envoy to Sweden in 1594 and 1598. Cf. *The Radziwill Coll.*, Arch. Glown. No. 8213, Warsaw. 47, 181

Lassius, Petrus. Headmaster of the High School of Gdańsk. 218^n

Lassota von Stebelow, Erich (c. 1550–1616). Silesian nobleman in the service of Arch-duke Maximilian. Ambassador. Cf. *Allgemeine Deutsche Biographie*, 17, 793–794. 83–91

Lassota von Stebelow, Friedrich. Brother of Erich L. von S. 84

Lassota von Stebelow, Ludwig. Younger cousin of Erich L. von S. 84

Laurentz, harpist. Musician at the court of John III in Stockholm. 139

Lauritz Schriffuer. Lorenzo the town-clerk of Elsinore. 113

Lauritzenn, Hanns. Organ-grinder at Fredriksborg Castle in 1579. 114

Leall, Henry. Scottish captain of horse and head of the Scottish squadron of mercenaries during the Swedish-Russian war 1592. Cf. *Cal. Car. IX*, 73 and 76. 185

de Lébéron, Charles (d. 1600). Nephew of Jean de Montluc. Accompanied him to the Royal election in Poland 1573. Abbé de Saint-Ruf 1573. Received the degree of Doctor of Law at the University of Valence. Acting bishop of Valence 1575–1579. Bishop 1580–1600. 175, 176

Lee. Sir Henry. 69

Lee, Sir Richard. English ambassador to Russia 1600–1601. 165, 213–216. Cf. Plate 6.

Leicester. See Dudley.

Leicester, Lady. 112

Leijonhufvud (Lewenhaupt), Axel (1544–1619). Councillor of state. Governor of Westrogothia. Removed from office. 84

Leijonhufvud (Lewenhaupt), Maurice (Moritz, Mauritz) Stensson (1559–1607). Count. Councillor of state. Lord Treasurer of Sweden, *m.*, Amalia von Hatzfeld (q.v.); Entry 1595 in the album of Morten Bornholm, *Rostg. 28, 8°,* fol 44^v, Danish KB. 47, 69, 70, 102, 103^n, 145, 155, 165. Cf. Plate 5 b.

Lewenhaupt. See Leijonhufvud.

L(-ille) (Little) Philip. See Gibson.

Lindeinern, of Schleywitz, Ernst. Accompanied Erich Lassota on the embassy to Russia in 1590. 85

von der Lithe, Luder. 64

Lodewijk, Willem (1560–1620). Count of the Netherlands. Governor of West Friesland, *m.,* Anne of Nassau (1562–88). 187

von Lodron, Hieronymus. Count. Colonel of a regiment in the force raised by Philip II in Germany 1579. 84

Lodskin, Otto. Secretary to Helena Northampton. 33

Louis (Ludwig) (1537–1604). Landgrave of Hesse-Marburg in 1567. Younger brother of William IV, the Wise. Uncle of both of Duke Charles's wives Mary of the Palatinate and Christine of Holstein. 67, 68

von Lubeck, Claus. Rider in the suite of Princess Christine of Holstein to Nyköping at the wedding with Duke Charles August 26th–28th, 1592. 64

Lyly, John (c. 1554–1606). Playwright and the oldest of 'the University Wits'—a little apart from the others. 32, 161

M

Magnus (1543–1603). Duke of Saxony-Lauenburg. Cousin of King Eric

1619). Dutch statesman and merchant prince of Rotterdam. 187

Olifant, Davidh. Scottish captain. Entered Swedish service in 1592. His widow, Magdalena Hum (or Hem), is mentioned in *Res. Staat. Gen.*, 10, 661. 189

Olaf the Carpenter. See Oloff Snickare.

Oloff Snickare (Olaf the Carpenter). Worked on the 'Play-yard' (Spelebannen) at Nyköping for three weeks in 1592. 50

Olsson, Franns (Francis). Bassoonist in King John III's service. 139

Olsson, Siffredh (Sigfrid). Clerk to the Swedish Royal Wardrobe. 178

Oxenstierna, Christian (1545–1592). Councillor of state in 1586. 88

Oxenstierna, Gustavus (1551–1597). Councillor of state in 1590. 88

P

Paalack (Pålack), Hans. Swedish Trumpeter. 43

Pahr, Dominicus. Son of Franciscus Pahr (q.v.). German architect, active in Kalmar and Borgholm. 88

Pahr, Franciscus (d. 1580). German architect, active in Uppsala. 88

Pahr, Johan Baptista. Son of Franciscus Pahr (q.v.). German architect, active in Kalmar. 88

Palm, Ambrosius. Secretary to King John III. 87

Pape. See Pope.

Papst. See Pope.

Paravicinus, Barthol. Curia-Rhaetus. 174

Paravicinus, Daniel. Volturens-Rhaetus. 174

Parkins or Perkins, Sir Christopher (c. 1547–1622). Diplomatist. Master of requests and dean of Carlisle. English ambassador to Poland in 1591–92. Cf. *DNB*, 45, 5 ff., and Pollard, 'Sir Edward Kelley', *Lives of Twelve Bad Men*. Entry in the album of Johan-

nes Opsimathes of Moravia, M. S. Bibl. Egerton 1220, fol 51, BM. 17

Parr, William (1513–1571). Brother of Queen Catherine P. (q.v.), Cf. *DNB*, 43, 367 f. 32, 33, 166, 171, 172

Patavin, Dorotea. See Francklyn, Dorotea.

von Paumgartner, Balthazar (fl. 1592). Citizen and merchant of Nuremberg. 137–139

Peele, George (1558–1596). Playwright, one of the 'University Wits' from Oxford. 161

Pelerini, Johan Baptista. Merchant of Venice living in Stockholm. 199

Pembroke, Mary. See Herbert, Mary.

Percy, Richard. English musician engaged by Duke Charles's court in Nyköping 1599/1600. Cf. H. 12. 69, and Chamb., *Sir Henry Lee*, 205. 132

Percy (Persj, Persten), Robert (Rupert) English player engaged in Denmark 1586 and in Saxony 1586/87. Cf. Nung., *Dict. of Actors*, 273. 130–132

Persdotter, Agda. Daughter of a prosperous burgher of Stockholm, 'Peder i Porten'. Mistress of King Eric XIV. Mother of Constantia Eriksdotter Francklin (q.v.). 22[n], 170

Persenn, John (Johan). English player in Denmark 24.6.1579–18.11.1586. Returned April–June 1586 to England in the suite of Henry Ramelius. 114–120

Persj, Robert. See Percy.

Persten, Rupert. See Percy.

Peter. Holstein trumpeter. 64, 65

Peter. Swedish player. 54

Petevine, Thomas. Entry in Henry Francklin's album 2.6.1591. 27, 207

Petreus Stockholmensis, Joannes. 216

Philip of Nassau (1555–1618). Elder half-brother of Maurice of Orange-Nassau, *m.*, Eleanor of Bourbon-Condé in 1596. 192

Philip II (1527–1598). King of Spain. 37, 84, 204

It is signed S.W.R. Cf. *DNB*, 47, 186 ff. Entry in Captain Francis Segar's album amicorum, H.M. 743, fol 110[n], Henry E. Huntington Library San Marino, Cal., U.S.A. 22, 33, 34, 97, 99, 108, 147, 162, 167, 169, 170, 171, 172[n]

Ramelius (Ramel), Henry (Henric) (c. 1550–1610). Councillor of the realm. Son of Gert Ramel of Wusterwitz, Pomerania Ulterior (d. not earlier than 1581) and Margaret von Massow, *m.*, 1. Anne Rantzau (d. 1596) at Flensburg, 2. Elsa Brahe in 1599 at Vittskövle. Journeyed abroad extensively in his youth. Studied in Padua in 1568. Believed to have served for a time at the Sultan's office in Constantinople. Been a deputy judge at the Imperial Court in Speier and served King Stephen Bátory of Poland. Returning home, was probably engaged by Duke John Frederick of Pomerania but soon moved to Denmark, no doubt assisted by the von Below family, with whom he was closely associated, and Queen Sophie of Denmark, who was born in Mecklenburg. In 1581 bound himself to serve Frederick II and Denmark for the rest of his life. Appointed court chamberlain in 1582 and head of the Danish king's 'Latin and German Chancellery' in 1583, in which office he performed several diplomatic missions. Appointed tutor to the young Prince Christian in the same year, a clear indication of how high he stood in the royal couple's favour. In 1584 the Danish king granted him Bäckaskog's monastery in Scania (Villand's parish) at the same time as R. repeated his promise to serve Denmark for the rest of his life and was naturalized as a Danish nobleman. R. maintained his connections with his native German-Polish district, as witnesses his strong support of Sigismund Vasa during the royal election of 1587 in Poland. Sigismund granted him estates in Poland in return. In 1586 R. was sent by Frederick II of Denmark on an embassy to England to offer Queen Elizabeth I the Danish King's "Bona officia" in view of the threat from Spain and to try to negotiate a peace between Elizabeth and Philip II. R. was a close friend of Tycho Brahe (cf. Tycho Brahe, *Opera omnia*, T. VI, p. 246: 30, 'Henric Ramel my very good friend'). R. soon became indispensable in Danish foreign policy and as head of the German chancellery thanks to his extensive knowledge of European politics, his diplomatic experience and negotiating skill, all based on great fluency in Latin and German. His foreign birth, however, elicited strong national opposition to him within the Danish nobility. At Frederick II's funeral in June 1588 the nobles requested that he should be released from his guardianship during the minority of the new king, Christian IV. The council of the Realm refused and R. received powerful support from the Dowager Queen, to whom R. was chief adviser. When the nobles met at Kolding in August 1590, however, R. was forced to relinquish his post as tutor to the young King, though he remained in charge of the German chancellery for a salary in the form of the county of Åhus in Scania. R. was very skilful in manœuvring between the Dowager Queen and the Council of State when they disagreed and it was he who brought them to terms again, whereupon he was admitted to the Council of the Realm in June 1596 shortly before the coronation of Christian IV. His activities during the early years of the new reign were chiefly diplomatic. R. participated in the negotiations that led in August 1597 to a contract of marriage between Christian IV and Princess Anne Cathrine of Brandenburg. Negotiated in 1599 with Duke Charles in Jönköping and in 1600 with an English embassy in Emden. Accompanied Christian IV in 1603 to Hamburg for a ceremony of homage. Was sent to England on another embassy in 1605. Accompanied Christian IV on his journey to England on 1606 and to Brunswick-Luneburg and Saxony in 1608–09; in 1597 he had been granted the parish of Villand and in 1607 Hörby in the parish of Frosta, both in Scania. His second marriage made him the owner of Vallengaard on Bornholm. Entry in Balthasar Fuchs von Bimbach's album amicorum, 580. Die Stadtbibliothek zu Königsberg. 98, 118, 120, 121, 124, 126, 127, 129, 141, 143, 164. Cf. Plate 4.

Rantzo[u]w, Matthias. 64

Raph. See Raff.

Rasch, Nicholas (Nils). Secretary to John III of Sweden and to Sigismund III of Poland. 197, 209

Ratlen[-o-]w, Gotsche. 64

Rattger, Jost. German trumpeter. Accompanied Duke Henry-Julius of Brunswick-Luneburg to Kronborg Castle 1590. 133

Rebock, Casper. Swedish trumpeter. 42

Rebock, Jörgen (George). Swedish trumpeter. 43

Reeve, Raphe. English player. One of the patentees of Porter's Hall 1615. Cf. Nung., *Dict. of Actors*, 294. 57

Ribbing of Säby, Bo (1560–1640). Chamberlain to Duke Charles in Nyköping 1585. Chancellor 1598. State secretary 1602. Governor of Värmland 1605. Cf. *Elg.*, 6, 310 f., Tab. 72. 47, 59

Ribbing, Eric (1558–1612). Swedish councillor to King John III. Secretary of state in 1602. Governor of Westrogothia. Cf. *Elg.*, 6, 309, Tab. 68. 181, 209

Rich, Lady Penelope (c. 1562–1607). *Stella* (q.v.). Sister of Robert Devereux, Earl of Essex (q.v.). 167

Richardt. See Havell.

Richter, Johannes, Oppaw., Med. Dr. 216

Robustelli. 174

de Rode, Jacob. Dutch captain. Entered Swedish service 1592. 189

Rodenhausen, Johan. 64

Rogier, Claude. Lecturer of the faculty of law at the University of Valence. 176

Rondelet, Guillaume (William) (1507–1595). Physician and biologist. Active at the University of Montpellier. 177

Rosencrantz. One of *Dramatis personae* in William Shakespeare's *Hamlet*. Courtier at Kronoborg Castle, Elsinore, Denmark. 91

Rosencrantz, Jørgen (George) (1523–95). Danish councillor of state. After the death of King Frederick II one of the four councillors comprising the regency government 1588–96. 62, 133[n]

Rosencrantz (Rosenkrands), Jakob. Envoy in the Danish Embassy to Stockholm 1595. 154

Rosseter, Philip (c. 1568–1623). Lutenist at the court of James I in London. Associated with the actors there, composed some of the music to the *Book of Airs*, by Dr. Thomas Campion, which book Rosseter published in 1601. One of the patentees for the erection of Porter's Hall 1615. Cf. *DNB*, 49, 282, Nung., *Dict. of Actors*, 304 f., Pulver, *Biogr. Dict. Old*

271

Stenbock, Eric Gustafsson (1538–1602). Baron of Öresten at King Eric XIV's coronation in 1561. King John III's councillor 1569, governor of Westrogothia and Fort Elfsborg 1575, *m.*, Magdalene Sture (q.v.). 46[n], 66

Stender, Matz. Swedish player at Duke Charles's court at Nyköping 1591–92. 54

Stephen Báthory (1533–86). King of Poland 1575–86, *m.*, 1575 Anne Jagiello (q.v.). 14, 84, 85

Stephens, Thomas. See Stevens.

Sterneman, Johan. Accompanied Erich Lassota as interpreter on the embassy to Russia in 1590. 86

Stevens (Stephens, Stiwens), Thomas. English player. Engaged in Denmark 1586, where he served as payee for the company, and as player in Saxony, where he is called Tomas Stephan or Stephans. Cf. Nung., *Dict. of Actors*, 338 f. 120, 129, 130, 131

Sthen, Hans Christensen. Headmaster of the Latin school at Elsinore from 1565 onwards. 133

von Stiebendorff, Hans Sitsch. Maternal uncle of Erich Lassota. 84

Stiwens, Thomas. See Stevens.

Stofel, Georg. Maternal uncle of Erich Lassota. 84

Stoffuadt, John (Jann). English merchant shipmaster from London. 40

Store (Big) Philip. See Kingman, Philip.

Stow, John. 111

Strange, Lady. See Spencer, Alice.

Strange, Lord. See Stanley.

Strozzi, Hieronymus (Geronimus) (d. 1619). Count de Belvedere (an ancient Florentine family). Legate from Samuel Laski of Poland to Duke Charles in 1591. Imperial general. Took part in the wars in Hungary and Transsylvania in the 1580's. During the celebrations for Sigismund's coronation in Uppsala in February 1594, S. detected a plot planned by Sigismund, to murder Duke Charles. S. then left the service of Poland and joined Duke Charles with Sigismund's approval. The latter being unaware that S. had detected his plot until he (Sigismund) returned to Poland the following year. Cf. Riksregistraturen 14.8.1595, Pars I, fol 236 r; for S. death cf. Riksregistraturen 31.3.1619, fol 103 r. 47, 149, 181, 193

Sture, Anne. Sister of Charles Sture, *m.*, Hogenskild Bielke. 46[n]

Sture, Charles (Karl) (1550–1598). Duke Charles's councillor, most trusted adviser and good friend. Entry 1595 in the album of Morten Bornholm, *Rostg.*, *28*, 8°, fol 44[r], Danish KB. 46, 47, 66, 68, 74, 145, 154, 165. Cf. Plate 5 a.

Sture, Christine. Sister of Charles Sture, *m.*, Gustaf Axelsson Baner of Djursholm. 46[n]

Sture, Magdalene. Sister of Charles Sture, *m.*, Eric Gustafsson Stenbock (q.v.). 46[n]

Sture, Margaret. Sister of Charles Sture, *m.*, Ture Nilsson Bielke. 46[n]

Sture, Sigrid. Sister of Charles Sture; *m.*, Thure Pedersson Bielke. 46[n]

Sverkersson, Olof (Elfkarl). Personal secretary to John III. Sometimes in the King's, sometimes in Duke Charles's service. Nicknamed *Twacoat*. 87, 212

Sweveselio, Carolus Lucz A'. Colonel in Philip of Nassau's regiment. Commanded the Dutch mercenary regiment in Sweden 1592–93 as deputy for Willem van Bloys Treslong (q.v.) who was not permitted to leave Holland. 189, 192

Syll, Elizabeth (Lisabet). See von Zeulen, Elizabeth.

of the regency government 1590–93. Cf. *DBL*, 24, 492 ff. 62, 133[n]

Urania. Pseudonym for Mary Herbert, Countess of Pembroke (q.v.) in Edmund Spenser's *Colin Clout's come home again*. 167

V

Valkendorf, Christopher (1525–1601). Secretary of state. One of the four councillors comprising the regency government 1588–96 after the death of Frederick II of Denmark. Answered at the High Court of Denmark for the bad equipment of the ships to Scotland with Princess Anne of Denmark in 1589. Found not guilty, but 13 other persons 'who through their witchcraft had arranged the troublesome crossing of the North Sea' perished at the stake. Cf. *DBL*, 25, 58 ff. 133[n], 181[n]

Vaughan, Anne. Daughter of Sir Christopher Pickering, *m*., (1) John Vaughan of Sutton-on-Derwent, York (2) Sir Henry Knyvet of Escrick. Mother of Frances Vaughan (q.v.), who became Lady Burgh, and of Sir Thomas Knyvet of Escrick. Cf. *Compl. Peer*. 2, 424, and *DNB*, 21, 340. 31

Vaughan, Frances, Lady Burgh. Parentage, see Vaughan, John and Anne, *m*., Thomas, Lord Burgh (q.v.). 31, 147, 148

Vaughan, John. Owner of Sutton-on-Derwent, York. Father of Frances Vaughan (q.v.), who became Lady Burgh. 31, 148

Vaughan, John of Radnorshire/Herefordshire. Mentioned in the Exchequer Depositions 1590–91. Possibly identical with Johan Wahan (q.v.) who was an English trumpeter at Nyköping 1591–93. 148

Vaughan, Robert of Radnorshire/Herefordshire. Mentioned in the Exchequer Depositions 1590–91. Possibly identical with Robert Wahan (q.v.) who was an English trumpeter at Nyköping 1591–93. 148

Vaughan, Thomas. Owner of Porthamal in the county of Brecknock. Father of John Vaughan (q.v.). 31

Vaughan. See also Wahan.

Vheling. See Felingh.

Viting. See von Fitinghoff.

W

Wahan (Wahn, Wan, Vaughan), Johan (John). English trumpeter at Nyköping 1591–93. 42, 60, 71, 73, 75, 78, 79, 144, 148

Wahan (Wahn, Wan, Vaughan), Robert (Rubertt). English trumpeter at Nyköping 1591–93. 42, 60, 71, 73, 74, 78, 144, 148

Wahn. See Wahan.

Waimer, Philip, D. Law. Active at the High school of the city of Gdańsk. German playwright. 145

Walker, Henry. Citizen and minstrel of London; Cf. Chamb., *W.Sh.sp.*, 2, 154 ff. 57[n]

Walsingham, Sir Francis (c. 1530–1590); secretary of state; cf. *DNB*, 59, 231 ff. 14[n], 19, 34, 94, 112, 121, 124

Walter, Thomas. English shipbuilder engaged at Nyköping 1591 through Severine John (Söffring Jönsson). 43

Waltkirch, Henrico (fl. 1606). Publisher in Copenhagen, Denmark. 165

Wan. See Wahan.

Warrinn, Thomas. English player and intrumentalist. Engaged in Denmark 10.4.1583–18.11.1586. 116–119

Warwick, Anne (Mary), Countess of. See *Theana*.

Watz, Antonius. German masterbuilder from Breslau. Carried out work on Uppsala Castle in Sweden. Decorator, plasterer. 88

Weßgiöthe of Skedvi, Laße, (d. 1599). Governor of Nyköping Castle and the county of Nyköping. 40, 41[n], 89, 90

Westermacher. 37[n], 51

Whitgift, John (c. 1530–1604). Archbishop of Canterbury 1583. Privy Councillor. Cf. *DNB*, 61, 129 ff. 14, 94[n]

William IV, 'the Wise', (1532–92). Landgrave of Hesse-Cassel 1567–92, maternal uncle of both of Duke Charles's wives, Mary of the Palatinate and Christine of Holstein. 67, 68, 70, 71, 162, 163

Willam. See Coper.

Witt, Petter. English merchant shipmaster from London. 40

Wogesserius, Georgius (Woritz, Jöran). Chamberlain at Duke Charles's court at Nyköping. Entry in Henry Francklin's album 20.8.1592. 211

Wolley, John, Esq. (d. 1595); secretary for the Latin Tongue; Chancellor of the most Honourable Order of the Garter; cf. *DNB*, 62, 316f., and Sarg., *Edw. Dyer*, 128. 27, 28, 94[n]

Wordsworth, Joan (d. 1623). Stepdaughter of Philip Henslowe (q.v.), *m.*, Edward Alleyn (q.v.) 22.10.1592, *DNB*, 1, 327 ff. and 26, 136 ff., and Nung., *Dict. of Actors*, 4 ff. and 188 f. 138[n]

Woritz, Jöran. See Wogesserius, Georgius.

Wroth, John (fl. 1595). English private banker. London agent of Landgrave Maurice of Hesse-Cassel. Entry in Francis Segar's album amicorum, Henry E. Huntingdon Library, San Marino, Cal. 91108, USA, H.M. 743, fol 96. 55

Wulf Cantor [Hans Wulff]. Rider in the suite of Princess Christine of Holstein

to the wedding with Duke Charles at Nyköping, August 26th–28th, 1592. Later singingmaster of Duke Charles at Nyköping. Had 18 singers under him according to Kungl. hofförtärningen 93. 54, 64

Wymblish, Thomas 30

Y

Youngh (Jungh), Abraham. Scottish captain. Entered Swedish service 1592. 189

Z

Zamoyski, Jan (1542–1605). Polish politician. Contributed to the election of Sigismund Vasa as King of Poland. 85

von Zeulen (Zulen, Syll). Elizabeth (Lisabet). Lady-in-waiting to Princess Elizabeth of Mecklenburg. Married in 1596 James Hill (q.v.). Cf. *Cal. Car. IX*, 127. 95, 96, 106, 108, 109

Zion (Master Zion). First Swedish player at the court of Duke Charles at Nyköping. Cf. *Sth. st. tänkeböcker 1596–99*, 326 ff., and 410. 54

Zoëga, Matthew (Mathias). Italian player and dancer from Verona. Engaged in Denmark 1580. Cf. Chamb., *Eliz. Stage*, 2, 271 ff. and *DBL*, 26, 486. The Zoëga family, chiefly associated with the clergy of South Jutland, traces its ancestry to this Matthew Z., subsequently 'Gehejmekammertiener' at Gottorf Castle, according to tradition a nobleman exiled from Verona. Z. was the father of 'Pfennigmeister' Johann Adolph Z. 115

von Zulen. See von Zeulen.

INDEX

of places and subjects &c.